CIRCLED WITH STONE

CIRCLED WITH STONE

EXETER'S CITY WALLS 1485–1660

Mark Stoyle

UNIVERSITY
of
EXETER
PRESS

First published in 2003 by
University of Exeter Press
Reed Hall, Streatham Drive
Exeter, Devon EX4 4QR
UK
www.ex.ac.uk/uep/

British Library Cataloguing in Publication Data
A catalogue record of this book is available from the British Library

ISBN 0 85989 727 3

Typeset in New Baskerville 11/13 by
Exe Valley Dataset Ltd, Exeter

Printed in Great Britain by
Short Run Press Ltd, Exeter

To Chris Henderson, in memoriam
1946–2001

CONTENTS

ILLUSTRATIONS

Maps

Figures

Plates (between pp. 80 and 81)

PREFACE

Like generation upon generation of Exeter folk before me, I have grown up in the shadow of the city wall. One of my most vivid childhood memories is of standing at the bottom of Mary Arches Street—gazing out across the deep-cut valley of the Longbrook to the soaring spire of St Michael's Church beyond—as my father explained to me that the pavement beneath our feet had been built on top of the ancient Roman rampart: a rampart whose strength and solidity could still be plainly seen if one craned one's neck over the iron railings beside the walkway and looked down on the courses of neatly hewn stone rising up from the grass of the overgrown cemetery beneath. Over the succeeding years, the city walls became a familiar backdrop to my everyday life. Dusty-red and topped with plumes of purple buddleia in summer, sullen-dark and slimy to the touch in winter, the walls, like the seasons, followed a sempiternal round. As a child, I walked beside them, played beside them and picnicked beside them in Rougemont Park and Northernhay Gardens. Later, grown older and bolder, I clambered up on them and ran along the top of them in Post Office Street. As a teenager, I haunted the nightclubs which stood close beside (and, in one case, practically on top of) the town walls in Castle Street and Quay Lane. It was almost inevitable that, when I left school and started work as a temporary digger with Exeter Museums Archaeological Field Unit, I would be assigned to an excavation in the lee of the city wall.

During the bitter winter of 1984–85, as the snow drifted down on our trenches, I worked as hard as I have ever done in my life: labouring alongside dozens of others to uncover the foundations of the Roman rampart in Paul Street. As I delved into the physical remains of the walls by day, I delved into their literary remains by night: keen to find out more about the ancient fortifications on which we were working from whatever general histories of the city came to hand. Gradually I got to know Chris Henderson—the Director of the Field Unit and a man who had made the historic defences of Exeter his life-long study. Under his beneficent influence, my interest in the subject took flight. At Chris's suggestion, I laid down my pick-axe and Devon shovel—with which, truth to tell, I had never become very adept—and transferred my activities to the civic archives. Over the next few months, I was introduced to a treasure-trove of original documents: a treasure-trove from which—to my surprise and delight—I was paid to quarry out extracts relating to the fortifications. Thus it was that I first entered the service of the city wall. In a sense, I have never left it since. This book is the result.

Why have I been so fascinated by the city wall for so long? The answer, I suppose is because—like all city walls—it is far more than a purely military structure. Instead, it is a symbol, a physical embodiment, of the community which it surrounds and protects. So it may be argued that—for all the terrible destruction which the city has undergone during the last 60 years—Exeter will always remain recognizably Exeter as long as it retains its unique city wall. And equally, I would suggest, for Exeter people who wish to understand their city's past—and thus, by extension, their own histories—the city wall, so often taken for granted, will always be found to repay fresh scrutiny. T.S. Eliot once wrote that:

> We shall not cease from exploration,
> And the end of all our exploring
> Will be to arrive where we started
> And know the place for the first time.

Perhaps his words justify my motives in undertaking this study better than I can myself.

Exeter, December 2002

ACKNOWLEDGEMENTS

I have incurred many debts while writing and researching this book. First, I would like to thank the staff of the various libraries and record offices which I have visited, including the Bodleian Library, the British Library and the Public Record Office. John Draisey and his staff at the Devon Record Office, Ian Maxted and his staff at the West Country Studies Library, Angela Doughty at the Cathedral Archives Office and the librarians of the Devon and Exeter Institution deserve special praise for their helpfulness and their forbearance over many years. Second, I am grateful to the bodies which have provided me with financial assistance. The Arts and Humanities Research Board made me an award under the terms of the research exchange scheme which allowed me to carry out vital work during winter 2000–1. Exeter City Council provided a financial subvention to assist with publication costs. I am also indebted to Exeter City Council for permission to publish transcripts and photographs from the civic archives. Third, I would like to thank the many scholars who have given up their time to discuss various aspects of the project with me: in particular George Bernard, Alastair Duke, Brian Golding, Frances Griffith, Vanessa Harding, David Hinton, Maryanne Kowaleski, John Oldfield, David Palliser and Ivan Roots. I owe a special debt of gratitude to John Allan, Stuart Blaylock, Bob Higham and Andrew Saunders, all of whom read the original draft text. Their comments have been invaluable. This is the fourth book which I have published with the University of Exeter Press. It has been a great pleasure to work with Simon Baker, Genevieve Davey, Anna Henderson and Nicola Sivills once again; I would also like to thank Barrie Behenna and Emma Catherall for their work on the book. I am deeply grateful to them all for their energy, their enthusiasm and their commitment. No author could wish for more congenial publishers.

This book was written and researched under the auspices of Exeter Archaeology (formerly Exeter Museums Archaeological Field Unit) and almost everyone who has worked for that organization over the past thirty years has contributed something to it. Among the many past and present employees of Exeter Archaeology who have provided information, advice and technical support, I would especially like to thank Jon Bedford, Jane Brayne, Tony Collings, Tony Ives, Mark Knight, Richard Parker, John Salvatore, Sandra Turton and Pam Wakeham. David Garner undertook the photographic work required for this volume with his customary dedication and professionalism. Paul Thomas and the late Paul Staniforth made preliminary transcriptions from original documents. Stuart Blaylock was generous enough to share his unrivalled knowledge of the fabric of the city walls with me, and to provide expert guidance on a host of other subjects. Peter Weddell, the present Director of Exeter Archaeology, has been unfailingly supportive of the project throughout. For this, and for his friendship over many years, I thank him with all my heart. Jannine Crocker helped me to negotiate my way through the city archives, carried out much of the work of transcription and typed up the entire text as well. This book is hers as much as it is mine, and I am more grateful to her than I can say.

My greatest debt is to the late Chris Henderson, the former Director of Exeter Archaeology and the man who first inspired my interest in Exeter's city walls. Chris encouraged me at every stage of the book's completion and read much of the text in draft during his final illness. He was the only begetter of this work; I dedicate it to his memory.

MARK STOYLE

PART I

THE HISTORY OF THE CITY WALLS

INTRODUCTION

The city of Exeter was one of the great provincial capitals of early modern England. From the accession of Henry VII to the eve of the Civil War, Exeter consistently ranked among the five or six most populous English provincial cities, with a population which steadily increased from around 8,000 in 1525 to perhaps as many as 12,000 by 1642.[1] Ruled by a group of wealthy urban oligarchs—who were collectively known as the 'Chamber', or the 'Council of Twenty-Four'—Exeter had grown fat on the profits of trade.[2] The city stood at the lowest crossing point on the River Exe and was ideally placed both to dominate and to exploit its own rich agricultural hinterland and to pursue a vigorous overseas trade through the port of Topsham (which lies at the head of navigation of the Exe, some three miles to the south of the city itself) [*see map 1, and map 6 on p.63*].

During the final quarter of the fifteenth century, Exeter had enjoyed an unprecedented economic boom.[3] The city's size and wealth—together with the fact that it lay in a part of the kingdom which was not only remote but also considered to be unusually vulnerable, both to foreign attack and to domestic disturbances—made it a key strategic position, and it possessed a system of fortification that was fully commensurate with its own importance. During the late second century AD a substantial town wall had been built around the site of the Roman city, and over the succeeding centuries this original defensive circuit, or enceinte, had been repeatedly repaired and improved.[4] At the beginning of the Tudor period, Exeter lay encased within a protective carapace of stone, studded with towers and gates and flanked by deep-cut ditches [*see map 2*]. It is this system of fortification and its history between 1485 and 1660 which forms the subject of the present book.

Town walls are no longer the 'neglected branch of military architecture' that once they were.[5] Ever since the publication of Hilary Turner's pioneering survey of town defences in England and Wales in 1971, a succession of new books and articles on this subject has appeared: some of them dealing with the fortifications of individual urban communities in depth, some of them examining the position across the kingdom as a whole.[6] Over the same period, there has been an explosion of interest in the history of town defences across Europe, the Americas and the wider

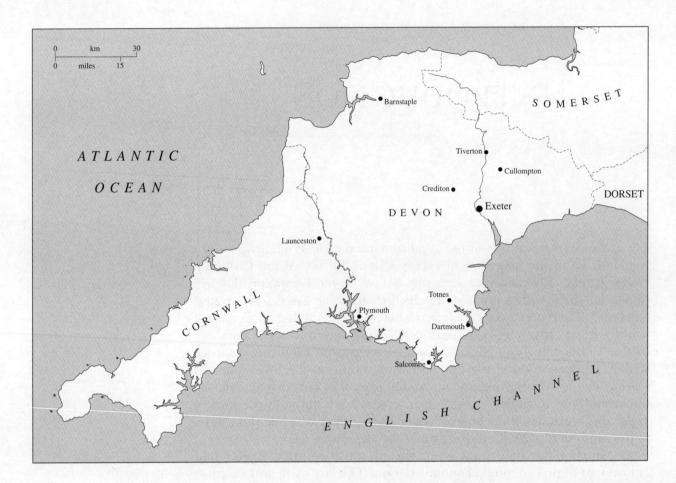

Map 1   Exeter and its region

world beyond.[7] As a result, scholars are now better informed about the nature and purpose of pre-modern urban defences than they have ever been before—and, at Exeter, the rate at which understanding of the city fortifications has improved over the last quarter century has been particularly dramatic.

As late as 1975, the sum total of published work on Exeter's post-Roman defences consisted of a few short essays on the Castle,[8] a clutch of early twentieth-century articles on the city walls and ditches,[9] and a disparate collection of pieces by local antiquaries on the city's gates and towers.[10] This situation first began to change in 1977, with the appearance of an article by Ian Burrow which gave a careful, scholarly account of the defences as a whole.[11] At the same time, the extensive programme of excavation and documentary research which had been commenced in 1972 by Exeter Museums Archaeological Field Unit (latterly Exeter Archaeology) under the direction of the late Chris Henderson was uncovering a vast amount of new information about the defences. During the 1980s and early 1990s much of this material was made available in a series of limited-circulation archaeological reports.[12]

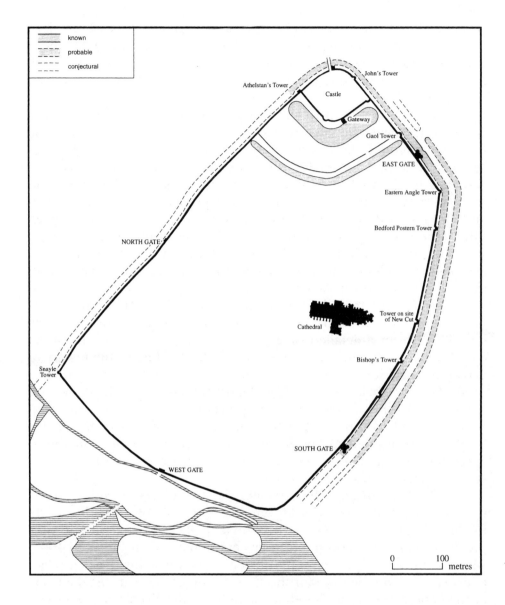

known
probable
conjectural

John's Tower

Athelstan's Tower
Castle
Gateway
Gaol Tower
EAST GATE

Eastern Angle Tower

Bedford Postern Tower

NORTH GATE

Tower on site
of New Cut
Cathedral

Snayle
Tower

Bishop's Tower

SOUTH GATE

WEST GATE

0   100
└──────────┘ metres

Map 2   The medieval
defences of Exeter

This process reached its climax with the appearance, in 1995, of Stuart Blaylock's *Exeter City Wall Survey*: a work which not only provided the definitive history of archaeological investigation of Exeter's defences, but also contained a minutely detailed description of those sections of the city wall—some 72.5% of the original city circuit—which still survive as visible standing fabric today.[13]

The essential lineaments of the system of fortification at Exeter have already been firmly established, then: the nature of the physical construction of the defences (or at least of those portions of them which survived into the twentieth century) is becoming increasingly clear, as is the broad outline of the system's development over time. What remains to be done is to fill in the details of the story: to add historical flesh to the archaeological bones, as it were, by exploring the many roles which the fortifications have played—and, indeed, which they continue to play—in the life of the urban community at Exeter. The early modern era is especially deserving of study in this respect, for during the Tudor and early Stuart periods Exeter not only reached the zenith of its wealth and importance, it also experienced an unprecedented series of military emergencies.

Between 1485 and 1660, the inhabitants of Exeter underwent five major sieges. Over the same period, they were affected—like people all over the kingdom—by a series of more or less serious invasion scares (most notably, perhaps, in 1539–40 and 1545). These episodes led to a vast amount of work being carried out on the city's walls and gates—and to an increasing degree of reliance being placed upon artillery pieces and, latterly, earthworks, as the town governors made determined, albeit fitful, efforts to keep up with the latest advances in military technology. Work on the fortifications of Exeter during these years is quite exceptionally well documented. Indeed, there are few provincial English cities, if any, which can boast such rich civic archives for the medieval and early modern periods.[14] Thus the history of Exeter's fortifications under the Tudor and early Stuart monarchs is by no means of purely local interest, for a detailed study of the fortifications of this one urban community can do much to deepen our understanding of the history of urban fortifications across early modern England as a whole. In particular, it can help to underscore the point that—partly thanks to civic pride, partly thanks to a keen appreciation of the local political advantage that control of the town walls could afford—ruling elites frequently continued to lavish care and attention on their medieval enceintes even after these ancient defensive structures had become, in strictly military terms, anachronistic.

This book subjects the city walls of Exeter to close scrutiny: closer, perhaps, than has ever been applied to the walls of any other early modern English city. The book is divided into two parts. The first provides a narrative account of the city enceinte between 1485 and 1660. The second reproduces those portions of the civic archives which relate to expenditure on the town fortifications during these years. At the heart of the book, figuratively as well as literally, lie the Exeter city receivers' (or treasurers') accounts: a uniquely rich series of documents which run, in an almost unbroken sequence, from 1485 to 1660 (for only nine of these 185 years are the accounts entirely missing).[15] A discussion of the receivers themselves and of the nature of their office, is provided in the introduction to Part II.

The receivers' accounts provide the bulk of the evidence on which our knowledge of the early modern town defences is based, and extracts from these records take pride of place among the transcripts which appear in the second part of this volume [*see document 1*]. Alongside them are reproduced copies of a number of other important documents relating to the city defences. These include a series of extracts from the Chamber act books concerning expenditure on the city enceinte between 1509 and 1545; an account of monies laid out during Perkin Warbeck's assault on Exeter in 1497; two newly discovered 'bills' for expenses incurred during the Prayer Book Rebellion of 1549; two detailed inventories of the city's ordnance compiled in 1556 and 1643; and a list of 'instructions for the defence of the city' which was drawn up by the Parliamentarian authorities in Exeter during the English Civil War [*see documents 2–8*]. The transcripts are accompanied by a glossary which explains some of the more recondite terms used by the fifteenth, sixteenth and seventeenth-century scribes. A list of suggestions for further reading is also provided: one which directs the reader to some of the most stimulating works on urban fortification in medieval and early modern England to have been published over the last 100 years.

The introductory essays with which the book begins are designed partly to set the documents in context, partly to serve as a free-standing history of the town defences at Exeter between the end of the Wars of the Roses and the Restoration of Charles II. Chapter 1 conducts the reader on a virtual tour of the city circuit and explains the nature and significance of the multifarious structures—some dourly defensive, others cheerfully domestic—which are alluded to in the financial accounts. Chapter 2 considers the many different roles which the fortifications played in the life of the early modern city, while Chapter 3 surveys the complicated processes by which the defences were maintained and repaired. Chapters 4 and 5 provide a chronological history of the city defences between 1485 and 1660: a history which explores the fluctuating pattern of expenditure on the defences over time and seeks to explain why that pattern altered as it did. Finally, the many maps, figures and plates which accompany the text help to illuminate the story told by the documents and to bring the city fortifications to life. Together, essays, documents and illustrations provide a minutely textured portrait of the town defences of Exeter between 1485 and 1660: a portrait which registers and reflects back to us—albeit in miniature—the anxieties which flickered across the countenance of the kingdom as a whole during these uniquely troubled years.

CHAPTER I

THE NATURE OF
THE CITY DEFENCES

The Topography of the City Circuit

At the dawn of the Tudor age, Exeter was a self-contained city: one in which the great majority of the inhabitants still dwelt within the town walls. Admittedly, there was already a good deal of extramural development in 1485—most notably in St Sidwell's parish to the east of the city and in Holy Trinity to the south—and the suburbs would grow increasingly populous and extensive as time went on.[1] Nevertheless, anyone walking around the circuit of the city walls at the beginning of the Tudor period would have found that, generally speaking, they were looking out over open ground: over St John's Fields and Southernhay to the east and south, over Bonhay and Shilhay to the west and over Friernhay and Northernhay to the north [*see maps 3–4*]. The city itself stood on an eminently defensible site. The Roman fortress and town had been established on a broad, sloping spur on the eastern bank of the River Exe, and the river helped to guard the city's western flank. To the north lay the steep-sided valley of the Longbrook, and the Roman engineers who had overseen the construction of the original town wall had taken full advantage of this natural defensive feature. From the high bluff at the western corner of the city—the spot known during the early modern period as Snayle Tower [*see map 4*], which overlooks both the river to the west and the Longbrook to the north– the Roman wall had been run along the crest of the Longbrook valley for a distance of some 870 yards as far as the volcanic hillock of Rougemont. This prominent knoll—literally 'the red hill', or 'red mountain'—formed both the northern angle of the city circuit and its strongest point [*see map 5*].

From Rougemont, the wall ran in a south-easterly direction for some 325 yards across the narrow neck of land which connects the spur on which Exeter stands to the similarly high land to the east. At the spot in present-day Post Office Street where the remains of the medieval bastion known as the eastern angle tower now stand, the wall changed direction once again. From here, it headed back in a south-westerly direction towards the river, running at first across almost entirely level terrain and then, for some 490 yards, along the top of a low ridge between two valleys. (As a result the smaller of these two features—the Combe valley, which lay on the site of present-day Coombe Street—was

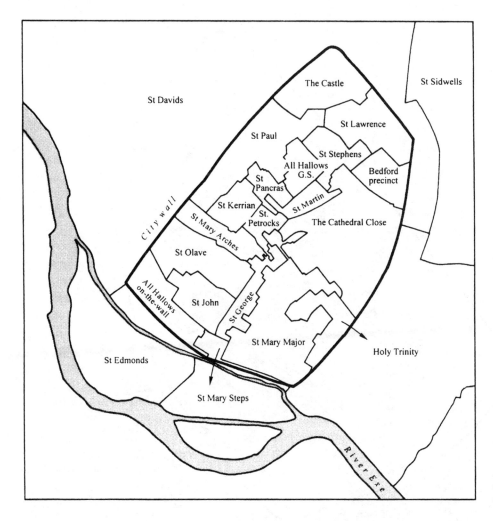

The following labels appear on the map:

The Castle

St Sidwells

St Davids

St Lawrence

St Paul

St Stephens

All Hallows
G.S.

St
Pancras

Bedford
precinct

St Kerrian

St Martin

St.
Petrocks

St Mary Arches

The Cathedral Close

St Olave

All Hallows
on-the-wall

St John

St George

City wall

St Mary Major

Holy Trinity

St Edmonds

St Mary Steps

River Exe

Map 3 Exeter in the sixteenth and seventeenth centuries: parishes

entirely enclosed within the city walls.) Upon reaching a point immediately above the Exe, at today's Quay Hill, the wall changed direction for the last time, running back towards Snayle Tower along the bluffs which overlook the river. The complicated network of water-channels and marshes which lay beneath the walls here made this side of Exeter even more well protected than was the north. It was the southern and eastern sides of the city which were most vulnerable to attack, and—as this chapter will show—it was those same sides of the city which were subsequently provided with the most impressive and elaborate defences.

The Walls

Any attempt to delineate the physical structure of Exeter's early modern fortifications must begin with the town walls. Although they formed but one part of a sophisticated 'defensive ensemble'—an integrated system of fortification which also included ramparts, gates, towers, ditches and, latterly, artillery pieces—the walls were the essential framework which bound all the other component parts together. It was the ancient

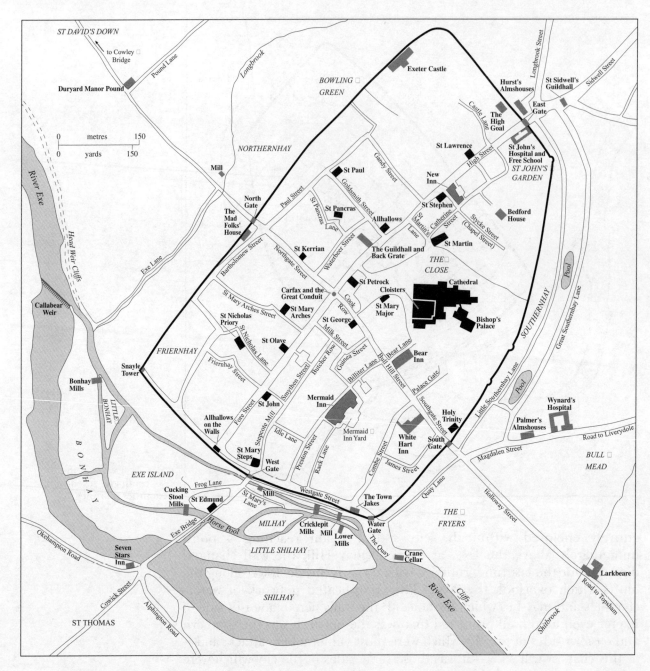

Map 4   Exeter in the sixteenth and seventeenth centuries: place names

KEY:

■ Ecclesiastical buildings
▬ Other buildings
— City wall

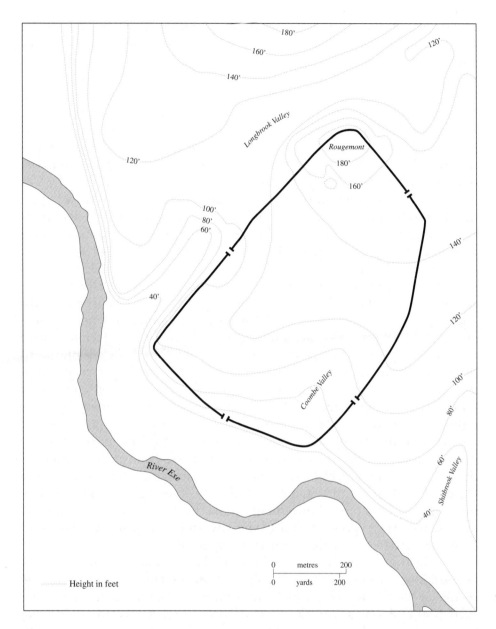

Map 5 The topographical setting of Exeter

masonry enceinte which provided the permanent core of the city fortifications while other, more transient, defensive features ebbed and flowed around it. The town wall which the inhabitants of Tudor Exeter had inherited from their forebears was a gallimaufry in stone: a structure which exhibited an intriguing diversity of materials and architectural styles. To the original Roman wall, which had been built almost entirely in the grey volcanic lava known locally as 'trap', the stonemasons of the Middle Ages had added a colourful patchwork of repairs in pink and white Triassic sandstone from south-east Devon and in red breccia derived from the quarries around Heavitree and Exminster.[2] A good impression of the wall's general appearance is provided by the nineteenth-century antiquary Alexander Jenkins, whose *Description of the City of Exeter* (1806) gives one of the first detailed descriptions of the city's walls and gates. The wall, wrote Jenkins, 'consists of small unhewn stones, as they were dug from the quarry, the interstices filled up with . . . lime and rough sand, and faced with ashler work of hewn stone, [while] the whole [is] strengthened by strong buttresses'.[3] Several of these buttresses—thick stone piers which were built against the outside of the wall to strengthen and support it—may still be seen around the city circuit today [*see plate 19*], and the receivers' accounts contain a number of entries referring to their construction.

The total circuit of the town walls was around a mile and a half. It has been calculated that the original Roman wall was about 11 feet thick at its base, narrowing to about 6½ feet thick at the top, with a wall-walk probably 16 feet above ground level.[4] The Tudor town wall appears to have been of broadly similar height, though those sections which had been entirely rebuilt during the post-Roman period may well have been considerably thinner. In 1527–28 the receiver paid a mason £24 for 'makynge of a pice of walle' near West Gate, containing 'in lenght 61 fote & in height 18 fote . . . and 5 fote in thyknes by the fundacion'. These figures perhaps reveal what were considered to be the basic specifications of the city wall during the Tudor period. The wall was crenellated throughout its entire length and the broad stone merlons, the solid tooth-like portions 3 feet high and up to 6 feet long, which stood on either side of the embrasures were commonly referred to as 'garrets'.[5] The embrasures themselves were known as 'loupes' or 'garret holes'.[6] There are no longer any original garrets standing clear of the parapet of the city wall, but blocked crenellations remain visible at Northernhay Gardens and at Trinity Lane, behind the Southgate Hotel.[7] Some impression of how the battlements looked may be derived from the earliest pictorial representation of the city wall, a map of the lower end of St Mary Arches Lane drawn in 1499 [*see plate 2*].

On the top of the wall, behind the battlements, lay the wall-walk or mural way. Access to this was gained from the city gates, or from 'the steares of the towne wales' which lay at intervals around the circuit.[8] One such flight of stairs was situated at West Gate, a second beside the Church of All Hallows-on-the-Walls and a third at Friernhay.[9] A fourth set of steps is shown leading up to the wall near East Gate in a map of 1617 [*see plate 10*]. The mural way was paved with flagstones. The paved section of walkway which still survives today in the south-western corner of the city circuit, at Bartholomew Terrace, perhaps provides an idea of how the entire wall-walk once looked [*see plate 18*]. The paving not only made it easier and safer for people to pass along the top of the wall, it also helped to protect the fabric of the structure itself. In 1562 the inhabitants of the West Quarter complained that 'there is no pavement nor cawsey [i.e. causeway] made uppon the cyttyes walles behynde Allhallowes Churchye to avoyd the poryinge water, by reason whereof the reigne & water soketh in the wales'. Eight years later, similar complaint was made about the 'unpayved' state of the city walls in St Paul's parish.[10]

It was probably in order to provide a temporary solution to this problem of broken pavements that the receivers occasionally paid workmen to cast gravel and sand upon the walls.[11]

The Rampart

Immediately behind the city wall stood a broad earthen rampart, first constructed by the Romans and later known as 'the barbican'.[12] The crest of this feature lay some 5 feet beneath the level of the wall-walk, but the wall and the rampart were sometimes referred to by contemporaries as if they were one and the same. (In a legal agreement of 1562, reference is made to the 'muraly waye or walke upon the walls of the cittie . . . called the barbycan': a formulation which nicely illustrates how the wall-walk and the earthen rampart which lay immediately beneath it were sometimes conflated in early modern documents.[13]) During the late medieval period many stretches of the barbican had been leased out by the town governors to private individuals, who had established gardens, and even houses, along 'their' portions of the rampart, while a chance reference of 1559 to '[the] walles of the barbeygan between the Southgate & the [Water Gate]' suggests that, here at least, the bank may have been bounded on its inner side by a permanent retaining wall.[14] Between East Gate and South Gate the barbican is known to have been 16 feet wide and it was probably of similar dimensions elsewhere along the circuit.[15]

The barbican served three purposes. First, it provided a fighting platform along which men and equipment could be swiftly moved in times of crisis. Second, it reinforced the town walls and made them far more resistant to cannon-fire. (This explains why, in 1622, it was observed that 'the barbicans and rampards are a farr greater strength and defence to the cittie than the walles'.[16]) Third, the barbican facilitated what one Elizabethan document termed 'the mendyng, sustaynyng, repairyng and walkyng up and uppon the . . . cities walls when and as often as nede schall requyer for the overseith and surveying of the same'.[17] In other words, the rampart not only made it possible to carry out detailed inspections of the wall but it also served as a convenient means of access to any part of the structure which might need repair. For all of these reasons, the Chamber was anxious to ensure that the barbican was kept free of encroachments—or at least of encroachments which could not be swiftly removed. However, this was not always easy to achieve, especially in that part of the city circuit which adjoined the Cathedral Close.

During the Middle Ages, the Bishop of Exeter and three other senior cathedral clergymen had effectively appropriated those sections of the barbican which ran along the ends of their gardens. More inconvenient still, as far as the city authorities were concerned, they had established the right to erect substantial partition walls across the rampart in order to divide their properties from those on either side: partition walls which rose to the top of the city wall itself and abutted on to the crenellations, thus blocking the mural way [*see plate 17*]. The Chamber had retained the right to re-enter the gardens whenever the city walls in this area needed to be repaired, however. Furthermore, in order to enable the citizens to carry out their periodic inspections, a series of 'posterns' had been made in the partition walls along the wall-walk: doors which were opened to the citizens, by the joint consent of the Chamber and the cathedral clergy, at least once a year.[18] (One of these posterns may be seen in a map of *c.*1560 depicting the Archdeacon of Exeter's garden [*see plate 3*].) A similar kind of agreement seems to have been arrived at between the city authorities and the monks of the Blackfriars, who, until the Reformation, held the district which lay next to the town walls between Frerenlane (present-day Chapel Street) and St John's Hospital. The Blackfriars' postern gates were subsequently inherited by the Russells, Earls of Bedford, who acquired the site of the monastery in 1539. The locks and keys of these 'doors next to the south walls' are occasionally referred to in the receivers' accounts,[19] and an early Stuart map shows a series of seven or eight posterns built along the mural way between East Gate and South Gate [*see plate 11*].

The Gates

Only at the gates of the city was the protective circle of wall and rampart breached. In 1485, as for many centuries before, Exeter possessed four city gates: East Gate, North Gate, South Gate and West Gate. Of these, the largest and most impressive was South Gate, which stood near the bottom of present-day South Street, beside old Holy Trinity Church [*see figures 1–2*]. Because this was the side of Exeter which—owing partly to its lack of natural defences and partly to its proximity to the sea-coast—was most vulnerable to attack, South Gate was regarded as a strong-point of particular importance. During the early fifteenth century the medieval gateway here had been extensively remodelled, if not entirely rebuilt. Two great stone drum towers had been erected, one on the south-west side of the gate and the other on the north-east, both projecting boldly outwards from the line of the city wall. At the same time, extensive new chambers and lodgings had been constructed over the gateway itself. During the sixteenth century, the complex of buildings within and behind the gate became ever more elaborate as, first, an inner archway was built over South Street (to connect Holy Trinity Church on the east side of the street with a house belonging to the verger on the west) and, second, a new prison, or 'Counter', for the city was established on the site.[20]

Late sixteenth- and early seventeenth-century drawings provide a good impression of how South Gate looked at this time. Its twin towers were pierced with arrow-loops and windows and topped by domes of lead, while between these two lofty structures—behind the battlements above the gateway—rose the slated roofs of the various ancillary buildings. Just outside the gate lay a sturdy wooden bridge across the city's defensive ditch. Just within it lay the elegant tower of Holy Trinity, a building which stood so close to the battlements that, from a distance,

Figure 1   South Gate, exterior view, 1822

it almost seemed to be part of the gate complex itself [*see plates 4 and 6*]. Alexander Jenkins provides the best eyewitness account of South Gate: an account which, although it was written in *c.*1800, nevertheless helps to convey something of the impression which the structure must have made on those who saw it during earlier centuries. 'The gate is a massy building of hewn stone', wrote Jenkins,

> [and] the entrance from the suburbs is through a lofty pointed arch, flanked by circular towers, [while] over the gateway is a niche . . . [with] a mutilated statue in a magisterial robe. This front is likewise decorated with angels, supporting the royal and city arms; [while] the interior arch of the gateway . . . [is in] semi-circular form . . . [and] on the tops of the towers are battlemented leads, which command a fine prospect.[21]

The second of the city's principal gates was East Gate, which lay at the eastern end of High Street, on the site now occupied by Boots the Chemist [*see figures 3–4*]. Like South Gate it was approached by way of a timber bridge over the defensive ditch which lay immediately outside the city walls. In 1485 a single tower, apparently known as 'the wacchehouse',

Figure 2   South Gate, interior view, 1819

stood above the gate-arch here.[22] The roof of this structure was crenellated and covered with lead, while the main chamber within it was well-appointed and periodically let out to tenants. To the rear of the tower and immediately adjoining it above the roadway stood the chapel of St Bartholomew, which effectively formed an extension of the gate. Other houses adjoined the tower, and it is clear that the medieval East Gate formed an impressive complex of buildings.[23] It was to become more impressive still after 1511, when the Chamber ordered 'that Estgate shalbe taken downe & . . . newe bildyed agayne'.[24] By the time that this programme of work came to an end, in 1514, East Gate had been provided with two massive projecting towers of the type which had previously been erected at South Gate. The chapel and a number of other old buildings seem to have survived at the rear of the structure, but the outer façade was completely new. Later drawings by Exeter's Elizabethan Chamberlain, John Hooker and by Robert Sherwood, the city's early Stuart surveyor, show that the towers of the Henrician East

Figure 3   East Gate, interior view, 1785

Gate, like those of the medieval South Gate, were furnished with gun-loops and battlements and topped with great, dome-shaped lead roofs. Jenkins observed of the Tudor East Gate that:

> this gate . . . consisted of a curtain flanked by two bulwarks. The exterior arch was very strong and lofty, over which, rested a statue of King Henry 7th . . . Near the bottom of the flanking towers, were portholes for the great port cannons; and lookouts on each story . . . [while] in the centre of the gateway was a strong semi-circular arch'.[25]

Of the two remaining gates, the more important was North Gate, which lay at the bottom of North Street, beside the present day City Gate public house, and looked out over the steep ascent into Exeter from the Longbrook Valley [*see figure 5*]. Documentary evidence shows that a single defensive tower stood above the gate-arch here in 1485, and that the tower itself incorporated a large room or chamber.[26] Early Tudor references to '[the] house in North Gate', and 'the house over the North Gate' suggest that here, as at East Gate, the original tower had been extended in order to provide permanent accommodation.[27] Like East

Figure 4   East Gate, exterior view, 1785

Gate, North Gate was substantially rebuilt during the sixteenth century. In 1558, the Chamber noted that the gate was in poor repair and ordered the receiver 'to make and byld over the said gate such defensable byldings as shalbe thought resonable'.[28] The resultant structure, the product of some five years' work, is illustrated in many later drawings. Braun and Hogenberg's map of 1618, which incorporates the earliest surviving view, depicts a single crenellated structure projecting outwards from the city wall, to which is joined, at the rear, a large building with a tiled roof extending backwards over the roadway behind the gate [*see plate 4*]. According to Jenkins, North Gate

> had no flanking bulwarks, but projected from the wall, with two small curtains, in which were stairs that led to two guard rooms. They had orillons for the defenders to discharge their missile weapons on any attacking enemy. On the top of the gate, was a square platform, with a lofty battlemented curtain.

In Jenkins' own time, the interior of North Gate 'was occupied as a public house, which, from the darkness of its rooms, was, ironically, termed Hell'.[29]

Figure 5 North Gate, exterior view, 1831

The last of the city gates was West Gate, which stood at the bottom of Stepcote Hill and commanded a fine prospect over Exebridge and the River Exe. West Gate was the main entrance to the city for travellers from Cornwall, and the inn known as the Cornish Chough—a welcome sight for Cornish folk—lay only five minutes' walk away up Smythen Street.[30] Perhaps because this side of Exeter was so well protected by the river, the town governors lavished less attention on West Gate than they did on the other city gates. Unlike the other gateways, it does not appear to have been substantially redesigned or remodelled during the early modern period. In 1660, as in 1485, West Gate consisted of little more than an archway cut through the town wall, surmounted, to the rear, by a modest stone tower [*see figures 6–7*]. This tower contained a single chamber which, like the similar rooms over the other gates, was leased out by the Chamber to a series of private individuals.[31] The receivers' accounts show that the double gates within the archway were made of stout timber and liberally studded with iron. One of the gate leaves incorporated a 'wicket', or postern door, which—at West Gate, as at the other city gates—permitted pedestrians to pass through when the main gates were closed.[32] Jenkins found the West Gate unimpressive. He described it as 'a very ancient, but . . . mean structure, and inferior in point of architecture to the other city gates', adding that: 'it consists of a square tower, something loftier than the walls, without any projection on the outside, or flanking bulwarks'. 'In this tower', he concluded, 'is an ill contrived room, with a small window looking towards the suburbs; on the interior front is the remains of an inscription now

Figure 6 West Gate, exterior view, 1831

obliterated; the entrance into the city is through an irregular pointed arch'.[33]

Beneath the roadway under West Gate lay a large, stone-lined drain—variously described in the receivers' accounts as 'the conduit', 'the gutter', or 'the vault'—through which the waste water which would otherwise have accumulated in this low-lying part of Exeter was channelled out through the town wall.[34] Iron grates were placed at the mouth of the drain in order to prevent it from becoming clogged up with debris, but the fact that men were regularly paid for 'ridding', or cleaning out, the grates suggests that blockages were frequent.[35] Even when the drain was clear, it does not appear to have functioned very effectively. In 1570 the inhabitants of the West Quarter complained that 'the grates at Westgate' were 'to[o] littell to receave the water at great floudes' and added plaintively that there was 'great smell under the same'.[36] The proximity to the West Gate of this dark, noisome tunnel—its foetid entrance colloquially known during the Middle Ages as 'le Mouthe'—did nothing to improve the dignity of what was always regarded as Exeter's least splendid gateway.[37]

The Towers

In addition to its four great gates, medieval Exeter possessed a number of defensive towers which were built along the city wall. In all, seven such mural towers are documented. The date of their construction is unknown, but they probably dated from the thirteenth century: certainly,

Exeter

Inside view of West gate
remarkable in the seige in Edward VI time

Outside view of West gate, thro it is seen
the sea S.t Mary-Steps.

S.t Mary Stafses

Outside view of D.o taken sideways

Figure 7   West Gate, interior and exterior views, 1792

none of them seems likely to have been built after 1330.[38] Working in a clockwise direction round the enceinte, the first of the city towers was the semi-circular bastion which stood some 130 feet to the north-west of East Gate: a structure of which nothing now survives. Calculations made from the Chamber map book (a collection of surveys of the city's properties drawn up in *c*.1758) suggests that this 'hollow tower . . . in the . . . walle', as it was described in 1642, may have been about 20 feet wide.[39] Little is known about the structure, but it is clearly shown on several of the earliest maps of the city. A bird's-eye view of Exeter drawn up in around 1590 depicts it as a crenellated building with several loopholes or embrasures, while a rather later plan provides a rear view [*see plates 5 and 13*]. Not a single reference survives to work being carried out on this tower by the city receivers during the early modern period.

The section of the town wall which ran between East Gate and South Gate was the weakest part of the city defences. Five towers had consequently been built here during the medieval period. The first was the eastern angle tower, or hospital tower, which stood at the north-eastern corner of the city circuit, behind St John's Hospital. This tower is known to have been in existence at least as early as 1341 and its remains still stand today [*see plate 21*].[40] The structure is pentagonal in shape, and about 23 feet wide at its base. The parapet and allure which survive at the top of the tower probably date from the time of the Civil War.[41] Sixteenth- and seventeenth-century drawings suggest that, like all the other towers along this section of the wall, the eastern angle tower was crenellated and furnished with windows and arrow slits. Before the Reformation, the tower was leased out by the city authorities to the prior of St John's Hospital. Thereafter, the structure passed into other hands, and it is possible that the maintenance of the tower became the responsibility of the new tenants.[42] Certainly, there is no record of the Chamber laying out any money on repairs to the building during the century between the Reformation and the Civil War.

Some 45 yards to the south-west of the hospital tower, half-way along present-day Post Office Street, stood a second projecting pentagonal tower. Jenkins, who inspected this structure before it was demolished in the nineteenth century, drew a sketch of it [*see figure 8*] and provided a valuable description. 'In its original state', he wrote, this tower 'consisted of three stages, or floors, for the defendants to stand on. It is 42 feet in height, from the present scalp of the [city] ditch, having orillons in front, and on each side, to flank the ditch. A doorway was made here (now walled up) and called Bedford postern, it being a passage for the conveniency of Bedford House.'[43] (This was the former house of the Blackfriars, purchased by the First Earl of Bedford in the 1540s, which lay immediately behind the tower, inside the wall.) The doorway to which Jenkins refers may be clearly seen at the foot of the tower in his sketch. It had been made during the Prayer Book Rebellion of 1549, when the Earl of Bedford had ordered that 'a little low doore' should be 'made through the wall' here in order to facilitate sallies against the rebels.[44] According to an early seventeenth-century document, the postern could only be reached *via* 'a descent of many degrees' (by which a steep flight of steps within the tower was presumably meant). The key to the door was always kept in the possession of the Chamber.[45] Two of Hooker's maps show a small, railed footbridge issuing forth from beneath the postern door and passing over the city ditch into Southernhay [*see plates 5 and 7*]. The rails and boards of this 'postern bridge' were kept in a storeroom at Bedford House, and are referred to in an inventory of 1594.[46]

The fourth tower along the line of the enceinte stood 175 yards to the south of the Bedford postern tower, roughly on the site of the present day 'New Cut' [*see plates 15 and 17*]. During the medieval period, St Martin's Lane extended much further southwards than it does today, stretching all the way from High Street to the city wall. At the place where the lane ended, 'a grete defensable towre' had been built athwart the wall.[47] References to this structure exist from as early as 1284, making it the earliest documented tower on the city circuit.[48] The tower stood next to the house of the Archdeacon of Cornwall and had been leased out by the city to the holder of that office, on condition that he keep the interior parts of the structure in good repair.[49] During the 1440s a dispute had blown up between the Chamber and the cathedral clergy over access to the tower. The citizens had alleged that, owing to an encroachment made on St Martin's Lane, they could not 'have theyre way, as theym ought to have, to the towne wallys and ye towre aforesaid'. To this, the bishop had retorted that the citizens always had had, and always *would* have, 'unhindered comyng and going to repair the said towre and walles'.[50] Matters do not appear to have been resolved, and, as the dispute rumbled on over the succeeding decades, the tower fell into increasing disrepair and, eventually, collapsed.

In a petition submitted to Bishop John Veysey, probably during the 1530s, the citizens complained that the tower was

> of late . . . utterly decayed and fallen down and so remaineth to the great danger and deformity of the . . . city. And albeit that diverse . . . requests have been made to the . . . Dean and Chapter by the mayor . . . to reedifie the same tower . . . they so to do have utterly refused, and yet do.

Presumably the clergymen continued in their recalcitrance, for the tower is never mentioned again.[51] A payment of £20 made by the receiver in 1541–42 'for making and repairing the City Wall next to the Archdeacon of Cornwall's garden' may well record the construction of a new stretch of curtain wall to replace the ruined tower.[52] Late Tudor maps show no trace of a structure on the spot where the archdeacon's tower had previously stood.

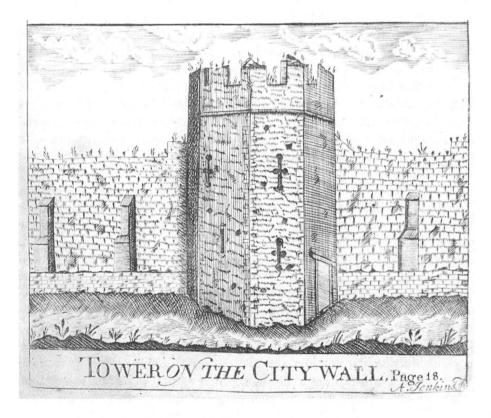

Figure 8 The Bedford Postern Tower, exterior view, 1806

The grandest of Tudor Exeter's mural towers lay 80 yards to the south-west of St Martin's Lane, in the section of the city wall which adjoined the garden of the Bishop's Palace [*see figure 9*]. In 1447 this structure had been described as 'the moste costelew defence and most stately towre of alle the city . . . well heled [i.e. roofed] with led, and housed for a right gode mansion to be ther yn'.[53] Late sixteenth-century plans depict it as an impressive building, three storeys high [*see plate 6*], while a document of the 1630s refers to it as 'an ancient castle', rather than a tower.[54] The face-work of the semi-circular bastion which today stands on the site is modern, but earlier work still survives in the interior of the structure. The building was 29 feet wide and probably rose to a greater height than any of the other towers along this section of the wall.[55] Although it officially belonged to the city, the tower had been effectively appropriated during the Middle Ages by the bishops, who used it both as a store house and a prison.[56] Despite the best efforts of the Chamber, the bishops managed to retain possession of the tower throughout the early modern period. As a result the structure was generally referred to in the receivers' accounts as 'the bishops tower', or, more pointedly, as 'the tower called the bishops'.[57] Today, it has come to be known as 'the Lollard's Tower', or 'the Lollard's Prison'.

The final tower along this section of the wall lay 74 yards to the south-west of the bishop's tower and 120 yards to the north-east of South Gate. Contemporary drawings depict it as a crenellated structure, two storeys high, provided with gun-loops and embrasures [*see plates 6 and 11*]. (The semi-circular bastion, 30 feet wide, which stands on the spot today was rebuilt as a ruin in 1912.[58]) Like its northern neighbour, this tower lay beside the garden of the Bishop's Palace and had fallen under the bishops' *de facto* control during the medieval period. As a result it is difficult, if not impossible, to distinguish entries in the documentary record which relate to this tower from those which relate to the larger structure to the north. Both buildings were almost certainly referred to as 'the bishops tower' at different times. All that can be said with confidence is that, owing to the intense reluctance of successive bishops to admit the city's workmen into the Palace grounds, comparatively little work was carried out on either of these structures during the years before the Civil War.[59]

The last of Tudor Exeter's mural towers was the structure known as 'Snayle Tower', which stood on the site of present-day Bartholomew Terrace, at the north-western corner of the city [*see map 4*]. This was one of the largest and most important of Exeter's defensive towers. The etymology of its peculiar name is uncertain, though it has been suggested that the appellation may derive from the tower's 'colour and perhaps odd shape'.[60] The earliest reference to the tower dates from 1348, while the receivers' accounts contain a number of entries relating to work on the structure (which, unlike the other towers, does not appear to have been let out to, or appropriated by, private individuals, and was therefore the responsibility of the citizens alone).[61] Braun and Hogenberg's map of 1618 depicts Snayle Tower as a hollow, circular building topped by crenellations [*see plate 4*]. Later plans suggest that it possessed a conical

Figure 9   The 'Lollard's Tower', exterior view, 1870

roof turret as well, while a drawing of 1662 provides a good impression of the way in which the structure dominated the city defences in the north-western corner of Exeter [*see figure 10*]. Snayle Tower was demolished in the nineteenth century and no vestige of it now remains.[62]

The Ditch

Beyond the circuit of walls, gates and towers lay Exeter's outer line of defence: the city ditch. This deep defensive feature, which probably dated back to the late Saxon period, extended right around the vulnerable south-eastern corner of the city, from East Gate to South Gate.[63] During the Middle Ages it had been commonly known as the town 'fosse': during the early modern period it was more often termed 'the dyke'.[64] The precise length of the ditch is unknown, but archaeological excavation has located it at several points in Southernhay, as well as just outside East Gate. The ditch was some 45 feet wide and lay close to the base of the city walls.[65] In 1633 a witness in a law case deposed that the ditch 'doth lye at the foote of those bankes whereon the walles of the . . . cittie are . . . built, and nothinge doeth devide it from the said . . . walles, but the said banckes'. A second witness provided a similar picture, testifying that the 'said ditches are distant in some places twentie feete and in some places thirtie from the sayd walles on the outside'.[66] By 1485 the medieval ditch had become partially silted up, and by *c*.1580 it was almost entirely covered over with brambles, thistles and nettles. Nevertheless, it remained a distinctive part of the local scene. During the Elizabethan period, much 'offence' was caused to passers-by 'by reason of the stinckinge water that stood in diverse places of the said ditch, and of the carrion and other noysome thinges which were . . . throwen into it'.[67] Exeter possessed at least two other defensive ditches during the Tudor period. One of these was situated in Northernhay, and probably extended from North Gate to Rougemont. The other was the 'Crolleditch', an ancient earthwork which lay in Southernhay, some distance beyond the main city ditch, and which had fallen into disuse long before 1485.[68]

The Castle

The strongest part of Exeter's defences was the Castle [*see figure 11*]. This imposing fortress, which stands on the summit of Rougemont Hill in the north-eastern corner of the city, had been founded by William the Conqueror in 1068 and extended and improved by subsequent monarchs. The Castle lay under the jurisdiction of the Crown, rather than of the city authorities, and it was the Crown which was responsible for the structure's upkeep and repair. As a result, the receivers' accounts contain practically no references to work there. During the early modern period, as today, the Castle was separated from the rest of Exeter by a high stone curtain wall, which transformed the north-eastern part of the city circuit into a separate citadel. At the foot of this wall lay a steep bank and a deep ditch which could only be crossed at one point: at the head of Castle Street, or Castle Bayley Lane, where a fortified drawbridge ran up to the main Castle gate. Immediately beside this gateway lay the old Norman gatehouse, which had been blocked up during the late Middle Ages but retained as a mural tower [*see plates 9 and 10*].[69]

This was just one of the strongpoints which bristled along the Castle walls. To the north-east of the main gate, where the Castle curtain wall met the inner face of the city wall, stood a corner tower. To the north-west of this structure stood the semi-circular bastion known in later centuries as 'John's Tower', while a further 75 yards along the wall stood a second gateway. A lofty tower rose up here, flanked by a lower gateway, or 'sally port', from which two parallel walls, cut through with loop-holes, extended to form a 'covered-way' which was colloquially known as 'the Devil's Cradle'.[70] This in turn led to a wooden drawbridge which crossed

Figure 10   Exe Bridge and the city walls at Snayle Tower, 1662

the outer ditch of the Castle into Northernhay [*see plates 9 and 10*]. Around 65 yards to the south-west of here stood a rectangular tower, today known as 'Athelstan's Tower', which defended the junction of the shared city and Castle wall with the north-west end of the Castle's inner curtain wall. From this point, the curtain wall ran back, first to the south-east, and then to the north-west, until it finally rejoined the gatehouse at the main entrance.[71] The fact that Richard III took the trouble to inspect the Castle during his brief visit to Exeter in 1483—the occasion of the King's famous discomfiture on recalling the prophecy that '[he] should not live long after [he] saw Richmond [i.e. Rougemont]'—suggests that at this time it was still regarded as a key position.[72] Thereafter, the Castle defences—like those of similar urban fortresses all over England—appear to have been indifferently maintained, if not entirely neglected.[73]

Artillery

More significant than Richard III's visit to Rougemont Castle, in terms of the evolution of the city defences, was the fact that that unfortunate monarch's reign also coincided with an increased use of artillery at Exeter. During the 1300s Exeter is known to have been provided with 'springels', or catapults, but, by the late fifteenth century, at the very latest, these old-fashioned weapons had clearly been replaced by guns.[74] In 1483–84 the citizens purchased a large quantity of gunpowder, while in 1484–85 the receiver paid one man for making 'gunstones' and another for 'attending' a gun at the Guildhall.[75] Over the next sixty

Figure 11 The Castle, exterior view, 1744

years, the citizens placed increasing reliance on guns: initially borrowing artillery pieces from local noblemen to defend the city during specific military emergencies, but eventually purchasing an entire suite of ordnance of their own to serve as a permanent part of the city defences.

In 1545 the Chamber bought a substantial collection of artillery pieces [*see document 4*] and from this time onwards fees were regularly paid to the men charged with looking after these weapons. From around 1550 onwards, the civic ordnance was kept in a special chamber known as 'the gonnehouse', which lay within the former monastic complex of St John's Hospital.[76] Gunpowder was kept in the 'common storehouse' at the Guildhall, and the receivers' accounts contain many references to powder being carried back and forth from here.[77] Only in times of genuine crisis were the guns brought out of storage and deployed around the city circuit. In such emergencies, the 'great port pieces'— guns which fired hail-shot and were used to protect narrow passages— were positioned within the gates. The other artillery pieces were placed on temporary earthen 'mounts', or batteries, constructed on the barbican behind the city wall. Experts were, of course, needed to serve the guns, and references to the payment of such men became increasingly frequent in the city records during the mid-Tudor years.[78]

Citizens and Soldiers

What of those who manned the city defences? The history of the town militia at Exeter during the early modern period forms a discrete subject of its own, and it is not one that can be explored in depth here. In essence, however, the position was very simple. Throughout the Tudor and early Stuart periods—except, perhaps, during the wholly exceptional years of the Civil War—the citizens were primarily responsible for their own defence. They might be assisted from time to time by noble retinues, or by other forces from outside, but, generally speaking, it was they themselves who shouldered the burden. 'In tymes of warres and trobles', as Hooker put it, Exeter's first line of defence were 'the watchemen and wardesmen'.[79] These were respectable citizens who were appointed to patrol the streets and guard the gates: the watchmen by night and the wardsmen by day.

Should more substantial forces be required, the town governors could summon up an impressive body of citizens in arms. Every able-bodied male inhabitant of Exeter above a certain level of income was required to maintain weapons for the city's defence. To ensure that the citizens were fulfilling these military obligations, a formal review was held once a year on Midsummer Day, at which the mayor inspected the menfolk of the city drawn up in full battle array. The citizens were also obliged to turn out at musters: periodic assemblies of the city's able-bodied men which were summoned by the Lord Lieutenant at the behest of the Crown. A muster held in 1538 resulted in an appearance of over 1,000 men, while, a century later, the Deputy Lieutenants reported that there were 1,350 'able men' in Exeter 'which are fitt for supplies of the trayned bands there'.[80] The 'trained bands'—four companies of 100 men apiece, each company recruited from a different quarter of the city—were Exeter's 'elite troops'. These were the men who were provided with regular training, and upon whom the chief responsibility of defending the city would fall in times of crisis. Each company was commanded by a captain, invariably one of the civic elite, while, from the 1580s onwards, the Chamber also retained a 'muster-master' to oversee the drilling and the organization of the city's soldiers.[81]

The Porters' Lodges

In addition to the chief component parts of the city defences, there were various non-military structures which stood either upon or immediately behind the walls: structures which are frequently referred to in the receivers' accounts. The most important of these were the houses belonging to the city porters. Of all the inhabitants of early modern Exeter, the porters were the individuals whose day-to-day lives revolved most closely around the town defences. Writing in 1600, Hooker described them as the officials in whom 'the greatest trust is committed for the salffe keepinge of the gates and the preservation of the whole citie'.[82] The duties and responsibilities of a porter were surprisingly wide ranging, and were summed up by Hooker thus:

> He is to . . . shutt the gates . . . at . . . [10pm] in the sommer and [9pm] in the wynter. And in the morninge to open theym at . . . [4am] in the sommer and . . . [5am] in the wynter . . . Also every . . . straunger [is] to be receaved [by the porter], and all lewd and suspecte persons to be apprehended [by him] and committed to the warde. The gates upon hewe and crye and upon tumoltes must be shutt [by him]. And all faultes founde [by him are] upon every Monday to be presented [to his superiors].[83]

The porters were appointed directly by the Chamber. Should they misbehave themselves in any way, they were liable to face severe censure, and several porters were summarily dismissed, either because they were felt to be unreliable or because they had grown too old to carry out their duties.[84]

Between 1485 and 1560 the porters of the four city gates received an annual pension, or retaining fee, of 3 shillings apiece. This sum was raised to 4 shillings in 1560–61, and remained fixed at that rate thereafter.[85] In addition, the porters of North Gate and West Gate received an extra 6 shillings and 8 pence and 4 shillings respectively, for cleaning out the drains which lay beside 'their' gates. Following the construction of Quay Gate, or 'Water Gate', in 1564–65 [*see figure 12*], the Chamber decided that a fifth porter should be appointed to oversee this new entrance to the city. 'Thomas Rawlyns, taylor' was chosen to be the first porter of the Water Gate, and over the following years he received an annual fee of 6 shillings and 8 pence.[86] The office of fifth city porter did not endure for long, however. Perhaps because the new gate proved to be a less busy thoroughfare than had originally been anticipated, the town governors later decided that the keepership of Quay Gate and West Gate should be combined. Accordingly, in 1599, the Chamber ordered that one Thomas Slingsby should be 'sworn porter bothe for the Westegate and the Keyegate' and should receive the accustomed pensions for both offices.[87] Half a century later, the porter of West Gate was still receiving 6 shillings and 8 pence *per annum* 'for keeping of the Keygate'.[88]

Like many of the other civic functionaries, the porters enjoyed the right to wear the city's livery. In 1591 the Chamber directed that the porters should be provided with cloth to make formal gowns at the city's charge and, thereafter, each porter was presented with a seven-and-a-half yard length of black kersey cloth every three years.[89] Whenever a sudden emergency meant that an especially close watch had to be kept on the gates at night, the porters were supplied with candles—or, more commonly, were reimbursed for having purchased extra candles themselves.[90] Finally, as has already been indicated, the porters were

Figure 12   Quay Gate, exterior view, 1822

provided with on-site lodgings: lodgings which stood either above, or within, the gates and for which the porters paid the Chamber an annual rent.

At North Gate the porter lived in the 'house' or tenement above the gateway itself.[91] At Quay Gate, it is not clear that a gate-keeper's house was ever provided. At the other three gates there were purpose-built 'porters' lodges', at least from the end of the sixteenth century. A city rental of *c*.1603 records that one John Weste then held 'a littel tenement under the [South] Gate called the porter's lodge', while Thomas Slingsby occupied 'the porters lodge late newly bilded' at West Gate, at a rent of 10 shillings a year.[92] The porter's lodge at East Gate is referred to in the receiver's book for 1602–3, when a workman was paid for repairing a chimney there.[93] It was clearly a sizeable building. When a young Exeter man staggered into the lodge at East Gate after a night on the town in 1618, he found there not only 'Humfrye the porter', but also 'two worsted comers & a boy playing at cardes for drincke'.[94] The porters' families lived with them 'over the shop', and when a porter died in office it was not unknown for his widow to be permitted to serve in his stead until she could find somewhere new to live. This happened at West

Gate in 1698, for example, and may also have happened at South Gate in 1640.[95]

Houses and Privies

The porters' lodges were by no means the only buildings with a non-military purpose incorporated into the city enceinte. First, there were the houses belonging to private individuals, which in certain parts of Exeter stood right next to, and partially on top of, the town wall. Most of these were situated in the West Quarter, along the stretch of the wall which ran between West Gate and All Hallows-on-the-Walls Church [*see map 4 and figure 13*].[96] Second, there was 'the little house upon the walls by . . . North Gate' which was built in 1590–91 [*see map 4*]. This structure was termed the 'madfolkes house' and was clearly intended to serve as a place of incarceration for the mentally disturbed.[97] The roofer whom the receiver paid in 1619 for 'repayreinge the darke house by the walles being much torren with the winde' had probably been at work on this building: in contemporary parlance, a 'dark house' was a place in which madmen were confined.[98] Third, and most frequently referred to of all in the receivers' accounts, there were the city's *communas latrinas,* or public lavatories.

Exeter's first recorded public lavatories lay at the bottom of Coombe Street, halfway between South Gate and West Gate, at the point where the Coombe Stream passed out through the city walls and into the river below through a drain known as 'the Water Yeate'.[99] This outfall took the form of a substantial archway, made of grey volcanic stone, one side of which may still be seen high up on the city walls near Cricklepit [*see figure 14*]. Together, the stream and arch provided a convenient means of flushing away sewage and a cluster of privies had been built here during the Middle Ages. The privies were housed in a purpose-built timber structure which stood immediately behind the city wall, above the drain. During the Tudor period this building was known as 'the towne jakes' or 'the towne sege' (i.e. 'the town seat', or perhaps one should say 'the town throne').[100] A second public lavatory stood in Friernhay, near Snayle Tower.[101] This privy appears to have discharged its contents straight over the town wall on to the ground below, from where the waste material presumably trickled downhill into the Exe. In 1528 the Chamber directed that '2 new syttes & 3 wherelgogges' should be erected here: quite what the 'wherelgogges' were remains unclear.[102]

Forty years later the town governors initiated a major overhaul of Exeter's public lavatories, when they ordered that three communal jakes or 'widraughtes' (i.e. 'draught-houses'—so-called for obvious reasons) were to be made: one in Friernhay, one 'at the townewalle' in St Paul's parish and one 'about the Watergate'.[103] The 'newe beldyng of the prevy by ye Watar Gete', recorded in the receiver's book for 1571–72, was clearly a direct result of this order.[104] It is evident that the 'widraughtes' which the Chamber had ordered to be built at Watergate and Friernhay were intended to replace the derelict privies which already stood on those sites.[105] The jakes 'at the townewalle in St Pauls', on the other

Figure 13 City walls at Rack Lane, 1849; the horse and cart in the middle of the picture are emerging from West Gate

hand, may well have been an entirely new structure. Few references survive to the privies in St Pauls, but they may be identifiable with 'the howses upon the walls at the end of Mr Birdalls garden' which were repaired by a city workman in 1629.[106]

Vaults, Drains and Gutters

In addition to the various buildings which stood on top of the town wall, there was also a complex series of 'vaults', drains and gutters which lay beneath it. These subterranean structures served two major purposes; they brought fresh water into Exeter through the barrier formed by the city enceinte and they channelled waste water and sewerage back out again. The largest and most elaborate of the Exeter vaults were the two stone-lined inspection-tunnels—or 'underground passages' as they are known today—which had been built to accommodate the water-pipes of the city and cathedral aqueducts as they passed beneath the town

Figure 14   The city walls at Quay Gate *c.* 1570;
note the outfall of the Coombe Stream on the left-hand side of the gate

defences on their way into Exeter from the springs in St Sidwells. The first of these passages belonged to the citizens and crossed into Exeter directly beneath the East Gate. The second belonged to the Dean and Chapter and passed into Exeter beneath the wall near the hospital tower. Very similar in function, if far less impressive in appearance, was the little vaulted chamber which had been cut through the city wall to the north of the Bedford postern tower in order to admit the pipes of the aqueduct which supplied the Blackfriars monastery.[107] Another 'pipe-vault' lay in the vicinity of the Bishop's Palace. Here, a stone 'arch' had been built beneath the town wall to admit the pipes of the aqueduct which fed the conduit in Southgate Street [*see plate 12*].[108]

Far more numerous than the structures which let water in were those which channelled it out. These 'drainage channels' may be divided into three main groups. First, there were the many small gutters which had been surreptitiously driven through the city walls by private individuals in order to drain off water from their own premises. This practice was frowned on by the Chamber because of the damage it caused to the walls and people who had built such gutters were frequently hauled before the authorities. In 1630, for example, a certain Zacharie Searle was presented 'for a noysom gutter through the citties walles neere Westgate'. He was ordered 'to divert and turne the water another waye, and not to suffer any water to runne from his house through the walles againe'.[109] The second group of drainage channels were those which carried water away from beneath the gates. The most substantial of these lay at North Gate and West Gate, which, unlike East Gate and South Gate, stood at the bottom of steeply sloping streets down which water and ordure constantly flowed. The drain at West Gate has already been described. The drain at North Gate was of similar construction, consisting of a stone-lined 'gutter' which began some way within the gate and discharged its contents some way without.[110] The channel was covered over with earth and paving stones and fitted with stout iron grates at both ends. It seems probable that there was some way of lifting these metal grilles out of the timber frames in which they were set to permit the periodic 'ridding' of the drain.[111] At both gates, the term 'the grate'—which had initially been applied only to the grilles— later came to refer to the drain as a whole.

Last but not least, there were the structures designed to vent sewers through the town walls and out into the city ditch. In 1485 there were at least three such outfalls. The first was the arch at 'Water yeate'. The second lay in St Martin's Lane. Two 'grete comyn guttor[s]' served the ecclesiastical establishments in this part of Exeter during the Middle Ages: one running down Frerenlane (present-day Chapel Street), the other running down St Martin's Lane itself. Until the mid-fifteenth century the gutter in Frerenlane did not possess an outfall of its own. Instead, it altered course abruptly just before the lane reached the city wall: turning to the southwest and running along parallel with the wall through the Archdeacon of Cornwall's garden, until it eventually debouched into the gutter in St Martin's Lane.[112] The contents of both water-courses then passed out through the walls together *via* the same outfall [*for a later view of this outfall, see plate 15*]. It was not a very satisfactory arrangement. The gutters periodically flooded, causing rainwater and what was euphemistically known as 'other water' to accumulate behind the city wall. Accordingly, in 1458, the Chamber had authorized one of the cathedral canons 'to conduct the said waters through . . . [Freren] lane, and to break down . . . the wall there at the end of the lane . . . for an adequate . . . discharge of the . . . water . . . into the [city] ditch'.[113] Thereafter, two separate outfalls existed: one on either side of the Archdeacon's garden. No references to work on these outfalls survive in the city accounts, possibly because the structures were maintained by the cathedral clergy, but it is clear that the drain in St Martin's Lane was still functioning on the eve of the Civil War.[114]

Two further sewerage outfalls were constructed along the line of the enceinte during the mid-sixteenth century. The first lay beneath South Gate, and was probably built during the 1550s. Its purpose was to vent the contents of the lavatories of the new city prison there into the town ditch. The outfall consisted of a stone 'vawte' beneath the prison from which waste material passed into the ditch *via* a stone 'gutter' guarded by iron 'grates'.[115] The porter of South Gate was frequently paid for unblocking these grates: an unpleasant task, but not nearly as unpleasant as that which faced the labourers who periodically had to descend into the depths of the vault itself in order to clear out the accumulated filth by candlelight.[116] In 1651–52 'two poore men' spent many days 'clensing the vautt under the prison'; after the work was completed, the Chamber munificently agreed that they could keep 'the dunge' which they had removed.[117] Jenkins, who inspected the felons' prison in the west tower of South Gate in *c.*1800, gave a lively account of the hardship endured by the prisoners here, observing that 'to add to their miserable state, the common sewer . . . from Southernhay runs directly under them, into which an opening being made for their own conveniencies, a very noisome smell commonly arises'.[118] It seems probable that these (in)sanitary arrangements dated back to the early modern period.

The second major sewerage outfall constructed during the mid-sixteenth century was also designed to serve a prison: in this case the county prison, or High Gaol, which stood close behind the city wall upon the former outworks of the Castle [*see plate 10*]. (Because the Gaol lay within the Castle precinct, it fell under the jurisdiction of the Crown, rather than the Chamber, and as a result the citizens sometimes found it difficult to secure access to the city wall in this area: a fact which may help to explain the lack of expenditure on the nearby mural tower.) During the 1550s a huge latrine-pit was dug in the barbican next to the city wall here for the disposal of the prisoners' waste. In 1560 the inhabitants of the East Quarter made a complaint against Mr Denys, the keeper of the Gaol, for 'castyng of fylth . . . yn a grette pett that he hath made betwyne the Gayle & the cetyes walles, where[by] the walles peryshe'.[119] A legal dispute followed, the result of which was that, in 1562, Sir Robert Denys agreed to build a 'cesspool in Northernhay ditch for the sewerage of the prison'.[120] Soon afterwards, Denys paid for an arch to be constructed through the city wall, and from this time onwards he and his heirs paid the Chamber a yearly rent for this structure: described in a rental of 1600 as 'a vaut conveyed out of the Gaol throughe the cities wales into . . . Northinghaye for ridding of the ordure of the prysoners'.[121]

From the heights of 'cloud capp'd towers' to the depths of stinking sewers; the sheer variety of structures which have been encountered during this short peregrination of the city circuit helps to illustrate just how complex and sophisticated an organism the defensive enceinte of early modern Exeter was. Yet what was the purpose of that enceinte? How did the town governors make use of the fortifications? And how did the ordinary townsfolk incorporate the defences into their day-to-day lives? These are some of the neglected questions which the following chapter will explore.

CHAPTER 2

PURPOSE AND FUNCTION

Had one stopped a member of the Tudor Chamber in the street and asked him to explain what the city wall was for, his answer—once he had overcome his initial surprise—would probably have been that its function was primarily a defensive one: that it served to protect the city itself against attack and that, by doing so, it upheld the local authority of the Crown. This dual defensive purpose was frequently alluded to in contemporary documents. When the city councillors asked the inhabitants of Exeter for money to fund repairs to the town walls in 1544, for example, they justified their request by observing that the walls were vital both 'for the defens of the cetie & the kingyes survys yn the tyme of the warrs'.[1] Five years later Lord Russell declared that, by closing their gates against the Prayer Book rebels, the citizens had preserved both 'the King's Majesties honour and your owne common welthe'.[2] A precisely similar view of the city enceinte—as a structure whose primary purposes were to further the Crown's service and to ensure the 'safetie of this cittie'—continued to be propounded in official documents through-out the early Stuart period (though with a novel twist during the Interregnum, when it was recorded in the Chamber act book that the walls and gates had been repaired 'for the service of *the Parliament* [and] the defence of the cittie').[3] The pattern of civic expenditure bears out the official rhetoric. As Chapters 4 and 5 will show, financial outlay on the city enceinte during the early modern period tended to wax and wane in accordance with the severity of perceived threats to local and national security. But if the defence of the city—and, by extension, the Crown—against military attack was considered to be the chief purpose of the wall, it possessed a remarkable variety of other functions as well. This chapter will explore some of the myriad ways in which Exeter's walls and gates were utilized during the early modern period—not only by the town governors, but by the inhabitants at large.[4]

Official Functions

On a day-to-day basis, perhaps the most important function of the city enceinte was to control the movement of people and goods. The town walls were designed to ensure that no one could pass in or out of Exeter except by way of the gates, and this helps to explain why breaches in the wall were usually very swiftly repaired. (To illustrate the point, it may be observed that, in 1647, a workman was ordered to block up a gap in the town wall because 'sheepe staylors and other ill-affected persons made a thoroughfare of it to the damage of the citty'.[5]) During daylight hours, the porters—assisted, in 'tymes of trobles', by the wardsmen—would keep a close eye on the gates, and would interrogate, and if necessary detain, anyone who aroused their suspicions. Should any violent crime or public disturbance take place within the city, the porters would close the gates as soon as they heard the 'hue and cry' and would do their best to prevent the perpetrators from escaping. [6] At night the gates were shut in order to keep out suspicious persons and 'night walkers', and only those who were prepared first to hammer at the gate and then to satisfy the porter as to their *bona fides* would be permitted to pass through.[7]

The fact that all traffic was channelled through the city gates conferred inestimable advantage on the Chamber. The gates facilitated the collection of tolls and customs on goods passing in and out of Exeter, and thus made a vital contribution to the city's revenues.[8] They made it possible for a round-the-clock guard to be mounted in times of pestilence—as, for example, in 1640, 1645 and 1665–66—in order to keep infected goods and persons out of the city.[9] They made it possible to prevent prohibited foodstuffs from being brought into the city during Lent.[10] They made it possible to deny entry to anyone who was considered to pose a threat to the public peace.[11] They even made it easier for the city's officials to uphold standards of public morality. In 1619 Cyprian Sheer, one of the watchmen, informed the Exeter sessions court that 'this last night, about twelve of the clock, James Mendust came into Eastgate in the company of one Avis Major', adding piously that, to his certain knowledge, Mendust had 'a wife at Denbury'.[12]

As well as playing a vital role in the defence and policing of early modern Exeter, the walls and gates possessed immense symbolic value. First, they underlined the city's local pre-eminence. There were only a handful of walled towns in Devon and Cornwall during the early modern period,[13] and the looming presence of the city enceinte constituted a permanent physical reminder of Exeter's age-old status as 'the centre, heart and head of the West'.[14] Second, by their magnificent appearance, the walls and gates added lustre to Exeter's reputation for opulence and wealth. Contemporaries clearly regarded the Exeter city circuit as a structure of considerable beauty in its own right. Leland, writing in the 1530s, described both the gates and the mural towers as 'fair', while the seventeenth-century author Tristram Risdon was equally impressed, observing that the city walls were 'beautified with battlements and many turrets'.[15] The townsfolk went out of their way to make the city circuit appear more splendid still by adorning the gateways with elaborate decorations: with coats of arms, with carved angels, with gilded weather vanes and with ornate representations of monarchs and magistrates.[16] On special occasions these elaborate decorations could be augmented with temporary additions; in 1451, South Gate was bedecked with painted linen cloth in order to welcome King Henry VI to Exeter.[17] As the city reached the height of its prosperity, during the late sixteenth and early seventeenth centuries, further decorative features began to appear around the enceinte. A 'dyoll', or clock, was set up in the tower above North Gate, for example, while date-stones began to be incorporated in the fabric of the city wall in order to commemorate major pieces of repair work.[18] The date-stones themselves were of painted Purbeck stone, while the words and letters of the inscriptions were either painted or picked out in lead.[19]

One of the most important symbolic functions of the city defences was to act as the physical embodiment of both civic and royal authority: to represent to local people the power of the city and the Crown, and to hammer home the message that the two were inextricably conjoined. Above each of the main gates at Exeter, royal coats of arms were prominently displayed alongside those of the city itself.[20] Whenever printed royal proclamations were sent down to Exeter from London, they were 'sett up upon the gates of the citie' in order to make it plain that central and local government spoke with one voice, and to give the widest possible circulation to the Crown's message.[21] (The receiver's roll for 1532–33 records a payment of one penny made to 'Robert Dole, for paste to putt up the Kynges wretyn at every gatt'.[22]) The mangled remains of traitors were also displayed at the city gates, for much the same reasons. In 1483–84, 'stapells', a 'soket' and a pole were 'fixed in the [city] wall' in order to carry 'James Newham's head', while in 1617–18 workmen received a total of 2 shillings and 6 pence 'for removying the traytor his quarter from Snail Tower to Nor[th]g[ate]'.[23]

Because the gates were the most impressive and forbidding structures which the Chamber possessed, and because they stood guard over the city's busiest thoroughfares—streets that were teeming with potential wrongdoers at all times of the day and night—they frequently served as a backdrop to the theatre of civic punishment. 'Cages', iron-work contrivances in which drunks, brawlers and other minor offenders could be restrained for hours at a time, stood either immediately within or immediately without each of the four main city gates.[24] The more familiar 'stocks'—'instrument[s] of punishment in which the person to be punished was placed in a sitting posture in a frame of timber, with holes to confine the ankles'—stood at South Gate.[25] Offenders against the city's harsh moral code were also frequently punished in the vicinity of the gates. In 1619 Claire Robbins, a young woman convicted of 'whore-dome', was ordered by the city justices 'to be whipt at the cartes tayle' from the Guildhall to West Gate, and from there back to the Guildhall by way of Southgate Street.[26] Two years later, it was decreed that the mother of an illegitimate child should be whipped along the entire length of High Street 'from East Gate to Weste Gate'.[27] When Exeter secured the right to set up a prison of its own in the mid-sixteenth century, it was the largest of the city gates, South Gate, which was eventually chosen as the site for the new establishment.[28] The perceived link between control of the town defences, the exercise of local authority and the punishment of offenders was underlined once again during the Civil War, when the parliamentary authorities in Exeter erected 'a galo[w]s on Estgate . . . to hang such as they disliked'.[29]

If the proud display of the royal arms and emblems above the gateways of Exeter was, in part, a device to bolster the prestige of the civic authorities, by recalling the very considerable powers which the Crown had delegated to them in their own sphere, it was above all intended to express the city's loyalty to the Crown. Nor was this the only way in which the citizens of Exeter made use of the walls and gates to protest their devotion to the reigning monarch. The repeated assertions that the Chamber maintained the town defences for the good of the Crown, as well as for the good of the city, have already been alluded to. When influential men who might be regarded as personal representatives of the reigning monarch visited Exeter—as the Earl of Bedford did in 1558, for example—the town councillors assembled at one of the two main city gates to greet them. By ushering their noble visitors in through the portals of these, the most powerful military strongpoints in Exeter, they made a symbolic gesture of submission to the Crown.[30] The town cannon were also deployed to salute such noblemen: an action which not only demonstrated the citizens' respect for the visitors themselves, but also made it clear to the Queen's representatives that the city was taking its military responsibilities seriously.[31] When Queen Elizabeth herself died, in 1603, cannon were fired off once again to mark the passing of 'our laet most vertuos Queen', and to demonstrate the citizens' sense of loyal grief.[32]

When Exeter was visited by a reigning monarch, elaborate ceremonial receptions were staged at the city gates in order to welcome the royal visitor. John Hooker records that, when Richard III made his accession to Exeter in 1483, 'the Mayor and his brethren yn all theire best and most seemly arraye mett & receved the Kinge at the gate of the citie, where the Recorder made unto him his gratulatorie oration'. After Richard had patiently sat through this speech, the Mayor 'presented unto his grace 200 nobles yn a purse' and 'delivered unto hym . . . the keyes of the cities gates'.[33] This last was a richly symbolic act, of course: one which was designed to make the clearest possible statement about Exeter's willing submission to royal authority. Similar receptions were laid on for subsequent royal visitors. When Henry VII arrived at Exeter in the aftermath of Perkin Warbeck's rebellion in 1497, he was met by the town councillors at one of the main entrances to the city, just as his late rival had been, and presented with the keys to the city gates (which had been specially 'fourbished', or polished up, for the occasion).[34] When Charles I passed through Exeter in July 1644, on his way to do battle with the Parliamentarian army in Cornwall, the Chamber again organized a reception at the city gate. Charles' secretary, Sir Edward Walker, recorded that the King was met at the gate 'by the mayor and aldermen, and a very great confluence of people, with much joy and acclamation'.[35]

How else did the Chamber make use of the city fortifications? The buildings next to, and immediately above, the town gates—which were not only spacious, but which must also have been regarded as prestigious places in which to live—were rented out to private individuals at substantial rents. In 1562–63 the city treasurer noted that he had received annual rents of £4 apiece from 'Sir Roger Blewet, knight, for the tenemente over the Eastegate of the citie' and from 'James Kyrkham for the howse new buylded over the Northgate'.[36] Fifty years later, the gate complex at South Gate was let out to one William Marks at the very substantial rent of £8 *per annum*, while in 1647–48 a payment of £1 and 10 shillings was received from 'Hugh Bidwell for the rent of the tenement next unto the Westgate and the roomes over the said gate'.[37] With the agreement of the tenants, the buildings at the gates were used for a variety of civic purposes. Banquets were regularly held in the 'house' over South Gate, as we shall see, while in 1631 plans were set in motion to convert 'the roomes over the Eastgate' into a school.[38]

Several of the towers along the city walls were also rented out. At other times, they were used to store weapons and munitions. In 1448 it was noted that one of the towers adjacent to the Bishop's Palace had been provided with a 'right . . . stronge dore' and a stout lock and key, 'to this entent, ther to bryng yn stuf for the werre and defence of the Cite, and other thyng more of the saide Cite, ther to be kept stronge, saf[e] and sure'.[39] Almost two centuries later, on the eve of the Civil War, the Chamber ordered that the eastern angle tower should be converted into a gunpowder store.[40] The ammunition seems to have been removed from the tower once the conflict had actually begun—presumably because the tower's position on the wall made the powder very vulnerable to a direct hit—but during the Interregnum steps were taken to restore the structure to its former use. In 1657, the Chamber ordered two of its number 'to take a particular vewe of the powder house uppon the cities walles neere to the hospitall, and to give their report . . . of the fitness and convenience of the place for the safe keeping and laying upp of powder therein'.[41] Soon after the Restoration, the structure was cleansed and stocked with powder, and it probably continued to be used as a powder store for many years afterwards.[42] (In the Chamber map book of *c.*1758, the eastern angle tower was still referred to as the 'powder room'.[43])

As well as renting out the gates and towers, the Chamber leased extensive sections of the barbican and the silted-up city ditch to private citizens—always with the proviso that the city's workmen should have access to those properties 'at all tymes . . . for any thinge there to be done for the repere or buildinge of the cities walles'.[44] There can be no doubt that the Chamber sometimes made use of these rights of access as a pretext, in order to assert its authority over the inhabitants of the Cathedral Close and the Castle precinct. On one occasion it was claimed that the Council of Twenty-Four had sent workmen into the bishop's garden 'under pretence of mending their wall', when their true purpose had been to mount an open 'challenge' to the ecclesiastical jurisdiction.[45] Possession of the barbican offered the Chamber both pecuniary and political advantage, as well as helping to ensure Exeter's military security.

This helps to explain why the city's rights to the rampart were so jealously guarded.

Before concluding this discussion of the 'official' functions of the city defences, it is important to consider the unique case of the Castle. As has already been observed, the Chamber took great care to stress in its formal pronouncements that the chief purpose of the enceinte was to defend the joint interests of the city and the Crown. That those two interests might one day cease to coincide was a possibility which, in public at least, no town councillor would have dared to entertain. It was also a possibility which no wise monarch could have dared to ignore. Fortunately for the rulers of early modern England their medieval forebears had bequeathed them Rougemont Castle to act as a local insurance policy. Although the Castle helped to strengthen the city defences, and could also have been used as a place of refuge if the rest of Exeter had fallen into enemy hands, its primary purpose—a purpose which was seldom, if ever, acknowledged—was to overawe the citizens by providing a constant, visible reminder of the strength of royal power. No rebellion against the Crown in Exeter could succeed as long as the Castle remained in loyal hands—a fact which doubtless helps to explain the keen interest which Richard III evinced in Rougemont in 1483.

After Richard III's death, relations between Exeter and the Crown remained consistently good for some 140 years. In consequence, the potential threat posed by the Castle was all but forgotten. Far from regarding the Castle as an over-mighty neighbour, the inhabitants of Tudor Exeter several times complained to the Privy Council about its 'ruinous' condition.[46] During the unquiet reign of Charles I, however, fears of the ancient fortress at Rougemont as a cuckoo in the nest—as a defensible island of privileged jurisdiction within the city walls, by means of which a tyrannous authority might one day be imposed upon Exeter—began to resurface. The Civil War saw those fears being effectively realized, as first the Parliamentarians and then the Royalists installed powerful military garrisons in the Castle. The end of the war did not bring an end to the military presence. On the contrary, Parliamentarian soldiers remained permanently stationed at Rougemont throughout the period 1646–60. During these years, the Castle reassumed its long-dormant role as a bridle and a curb upon the city. Not only this, the Castle soldiers now assumed much of the responsibility for defending Exeter itself against outside attack. In 1647, a sergeant in the Castle garrison boasted that 'himselfe and the rest of the souldiery of the castle kepte guard for a company of rascalls, meaning the cittizens . . . and that . . . the said cittizens would never leave to meddle with the souldiers untill there braynes were knockte out'.[47] It was a comment which perfectly encapsulated the uncomfortable situation in which the citizens now found themselves: both entirely dependent on the Castle garrison for protection, and entirely exposed to the coercive power of that same garrison should they dare to step out of line. All in all, it seems fair to suggest that no part of the enceinte saw its day-to-day role change more dramatically over this period than did the Castle.

Secondary Functions

For every one of the official functions which the city enceinte was designed to perform, there were dozens of other incidental uses to which the defences were put simply because they were there. Early modern Exeter was an intensely cramped and overcrowded place: a community in which some 10,000 men, women and children were crammed together, hugger-mugger, within the narrow confines of the city circuit. With space at a premium in this busy, bustling world, it was inevitable that the town defences themselves would come to be used for a multiplicity of everyday purposes by those who lived and worked around them. Over the following pages these secondary functions of the city enceinte will be considered in more depth.

One incidental function of the town wall which it is very easy to overlook, but which impinged upon the lives of almost everyone who dwelt in the city, was to serve as a parish and property boundary. Just as the city circuit as a whole formed the boundary between the intramural core of Exeter and the extramural suburbs, so individual stretches of the city enceinte formed the boundary between different parishes and between individual properties. Literally hundreds of early modern property deeds still survive which note that the premises to which they relate were bounded, on one side or more, by the city walls, the city barbican, the city gates or the city ditch. Indeed, it might not be going too far to suggest that, for much of the period under discussion, many of the inhabitants of Exeter would have tended to regard the city enceinte more as a glorified garden wall than as a primarily defensive structure.

They would also have regarded it as public space set aside for recreation. Throughout the Tudor and early Stuart periods, the city walls and the so-called 'city wastes'—the banks and ditches which lay immediately beyond them—were used by the citizens, 'both men and women', for sports and exercises of every conceivable kind.[48] In Southernhay, a fair was held every year, and 'tryumphes' and shooting contests were staged.[49] Southernhay was also the accustomed venue for musters and military training, 'there beinge noe other such convenient place for that . . . purpose in or about the . . . cittie'.[50] Both here and in Friernhay, butts were erected to enable the citizens to practice their archery.[51] In Northernhay, the counterscarp bank of the Castle was levelled during the early seventeenth century, and pleasant walks and avenues were laid out in its place. Trees were planted here, seats provided and a bowling green established [*see plate 10*]: all at the Chamber's expense.[52] Over the following years, every respectable inhabitant of Exeter, from the Mayor downwards, became accustomed to taking the air 'upon Northenhay hill'.[53] The city walls themselves were also used for promenading. People regularly strolled along the top of the wall-walk in order to enjoy the view, while those who had access to sections of the wall which were usually shut off to the general public established what were, in effect, private walks and gardens.[54] In 1562 it was reported that Mr Humphrey Orchard 'hath made a garden upon the . . . turrett uppon the walles by

St Johns Garden'.[55] Thirty years later, the Chamber agreed that a certain Mr Leche should 'have libertie to take away a garret of the walles of the cittie to have a prospecte oute of his garden into Southinghey'.[56] Seventeen years after this, in 1608, the Chamber granted permission to Dr Barrett, Archdeacon of Exeter, to make a flight of stairs up from his garden, so that he too could 'walk on the . . . walls and enjoy the prospect'.[57]

Women frequented the city walls just as men did. In 1644 Dorothy Jeffrie, a suspected thief, assured the town magistrates that she had found the money and the silver whistle which had been discovered on her person while walking 'uppon the towne walles of this cittie'.[58] Lovers also met in the hidden corners of the city circuit to take their furtive pleasures. During the 1650s one Exeter couple enjoyed a passionate encounter in 'the battery at Southernhay'(almost certainly one of the ancient mural towers, all of which had been converted into gun batteries during the Civil War). Nine months later, a child resulted from this brief liaison, leading to the discovery and disgrace of the two parties involved.[59] Children used the town walls as a playground. During the 1530s, the young Peter Carew terrified his tutor by clambering to the very top of one of the city turrets—in all likelihood the eastern angle tower—while 'meechinge', or playing truant, from school.[60] Over a century later, in 1654, the receiver ordered that a gun battery which had been built at Snayle Tower should be removed 'for prevention of danger of children from falling out over the walles of the cittie there'.[61] Some combined walking on the walls with petty theft. In 1647 John Breall, a city fuller, deposed that while 'standing in the streete . . . betweene Westgate and the Key Gate, he sawe a man . . . standinge neare the walles of this cittie' who was acting very suspiciously. When the stranger scrambled up 'uppon the barbiganes of the said walles', Breall went after him. Upon being confronted, the man shamefacedly took a stolen piece of cloth from 'out of his breeches & threwe it downe uppon the garretts'.[62]

For those who preferred to spend their leisure hours watching the world go by, rather than indulging in more vigorous activities, the city gates provided congenial places in which to meet. Here, idlers could loll on the benches which stood beside the gates, and be sure of company at almost any time of day. Writing in *c.*1800, Alexander Jenkins recorded that, in front of St Mary Steps Church, just within West Gate, there had formerly been 'a stone bench, which extended from the watch house to the entrance of the church, and [which was] supposed to be designed for the accommodation of . . . soldiers'. This seat, Jenkins went on, 'being much resorted to by idle and disorderly persons, obtained the name of *Pennyless Bench*, and at length becoming a public nuisance, it was taken down about the year 1757'.[63] Both the bench and its soubriquet may well have been familiar to the inhabitants of early Stuart Exeter: references to a seat at West Gate go back at least as far as 1604.[64]

During the early seventeenth century, East Gate became an increasingly popular place of resort for the city's roisterers. By 1618 people are known to have been gathering in the porter's lodge there to drink and play cards [*see page 31, above*], while three years later a certain Mr Newberry was presented to the city aldermen 'for keeping of ill-rule in his howse over East Gate [both] day and night, by report of his neighbours'.[65] The gate's transformation into a *de facto* tavern became more evident still shortly before the Civil War, when a 'wyne bushe' was 'sett upp att the Eastgate in the outer parte', indicating that drink could be brought there.[66] The Puritan town councillors were outraged. Having condemned the erection of this bacchanalian symbol as 'both hurte[ful] to the gate, and disgracefull to the cittie', they decreed that 'some course be taken for the pulling downe of the same'.[67] Presumably this order was obeyed, but in the long run commercial pressure to develop East Gate as an alehouse proved irresistible: by the eighteenth century 'the gate was occupied as a public house, known by the sign of the Salutation'.[68]

Because of their role as meeting places, the gates were frequently sites of confrontation as well as of conviviality. Disputes regularly blew up at the gates between the porters and the city watchmen on the one hand, and those whose passage they tried to bar on the other. In 1533 John Scobell, porter of West Gate, heard two men knocking on the gate at midnight. When he asked them what they wanted, they gave a plausible reply and so, he later recalled, 'I awpenyd the gaytt, and I lett them yn'. It was unfortunate for Scobell that he had not questioned them more closely; as soon as they had passed through the gate, one of the importunate travellers struck the unsuspecting porter on the head with his sword, and the two men promptly disappeared into the night.[69] A century later, on the eve of the Civil War, West Gate was the scene of a more violent confrontation. Late one night in October 1642, a group of men approached the gate from the direction of Exebridge. The watchmen stationed at the gate did not recognize any of them and so, as they later informed the city magistrates,

> they willed . . . [the strangers] to stand, and to give them an accompte from where they came, but the said . . . [strangers] obeyed not the command of these informants, but came in violentlie uppon them, and endeavoured to seize on . . . [their] weapons, which caused a great tummulte.

Reinforcements had to be summoned to overpower the watchmen's assailants, who were eventually flung into prison.[70]

Incidents like these—which tended to involve drunks, petty criminals and those who simply enjoyed a good punch-up—were relatively commonplace. Far more unusual, and far more serious, were the confrontations which occurred when disaffected groups of citizens tried to seize control of the city gates in order to reverse or defy official Chamber policy. This happened on at least three occasions during the early modern period: in 1549, when religious conservatives made an unsuccessful attempt to let the Prayer Book rebels in at South Gate; in 1642, when pro-Royalist citizens made an equally unsuccessful attempt to prevent Parliamentarian troops from entering the city at East Gate; and in 1659, when mobs of 'apprentices and others'—enraged by the Chamber's apparent reluctance to support General Monk's call for a free parliament—went on the rampage through the streets of Exeter and managed to seize the keys to each of the city gates.[71] These three dramatic episodes help to illustrate the enormous political significance which the gates possessed in early modern Exeter. It was clear to all that whoever controlled the city gates effectively controlled the city itself, so—for any determined political or religious faction which found itself in a minority on the Chamber—the gates were the obvious places at which to attempt an armed coup.

If the gates were a prime location for violent confrontations, they were also a prime location for violent accidents. The ceaseless passage of traffic through the narrow roadways under the gate arches made the occasional crushing or maiming of unwary bystanders almost inevitable, and several people met with unpleasant ends at the entrances to the city.[72] Other parts of the circuit had their dangers, too, especially in the aftermath of the Civil War, when the temporary earthworks which had been thrown up around Exeter during 1642–46 began to moulder and decay. In 1652–53 a man named Gould was drowned in 'a deepe trench without Southgate' which was subsequently filled in by the city's work-men.[73] During the same year the Chamber was forced to pay £2 in compensation to one James Ellys 'towards his losse of a gelding breaking his legg att the drawe bridge without South Gate'.[74] The receiver's concern to prevent children from tumbling off the walls near Snayle Tower has already been noted—and the city ditch was also thought to present a threat to youngsters. One of the considerations which prompted the Elizabethan Chamber to fill up part of 'the town dyke' in Southernhay during the 1580s was the fact that 'the said ditch was . . . dangerous for children, and others that passed that way'.[75]

After the ditch had been filled in, cottages and gardens were built on the site.[76] This underlines the fact that, for some Exeter folk, the most important of the city circuit's many secondary functions was to provide them with a place in which to live. The porters in their lodges; the men and women who occupied the chambers above the gates; the families who rented out the tenements 'upon the walls' between West Gate and All Hallows Church; the newly established householders in Southernhay: for all of these people, the city circuit was, in effect, home. And as Exeter's population grew, during the late sixteenth and early seventeenth centuries, so did the number of people who lived either on top of or immediately beside the fortifications. From *c.*1560 onwards, South Gate was home to the keeper of the city gaol, as well as a place of incarceration for dozens of unwilling inmates.[77] Many more prisoners spun out their daily lives in the shadow of the town defences at the High Gaol, near the Castle: periodically emerging from their cells to take the air in the enclosed garden which lay between the prison and the town walls.[78] In 1590–91, as we have seen, a 'little house' was built for the confinement of 'mad folkes' on the city walls near North Gate, while at around the same time Mr Jerome Helliar financed the construction of an almshouse 'for the harbouring of 2 poore people' on the wall near Quay Gate.[79] Helliar's almshouse was erected on the stretch of the city wall which marked the boundary between the parishes of Holy Trinity and St Mary Steps, leading to some confusion as to where the almspeople should be buried when eventually they died. In August 1597, the clerk of Holy Trinity recorded the death of Joan Wooulcott 'some tymes dweller in this parrish, and after wards dwelled upon ye walles in Mr . . . Helliers Almes house, but [that house] being newlie made it was unknown to what parish they weare in, therefore we thought good to register her name'.[80]

The town defences were also made use of as a *de facto* rubbish dump. One of the great benefits of living either on top of or close beside the city wall, as far as many Exeter people were concerned, was that it enabled them to get rid of all sorts of waste material by the simple expedient of chucking it over the battlements. Formal complaints, or 'presentments' made to the Exeter court leet show that a constant battle had to be waged against those whose careless disposal of rubbish threatened to turn the banks and ditches at the foot of the city wall into a stinking midden.[81] In 1559, for example, the inhabitants of the West Quarter presented 'all them that dwell upon the walles betweene West Gate and Allhallow Churche for casten out of rubble and fylthe over the walles very evyll', while during that same year the inhabitants of the East Quarter reported five individuals (including 'Archdeacon Kente', one of the cathedral clergy) 'for casten of rubble out of ther gardens over the walls' near East Gate.[82] Three years later complaint was made about a 'depe pytt' which had recently been dug between the High Gaol and the city walls 'wherein the fylth and garbage of the prisoners . . . [is] caste, which is nowe very dangerouse and hurtfull'.[83] Here, as so often, it was the illicit disposal of sewerage which had aroused particular alarm. In 1620 the scavengers, or street cleaners, of the West Quarter presented Elizabeth Brounscombe and her daughter Agnes for 'emptyinge of . . . [a] vaute or privie' and then strewing its contents around the immediate neighbourhood: 'some parte in the streate agaynste Mr John Peters house, and the reste they caste over the towne walls very noysome, about nyne a clocke at nighte'.[84] A decade later, three more inhabitants of the West Quarter were reported 'for castinge of filth over the walles . . . to the annoyance of his Majesty's leige people'. The offenders were subsequently fined 3 shillings and 4 pence apiece.[85]

Some regarded the city enceinte as a suitable place to dump animal carcasses; in 1557 a man was presented 'for casting a ded swyne over the cyttye walls into Northynghaye'.[86] Sixty years later, a woman threatened to go one better by hurling a live animal over the ramparts— though her rage was perhaps understandable. While sitting with a friend who was on the point of giving birth in a house in All-Hallows-on-the-Walls parish, Mrs Agnes Barrons was amazed to see the attendant midwife, one Alice Dodridge, going to the door to answer a query from a small boy about a 'pretty little whelp' which was having trouble giving birth to puppies in a neighbouring house. Amazement turned to fury as Barrons heard the midwife advise the boy to 'bid his mother to lap [the dog] in a cloth and send it down to her' at the pregnant woman's bedside. Advancing on Dodridge, Barrons assured her that 'if there were a bitch brought thither . . . [she] would take it and throw it over the towne walles'. Doddridge's reply—'Noe, by God, not so [for] many a boddy loveth a dogg, & soe doe I'—was hardly calculated to ease the situation, though in the end the midwife agreed, reluctantly, to devote her attentions to the job in hand.[87]

One sinister story suggests that human bodies, too, may occasionally have been disposed of around the city enceinte. In 1609 a prisoner named George Close was accosted in the garden of the High Gaol by the gaoler, William White, who

> calling . . . hym . . . neere unto the . . . pryson wall, and takeinge out of his pockett a cord or halter of hempe did . . . sweare . . . unto . . . [him] that if hee would not follow . . . the same gaoler's . . . directions, then the said gaoler would there ymediately with the said corde strangle . . . [him] and would afterwardes cast him into a deepe ditch which was therunto adioyninge for the cleansynge of the said prison.[88]

(This was the 'pytt' alluded to above, from which sewerage passed under the city walls into Northernhay *via* a stone vault.) Fortunately for Close, he eventually managed to escape from his tormentor, but it is possible that other recalcitrant prisoners were less fortunate—like many early modern gaolers, White possessed a black reputation.[89]

For those who could not be bothered to sling their rubbish over the garrets, an easier alternative was simply to dump it against the inner face of the wall. In 1559 'fylth and rubble' was reported to have been cast 'agaynst the barbygan' near North Gate, while during the 1580s a certain Nicholas Grenrye of East Gate was taken to task 'for feylth lyeinge against the tower of the gate'.[90] Dung heaps, presumably composed of a mixture of human and animal waste, were a common sight around the city enceinte throughout the early modern period. In 1583 complaint was made about 'a fyltye dunge heape agaynste the cyties walles by William Dodryges house', while thirty years later the scavengers of the South Quarter presented a man 'for [a] great heape of dunge lyinge in the backe streate nere the cyttie walls'.[91] At other times, stones, earth and soap-ash are all known to have been heaped up against the foot of the wall.[92] The citizens' fondness for keeping pigs in the intramural gardens which ran along beneath the rampart—a practice which flourished, despite being strictly forbidden—undoubtedly led to further quantities of dung being deposited on the barbican.[93] Pigs were also put out to forage—again, it would seem, illegally—on the ditches and banks which lay beneath the outer face of the wall. In 1621 William West, a butcher, was reported to the court leet 'for keepinge of piggs and filthie dunge agaynste the cyttie walles without Westgate'.[94]

Pig-keeping aside, Exeter's walls, banks and ditches were appropriated by the townsfolk for a wide variety of other agricultural and industrial purposes. During the early modern period, as for centuries before, the open ground 'around the walls of the town' was rented out to private individuals for the purpose of grazing sheep and cattle.[95] The bishops of Exeter, for their part, kept deer and rabbits in the gardens behind the Palace which bordered on the city wall.[96] Great 'timber trees', mostly elms and ashes, were planted on the city's wastes; nearly 200 were growing in Southernhay on the eve of the Civil War, and 100 more in Northernhay.[97] Fruit trees were planted in the Castle ditches, and on the stretch of the barbican which ran behind the Bishop's Palace; by 1570 an entire orchard had become established in the bishop's garden.[98] (This was probably one of the orchards which was said to be encroaching upon the rampart on the eve of the Civil War.[99]) The little gardens which nestled everywhere, on both sides of the enceinte, were almost certainly used to grow fruit and vegetables, as well as to present a pleasing spectacle and to provide some space for recreation. To the grave displeasure of the city authorities, such gardens were also occasionally exploited in order to quarry stones and earth from the foundations of the city walls.

This problem seems to have become increasingly acute as Exeter's population expanded during the latter half of the sixteenth century. In 1561 an official complaint was laid against one William Monsdon 'for that he makes his garden under the walles hurtfull and dangerous, & goyth lower than the foundacion, & selleth away the stones'.[100] (That Monsdon was the man whom the Chamber retained to ensure the good condition of the city walls made his conduct especially reprehensible.[101]) A year later two men were presented to the court leet for undermining the mural walk in their gardens, while in 1579 it was noted with alarm that large quantities of earth were being removed from the foundations of the city walls in Southernhay.[102] The assault upon the 'town banks' in this area—an assault which appears to have been connected with the recent conversion of the adjoining stretch of the city ditch into gardens—quickly prompted a Chamber order that '[no] person having any garden adioyninge to the cities walles shall . . . pull or drawe downe any earthe from the walls'.[103] This decree brought a halt to the large-scale excavations in Southernhay, but the stealthy removal of material continued to go on. In 1583 a certain William Simmons was informed against for having 'abbatted the grownd in his garden agaynste the cities walles', and stones and earth continued to be surreptitiously taken away from the town defences throughout the early seventeenth century.[104]

One of the more surprising uses to which the city wall was put by those who dwelt around it was, in effect, that of a giant stone washing-line. The cloth industry on which early modern Exeter's prosperity depended had its chief centre of operations amid the mills and workshops of the West Quarter, and the Chamber had long leased out the open ground which lay next to the city walls in this area for the purposes of stretching and drying cloth.[105] Towards the end of Elizabeth's reign, John Hooker recorded that the Chamber possessed sixteen racks 'under the wall betwene West Gate and Watergate', eleven racks 'without the West Gate betwen the sayed gate and Snayle Towre' and a further, unspecified, number of racks in Friernhay [*the racks in Friernhay can be plainly seen in plate 12*]. All of these racks were leased out to textile workers, who also paid the Chamber a yearly rent 'for the use of the garrets [of the city wall] to hange their clothes upon'. [106] The practice of draping cloth over the battlements—where it must have swiftly dried out in the wind and the sun—presumably dated back to the medieval period and continued to flourish at Exeter until the eve of the Civil War. In November 1640 the Chamber ordered that the practice should be discontinued because of the damage which it caused to the walls.[107] Quite how long this interdict remained in force is unclear, but the ban must have been lifted by 1655, at the latest, for in that year the Chamber agreed that Richard Hooper, fuller, should have 'the use of the citties walles betweene the Widdow Sowtons house and Walter Stranges . . . house to dry clothes on [namely] serges & kersies' at an annual rent of 18 shillings. A supplementary note in the Chamber act book—that Hooper was only to enjoy the use 'of the *inside* of the said walles'—suggests that the outer face of the wall may have been rented out to someone else, thus doubling the city's profit.[108]

Nor was it only the town councillors for whom the city defences represented a useful source of funds. Throughout the early modern period, scores of local people earned a significant part of their yearly income from the work which the Chamber paid them to carry out upon Exeter's fortifications. The porters who kept the gates; the beadles who swept the mural walk; the men who kept the walls free of ivy; the labourers who unblocked the grates; the quarrymen who excavated and dressed the building-stone; the carriers who transported stones, earth and sand; the masons who constructed the walls; the blacksmiths who supplied the ironwork for the gates; the carpenters and plasterers who fitted out the chambers in the gate-towers; the 'helliers' who laid the slates overhead; the plumbers who repaired the roofs and gutters; the sculptors who carved the mural decorations; the painters who embellished them; and last, but by no means least well-rewarded, the overseers who directed major defensive projects: all of these individuals were not only the servants of the city enceinte, but also—in a sense—the recipients of its bounty.[109] The following chapter will explore how this huge cast of players went about its work, and how the upkeep of the city fortifications was organized and financed.

CHAPTER 3

MAINTENANCE
AND REPAIR

Keeping the city defences of early modern Exeter in a more or less adequate state of repair was a never-ending task: a continuous struggle to counter the damage wrought by time, by the elements and by miscellaneous human agency which, on occasion, stretched the town governors' resources to the very limits. At Exeter, as at many other English cities, much remains to be discovered about the precise mechanics by which this ongoing struggle was waged.[1] During the Middle Ages royal orders had regularly been sent down to the citizens of Exeter in times of war, commanding them to repair their walls and gates.[2] Similar interventions from the centre occurred during the major military crises of the early modern period, as Chapters 4 and 5 will show. Yet, as far as it is possible to tell from the surviving evidence, the vast bulk of the work carried out on the defences between 1485 and 1660 was initiated, as well as carried through, by the citizens themselves. What were the methods which they adopted? How were defects in the city enceinte detected in the first place, for example? Who authorized the necessary repairs? What sort of repairs were carried out? Who were the workmen—and, very occasionally, the workwomen—who carried out those repairs? How were they organized? What sort of wages did they receive? Where did they get their materials from? Finally, and perhaps most crucially of all, how did the city authorities find the vast sums of money which were needed to pay for it all? These are some of the questions which the present chapter will address.

Surveying the Defences: the Mural Walk

The importance which the Chamber attached to the upkeep of the city enceinte received its most powerful and visible expression in the annual perambulation of the town walls, known as the 'murally walk': an elaborate civic ritual which was one of the highlights of the festive year at Exeter. Deriving its peculiar name from the old French word *muraille*—meaning of, or pertaining to, a wall—this custom was already well established by 1322, at which time it was observed that the perambulation of the walls was traditionally undertaken by the citizens 'on some convenient day between the Feast of St Michael [i.e. 29 September] and the Festival of All Hallows [i.e. 1 November]'.[3] Nothing was to change in this respect for the next 500 years.[4] The mural walk is alluded to in several later documents, including a petition of the 1530s which records that 'once in a yere . . . [the citizens] do viewe the . . . walles & towers . . . [to see if] they be sufficiently repayred & maneteined for the defence of the . . . Citie or not'.[5] But the first detailed description of the procession appears to be that of John Hooker, written during the Elizabethan period. Hooker noted that, according to the custom of the city, each newly elected mayor was 'yerely within eight dayes after the feaste of St Mychaell . . . to take his muralie walke and perambulation rounde about the Citie beinge accompanyed with the Aldermen, officers & good citisens to take the viewe of the walles, and, the faultes then founde, to take order for the reperation of the same'.[6]

Hooker did not bother to specify the form which the procession took, but—because the basic lineaments of the ritual appear to have changed comparatively little over the years, as we shall see—it is probable that some flavour of the early modern mural walk may be derived from surviving descriptions of its nineteenth-century descendant. According to James Cossins (an Exeter man who witnessed the very last perambulations around the walls, which took place during the 1830s) the procession was:

> headed by the . . . constables, about twenty-four in number; then the staff and mace-bearers; [the] sword bearer; the mayor-elect walking uncovered, with his hat in hand; [the] Aldermen, with scarlet robes and three-cornered hats, followed by members and officials; in the rear being three . . . [officials] named Mayor's stewards (the outside one called gutter steward[7]), wearing long black robes, with tufts and three-cornered hats. Some of the . . . inhabitants would [also] accompany the procession, and give vent to their feelings by an occasional cheer.[8]

There is no reason to believe that the procedures adopted 200–300 years before had been significantly different.

The route which the procession followed during the Elizabethan and early Stuart periods can be roughly established from the records of minor expenses incurred during the perambulation which are preserved in the receivers' accounts.[9] The mayor, and the other members of the civic party first assembled at the Guildhall [*see map 4*]. From here, they seem to have made their way to the city walls in St Paul's parish, probably by way of Goldsmith Street (effectively destroyed during the 1970s) and the little lane opposite, which appears on eighteenth-century maps as Maddox Lane, or Maddox Row.[10] During the sixteenth century this alleyway was called 'the murally lane', presumably because of its association with the annual perambulation.[11] Having ascended the rampart, the mayor and his companions next made their way along the wall-walk, or 'mural way'—which had previously been swept clean by the city beadles—as far as the Castle.[12] Here, the party descended into the

Castle ditch and coasted around the south-west side of the Castle enceinte to Castle Lane. Crossing over the lane, the processors then passed through the courtyard of the High Gaol in order to get back to the city wall.[13] A gratuity was usually given to the prisoners incarcerated here, and sometimes to the poor folk of Castle Lane as well, before the mayor and his followers moved on.[14]

Having clambered back on to the wall-walk behind the Gaol, the members of the civic party next proceeded to East Gate and from there to the stretch of wall behind St John's Hospital. Small sums of money were sometimes distributed here, as at other points around the circuit, to 'companies of poore maides' who had been 'set on work' at knitting nearby.[15] Following the establishment of a Free School at St John's during the 1630s—an achievement of which the Chamber was inordinately proud—the procession made a regular halt at the former hospital building in order to listen to a speech given by one of the 'blue boys'.[16] (The schoolboys of the new foundation were so called because their gowns and caps were made of blue kersey cloth.[17]) In 1634–35, the receiver paid 5 shillings 'to a scholer of ye Freeschoole which made an oration', while during the following year no less than 10 shillings was presented 'to the 2 schollers in the Free Schoole which made orations to Mr Maior & the Ald[ermen]' during the mural walk.[18] Sometimes the usher of the new school received a gratuity as well.[19]

From St John's the mayor and his company processed along the wall as far as the boundary of the Bedford Precinct—the extensive property within the south-eastern corner of the enceinte which belonged to the Earls of Bedford—where a postern gate was opened to admit them to the stretch of wall-walk which lay within. Emerging from the garden of Bedford House through another postern near the head of St Martin's Lane, they then passed through the whole series of similar posterns which were incorporated within the garden walls of the cathedral clergy on top of the rampart behind the Bishop's Palace [*see plate 11*] until they eventually attained the South Gate. Here, the civic party—whose older and less agile members were doubtless beginning to flag a little by this time—enjoyed a break for refreshment. Having distributed still more money to the prisoners held in the City Gaol, or 'Counter', within the gate, the processors then repaired to the gaoler's 'howse' in one of the upper chambers, where they were provided with fruit, wine and beer.[20]

After 1588 the entertainment became more elaborate still, and a formal 'banquet'—in sixteenth-century parlance, a light meal or repast, rather than a full-blown feast, as today—was laid on for the mayor and his party by the gaoler—or, perhaps more accurately, in most cases, by the gaoler's wife.[21] The idea of holding a banquet in a prison at first sight seems a rather odd one, but there were sound reasons for the Chamber's choice of venue. As was observed in the previous chapter, South Gate was the strongest and most impressive of the civic buildings: the closest thing which the Chamber possessed to a castle of its own. What better location could there be for the 'murallye banquet' than the miniature fortress which lay at the heart of the very defensive system which the perambulation was designed to uphold? The accommodation over the prison appears to have been much extended and improved during 1585–87: perhaps, in part, with the specific aim of making it suitable for civic functions.[22] Finally, the views out over the city and the surrounding countryside from the chambers above the South Gate must have been superb: something which it is still possible to appreciate if one stands on the footbridge over Western Way near where the gate once stood.[23]

With the banquet over, the mayor and his companions resumed their progress, passing along the mural way to Quay Gate, where sixpence was sometimes given to 'the poore on the walls' at Helliar's Almshouses.[24] Apples were also distributed at this point, almost certainly hurled by members of the procession from the gate-arch to a scrum of eager boys gathered below.[25] It is clear that swarms of children accompanied the civic officials on their perambulation and the receivers' accounts contain many references to the apples, pears and nuts which were bought to throw among the youngsters.[26] Surprisingly large quantities of fruit appear to have been 'cast abroad' in this way. No fewer than 200 apples were bought in 1612–13, for example, while so many apples were provided for the procession of 1659–60 that the receiver later had to pay someone 'for carriage of aples and attendance at ye murallie walke'.[27]

About the final stage of the perambulation—from Quay Gate to North Gate and then back into the city centre again—little is known. Clearly, this part of the walk was attended with scant ceremony. It may be that, as the procession moved off along the stretch of the enceinte which passed through the poorest districts of Exeter, many members of the civic elite made their excuses and went home, leaving only the mayor and a hard-core of processors to complete the circuit.[28] What is certain is that, for those who stayed the course—including the ubiquitous flocks of children—the mural walk always concluded with some kind of celebration at the mayor's house. Usually this involved another distribution of apples or pears. In 1587–88, the receiver spent 2 shillings on 'appells for the chyldren cominge from the muralye at Mr Brewtons doore', while, in 1601–2, 1 shilling and 3 pence was laid out on 'appells provided & geven the boyes at the retorne of Mr Maior from the mewerawly walcke'.[29]

The itinerary of the nineteenth-century procession shows how long the basic pattern laid down during the early modern period continued to be adhered to. During the 1830s, according to Cossins, 'the route was from the Guildhall . . . up High Street . . . to the Mayor's Chapel, [in] St John's Hospital'.[30] Here, on one of the last occasions that the mural walk was staged (in 1831–32) £2 and 2 shillings was presented by the receiver to 'the grammar school boys [for] declaiming before the mayor', thus continuing an oratorical tradition which had endured for almost 190 years.[31] From St John's the nineteenth-century procession continued, in Cossins' words:

on the walls down Southernhay . . . to Trinity Church . . . then . . . to Water Gate, Quay Hill, where a man was waiting with two large baskets of apples, which were thrown about for a general scramble. This amusement over, they proceeded through West Gate and Bartholomew Street to Snail Tower and Bartholomew Yard, where two more baskets of apples were distributed as before. From thence across North Street, up to S. Mortimore, Esquire's, where wine was waiting their arrival. On leaving they crossed over Maddox row . . . to Rougemont Castle [and] thence to Castle Street, making their exit at East Gate. The ceremony wound-up in the evening with the good old English custom of dinner.[32]

By the 1830s, of course, the mural walk had become an almost entirely symbolic custom: an enjoyable jaunt around the town which retained only the most vestigial connections with questions of civic security and control. Two and a half centuries earlier, this had most emphatically not been the case. Surviving presentments made to the Council of Twenty-Four by the jurors, civic officers and other assembled citizens who periodically attended the 'greate inquests', 'law days' or court leets convened at the Guildhall make it clear that, in Hooker's day, the perambulation had still served not only as a vital means of assessing the state of the city enceinte, but also of 'naming and shaming' those who had offended against it.

Surveying the Defences: Presentments

The records of the 'law jury', which sat at the court leet, reveal that, soon after the annual procession had taken place, a list of the defects which the processors had identified in the city's walls and gates was compiled. Those who were considered responsible for causing the damage, or for failing to carry out any necessary repairs, were then formally reported to the town governors. In October 1563, for example, the jurors presented 'Harry Ellacott & Richaurd Vilvayn . . . for a lane goyng to the walles which is very filthy & noysome' (this was the 'murally lane' referred to above); 'my Lorde Bysshop for that his conyes [i.e. rabbits] dystroy the walles';[33] and an unknown malefactor for 'a greyt pitt beyng made fast by the citye walle . . . which is very noysome for Mr Mayors walke & hurtfull to the wall'.[34] During the following year, the jurors complained about 'the decay of the wall of the citie betwene Mr Wolcott's garden and the jakes in the wall [at Watergate]'; 'the decay of the citie wall betwene the Estgate & Southgate'; and '[the] filthe cast over the city wall at St Mary Arches Lane end'.[35] Defects in the walls and gates were sometimes reported at other times of the year as well—the great inquest met several times annually in order to inquire into 'common nuisances' of all sorts—but it was always in the wake of the mural walk that the greatest number of presentments concerning the state of the enceinte was made.

Nor did this exhaust the Chamber's armoury when it came to assessing the condition of the walls and gates, for there were several other ways in which dilapidations could be identified. Sometimes the town councillors were alerted to the need for repairs by the evidence of their own eyes. In addition, concerned private citizens occasionally informed the Chamber about sections of the city wall which were tottering or on the verge of collapse. We catch a glimpse of this in a Chamber order of 1653, which directed that two of the Twenty-Four should inspect 'parte of the citties walle neere the Keygate which is . . . this day complayned of by Thomas Flood and others to bee ruinous and in great danger of fallinge'.[36] Finally, in times of pressing military danger, the Chamber could order 'extraordinary inspections' of the defensive perimeter to be carried out. This work was usually undertaken by small groups of councillors who were deputed to survey the condition of the enceinte and then to report back to their colleagues. When a 'committee for public safety' was established in Exeter on the eve of the Civil War, in September 1642, one of the first tasks that its members were given was to establish the state of the defences. Similar working-parties were ordered to inspect the walls in January and October of the same year.[37]

How long did it take for the recommendations of those who presented defects in the city defences to be acted upon? Reports from the emergency working-parties could kick-start remedial work in a matter of weeks, or even days. In the case of the routine presentments made by the law jury, response-times were more commonly measured in years. This is well illustrated by the long-drawn out saga of the latrine pit dug through the barbican behind the High Gaol which has already been referred to in Chapters 1–2. This pit was first presented as a nuisance at the law day held on 10 May 1557, when the jurors informed against 'Rychard Denys [keeper] of the Gayle for stoppynge of the murallye waye and the dystruceyon of the wall by reason of a jacks made yn the barbycan'.[38] Clearly nothing was done, for the jurors reported the nuisance caused by the 'Gayle jakes' again in October 1559, and yet again in October 1560. The Chamber now took up the cudgels, leading to an agreement of 10 October 1562 by which Denys agreed to fill up the pit, to replace it with a vault and to 'permit the old way to be opened and used by the Mayor &c as heretofore'.[39] The Gaol-keeper continued to drag his heels, however. Later that same month the law jury complained that 'Mr Denys, accordying to hys promysse & the inforcement made, hath not opened the murally at the Gaole', and as late as October 1564 the jurors were continuing to make angry representations against Denys 'for an [impediment] yn the murally way & mayntenying a notable filthy jakes [whereby] Mr Mayor and the commons cannot passe accordyng to the old [custom]'.[40] In the end, it took over seven years for the damage to the barbican here to be repaired.

This was by no means an unusual case. Following the demolition of the old town jakes during the construction of Water Gate in 1565, the jurors complained that 'we do fynd great anoysaunce for lacke of a draff [i.e. draught-house] at the newe gate'.[41] It was three years before the Chamber got around to ordering that a replacement should be built, and another three or four before the 'newe . . . prevy by ye Watar Gete' was actually finished.[42] Matters proceeded even more slowly when it came to the crumbling stretch of city wall between Water Gate and South Gate. First reported to be in poor condition in 1559, the wall here was not eventually rebuilt until 1579![43]

Initiating the Work

As the preceding discussion makes clear, only the town governors had the power to initiate work on the defences. Dealing with minor repairs was the province of the receiver, who was permitted to initiate such work on his own authority. Major projects, on the other hand, could only be embarked upon with the agreement of the Chamber as a whole, and throughout this period receivers were scrupulously careful to ensure that they had the blessing of their fellow-councillors before they dispensed any large sum of money on the defences. The receiver for 1528–29 made a point of observing in his end-of-year account that the work which he had ordered to be carried out on the city wall near West Gate had been undertaken 'by the counsell of the hole mastyres'.[44] Similarly, when the receiver for 1637–38 unexpectedly found himself having to lay out money in order to stave off an imminent collapse of the barbican behind St John's Hospital, he hurried off to seek retrospective approval from his colleagues. A few days later it was noted in the Chamber act book that

> whereas Mr Receiver hath of late bestowed on a sudden some monies in the repaire of the citties walles adioyninge to the Hospitall Chappel which was in danger of falling, it is this day agreed that he shalbe allowed of those disbursements uppon his account.[45]

Some forty formal 'orders' instructing work to begin on different parts of the city enceinte are recorded in the Chamber act books for the period 1509–1660, and doubtless many more such directives were issued orally for which no evidence now exists. The earliest of the written orders—those which relate to the 'new building' of East Gate between 1511 and 1513—are reproduced below [*see document 3*]. As these particular directives illustrate very well, the Chamber had three distinct methods of proceeding when it came to transforming into action an initial decision that work on the enceinte should begin. The first— usually employed in connection with major projects—was to contract all the requisite work out to an individual mason. Thus Robert Poke of Thorverton was engaged to 'bilde & make Estgate' in 1511, while in 1500–1, John Drake, mason, made an agreement with the town governors 'for rebuilding the city wall on the south side of West Gate': the deal being closed with liberal draughts of wine.[46] The second method was to appoint small groups of influential men to act as 'supervisors' of major projects. The Chamber selected thirteen individuals to oversee the rebuilding of East Gate in 1511, for example; five town councillors to oversee the rebuilding of North Gate in 1558; and nine councillors and nine 'commoners' to act as 'surveyors and devysers' of the construction of Water Gate in 1565.[47]

The third, and much the most common, method was to order the current receiver to set the necessary work in motion, occasionally under the supervision of a group of overseers. Thus, in 1558, it was noted in the Chamber act book that, because North Gate and the adjoining stretches of the city wall were in a sad state of decay:

> it is . . . agreed by the hole assent of the 24 that the Recever with all spede convenyent shall aswyll appoynt convenyent workemen for the reperacon of the said walles, as also to . . . [rebuild] the said Gate . . . by the oversight of [the mayor and others].[48]

Dozens of similar orders were to be issued over the succeeding century.

Although Exeter did not possess permanent officials whose job it was to supervise all work on the town walls, as a number of other early modern European cities did,[49] the receivers and the members of the specially constituted supervisory groups performed very much the same function: albeit on a strictly *ad hoc* basis. Occasionally, an acknowledged local 'expert' seems to have emerged. A good example was Mr Thomas Andrewe who, after having re-edified a portion of the city wall while serving as receiver in 1499–1500, was subsequently rewarded for his 'attendance' at East Gate in 1513.[50] During the early seventeenth century, both Thomas Bridgeman and Robert Sherwood acted as occasional 'overseers' of the city's works.[51] Generally speaking, though, continuity of personnel was far less marked among those who oversaw work on the defences than it was among the artificers who carried the work out.

The City's Workmen

Once the receiver had been ordered to start work on the enceinte, how did he set the ball rolling? The first step, as the order of 1558 acknowledged, was to 'appoynt convenient workmen'. This could be done in two ways: by making an agreement with a single master craftsman to carry out all the necessary work 'at task', as the receiver did in 1527–28 and 1528–29,[52] or by hiring a number of different artificers to work on the project at a daily or weekly wage, as was more usual. It was clearly expected that, wherever possible, the workmen whom the receiver engaged would be residents of Exeter. A Chamber order of 1580 instructing the receiver to 'provyde for the buyldinge' of the city walls near South Gate specifically directed 'that he shall hyre & reteyne such masons to be workers as be of this Citie'.[53] As far as one can tell from the surviving evidence, the great majority of those who were employed to work on the defences during the early modern period were, indeed, Exonians. Workmen are only known to have been brought in from outside the city on exceptional occasions. During the Prayer Book

Rebellion of 1549 a messenger was sent out of Exeter to summon in 'masons for the Cetie walles', while during the Civil War the Royalist Chamber hired William Plumer of Thorverton and Peter Martin of Teignmouth—both described as masons and 'maister workemen'—to work on the fortifications.[54] Such emergencies aside, the only 'foreigners' who received regular payment in connection with work on the defences were the carriers who supplied stones from the neighbouring quarries.

Of the artificers themselves, there is space to say only a very little here. Hundreds, probably thousands, of individuals worked on the city defences of Exeter between 1485 and 1660, including representatives of a score of different trades. The receivers' accounts show that among the different kinds of workmen employed throughout the whole period were blacksmiths, carpenters, carriers, glaziers, helliers (i.e. roofers), labourers, 'lymers', masons, painters, paviers, plumbers, quarrymen, sawyers, thatchers, tilers and 'wallers'. To these were added, during the 1640s and 1650s, 'lockyers', joiners and waggoners. A handful of these individuals, most of them masons, were employed by the Chamber on a semi-permanent basis. Between 1556 and 1563, for example, William Monsdon—the man whom we have already encountered purloining stones from the rampart—received a fee of £1 *per annum* for keeping the walls clean.[55] During the 1570s, the same task was performed by a certain Richard Coffield, while in 1589 the Chamber engaged John Davey, mason, to 'clence the citties walles this yere of the ives [i.e. ivy] & suche other hinderances of the walles'.[56]

Two years later the Chamber—emulating a practice which had long been followed at York, Chester and elsewhere[57]—took the decision to engage a 'dedicated' civic mason. In 1591 it was agreed that Richard Deymond, an artisan who was already well acquainted with the city enceinte, should be appointed to 'yerlye clense the cities walles . . . [and to] oversee the said walles . . . & [to] geeve notice yf there be any . . . decaye [therein] . . . & [to] certefie the Maier & Receiver . . . of the same'.[58] Deymond was to serve in this role for the next twenty years.[59] He finally stood down in 1611 and was succeeded as the Chamber's most favoured mason by William Lawrence; the latter had been admitted as a freeman of Exeter in 1599–1600, but is known to have been intermittently working on the city walls since as early as 1584.[60] Thereafter, the Chamber's 'masons of choice' were John Moody, active on the walls between *c*.1616 and 1630; William Lawrence (serving in the role for a second time), between *c*.1632 and 1640; John Lawrence (perhaps William's son), between *c*.1640 and 1650; and John Griffen, between *c*.1653 and 1660. Men like these must have built up a wealth of experience and come to know the city circuit backwards; certainly, no one played a more important role than they did in moulding and fashioning the early modern enceinte.

The vast majority of those who were paid for working on the city defences at Exeter between 1485 and 1660 were men. With this said, a few payments were made to women—particularly during the troubled years of the mid-seventeenth century. In 1643 over £5 was paid to

Katherine Jerman, Thomasine Peare and Temperance Whiterowe for 'carriage of turf', while a further 5 shillings and 8 pence was paid 'to divers women for carriage of stones to the citty wales'.[61] During the same year, both 'Thomasine Sheares, widow', and 'the Widow Kelly' were reimbursed for deal boards which they had supplied for use in the fortifications.[62] Other sources reveal that the women of Exeter laboured to build defensive outworks during the bitter winter of 1645–46 as the city prepared to resist the New Model Army.[63] Finally, it is intriguing to note that Honour Crutchett, widow, was paid on three separate occasions between 1650 and 1652 for nails, crooks, 'cramps', 'spukes', locks, keys and other assorted 'iron-work' provided for the city gates.[64] It is known that Honour's former husband, John—a blacksmith—had died during the Civil War, leaving her saddled with six young children and a number of debts.[65] Had she therefore decided to set up as a smith on her own? If so, she was the only woman to be paid for working on the city defences as an artificer in her own right over the entire 175-year period.

The Process of Repair

How did the city's workmen go about their duties? To attempt to describe all of the multifarious tasks which were carried out around the city enceinte would be impractical in a work of this scope.[66] Nevertheless, it is important to understand how the artificers employed by the Chamber undertook the single, most important task connected with the maintenance of Exeter's defences: that of repairing the city wall. On this subject, we are fortunate enough to possess the direct personal testimony of William Lawrence, one of the most experienced of the city masons. Towards the end of his long working life in 1633, Lawrence—by then aged '70 or thereabouts'—was asked to describe the procedures which had typically been adopted during his life-time in order to effect repairs to the wall. This was the old mason's reply:

> when the walles of the . . . cittie are in decaye or doe need amendment, the magistrates of the . . . cittie or their officers have brought, or caused to be brought, stones or other materialls towards the reparacion of the walles . . . and some . . . have fixed scaffolds about six foot from the said walles, both within and without . . . as there is occasion . . . and . . . [the workmen have] put their materialls on the banckes and ditches . . . as the same hath beene most convenient for the reparacion of the said walles.[67]

The receivers' accounts both confirm and amplify this picture—and make it clear that the building methods which Lawrence described during the 1630s were of very long standing. Throughout the early modern period, the city authorities regularly supplied three essential materials to those who had been appointed to work on the town walls: stones, lime and sand. The stones were used to build up the wall. The lime and sand were mixed together—usually in the proportion of one part lime to two or three parts sand—in order to create the mortar which was used to bind the stones into a solid whole. All three types of material were delivered straight to the section of the enceinte where the work was taking place, usually on the backs of packhorses. The lime and sand would then be mixed together on site, and the accounts contain many references to the tubs, barrels and bowls which—together with large quantities of water—were employed in this process. In 1579–80 a 'mortar house' was constructed at the same time as repairs were being carried out on the walls near Water Gate: presumably this structure was built in order to enable the mortar to be prepared under cover.[68]

Once all of the necessary materials had been assembled, the next step was to clear the existing walls of ivy, brambles and other encumbrances.[69] It was then possible to erect the scaffolds. These consisted of long wooden poles, to which were lashed the wattle frames, or hurdles, known as 'flakes'. These in turn served as platforms for the masons to stand on while they were carrying out their work.[70] 'Puncheons'—stout wooden supports—were placed at the foot of the scaffold poles in order to give them additional strength.[71] 'Penny-ropes' and twine were used about the scaffolding, both to lash the poles and flakes together and to fix the whole structure more tightly to the walls.[72] 'Slings' were also fashioned in order to lift large blocks of stone.[73] Precarious as these arrangements sound, no one is known to have been killed or injured while working on the city walls of Exeter during the early modern period, and the system must surely have been efficient, or it would hardly have endured for so long.

Organization and Wages

Typically, repairs to the city wall were carried out by a small group of artificers working under the direction of a single 'chief mason' or 'master workman'.[74] The size of these work gangs—or 'companies' as they were termed during the seventeenth century—fluctuated according to the nature of the job in hand. Minor repairs were often effected by the mason alone, or by the mason accompanied only by 'his servant', 'his man', or 'his boy'.[75] Larger jobs required more manpower, and it was common for masons to engage two, three, four or even more artificers to assist them in their task. In 1646, for example, John Lawrence hired Christopher Kennicke and Thomas Pole—both of whom may well have been masons themselves—to help him to repair the Quay Gate, while nine years later John Griffin assembled a company of seven men to work alongside him on the city wall behind the Bishop's Palace.[76]

In times of crisis, numbers rose much higher. During the invasion scare of 1539–40, William Downeman—a mason who had long been employed to carry out repairs to the city enceinte, and who was presumably regarded as an unusually experienced and competent craftsman—led a task-force of eleven masons 'workyn at the walles'.[77] It seems probable that similarly large parties were assembled in 1549, after masons had been summoned in to help strengthen the defences against the

Prayer Book rebels. The Civil War saw many different groups of masons working around the city perimeter at the same time: eight separate 'companies' are known to have been employed in 1643 alone.[78] Almost certainly there were more masons employed about the city's walls and gates during 1642–43 than there had been at any other time over the preceding three centuries.

The wages which the craftsmen received for their work rose steadily as the period progressed. During the 1480s and 1490s, masons employed on the city defences commonly received between 5 pence and 6 pence per day. By the late 1530s this had risen to 7 pence: the rate at which William Downeman was paid in 1539–40. By the beginning of Elizabeth's reign, the typical daily wage had risen once more, to 9 pence, while during the 1580s and 1590s Richard Deymond was able to command a shilling a day. Under James I and Charles I the city masons enjoyed a daily wage of 1 shilling and 2 pence, and this rose to 1 shilling and 4 pence during the first months of the Civil War. John Griffin, the last mason to be regularly employed by the Chamber during the period covered by this book, was also the most handsomely remunerated; he received 1 shilling and 6 pence per day during the late 1640s, and no less than 1 shilling and 8 pence per day during the following decade.[79]

Between 1485 and 1660, then, the typical wage of master masons at Exeter had risen more than threefold, and members of other craft groups in the city saw their wages shoot up at a similar rate. Carpenters and helliers, who had been paid—like the masons—5 pence per day in the late fifteenth century, were receiving—like them—1 shilling and 2 pence per day by the eve of the Civil War.[80] The tripling of craftsmen's wages at Exeter simply mirrored a national phenomenon, of course: the steady rise in the cost of living which took place across England as a whole during the early modern period.[81] Yet the fact that the inflationary pressures were general cannot have made the spiralling cost of artificers' wages any more palatable to the town governors—especially as the price of building materials was also going up.

The Provision of Materials

Most of the raw materials used to repair the city defences were drawn from a number of key sites within a ten-mile radius of Exeter [*see map 6*]. Only the 'heling-stones' (i.e. slates) which were used to roof the gates were imported from further afield. Sand was obtained by local labourers from the River Exe: presumably scooped up from the river bed with buckets and shovels.[82] Lime was procured from the little market town of Chudleigh, eight miles to the south-west of Exeter, which stands upon limestone rock. The rock was quarried and burnt in kilns nearby and then supplied to the city workmen ready-made, usually in sacks. Between 1538 and 1559 the city receivers bought large quantities of lime from one Nicholas Ball, 'lymer', who lived at Harcombe, just outside Chudleigh (a large double lime-kiln, known locally as 'the tramps' hotel', still stands at Harcombe to this day).[83] During the 1640s lime brought directly from

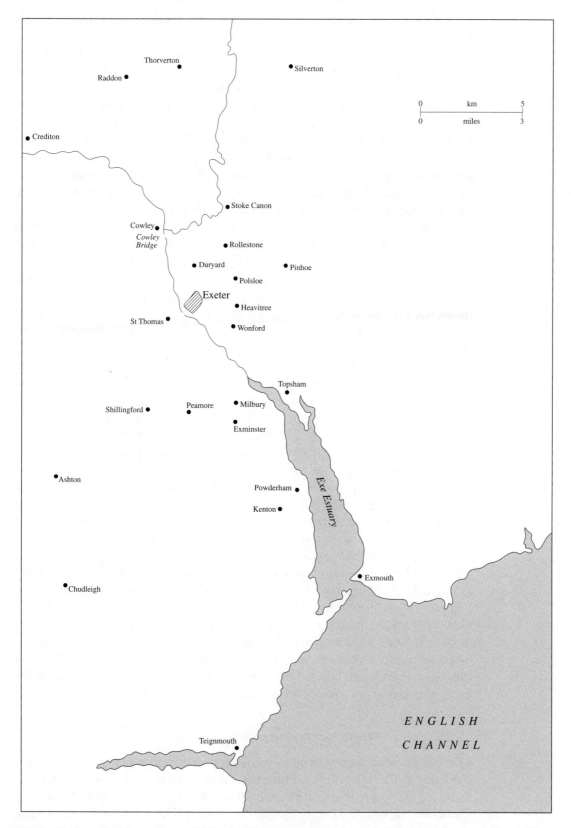

Map 6 Exeter and its immediate neighbourhood: this map shows those places outside the city which are mentioned in the text

Chudleigh was occasionally supplemented by supplies obtained from the lime-kilns at Weare, near Topsham.[84]

The most favoured stone for work on the city walls was red breccia.[85] Hewn from the quarries at Heavitree (or Wonford) to the east of the city, and from those at Peamore (in Shillingford parish) and Milberry (in Exminster parish) to the south-west, this was the stone which was used in the great majority of repairs to the city enceinte between 1485 and 1660.[86] During the earlier part of the period, considerable use was also made of volcanic rock, or 'trap'. Small quantities of trap from the quarries near Silverton, seven miles to the north of Exeter, were purchased by the city receivers as late as the mid-1580s for use on the walls at West Gate and East Gate.[87] During the Middle Ages, volcanic stone from the quarry at Raddon, near Thorverton, is also known to have been incorporated in the city enceinte.[88] No specific references to the purchase of Raddon stone for repairs to Exeter's walls and gates survive in the early modern accounts. But the fact that the man whom the Chamber engaged to 'new-build' East Gate in 1511 was Robert Poke of Thorverton is intriguing, and raises the possibility that the Henrician East Gate, which was chiefly built of stone from Heavitree, may also have incorporated some Raddon stone.[89]

Most of the timber which the artificers working on the city defences required—for scaffolding poles, for 'flakes', for the roofs of the gates and towers, for gate-leaves, for rafters, for planking, for doors, for stakes, and for a hundred and one other things—was procured from Duryard Wood, just to the north of Exeter. Duryard was the property of the Chamber and, throughout the early modern period, the town governors made use of it as a prime source of timber for all sorts of civic projects, including work on the fortifications. It was from here that the materials used to build scaffolding for the walls in 1538–40 came.[90] Over a century later, as the citizens feverishly prepared their defences on the eve of the Civil War, the Chamber directed that 'materialls . . . [should] be taken out of Duryard Wood of the toppes of the trees for the making of gabyons [i.e. wattle baskets] & such things for the carrying of earth'.[91] Three years after this, in 1645, beech trees were ordered to be 'taken downe in Duryard Wood for the making of stocks for musketts & other such like uses'.[92] Duryard made a crucial contribution to the upkeep of the city defences. The fact that apparently inexhaustible supplies of timber could be procured from here at little or no cost did much to reduce the cost of defensive work of all sorts. This was just as well, for maintaining the walls and gates was an extremely expensive task.

Paying for Work on the Fortifications

The Crown contributed little or nothing to the defences of Exeter during the early modern period; finding the large sums of money which needed to be regularly lavished on the city enceinte was the responsibility of the Chamber alone. Although routine repairs to the walls and gates were paid for by the annually elected receivers in the first instance, each receiver was eventually reimbursed from the sums of money which he and his successors-in-office had amassed in their roles as collectors of the city's revenues. Despite what was, in effect, a disguised loan from the receiver, therefore, the bulk of the money which was used to pay for work on the defences came, in the end, from the city's own annual income: an income which was itself derived from rents, from customs and from a variety of 'extraordinary' sources. However, the Chamber also made use of a remarkable range of other devices in order to supplement this central 'revenue stream'.

First, as we have just seen, the town governors sometimes contributed to work on the city defences by supplying raw materials free of charge: mainly wood from Duryard, but occasionally stone and timber from other sources as well.[93] An alternative strategy was to grant privileges to particular individuals in return for services rendered. Thus, in 1511, the town governors agreed that one Richard Andrew should be admitted as a freeman of the city *gratis* (i.e. without having to pay an entry fine) as a 'rewarde' to his father, Thomas, for his assistance with the rebuilding of East Gate. Similarly, in 1513, the Chamber ordered that Nicholas Abell, stainer, should be made a freeman of the city, '[he] paying nothing for his fyne' if he would agree to paint 'the tabernacle & the Kyng in the Est Gate'.[94] Such stratagems had their place, but the sums of money which they saved were infinitesimal compared with the sums which had to be raised. Far more important were the steps which the Chamber took to extract money for the maintenance of the city defences from the pockets of private individuals.

Particularly helpful in this respect were the tenants of the city's gates and mural towers. Although it was the city's responsibility to maintain the outer walls of these buildings, the tenants were bound by the terms of their leases to pay for any repairs to the main body of the structure themselves.[95] This could often save the Chamber a good deal of money. Following Perkin Warbeck's attack on Exeter in 1497, for example—during the course of which East Gate was badly damaged— Henry Grymston, clerk, the tenant of the gate, was forced to undertake 'diverse . . . repairs' on the structure. So great was the cost of this work that the city authorities later went so far as to excuse him from paying his rent, in respect of the 'expenses' which he had incurred.[96] Similarly, during the great invasion scare of 1539–40, the Chamber received a payment of £10 from Bishop John Veysey for repairs 'to the city wall opposite the [Bishop's] Palace': money which was almost certainly intended to be spent on strengthening the defences of the two mural towers in this area, which the bishops of Exeter had long treated as their own, although technically they belonged to the city [*see Chapters 1–2*]. The ambiguous status of these two towers appears to have confused this year's receiver, Thomas Prestwoode, who subsequently spent nearly £5 over and above Veysey's payment on work there. The gimlet-eyed civic auditors later noted that, as 'repairs to that [section of] wall belong or appertain to the . . . bishop', the receiver had exceeded his brief, and should not be reimbursed.[97] As a result, poor Prestwood ended up making his own, involuntary, contribution to the cost of repairing the city enceinte. It is hardly surprising that receivers, forced to operate in such an unforgiving climate, were so anxious to ensure that they had the Chamber's formal approval before they initiated any major repair work.

Pouncing on unauthorized items of expenditure was not the only way in which the Chamber contrived to wring more money out of the receivers. By long-established custom, each receiver was supposed to hold a feast for his colleagues in the Guildhall on St George's Day, while each of the city stewards was expected to provide similar feasts in their own houses soon after the election of the mayor. The custom was not always honoured, however—and this presented the city government with a window of opportunity. In 1539—as fears of imminent invasion pushed defensive expenditure to new heights—the Chamber decreed that in future, should any of the officials neglect to provide such a feast, they would be fined at the rate of £5 each: the money 'to be employed towardes the reparacions of the cities walles'.[98] This order had some effect, though it was quickly recognized that £5 was too steep a fine for the stewards—who were usually relatively young men—to manage. In 1542, £5 was handed over by that year's receiver, together with £3 6 shillings and 8 pence from one of the stewards, while in 1545 it was recorded that John Maynard—presumably another steward—had given £4 towards 'the reparacion of the . . . walls for his benevolens, by cause he kept not his dener'.[99]

Those who stumped up were in the minority; most of the civic officers appear to have concluded that it was cheaper to provide the feast than to pay the fine. In the wake of the Prayer Book Rebellion—which had necessitated further very heavy expenditure—the Chamber took steps to ensure that the receivers and stewards should no longer be given any choice but to contribute towards the cost of maintaining the defences. In September 1550 it was decreed that the dinners should be held no longer, but that, 'yn liewe thereof', every receiver should pay either £5 or £4 and every steward either £4 or £3 6 shillings and 8 pence 'towards the reparacion of the towne walls': the precise level of the fine to be determined at the Chamber's discretion. This order was duly entered into the act book, but for how long it continued to be enforced is uncertain.[100]

Useful as the one-off payments which the Chamber extracted from the receivers and the stewards were, the amounts of money produced by such 'dinner fines' paled into insignificance when compared with the huge sums which could be raised through loans, taxation, 'gifts' and assessment. Of these four 'emergency methods', loans were the most commonly employed. In times of crisis, every member of the Twenty-Four was expected to lend money to help pay for the city's defences. During the invasion scare of 1545, for example, each of the town councillors agreed 'of there [own] good willes' to lend money for the purchase of 'great gunnes'. Four years later, mayor John Blackaller and alderman William Hurst disbursed large sums of money out of their own pockets in order to pay for the defence of the city against the Prayer

Book rebels: money which they later claimed back from the common chest [*see document 5*]. Almost a century after this, in 1642–43, well over £5,000 was lent to the 'Roundhead' Chamber—both by individual town councillors and by other wealthy men and women—to meet the cost of defending Exeter against the Royalist army of Charles I.[101]

What of taxation? During the Middle Ages, the town governors had periodically received 'murage' grants from the Crown: that is to say, they had been empowered to raise tolls on local people to pay for repairs to the city defences.[102] Murage had fallen into disuse by 1485 and—perhaps rather surprisingly—formal taxation of this sort was rarely resorted to thereafter. During the Civil War, the Royalist authorities in Exeter imposed a 'garrison rate' on the inhabitants—and some of the money collected in this way may conceivably have been spent on building fortifications as well as on supporting the Cavalier soldiers.[103] Yet it is clear that the Chamber preferred to raise money through voluntary contributions wherever possible. Sometimes such 'free gifts' were exactly what their name suggests: contributions made entirely of the giver's own volition. This was true of the present of cannon and other weapons which the Earl of Bedford made to the Chamber in 1556, for example; of the legacy of £1 and 5 shillings which Joan Tuckfield, widow, left 'to the use of the city to amend . . . the city wall' a year or two later, and of the gifts of money, plate and labour which hundreds of individual citizens made towards the cost of fortifying the city against the King in 1642–43.[104]

With this said, the line between voluntary contributions and compulsory exactions could often be a fine one. When the Chamber 'invited' the citizens to contribute to extraordinary collections designed to meet the cost of emergency defence work—as they did in 1545, 1549 and 1642[105]—few can have been left in any doubt about how a refusal to make a donation would be construed. Those who declined to stump up not only risked public opprobrium, they also made themselves vulnerable to punitive 'assessments' which might eventually compel them to disgorge even more money than they had originally been asked for. In the aftermath of the Prayer Book Rebellion, Lord Russell—the commander of the royal army in the West—was informed that, although the defence of Exeter against the rebels had been 'vary chargeable', some of the citizens, 'for some synister affeccions they had in this cause', had refused to help with the cost. Russell promptly wrote to the mayor, empowering him to summon all such persons before him and to compel them to contribute.[106]

Enforced contributions of this sort reached their height during the Civil War. In June 1642, Charles I's opponents in London introduced the so-called 'Propositions of Parliament': a national scheme designed to raise finances for the Parliamentary war-effort by voluntary subscription. Over the following year, the inhabitants of Exeter 'voluntarily subscribed and advanced' the staggering sum of £4,892 on the Propositions, all of which was eventually spent on the defence of the city against the King.[107] Many local people refused to give anything, however, and in January

1643 the most prominent of these recalcitrants were arrested, 'assessed' and forced to contribute a total of £3,259 to the Parliamentary war chest.[108] A few days later, Parliament issued an ordinance which justified this action in retrospect by authorizing the mayor and other local Parliamentarians to assess all who had not yet contributed 'to pay such . . . sums of money . . . as the said assessors shall think fit'. Those who refused to pay the fines imposed upon them were to have their goods distrained and, if necessary, to be thrown into prison.[109] A further £992 was subsequently mulcted from various Exonians under the terms of this ordinance; most of the money went to pay Roundhead soldiers during the siege of summer 1643.[110] It seems highly probable that equivalent sums were exacted from the citizens by the King's supporters while they controlled the city during 1643–46—one Exeter man later deposed that he had been forced to contribute large sums of money towards the cost of 'fortifications' by 'both sides' during the Civil War[111]—but little hard evidence about the assessments which the Royalists imposed on the inhabitants has survived.

The exactions of the 1640s were exceptional. Generally speaking, money to pay for repairs to the city wall was more or less freely given—and the inhabitants of early modern Exeter were proudly aware of the fact that, by committing such huge resources of time and money to the maintenance of their own defences, they were helping—as they had helped for centuries before—to subsidize the defence of the entire realm. In a petition sent to Henry VI in 1447–48, the town governors observed—in distinctly self-congratulatory tones—that, as a result of the care which they and their predecessors had lavished on the fortifications, Exeter was able to provide 'socore to alle the Kynges puple' of the Western parts 'yn tyme of nede . . . [and] specially yn tyme of werre'.[112] Similarly, during the 1630s, the Chamber made a special point of reminding Charles I—whom they considered to be treating them unfairly over the matter of the 'city wastes' [*see Chapter 5*]—of the citizens' sterling work in maintaining the town walls 'as they . . . are bound to doe, and to their great yearely charge they have from tyme to tyme done'.[113] That the early Stuart Chamber should have expected their long-standing record of devotion to the city enceinte to win them credit with the King is hardly surprising: during the Tudor period, the defensive circuit, over which so many generations of Exeter people had sweated and toiled, had several times proved a vital bulwark of the royal regime. In the following chapter, the turbulent history of Exeter's fortifications between 1485 and 1603 will be examined in depth.

CHAPTER 4

THE CITY DEFENCES UNDER THE TUDORS

The association between the Tudor dynasty and the city of Exeter was quite exceptionally—even uniquely—close, for it was in Exeter that Henry Tudor had first been proclaimed as king. In October 1483, some two years before the battle of Bosworth, a group of local conspirators had backed the Duke of Buckingham in his ill-fated rebellion against Richard III and had publicly pronounced Henry's accession through the city streets.[1] At the time, the town governors' decision to stand by while this declaration of support for the 'usurper' was made had appeared a terrible misjudgement. Having captured and executed Buckingham, Richard had proceeded to Exeter in vengeful mood and had wreaked summary punishment upon his enemies. A number of leading rebels had been beheaded and their remains scattered about the city for the edification and the instruction of the inhabitants.[2]

For a time it seemed that Exeter might freeze in perpetual royal disfavour, but the city's winter of discountenance was turned to glorious summer by the unlooked-for events of August 1485. With Henry safely installed upon the throne and Richard's mangled body consigned to the crows, Exeter found itself transformed, at a stroke, from the most 'disloyal' to the most 'loyal' of English cities. It was the town governors' unbending determination to retain this new-found reputation for constancy which was to shape the course of Exeter's history over the following century, and which was eventually to lead the last of the Tudor line to bestow the title of *Semper Fidelis*—'Ever Faithful'—on the city which had first acclaimed her grandfather.[3] Nowhere is this determination better revealed, perhaps, than in the record of expenditure on Exeter's defences. The present chapter provides a detailed survey of the work which was undertaken on the city enceinte from the year of Henry VII's accession to that of Elizabeth I's death and demonstrates that, while the Chamber allocated small sums of money to the upkeep and maintenance of the town defences in almost every year, this pattern of routine expenditure was frequently interrupted by sudden 'spikes' in spending which were linked to specific military and political events.

The first years of Henry VII's reign were relatively peaceful ones for Exeter. Lambert Simnel's invasion of the North in 1487 was soon defeated, and the episode made little impact on the South West. The receiver's accounts for this year record no unusual expenditure on the enceinte. Between 1488 and 1490 considerable amounts were spent on the gates—over £2 on re-roofing 'the tower over Eastgate', for example, and almost £7 on 'the makyng of West yeate'—but these appear to have been just routine repairs.[4] In October 1492 Henry VII began his first major foreign war by leading an army into France and laying siege to Boulogne. The launching of this campaign may perhaps have been what prompted the citizens of Exeter to begin work on their town walls in 1492–93; almost £1 was spent on repairing 'the wall next to Snayltore'.[5] Within less than a month, though, Henry came to terms with the French. For the next two years, England remained at peace, and the Exeter receivers' accounts recorded no major outlay on the city defences.

Matters suddenly changed in 1495–96, when over £14 was spent on rebuilding the town walls 'on the north side of the city'. This was the largest single sum to have been laid out on the defences for more than fifteen years.[6] The sudden upsurge of work may well have been connected with the activities of another pretender to Henry VII's throne: Perkin Warbeck. In July 1495 Warbeck had attempted an invasion of the South East. Rebuffed here, he had moved on to Ireland, and had then established himself in Scotland, threatening to make further attacks on England all the while.[7] His erratic progress cannot have escaped notice at Exeter. Alternatively, the citizens may have been made anxious by rumours of unrest across the Tamar. In May 1497 a serious revolt broke out in West Cornwall, where the common people had been infuriated by Henry VII's demand for new taxes.[8] Soon afterwards a large body of rebellious Cornishmen appeared before the walls of Exeter and demanded to be let into the city. The citizens demurred; a few of the rebel leaders were allowed in, but the majority of their followers were kept outside. Trouble flared at the Guildhall when the Cornish 'capteynes, beinge offended and angrye that they were as longe kept out, beganne to quarell with the Mayer, and thretned to cutt of his hedd yn the same place'.[9] Despite these threats, the citizens held firm. They continued to deny admittance to the rebel host, and the Cornishmen eventually gave up and marched off. A few weeks later, the rebels suffered bloody defeat at the hands of the King's army at Blackheath—but Exeter's troubles were not yet over. Warbeck was still lurking in Ireland, and when news of the Cornish revolt reached him, he determined to take advantage of the confusion which it had caused. On 7 September 1497 the pretender came ashore near Land's End. He proclaimed himself king and quickly attracted an army of supporters. Ten days later, Warbeck arrived before Exeter with a force of some 6,000 men.[10]

Warbeck summoned the city to admit him, but the inhabitants—bolstered by the presence of the Earl of Devon who had ridden into Exeter with many local gentlemen—refused to do so. Angered by this intransigence, Warbeck launched a series of brisk assaults, hoping to scale the walls with ladders. These attempts were 'manneffully resysted' by the citizens and many of the attackers were slain.[11] The besiegers now tried a different tack and determined 'with fire to burne and breake open the towne gates, and so to enter yn'.[12] The first attempt was made at North Gate, which was successfully set afire. Yet 'before the gate could be fully consumed', the citizens blocked it up with faggots 'which they likewise set on fire, and so repulsed fire with fire; and in the meantime raised up rampiers [i.e. ramparts] of earth . . . to serve instead of wall and gate'.[13] When the flames finally died down and the attackers surged forward, they found themselves confronted with new defences, constructed inside the old gate. In addition, the ground was against them 'by reason that they were all to go up agaynst the hill, and that a fewe within were too good for many without'.[14] Warbeck's men could make no headway and were forced to retire. Soon afterwards the rebels launched another fierce attack, this time on East Gate 'which they brake open and with force entred yn to the citie'.[15] For a time it seemed that Exeter was lost. Warbeck's men poured through the gate, and rushed up High Street as far as Castle Lane. At this critical juncture they were met by a counter-attack, launched by the Earl of Devon from the Blackfriars (in present-day Bedford Street). For a few moments the struggle hung in the balance, then the citizens began to prevail. Eventually, Warbeck's men were driven back 'and with force compelled out of the gates'.[16]

That night, while the rebels licked their wounds, the citizens strengthened the ramparts in the gateways. The receiver's roll for this year, which includes a special section devoted to 'expenses within the city for repelling Perkyn Usbeck' [*see document 2*], records that labourers were paid for removing 'les bulworkes to let men into the City' and then for making them up again. The city's ordnance—some of which had clearly been procured in haste from ships at Topsham—was also looked to. Some 500 lb of lead were used to make 'pelettes' for the guns, while 1 shilling and 2 pence was spent on mending '1 gonne . . . by night'. In addition, wine and barrels of beer were sent to the gates to refresh the weary defenders.[17] Next morning the insurgents made further attacks on East Gate and North Gate. At both places they were repulsed with loss and this proved to be the rebels' last throw. Now, wrote the Earl of Devon, 'when Perkin and his company had well assaied and felt our gunns, they were faine to . . . geder theire company togeder, and soe to depart'.[18] Disheartened by their losses, Warbeck's followers began to melt away. By noon the remnants of the rebel army had quit the siege and trailed off to Cullompton. Three days later Warbeck abandoned his followers and tried to flee the country. Soon afterwards Henry VII himself arrived in Exeter with an army. He stayed in the city some time, busily engaged 'yn punyshynge of the rebells and quietinge of the countrie'.[19] The King also rewarded Exeter's loyal defenders.

Over the next three years, steps were taken to repair the damage inflicted upon the city by Warbeck. In 1497–98 over £17 was spent on 'remaking North Gate', burnt by the rebels during their attack, while further unspecified sums were laid out by the tenant of East Gate 'for diverse . . . repairs undertaken by him to damages caused by the assault of Perkin Wosbeck'.[20] Next year £32 was spent on 'the head' of the city's pipes and conduits, the source of Exeter's water supply, which may also have been destroyed by the besiegers. In addition, workmen were paid almost £5 for 'lifting up stones fallen from the [city] wall into the leat' near West Gate.[21] Further work in this area took place during 1500–1, when a mason received £31 for 'rebuilding the City Wall on the south side of Westgate'.[22] Once these repairs had been made, the citizens were able to reduce their outlay. The first few years of the sixteenth century were peaceful ones for England, and this is reflected in the receivers' accounts, which record no major work being undertaken on Exeter's defences between 1501 and 1506.

No detailed accounts of expenditure survive for the last four years of Henry VII's reign, nor indeed, for the first fourteen of his son's. Fortunately, the first surviving Chamber act book begins in 1509, and this reveals much about the most important defensive project undertaken during this period: the rebuilding of East Gate [*see document 3*]. John Hooker refers to the commencement of this work in his historical chronicle of Exeter (a work based partly on his own recollections, partly on his detailed study of the city archives, which he completed in around 1590). In 1510, Hooker records, 'the Eastegate of this Citie which was verie ruynose and yn decay and shrewdly shaken yn the late . . . assaulte of Parkin Warbok was now begonn to be pulled downe & new buylded'.[23] Although Hooker was a year out in his dating, the essential accuracy of his statement is borne out by the act book. The Chamber's decision 'that Estgate shalbe taken downe & . . . newe bildyed agayne' is recorded under the date 18 February 1511. On the same day thirteen men were chosen to be supervisors of the work.[24] Preparations went ahead quickly and the final details were soon being arranged. By 8 March a master mason had been chosen. It was agreed 'that Robert Poke of Thorverton shall bilde & make Estgate & the Cite to fynde all maner of stuffe & he to have for his labor £28 and to bilde 6 botores [i.e. buttresses]'.[25] Another man was hired to demolish the existing gate. The Chamber decreed that one Vawterd 'shall take downe Estgate & whan it is taken downe he [is] to caste all the sonde [i.e. sand] & rubbyll, havyng for his labour £1 6*s* 8*d*'.[26]

Hooker's statement that the repairs were undertaken in order to rectify damage which had been inflicted on East Gate fourteen years earlier, during Warbeck's attack, may well be correct, but why did the town governors suddenly decide to repair the damaged structure in 1511? Almost certainly, their order was prompted by considerations of state, and more particularly, by the foreign policy of England's new monarch. Unlike his more cautious father, Henry VIII was anxious to win glory in foreign wars. He dreamed of emulating the exploits of the Black Prince and of impressing all Europe with his military prowess. At Exeter, as at Coventry and other cities across the realm, the young monarch's vaunting ambition was to cost his subjects dear.[27] From the very beginning of Henry's reign, rumours of war had been circulating throughout the kingdom. By early 1511 these had become more insistent than ever, so a growing realization that war lay just over the horizon was probably what prompted the Chamber to begin rebuilding East Gate at this time.[28] Work on the new project continued throughout the entire year. In December the Chamber rewarded Thomas Andrewe 'for his attendance' at East Gate by making his son a freeman of the city and directed the receiver to pay him £30 for the money which he had laid out on the gate.[29]

Work recommenced in the following spring. In March 1512 the receiver was ordered to sell six acres of Duryard Wood to raise money for 'the bildyng of Estgate', and eight more men were selected to act as 'overseers of the bildyng'.[30] Construction at East Gate continued throughout 1512, and for much of the next year as well. By September 1513 the finishing touches were being added to the structure, which had already cost well over £60. High above the gate was placed a statue of Henry VII—perhaps in proud allusion to the events of 1483—and on 30 September a 'stayner' was engaged to 'paynte the tabernacle & the Kyng in the Est Gate with goolde lyce & oyle'.[31] By 29 October all was complete and East Gate was let out to a private individual at a rent of £3 a year. At the time of this lease, the premises were said to comprise 'all the newe bildyng & the olde with a garden belongyng to the olde bildyng'. The only part of the structure not included in the agreement was 'the dungyie [i.e. dungeon?] in the northe parte of Est Gate', which the Chamber appears to have reserved to itself.[32] It seems probable that the little 'blockhouse' which had been constructed at the bottom of the ditch outside the gate in order to protect the water pipes of the city aqueduct as they passed into Exeter beneath the main roadway was also retained by the Chamber.[33] Recent archaeological work has shown that a gun-port, or loophole, was built in the north side of this structure in order to provide flanking fire along the base of the city wall [*see figure 15*].[34]

For the next ten years almost no information about the city's defences has survived. The receivers' books are missing, the rolls are perfunctory, and the Chamber act book is uninformative, so it is impossible to tell whether any major work was undertaken. Not until 1527 do the mists begin to clear. In April that year repairs began to be carried out upon the city wall 'by Freren Hay'.[35] During 1528 the pace of work speeded up, with repairs taking place both at Friernhay and West Gate.[36] This quickening of tempo was preceded by a Chamber order of April 1528, the burden of which was that every receiver should 'for the tyme beinge . . . yerelye bestowe upon the reperacions of the townes walles the some of £10 . . . and that the mayor . . . shuld yerely apoynte four men . . . to be assistant to . . . [him] for the doinge thereof'.[37] This sudden solicitousness about the state of the defences undoubtedly stemmed from the fact that, in January, Henry VIII—maddened by Pope Clement VII's refusal to grant him a divorce from Catherine of Aragon—had declared war on the Pope's 'protector' and the Queen's nephew: the Emperor Charles V of Spain. Over the following years, the King's marital difficulties—and the drastic steps which he took to resolve them—would push the Exeter Chamber into ever-more lavish expenditure on the city enceinte.

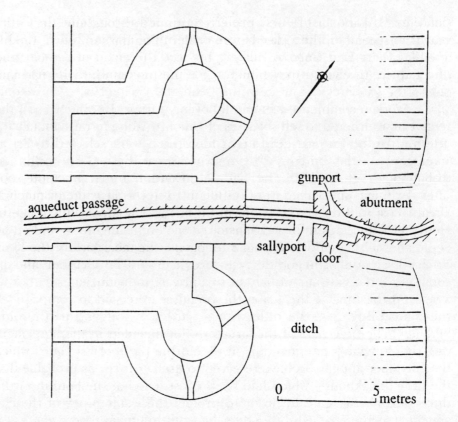

Figure 15 Plan of East Gate
in *c.*1513

The order of April 1528 was swiftly put into effect. In July it was resolved that the current receiver should be given £10 from the common coffer 'towards the buyldyng of the Cytie Walles now beynge in werk at the West Gate': presumably in order to reassure him that he would indeed be reimbursed for any further money which he laid out on the project.[38] Soon afterwards £24 was paid to Richard Towte, mason, 'for makyng of a pice of walle in the south parte of West Gate . . . with 2 botters [*i.e.* buttresses] to the same'.[39] Work continued near West Gate during 1528–29. Another mason was paid £3 for 'makeyng of the butteras yn the south syde' of the gate and 'makeyng of 6 garrettes'. Later that year, the same man received £16 for 'byll[d]yng of a pece of walle by the northe syde of the West Gate'.[40] Little work was carried out during 1529–30, but in the following year the receiver paid over £30 to Towte 'for the makeyng of [seventy-six] fotte of new wall yn Freren hayes'.[41]

This piece of work brought the sudden flurry of activity around the enceinte to a halt. Fears of an Imperial invasion had begun to fade, and between 1531 and 1537 the only defensive expenditure recorded in the accounts went on routine repairs to the gates. This is not to say that the state of the fortifications was neglected during this period. On the contrary, the town governors' continued determination to preserve the integrity of the city enceinte now led to them becoming entangled in a complicated lawsuit. In 1532–33 the receiver paid 6 shillings and 8 pence to 'Mr [Thomas] Denys', Exeter's recorder and legal adviser, 'for hys labour to speake with the Juges for making of the Towne Walles', while in 1534–35 Denys and Sir John Fulford were paid the very considerable sums of £1 apiece 'for suyng of the Wallys'.[42] Almost certainly, these payments related to the bitter dispute with the Dean and Chapter over who should pay for repairs to the ruinous mural tower on the site of the present-day 'New Cut' which was then in the possession of Archdeacon William Horsey. (Horsey, the former vicar-general of the Bishop of London was a notorious man. Suspected by many of having murdered Richard Hunne in the Lollard's Tower in 1514, he had left London under a cloud soon afterwards, and spent the rest of his life in Exeter.[43]) How the dispute was eventually resolved is unclear, though the clergymen later claimed that the Lord Chief Justice had found in their favour.[44]

As the city and cathedral authorities slugged it out in the latest round of their interminable battle for local authority and control, the old world was changing around them, and the monastic institutions whose power in Exeter had once rivalled their own were passing away. Henry VIII's escalating dispute with the Pope meant that the writing was on the wall for the monks of the Greyfriars, the Blackfriars, St Nicholas Priory and St John's Hospital and between 1536 and 1539 all four of these institutions—together with the extensive local properties which they had owned—passed into lay hands.[45] The Chamber was quick to take advantage of its rivals' misfortunes and within a few years the church of St John's had been converted into a storehouse for the city's artillery.[46] Rather surprisingly, there is no evidence to suggest that the massive rebellion against Henry VIII's 'Protestantizing' religious policies which took place in the North of England during 1536, the so-called 'Pilgrimage of Grace', sparked off any work on the town defences at Exeter.[47] Whether this was because the revolt was simply too far away to have caused any serious alarm, or because—in an England which was becoming increasingly divided along religious lines—at least some of the town governors secretly sympathized with the rebels, it is impossible to say.[48]

During 1538 the threat of foreign invasion began to assert itself once more, as the Catholic powers of Europe united against England's 'heretic king'. In June a ten-year truce was agreed between Charles V and Francis I of France. Matters were made still worse in December, when the Pope promulgated a bill of excommunication against Henry, pronouncing him to be deposed and absolving his subjects from their obedience. The early months of 1539 were thus a time of acute crisis in England. The country appeared to be facing triple attack: from Scotland, from France and from Spain. England was felt to be intensely vulnerable—a mere 'morsel amongst these choppers'—and Exeter was caught up in the general panic.[49] The receiver's roll for 1538–39, kept by one Robert Tooker, reveals that over £20 was spent on repairing the city walls in this year.[50] The roll does not specify where the work took place, but Hooker's chronicle fortunately does. Under the year 1538, Hooker comments that 'Robert Tooker, the receiver, buylded a peece of the towne walls in Southinghay'.[51] The repairs may well have been initiated by Lord John

Russell, who arrived in the West Country in 1539 'as Lorde President of the same'.[52] Fear of foreign invasion and internal unrest had prompted Henry VIII to send Russell into the West, with orders to 'settle' the region and to see to its defences. Hooker records that Russell 'travelled all the coastes and sea sydes commanding bullworkes & blockhowses to be made yn sundry places where he thought good and most meate for defense of the realme'.[53] It seems certain that he would have ordered a general overhaul of Exeter's fortifications at the same time.

Military activity continued at Exeter throughout 1539. Musters were held, considerable quantities of gunpowder were bought and more work was carried out on the defences.[54] In September a new receiver, Thomas Prestwoode, was appointed. During his term of office enormous sums were laid out on Exeter's fortifications. Hooker notes that, in order 'to contynue that which his predecessor . . . begonne', Prestwoode 'bought greate store of the stones of the howse of St Nicholas late dissolved and reedyfied a greate parte of the decayed cities walles yn Frerenhaye'.[55] Hooker's statement is amply borne out by the receiver's accounts for 1539–40. These record that £55 was spent on removing stones from the recently dissolved priory and incorporating them into the city wall in Friernhay. Nor was this all. A further £15 was spent on the city wall behind the Bishop's Palace, whilst £170 was laid out on repairs to the wall 'next to All Hallows-on-the-walls Church'.[56] To help pay for all this work, the Chamber devised the 'dinner fines' scheme discussed in Chapter 3.

Unfortunately, little information survives for the next year, and it is impossible to know if work on the defences was kept up. Probably it was not. The friendship between Francis I of France and Charles V of Spain was already cooling by March 1540. Soon the two men were quarrelling and, by August, the threat of imminent invasion had passed away. With France and Spain at loggerheads, the next three years were more peaceful ones for England. Hooker describes the period 1541–43 as 'quiet & out of trobles'.[57] This state of affairs is reflected in the Exeter accounts. Far less was spent on the city defences during these three years than in 1538–40. Nevertheless, at least one major piece of work was carried out during this period. In 1541–42 a certain Bernard Duffield was paid £20 for 'repairing the city wall next to the Archdeacon of Cornwall's garden'.[58] Duffield was Lord Russell's servant and he acted as keeper of his master's mansion house—the old Blackfriars monastery, soon to become known as Bedford House—while Russell was away.[59] The fact that it was Duffield, rather than one of the city councillors, who oversaw these repairs strongly suggests that they had been initiated by Russell himself—and thus that he was continuing to concern himself with the state of Exeter's defences. This was just as well, for another major conflict was soon in the offing.

In July 1544 Henry VIII embarked on his second great invasion of France. He possessed a powerful army and had been promised military support by Charles V. Initially, his chances of success seemed good. Yet within three months Charles had withdrawn from the fray, leaving Henry to face the French alone. As a result the English offensive collapsed. In October Henry returned to London, and much of his army was shipped home soon afterwards. Worse was to follow during winter 1544–45. Henry not only failed to make peace with France, but also managed to antagonize the Emperor. Once again England found herself completely isolated in Europe. The French began to concentrate all their strength against England and built up a fleet along the Channel coast. By June 1545 all was in readiness for a revenge attack. Panic on an even worse scale than that of 1539 now broke out, and with good reason; the threat which England faced in 1545 was 'greater than any which she had known for generations'.[60] At Exeter, fears were such that, on 18 June, the Chamber took a series of extraordinary measures designed to obtain 'ordinances or great gunnes' for the city [*see document 4*]. First, each of the Twenty-Four agreed to lend a sum of money for Exeter's defence. Second, provision was made for the councillors to be repaid once the crisis was over. Third, three men were chosen 'to receve the mony' lent, and to use it to buy a suite of guns. The requisite weapons were procured from ships at Dartmouth soon afterwards.[61]

Late in June, Lord Russell was again sent into the West to survey the local defences. He was unimpressed by what he found. Writing from Exeter on 4 July he noted that the sea-coasts were 'very unprovided for defence, and this town is very weak'.[62] Russell had little time to remedy the situation. Within days of his arrival, the French fleet at last set sail. On 19 July it entered the Solent, and on 21 July French troops landed on the Isle of Wight. Within hours they had re-embarked again. Nevertheless, the next few days were perhaps the most anxious of the whole reign for the people of England. A chain of warning beacons had carried news of the invasion all over the country and Exeter must have been alerted almost at once. The reaction of the town governors was to strengthen the city's defences still further. On 30 July the Chamber agreed that there should be a benevolence 'getherid amongst the commons of the Cetie for the mayntennance & makyng of the walles . . . which benevolens shalbe getheryd by the good wylles of the inhabitants'.[63] The members of the Council of Twenty-Four donated a grand total of £5 11 shillings and 10 pence: how much money was raised throughout the city as a whole is unknown. Sadly, the receiver's roll for this year is uninformative, merely stating that £47 was laid out on 'the city wall and le coysy [i.e. causeway] next to Cowlegh Brigge'.[64]

Whatever the success of the benevolence, the Chamber's defensive measures clearly took good effect. Russell was soon feeling far more confident of Exeter's ability to resist attack. On 18 August he wrote to the Privy Council that the townsfolk 'have long looked for the Frenchmen here and are daily better prepared for their coming'.[65] In the event, the long-feared invasion failed to materialize. The French fleet made no move towards the Devon ports. Instead, it sailed eastwards along the south coast, turning for home towards the middle of August. By early September the invasion scare was over. Nevertheless, work on the defences at Exeter continued. As late as 21 September petty sums derived from fines were being handed straight over to the receiver to be bestowed on 'the newe worke of the cety walles', rather than being deposited in the common chest as usual: clear evidence of persisting alarm.[66] The state of the fortifications continued to exercise the town governors during the following year. In June 1546 Nicholas Lymett, the new receiver, was ordered to 'make the barbigan with the wall from the newe worke att Freenhay unto North Gate yn such forme as . . . was before yn the last yere [done]'.[67] Sadly, no accounts survive for the last two years of Henry's reign, and the Chamber act book for this period is uninformative, so it is impossible to tell how much was spent on the ongoing defensive preparations.

Following Henry VIII's death in 1547 and the accession of his nine-year-old son, Edward, government passed into the hands of the Lord Protector, Edward Seymour, Duke of Somerset, under whose idiosyncratic rule the country rapidly became destabilized. Within two years of Edward's accession, England was in crisis. In June 1549 a major revolt broke out in Devon and Cornwall. The rebels had many different grievances, but were united by a passionate detestation of the government's zealously Protestant religious policies. By mid-June thousands were up in arms, demanding a return to the more conservative religious practices of Henry VIII's day. There was much sympathy for the rebels in Exeter, and many hoped that the city would open its gates to the insurgents, but—for the third time in half a century—the town governors remained loyal to the Crown.[68] On 15 June the Chamber ordered that forty 'honest' householders should keep watch by night in order to ensure the city's security. Seven days later, following the failure of an attempt by a group of loyal gentlemen to disperse the rebel army at Crediton, just six miles away, the Chamber ordered that the watch should be reinforced by armed men drawn from the city trade guilds.[69] Rebel emissaries, sent to invite the citizens to join hands with their 'honest neighbours' in the cause of 'the olde catholike religion', were twice rebuffed. Angered by this—and no doubt unwilling to march on to London with an unconquered enemy at their backs—the insurgents determined to take the city by force.[70] Exeter was about to face the most determined assault it had seen for centuries.[71]

As the rebels drew nearer, the inhabitants began to put the city into a posture of defence. This task may well have been less difficult than it sounds. Huge amounts of work had been carried out on the fortifications during the later years of Henry VIII's reign. The walls were in good repair and an entire suite of ordnance had been procured. All in all, Exeter was probably as well prepared for a sudden assault in 1549 as it was ever likely to be. Nevertheless, the defenders did their best to make the city stronger still. Hooker—who was an eyewitness of the siege and wrote the only detailed account of it—records that 'great peces of ordynunce were layed in everie gate and placed in all convenyente places of the walles'. In addition, 'mountes', or earthen mounds, were 'in sundrie places erected aswell for laying of ordynunce as for savinge of the soylders'.[72] Two newly discovered documents which list monies laid out for the city's defence during 'the Commotion', as contemporaries termed the rebellion, show that these 'mounts' incorporated stout wooden boards and 'maunds', or baskets. The extraordinary accounts also reveal that large quantities of gunpowder and brimstone were procured (together with bows and arrows), that timber was bought to provide platforms for the ordnance, that a parvis was constructed 'at the walls over West yeat' and that masons were sent for to work on 'the cetie walls' [*see document 5*]. No attempt was made to secure the extramural parishes, however, and the town ditch appears to have marked the outermost limit of the citizens' defensive perimeter. As a result the insurgents were able to occupy the suburbs as soon as they arrived before the city in force, on 2 July.

St David's Hill, St Sidwell's Church and the houses outside West Gate were all secured by the rebels. Doubtless they occupied the houses in the southern suburbs as well. From these positions the besiegers were able to harass the citizens with relative impunity. According to Hooker, the rebels lurked 'in sundry houses . . . neere the walls & would so watche the garrotes that if anye within the citie wolde loke out . . . [he] was in the daunger of theire shott: & some thereby were killed & many hurted'. To counter this threat, the defenders 'sett . . . parte of the suburbes on fire & some parte which was next to the wales they . . . brake downe, and so', Hooker concludes triumphantly, 'drave the rebells out of those holes'.[73] Among the properties known to have been destroyed in this way were a stable next to North Gate, and a house without West Gate 'lyyng next to the milleate', which, it was noted in 1562, had been 'burnyd yn the late Commosion'.[74]

Despite the success of such measures, Exeter remained under heavy fire. The besiegers had 'in sundrye places their greate ordynunces so sett . . . that in certeyne streetes & places none could go but in perill . . . of theire shott'.[75] A man dwelling in North Street was killed at his own doorway by a cannon ball fired from St David's Hill, and others must have been hurt in the same way. In order to counter this, the citizens constructed 'certeyne mountes to shadowe the streetes'.[76] Presumably, these were built on the barbican behind the city wall. The rebels, meanwhile, diversified their attack. They 'brake up the pypes & conduytes . . . for the takinge awaye [water] commynge to the citie, as also to have the ledd to serve for their shott'.[77] In addition, they managed to burn down the doors of the city gates, by pushing carts laden with hay against them. Yet this stratagem did not work on every occasion. At West Gate and South Gate, the rebels' approach being perceived, 'the great porte peeces were chardged with greate bagges of flynte stones & hayle shot'. As the rebels advanced, the gate was flung open and the 'porte peces dyscharged and so they were spoyled dyverse of theime'. Where the rebels had succeeded in burning down the doors, moreover, the citizens built earthen ramparts 'within the gate' to keep the attackers at bay.[78] The extraordinary accounts show that one of these 'rampyres' stood at North Gate.[79] Mining was another rebel ploy. 'In sundrie places', Hooker records, the insurgents 'did undermyne the walls myndinge thereby with goonepowder . . . to have blowen upp the walles & so to have entred in'.[80] Eventually, counter-mining by the citizens averted this particular danger.[81]

The siege dragged on for five weeks. During this time, traditional civic government all but ground to a halt. Entries ceased to be made in the Chamber act book from 22 June onwards, while business in the mayor's court was suspended from 1 July.[82] Both Hooker's narrative and the extraordinary accounts suggest that real power in the city now lay with a small group of individual loyalists, including the mayor, John Blackaller, the city aldermen, influential country gentlemen like Sir Roger Blewett and Lord Russell's steward, Bernard Duffield. These were the men who galvanized the city's defence and who frustrated the hopes of the pro-rebel faction in Exeter.[83] The insurgents found themselves unable to take the city by force, but as time went by it seemed that lack of provision would soon compel the inhabitants to surrender. Then, just as Exeter's fall seemed imminent, a royal army, sent down from the east under Lord Russell, broke through to the city's relief. The rebels who had been besieging Exeter took to their heels and fled, abandoning their trenches and their great 'camp' on St David's Down. On 6 August Russell himself finally arrived before the city 'to the great ioye and comforte of the longe captyveted citezens'.[84] The mayor marked the occasion by giving handsome cash 'rewards' to 'the trumpett[er]s that cam with [Russell]' and to the minstrels of 'my Lord Gray' (one of the chief commanders in Russell's army).[85]

Exeter now faced the task of repairing its shattered defences. Considerable sums of money had to be found for this purpose, but cash was in short supply. Well over £100 is known to have been spent on defending the city against the rebels and it seems probable that a great deal more money had been laid out during the siege of which no record survives.[86] In addition, the citizens had advanced no less than £1,000 to supply the wants of the relieving army.[87] Lord Russell, fresh from his final defeat of the insurgents in Cornwall, now suggested that the receivers' and stewards' dinners should be abolished altogether, and the money spent instead on the 'reperacions of the walles'.[88] His advice was taken and repairs began almost at once. Between 1549 and 1551 more than £58 was spent on rebuilding the walls and gates. In addition, £65 was spent on repairing the civic ordnance and a further £10 on re-roofing St Sidwell's church tower, the leads of which appear to have been stripped off during the siege to be melted down for bullets.[89]

Once the damage wrought by the rebels had been repaired, expenditure on the defences slumped. Only one more period of military activity is discernible at Exeter during Edward's reign. This was in spring 1551. On 21 April a watch was ordered to be kept every night, and the receiver was told to take an inventory 'of all the goone powder with the holle of the ordenanse & all other thengys apaytayning to ytt'.[90] Three weeks later the Chamber agreed 'that one Jacobe, a Duchman' should be paid £2 for overseeing 'the gunnys & ordynaunces of the Cetie' over the next year.[91] Quite why it was felt necessary to employ a gunner at this

PLATE SECTION

PLATE 1 Caleb Hedgeland's model of eighteenth-century Exeter, showing East Gate and the northern side of High Street in the foreground, with the city walls and the castle behind

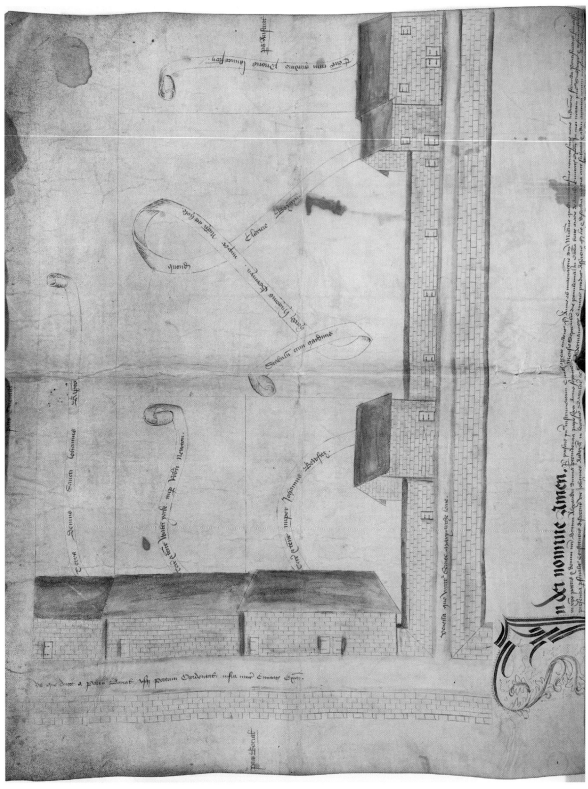

PLATE 2

PLATE 2 *The city wall at the lower end of St Mary Arches Lane, 1499*

This map was drawn up by Thomas Harres, public notary, in 1499, in connection with a disputed property in St Mary Arches Lane. It shows, on the far left, the crenellated city wall; immediately to the right of this, 'the road leading from North Gate towards West Gate' (present day Bartholomew Street East); and, running along the bottom of the map, 'the lane which is called St Mary Arche Lane'. The plot of land at the centre of the plan, on which a number of houses are depicted, today lies submerged beneath Mary Arches Car Park. [Source: DRO, ECA, ED/M/933]

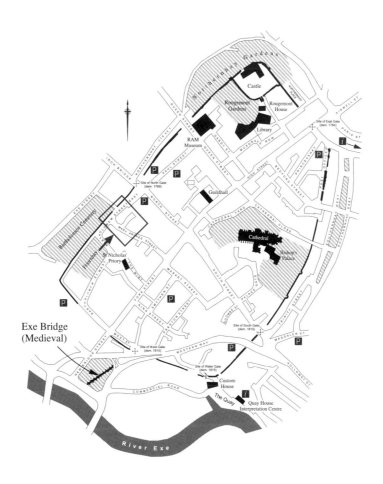

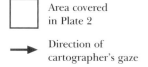

Area covered
in Plate 2

Direction of
cartographer's gaze

PLATE 3

PLATE 3 *South Gate and the south-eastern sector of the city circuit c. 1560*

This map—which was probably drawn up by the city chamberlain, John Hooker, in around 1560—covers the area between South Street and the Cathedral. It shows, on the far right, South Gate and Holy Trinity Church and, just above them, the crenellated city wall running along the back of the Archdeacon of Exeter's garden. The rampart walk is clearly depicted, as is the postern gate which had been built on top of the barbican in order to permit the citizens to pass through the Archdeacon's garden wall. The gatehouse to the Bishop's Palace, shown at the head of the lane in the centre of the drawing, still survives today. [Source: D&C, Exeter M/10]

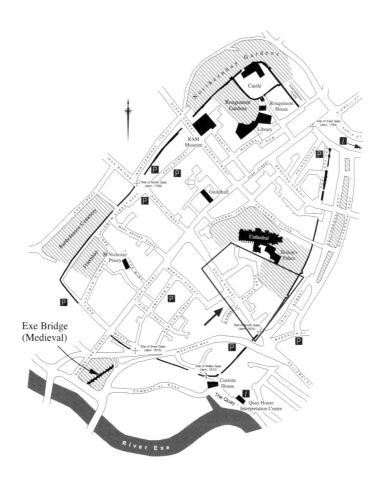

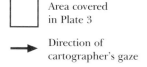

Area covered in Plate 3

Direction of cartographer's gaze

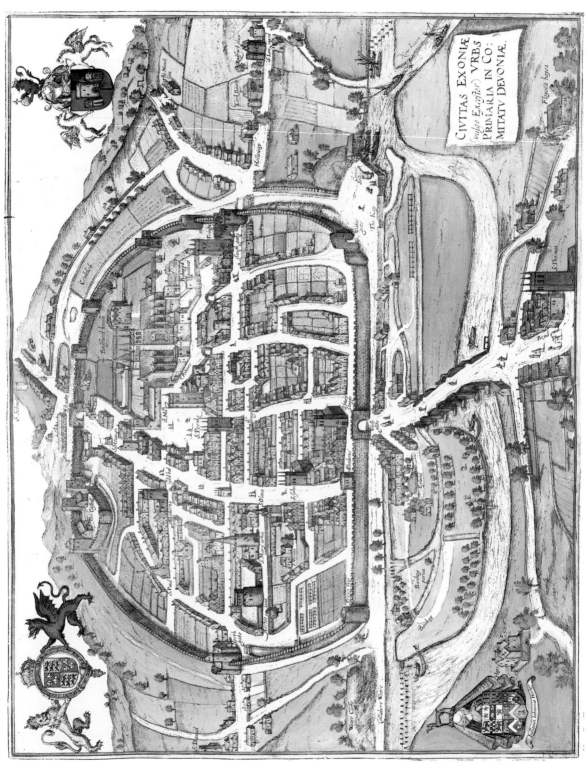

CIVITAS EXONIÆ
(vulgo Excefter) VRBS
PRIMARIA IN CO:
MITATV DEVONIÆ.

PLATE 4

PLATE 4 Map of Exeter dated 1618, based on an earlier survey of c. 1584

A bird's eye-view of Exeter from the west: first published in Braun and Hogenberg's *Civitates Orbis Terrarum* in 1618, but based on an earlier survey of *c.* 1584. The Castle, the city walls; the five city gates; and the various mural towers are all clearly shown. The structure depicted at the bottom left-hand corner of the city circuit is Snayle Tower. The square tower shown peeping over the city wall just to the left of West Gate is that of All-Hallows-on-the-Walls Church. Between Water Gate and South Gate, just outside the wall, may be glimpsed a section of the city ditch. [Source: Exeter City Museums and Art Gallery]

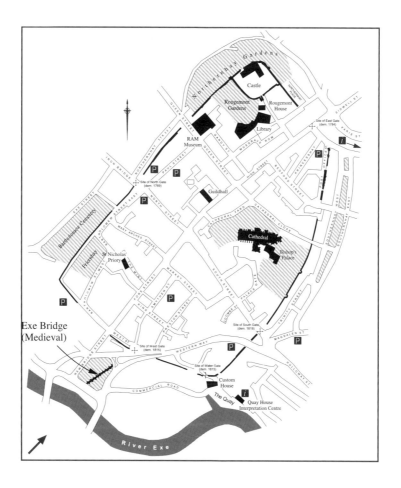

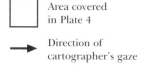

Area covered in Plate 4

Direction of cartographer's gaze

PLATE 5

PLATE 5 *Exterior view of the eastern side of the city circuit, c. 1590*

This map depicts the eastern section of the city enceinte as it might have appeared to someone viewing Exeter from St Sidwell's parish towards the end of Elizabeth I's reign. It was probably drawn by John Hooker. The plan shows, in the top left-hand corner, South Gate; next to this, the smaller Bishop's Tower; next to this, the larger Bishop's Tower; next to this, the Bedford Postern Tower (complete with drawbridge extending into Southernhay); next to this, the Eastern Angle Tower; next to this, East Gate (on the site of the present-day Boots); next to this, the Gaol Tower; and finally, next to this, the Castle. The broad road shown issuing forth from beneath the East Gate and running towards St Anne's Chapel (the little range of buildings set around a square courtyard in the middle of the drawing) is Sidwell Street. [Source: DRO, ECA, Drawer 2]

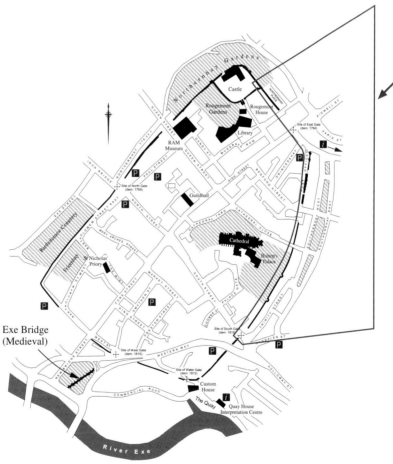

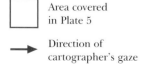

Area covered
in Plate 5

Direction of
cartographer's gaze

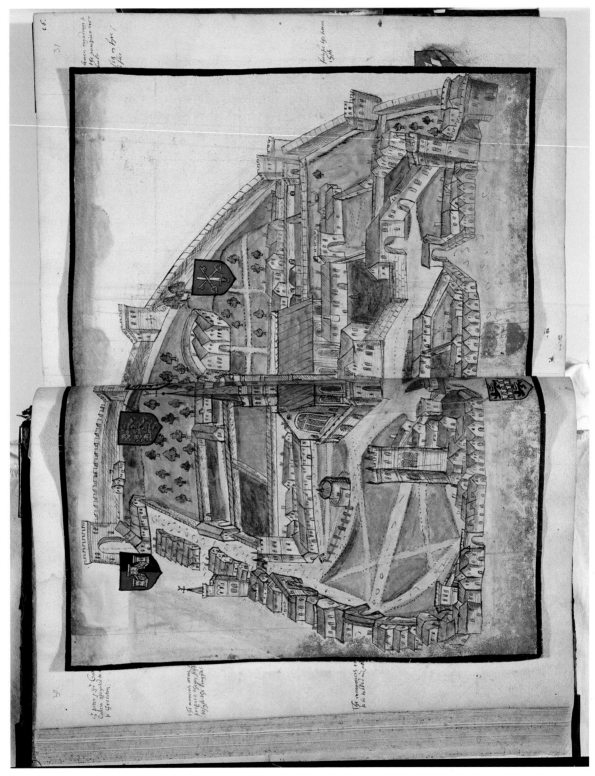

PLATE 6

PLATE 6 *Interior view of the eastern side of the city circuit, c. 1590*

This bird's-eye view of the Cathedral Close from the south-west provides a good impression of how the eastern section of the city circuit looked from the inside in *c.* 1590. East Gate is shown at the top of the map, towards the left. Moving along the city wall in a clockwise direction from here, the drawing shows: the Eastern Angle Tower; the Bedford Postern Tower; the larger Bishop's Tower; the smaller Bishop's Tower and South Gate. [Source: DRO, ECA Book 52]

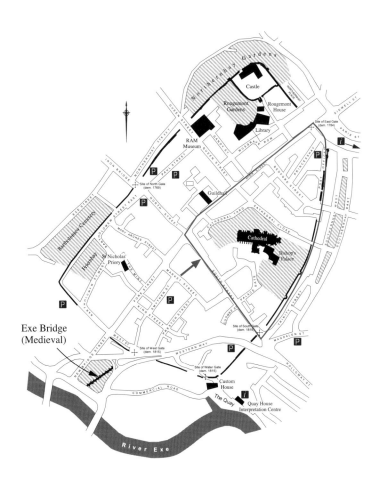

Exe Bridge
(Medieval)

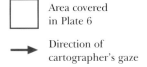

☐ Area covered
in Plate 6

→ Direction of
cartographer's gaze

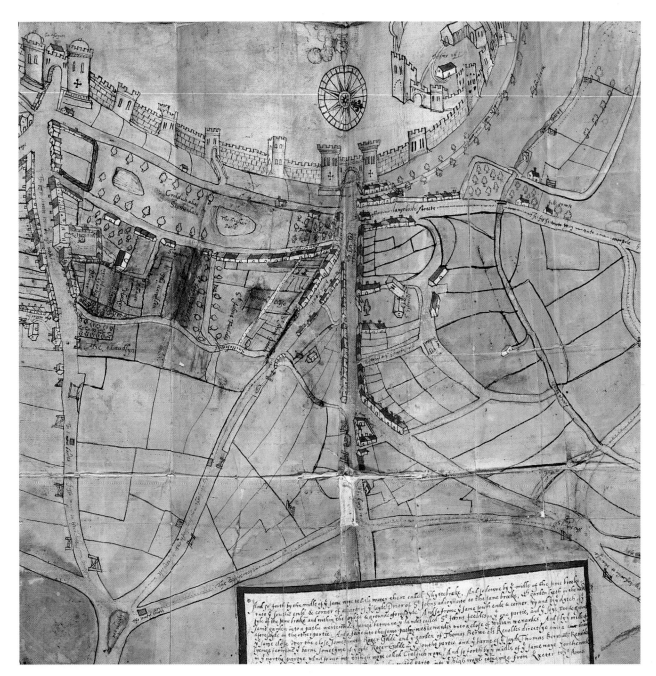

PLATE 7

PLATE 7 *A second exterior view of the eastern side of the city circuit, c. 1590*

'Platt of St Sidwells Fee'. Once again, it seems probable that this map was drawn up by John Hooker during the 1590s. The plan shows, in the top left-hand corner, South Gate; next to this, the smaller Bishop's Tower; next to this, the larger Bishop's Tower; next to this, the Bedford Postern Tower (with temporary drawbridge); next to this, the Eastern Angle Tower; next to this, East Gate; next to this, the Gaol Tower; and finally, next to this, the Castle. The crumbling northern sally-port of the Castle can just be picked out in the top right-hand corner of the map. [Source, D&C, Exeter 3530]

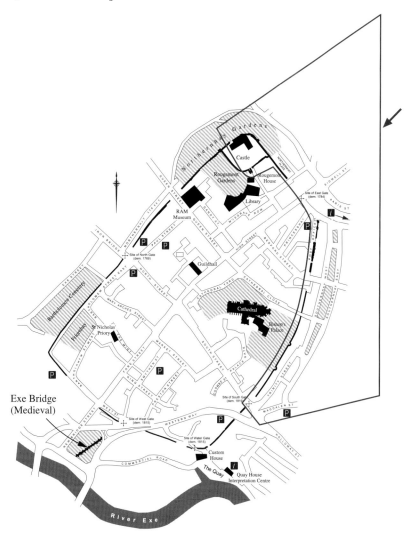

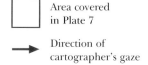

☐ Area covered in Plate 7

→ Direction of cartographer's gaze

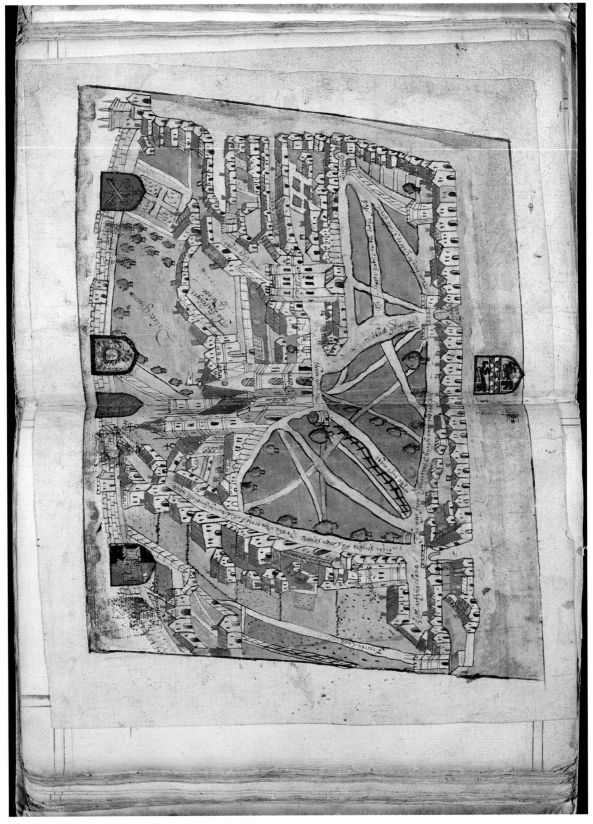

PLATE 8

PLATE 8 A second interior view of the eastern side of the city circuit, c. 1590

'A Platte [i.e. map] of the Churchyarde'. Another bird's-eye view of the Cathedral Close, this time from the north-west. The internal face of the city wall is shown running along the top of the picture. The turrets depicted along the line of the wall are (from left to right) the Eastern Angle Tower; the Bedford Postern Tower; the larger Bishop's Tower; the smaller Bishop's Tower and the tower of Holy Trinity Church. [Source: D&C, Exeter 3530]

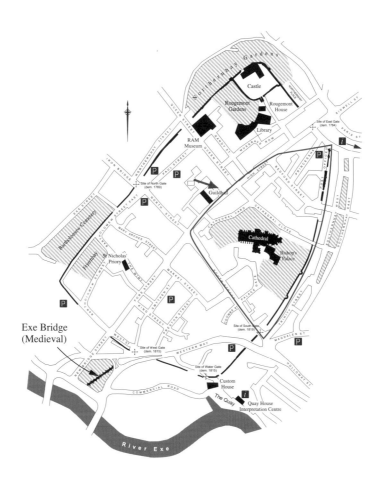

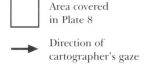

Area covered
in Plate 8

Direction of
cartographer's gaze

PLATE 9

PLATE 9 Map of the Castle, c. 1600

This plan of Rougemont Castle, which dates to around 1600, shows the line of the Castle walls (marked in light brown) together with the earth banks and ditches which encircled them (marked in green). The main entrance to the Castle from the city (labelled on the map 'ye latter port') is shown at the bottom centre of the drawing. The 'back entrance' to the Castle from Northernhay—complete with wooden drawbridge over the city ditch (marked in blue)—is shown at the top centre. The city walls proper, which adjoined those of the Castle, are depicted with crenellations. The section of the city wall which can be seen in the bottom right-hand corner of the drawing was that which ran between the Castle and East Gate. The section which can be seen in the top left-hand corner was that which ran between the Castle and North Gate. Also worthy of note are the two artillery positions – 'Mount Egg Pye' and 'ye cob battery', which are depicted on the outside of the Castle ditch at the very top of the drawing. [Source: BL, Add MSS, 5027, art.70]

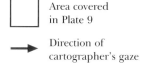

Area covered in Plate 9

Direction of cartographer's gaze

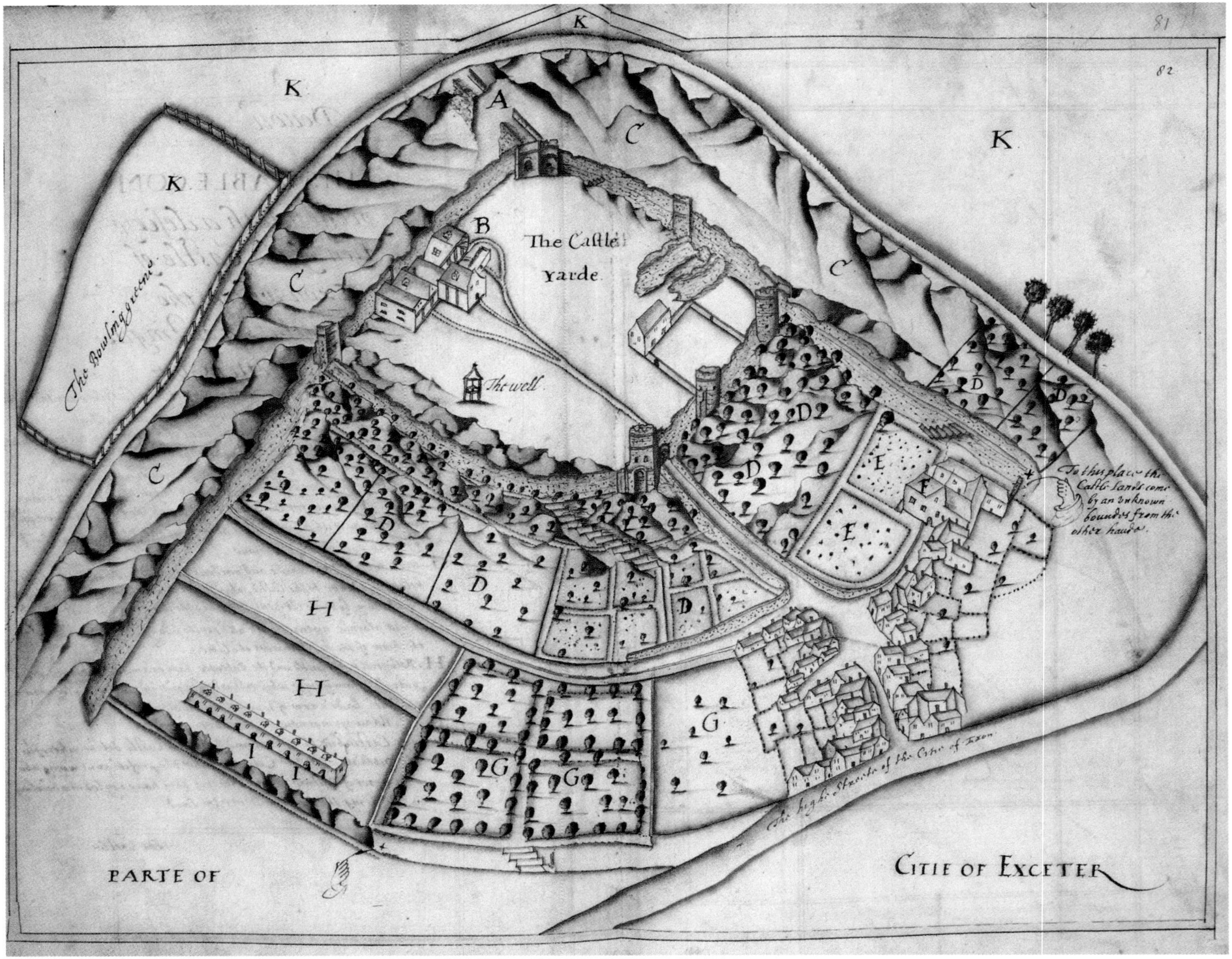
81
82
K
K
K
K
A
B
C
C
C
C
The Castle Yarde
The well
The Bowlinggreene
D
E
E
F
G
G
G
H
H
I
I
To this place the Castle Lands come by an unknown boundes from the other hande.
The highe Streete of the Citie of Exon
PARTE OF
CITIE OF EXCETER

PLATE 10

PLATE 10 *View of the Castle, 1617*

This bird's-eye view of the Castle from the south was drawn by the Prince of Wales's surveyor, John Norden, during his visit to Exeter in 1617. The main entrance to the Castle is shown in the centre of the drawing. The drawbridge into Northernhay ('A') is depicted as having broken down. The lane with houses clustering on either side of it, which is shown leading from 'the highe streete of the cytie of Exon' to the Castle, is present-day Castle Lane. The large building to the right of this lane ('F') is the County Prison. The row of houses in the bottom left-hand corner of the map ('I') stood on the site of the present day Arts Centre, in Gandy Street. [Source: BL, Add. MSS, 6027, f.81]

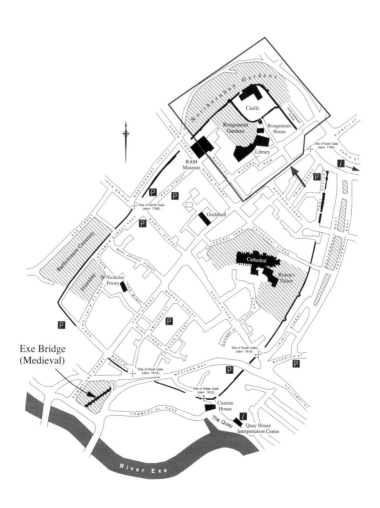

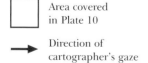

Area covered in Plate 10

Direction of cartographer's gaze

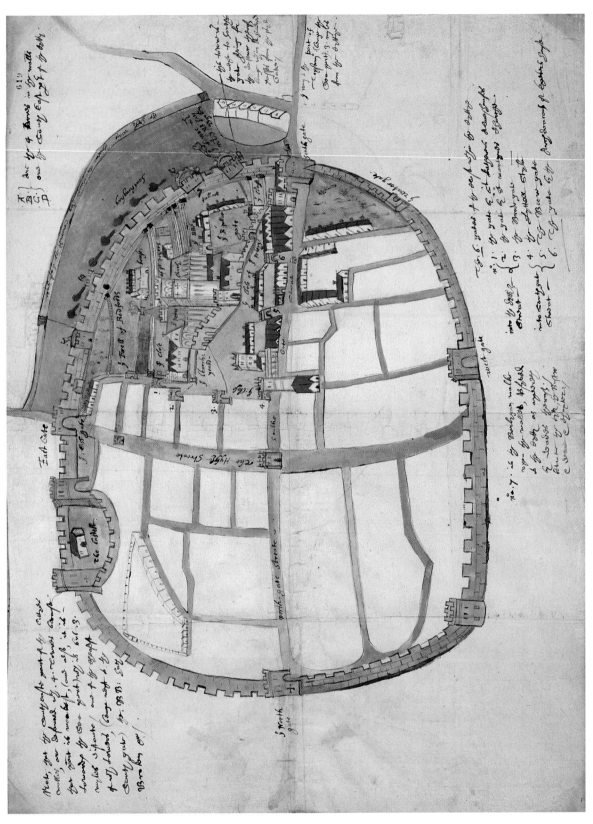

PLATE 11

PLATE 11 *View of the city circuit, with marginal comments, of c. 1622*

This bird's-eye view of Exeter from the west is anonymous and undated, but may perhaps have been drawn up by John Hooker in *c.* 1600. Many of the marginal notes relate to a dispute with the cathedral clergy over the maintenance of the city wall, which took place during the early seventeenth century. The postern gates on the barbican between East Gate and South Gate are shown as small black doors. [Source: DRO, ECA, Drawer 2, L 619]

The legend in the top left-hand corner reads: *'Note that the south easte part of the cittyes walkes, are defended with 4 Towres because that part is weakest, (and also, it is towards the sea port, which is but 3 myles distante) one of the cheafest of which towers (beinge next to the South Gate) the BB [i.e. the Bishop] hath broken &c.'*

The legend in the top right-hand corner reads: *'A.B.C.D. are the 4 towres in the walles one the South East parte of the Citty.'*

The legend on the right-hand side (above the road) reads: *'This towre is the next to South gate beinge for the defence thereof being within a hundred passes [i.e. paces] from the said Gate.'* Just to the left of this is a drawing of a hand pointing at the tower beside the gate with the legend: *'Ye Towre wch . . . ye BB hath broken.'*

The legend on the right-hand side (below the road) reads: *'Ye way to the port of Topsham (beinge the sea port) 3 myles from the cyttye.'*

The legend in the bottom right-hand corner reads:
The 6 gates of the Close within the Cyttye
In the High Streat	*No. 1—The gate by St Katherines Almeshouses*
	No. 2—The gate by St Martyns Churche
	No. 3—The Broade gate
In Southgate Streat	*No. 4—The Lyttell Style*
	No. 5—The Beare gate
	No. 6—The gate by the Archdeacon of Exeter's house'

The legend at the bottom of the map, in the middle, reads:
'No. 7 is the Barbygan walke upon the walles, reserved to the Cytty as apeereth by deades therof betweene the Cytty, the Bishop, & Deane & Chapter'.

Area covered
in Plate 11

Direction of
cartographer's gaze

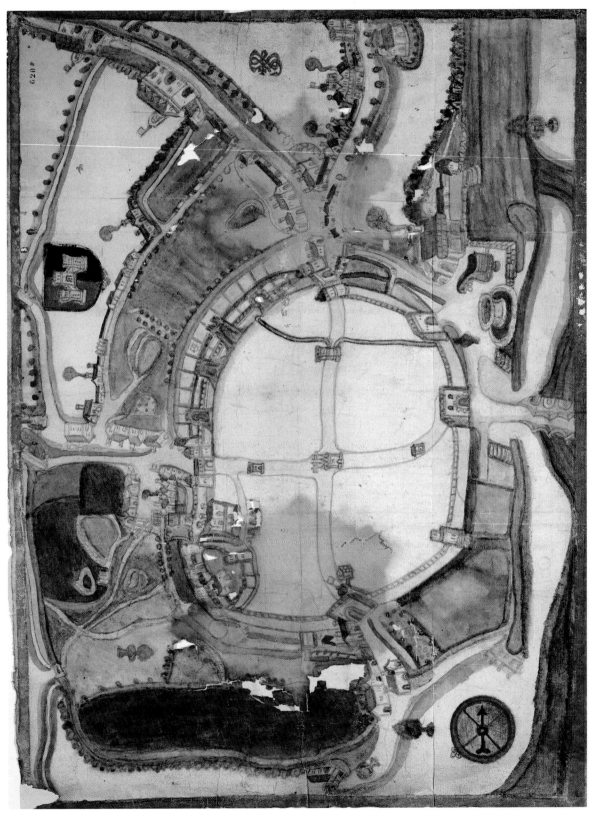

PLATE 12

PLATE 12 *View of the city circuit, c. 1633*

This bird's-eye view of Exeter from the west is by the city's early seventeenth-century surveyor, Robert Sherwood. It was probably drawn up in connection with the city's water supply, as the civic conduits and water courses are given particular prominence. The aqueduct which passed into Exeter from Southernhay is shown emerging from beneath the city wall via a tiny archway near the Bishop's Tower, then running down to the public fountain in South Street, before finally passing out through the walls again near Water Gate. [Source: DRO, ECA, Drawer 2, L 620]

Area covered
in Plate 12

Direction of
cartographer's gaze

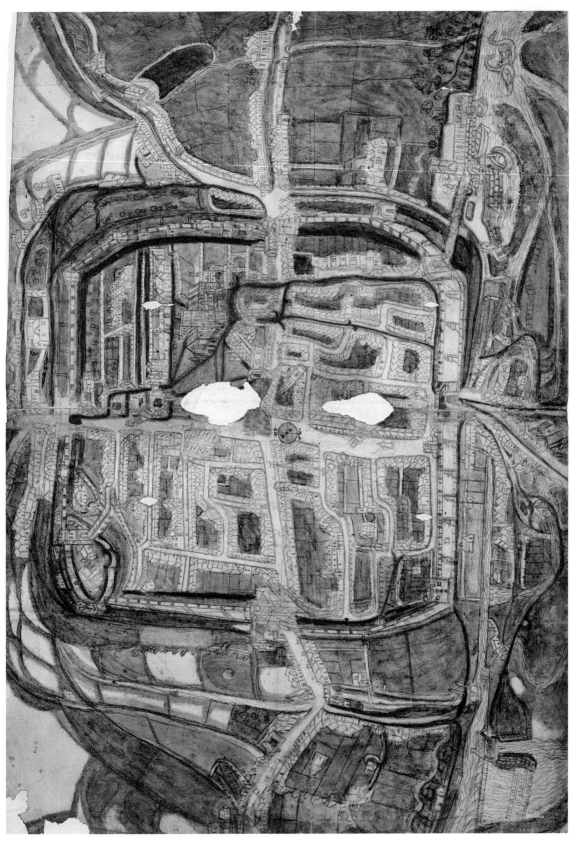

PLATE 13

PLATE 13 Map of Exeter in c. 1638

This immensely detailed plan provides us with an excellent impression of what Exeter looked like on the eve of the Civil War. It was drawn up by the city's surveyor, Robert Sherwood, and may well be the 'mappe' for which the Exeter Chamber granted him a handsome 'gratuity' of £1 and 10 shillings in March 1638. Like the previous plate, it shows the city from the west, with Bonhay, Exebridge and Shilhay in the foreground. The map affords a particularly good view of the stretch of the town wall which ran between Snayle Tower and Quay Gate and depicts the many stone buttresses which supported the wall in this area. [Source: DRO, ECA, Drawer 2, L 618]

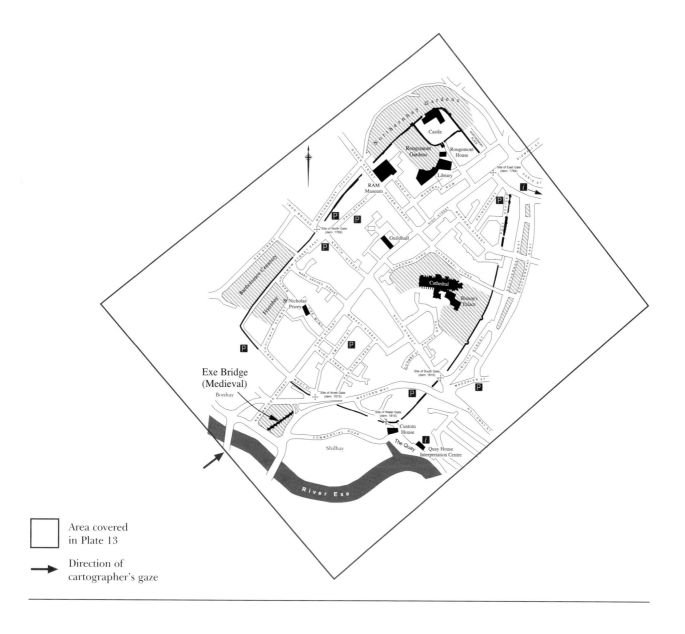

Area covered
in Plate 13

Direction of
cartographer's gaze

PLATE 14 East Gate in 1784

PLATE 15 Site of the Tower at New Cut, 1814, showing the doorway through
the city wall which was replaced by the present-day 'New Cut' (see Plate 17);
the culvert shown behind the seated workmen was that which emerged
from the base of the medieval tower which once stood on this site

PLATE 16 The city wall at Quay Gate: winter, *c.* 1580 (above); summer, *c.* 1620 (below)

PLATE 17 Ecclesiastical garden wall, rising to meet the city wall, next to St Martin's Lane

PLATE 18 The wall-walk at Snayle Tower (present-day Bartholomew Terrace)

PLATE 19 Buttress beside the city wall in Southernhay

PLATE 20 Houses on the city wall near West Gate
(in the foreground, present-day Western Way)

PLATE 21 The Eastern Angle Tower, off
present-day Post Office Street

PLATE 22 Houses on the city wall near
West Gate (detail)

PLATE 23 The back of the city wall in Paul Street

PLATE 24 Old Exe Bridge

PLATE 25 The city walls in Southernhay, behind the South Gate Hotel

PLATE 26 Walk-way beneath the city wall near Cricklepit

time is unclear, but the fact that over £6 was spent on repairing 'le gonnys' in 1550–51 suggests that Jacob was kept busy.[92] Unfortunately, the accounts record nothing about expenditure during the last two years of Edward's reign. The young king died in July 1553 and—after the collapse of the nine-day regime of Lady Jane Gray—was succeeded by his Catholic half-sister, Mary.

Within months of her accession, Mary faced a major crisis. In January 1554 some 3,000 men rose in Kent to protest against the new Queen's religious policies and her impending marriage to King Philip II of Spain—and there were attempts to provoke a simultaneous rebellion in Devon. The leaders of the intended *putsch* were Sir Gawen and Sir Peter Carew of Mohuns Ottery, both zealously Protestant gentlemen who had been prominent in opposing the Prayer Book rising. Towards the middle of January, a group of their servants ostentatiously paraded a wagon-load of arms through Exeter, while Sir Gawen himself took up lodgings within the city.[93] Alarmed by the rumours which were beginning to circulate about the Carews' intentions, the Sheriff of Devon, acting in conjunction with the town governors of Exeter, took swift and decisive action. On 19 January the gates of the city were closed and 'chayned'. Sir Gawen, presumably fearing that he was about to be apprehended, now took to his heels. Making his way to the Castle, he 'clymmed over the walles of the cittie . . . abowttes 12 of the clocke of the . . . nyght'—while still wearing his riding-boots, as an admiring servant later deposed—and disappeared into the darkness. Carew's dramatic 'skalynge of the walles' only served to increase local anxieties, and in the wake of his departure the citizens 'layed ordynaunce upon the walles [and] kepte watche and warde, as [if the city] . . . should be besieged by the Quenes . . . enemyes'.[94] The scare only lasted for a few days—the projected rising had little local support and quickly fizzled out—but the atmosphere of suspicion which had been engendered by the Carews' activities surely helps to explain the unusually large sum of money, some £73, which the Exeter receiver spent on repairs to the city's walls, 'gunnes and ordynances' in this year.[95]

The next major piece of expenditure on the defences came in 1556–57. During this year £3 was spent on the gates, whilst over £20 was laid out on the walls at Cricklepit Mills, on the western side of the city circuit [*see map 4*].[96] The heightened outlay was probably due to increased international tension. Phillip II was at war with France, and from late 1556 onwards Mary found herself under mounting pressure to intervene on her husband's side. In June 1557 she finally took the plunge. Initially, all went well, but in January 1558 the French captured Calais, Mary's last continental possession. Less than a month later, major defensive works were again initiated at Exeter. On 3 February the Chamber agreed that, because the North Gate was in 'decay', the receiver should 'with alle spede convenyent . . . make and byld on the . . . gate such defensible bylding as shalbe thoght resonable'.[97] Unfortunately, no accounts survive for 1557–58, so it is impossible to be sure exactly what was done. What is known for certain is that Lord Francis Russell, second Earl of Bedford, visited Exeter during 1558. His arrival suggests that French attacks were feared. Bedford quickly set to work on the local defences, and on 19 April he granted the Chamber 'halfe of all such his artyllyry as was then in the custody of the Cittie'.[98] An inventory of these weapons—which Bedford had left in the Chamber's care in 1556—is reproduced in Part Two [*see document 6*].

No attacks on the Devon coast materialized that summer, but the war with France continued. The Chamber therefore kept up its programme of repairs. In October 1558 the new receiver was ordered to 'contynew the buyldinge at the Northgate & to fynishe the same strongley'. He was to 'make the poyninge ende of the same house square up & to make garretts upon the topp of the same & to cover also the stayer with ledde'.[99] The very detailed receiver's book for this year makes it clear that the Chamber's orders were obeyed to the letter, and that over £66 was spent on roofing and flooring the new structure.[100] In November 1558 Queen Mary died. Her successor, Elizabeth I, made peace with France in early 1559. The end of the war brought a temporary halt to work on Exeter's defences and no expenditure was recorded between 1559 and 1561. Yet during 1561–62 work began again, with over £70 being laid out on a 'tenement on top of Northgate'.[101] Repairs continued in 1562–63. During this year, almost £28 was spent on the house over the gate, with considerable sums being laid out on the battlements, the Queen's arms, and on plastering and pointing the whole structure.[102] In September 1563 work finally came to a halt; the great rebuilding of North Gate was complete.

Soon afterwards, the Chamber initiated a project which would lead to the construction of an entirely new city gate. For many years Exeter's merchants had dreamed of bringing goods to the city by water, and during the early 1560s determined efforts were made to turn this dream into reality. In 1563 the Chamber signed an agreement with a Welsh engineer named John Trew. Under the terms of this agreement, Trew was to make the River Exe navigable from Exmouth to Exeter for vessels 'of a convenyent and reasonable wyght'.[103] Trew began work almost at once. By 1565 the project was well advanced, and it was becoming clear that facilities would have to be built at the proposed quay site—which lay at the south-west corner of Exeter—in order to cater for the anticipated flow of traffic. Accordingly, the Chamber agreed that 'a convenyent gate for cariege of all kyndes of wares & merchandyse' should be made 'yn the [city] wall at the place called the watergate' (i.e. at the outfall of the Coombe stream, where it was wrongly believed in Tudor times that an ancient gate had once stood).[104] Work on this project began around 25 August, when the Council ordered that a constant watch be kept 'at Watergate the whole night untyll the gate be buylded'.[105] Little is known about the gate's construction. The roll for 1564–65 merely records that £109 was spent on building 'the Key and . . . the new gate called the watergeate'.[106] Later drawings show that the structure was smaller and less impressive than the other city gates, consisting of little more than an archway cut through the wall [*see figure 12, page 31*]. Further sums were laid out at Water Gate in 1565–66 and work here was probably completed in that year.

The next major bout of expenditure on the defences came in 1570. Elizabeth's relations with France and Spain had recently grown very tense and the Pope's excommunication of the Queen in May heightened anxieties still further, raising the spectre of all Catholic Europe combining in a religious crusade against England. By July the country was in the grip of a major panic. Ships were set forth, beacons made ready and the militia chivvied into a semblance of preparedness. 'They are so alarmed here', wrote one contemptuous foreign observer, 'that they fear their own shadows.'[107] So matters continued until October, when the Privy Council finally decided it was safe to relax its precautions. These events perhaps help to account for the unusually large sum expended on Exeter's defences during 1570. Unfortunately, the receiver's book for 1569–70 is missing, but it is clear that work on the defences began in this year. In March 1570 the Chamber ordered that the city wall in Southernhay 'boundyng upon the Bishopps Palace or orchard being now fallen downe shalbe . . . new buylded'.[108] This task was not completed until 1570–71, when it was recorded that over £21 had been spent on repairs to the section of the enceinte lying next to the bishop's garden.[109]

Matters returned to normal in 1571–2: a year in which the only significant sum laid out on the city circuit was the £10 and 17 shillings which went on rebuilding the privy at Water Gate.[110] In 1572–73 the receiver bestowed less than 2 shillings on repairs to the enceinte, but this figure masks the fact that a minor scare took place at Exeter during that year. In August 1572 the massacre of St Bartholomew took place in Paris. Hundreds of Protestants were slaughtered, apparently with the connivance of the French Crown. News of the massacre at once revived fears of a Catholic attack on England, and the shockwaves clearly reached Exeter. In October, the Chamber took several significant decisions. First, it was agreed that the Queen should be asked to repair 'the decaied walles of the Castell . . . which nowe are very ruinose'.[111] Second, it was ordered that 'the newe mudd wall made from Southe Gate towardes the barbigans there'—which was obviously felt to encroach upon the defences—should be 'plucked downe'.[112] Third, the city sheriff was requested to 'vewe the artillarye of the cittie at St Johns & see the same bee newe trymmed': an instruction which led to a good deal of work on the arms stored at the former hospital complex.[113] No further steps were taken, however. It soon became clear that the massacre in Paris had not heralded a Catholic onslaught upon England and the fears which the episode had aroused quickly died away.

Not until 1578–79 was significant work again carried out on the city defences. The accounts for this year are missing, but in February 1579 it was noted in the Chamber act book that 'the walles which ar fallen downe neere the Water Gate and neere the Southgate' should be 'new buylded by Mr Recever . . . within the tyme of his yere'.[114] Why should it have been judged necessary to set to work on the defences with such speed at this time? Once again, the answer seems to be connected with foreign affairs. By 1579 England was facing new dangers from abroad. The situation in the Netherlands, where the Spanish were attempting to crush the rebellion of the largely Protestant Dutch, appeared particularly threatening. With the submission of the Walloon provinces to Spain in May 1579, the struggle in the Low Countries seemed to have been lost by the Protestants. It was common knowledge that Elizabeth was considering sending an expeditionary force to help the Dutch, for, with the Netherlands crushed, she feared that England would be next to feel the wrath of Spain. Such fears may well explain the sudden upsurge of expenditure on Exeter's defences in 1579.

The repairs begun in February continued into the next accounting year. In October 1579 the Chamber ordered the new receiver to complete the rebuilding of 'a certeine ruynous peece of the citties walles' near Water Gate which had 'begonne to bee erected by the late recever'.[115] Work here continued until November.[116] In January 1580 the focus of attention shifted, when a committee was directed to view the newly established gardens beside the city wall in Southernhay 'for redresse of the erthe there taken from the foundacion of the walles whereby they are like to decaye'.[117] A house and enclosures in Southernhay were also ordered to be demolished. In April work on the walls resumed when the receiver was told to 'provide for . . . fynyshinge of the Cities walls neere to Southgate & the Watergate'.[118] Over the next four months, some £40 was spent on this task. In 1580–81 defensive expenditure fell, but during the next year, it rose sharply, with £31 being laid out on 'the walls without Southegate next the Key'.[119] Expenditure in 1582–83 was even higher—some £88—most of which was probably spent on the walls near Water Gate.[120] Next year the receiver disbursed around £20 in repairs on all four sides of the city circuit.[121] This was to prove the last piece of major expenditure on the defences during Elizabeth's reign.

Little work was carried out on the enceinte between 1585 and 1587, and even less in 1587–88. At first sight, this seems rather puzzling. This was, after all, the year of the Spanish Armada: the year in which all England trembled in fear of imminent invasion. Exeter was certainly much disturbed during 'the troble of the Spanyerds beinge upon the coost', as one man later referred to Phillip II's 'great enterprise', and hundreds of pounds are known to have been raised by the townsfolk to fit out two ships and a pinnace to help counter the Spanish fleet.[122] In addition, a 'gunner' was admitted as a freeman of the city *gratis*—presumably because the Chamber hoped to make use of his skills—while large quantities of gunpowder were bought, and enquiries made about the purchase of a new gun.[123] So why was practically nothing spent on the fortifications? The speed with which the Spanish threat materialized (and subsequently receded) was probably the crucial factor, for it gave the citizens little time to set about the defences. They had, in any case, already spent so much on ships and soldiers that they can have had little stomach for laying out still more on the walls and gates: especially when they knew that the government itself was straining every nerve to protect the South West from Spanish invasion. Throughout the rest of the century, expenditure on the fortifications remained very low. Some £23 was spent on building the 'madfolks house' on the walls in 1590–91, but this can hardly be classed as defensive expenditure.[124] Even the invasion scare which gripped England in 1596, when it was feared that a new Armada was on its way, had little discernible effect.

The Elizabethan period had seen a steady decline in the amounts of money laid out on Exeter's fortifications: a decline which is especially significant given that this was a period of high monetary inflation. It is clear that, in real terms, less was spent on the walls and gates between 1570 and 1603 than at any other time during the sixteenth century. Nor was this the only sign that the town governors were becoming increasingly relaxed about the state of the enceinte. During the 1580s they abandoned their battle to prevent gardens from encroaching on the town banks in Southernhay and ordered the ditch there to be filled in.[125] Over the same period, they permitted an increasing number of domestic structures to be built upon the city walls: the privy at Water Gate, for example, and the madfolks' house at North Gate. No sustained attempt was made to upgrade the artillery pieces purchased during the 1540s, moreover, and the existing guns were gradually allowed to fall into disrepair. In 1590 a contemptuous witness described the civic ordnance at St John's as 'a few ship peces', which were more likely 'to kill the sho[o]ter of them than the enemye'.[126] That this was no exaggeration is strongly suggested by the fact that when the citizens decided to fire a salute to mark Elizabeth's death in 1603, cannon had to be procured for that purpose from ships at Topsham.[127] It was a tribute, in its way, to the increased sense of security which Elizabeth's long and comparatively stable reign had helped to engender. Yet as the events of the early Stuart period were to show, that sense of security would not endure forever.

CHAPTER 5

THE CITY DEFENCES
UNDER THE
EARLY STUARTS

By 1603 a generation of Exonians had grown up who had never experienced warfare and political turmoil at first hand. Elizabeth I had been securely on the throne since 1558, the region had been untroubled by internal disturbances since the Marian period and Exeter's defences had not had to withstand an assault since 1549. The kingdom had, it is true, been involved in wars with foreign enemies, but these disputes had largely been conducted at sea. By 1603, in any case, the international situation presented little cause for concern. The Spanish threat, so menacing to England during the previous thirty years, had now receded. Although the two countries remained technically at war until 1604, neither side attempted any major offensive operations during the early seventeenth century. This long period of calm lulled the citizens into a comfortable state of complacency, and the peaceful state of the realm is reflected in the receivers' accounts. Average annual expenditure on the city enceinte between 1600 and 1610 was less than £6. Even the death of the Queen in 1603 does not seem to have jolted the tranquil mood. Elizabeth's passing was marked with respect, as we have seen, but fears of a succession crisis were clearly not strong enough to motivate any work on the fortifications.[1] Following the trouble-free accession of James I and the subsequent peace with Spain, moreover, expenditure remained very low, and the little money that was spent on the fortifications went on routine repairs.

This pattern was to persist until 1612–13, when over £14 was laid out upon the 'reparacion of a tower in the Bishoppes Pallace'.[2] The 'tower' referred to was clearly one of the two which adjoined the bishop's garden. Indeed it is possible to be more specific still. On a contemporary plan of the city circuit—drawn up by an anonymous surveyor and now kept among the civic archives [*see plate 11*]—is a marginal note which states 'that the southeaste part of the cittyes walkes [*sic*] are defended with 4 towres . . . one of the cheafest of which towers, beinge next to the South Gate . . . [is] broken'.[3] Almost certainly, it was the latter, damaged, tower which was repaired in 1612–13.[4] Work in the area continued during 1613–14, when the receiver spent over £6 on 'reparacions upon the walls in the Bishopps Pallace'.[5] Quite why the tower was mended at this particular time is unclear. The kingdom was at peace, so the repairs may simply have been routine; the law jury had reported the dilapidated condition of the mural towers in Southernhay as long ago as 1570.[6] Yet it seems more likely that the work was connected with the Chamber's desire to assert its authority over the section of the town walls which ran alongside the Cathedral Close: a subject which is discussed in more detail below.

Further work took place in Southernhay in 1616–17. During that year, the receiver paid a workman for 'setting up the bridge in Minson's garden': that is to say, for putting together the collapsible wooden 'postern bridge' which was kept in the Bedford Postern Tower and reassembled whenever the Earls of Bedford or their guests wished to cross over the city ditch into Southernhay from the door in the tower's outer face [*see plates 5 and 7*].[7] In addition, £12 was spent on making a 'newe stone banke under the walls' near West Gate: probably in order to strengthen the wall's foundations in an area which was especially prone to subsidence.[8] The next sustained burst of expenditure came in 1618–19, when over £15 was laid out on repairs to the enceinte. Of this, almost £10 went on routine maintenance work at East Gate bridge.[9] No receivers' books survive for the years 1620–22, and between 1622 and 1624 only small sums were spent on the fortifications.

The terrible outbreak of plague which struck Exeter in 1625 brought all building work in the city to a halt. Thousands of local people died in 'God's visitation', as the sickness was termed, and for a time the whole structure of civic government seemed on the point of breaking down. Order was eventually restored, but 'watch and ward' continued to be kept up in Exeter throughout the first three months of 1626— presumably in order to ensure that no infected persons were able to enter the city. Only when these restrictions had been lifted could those who had survived the onslaught of the plague begin to rebuild their shattered lives.[10] During 1626 over £9 was spent on the city fortifications: the highest annual total recorded during the whole decade. The story behind this sudden rise in expenditure is of particular interest: not only because it provides a rare instance of the central government issuing a direct order concerning the city defences, but also because it reveals how the town councillors occasionally exploited periods of national emergency in order to further their own domestic agenda.

Shortly after his accession in 1625, Charles I led England into war with Spain. Though the succeeding conflict was a long one (hostilities continued until 1630) Exeter spent very little on its fortifications during this period. Clearly, the Chamber regarded the Spanish threat as negligible. Nevertheless, in early summer 1626, the town governors asked Exeter's aristocratic patron, Lord Russell, to inform the Privy Council that, in their opinion, the ancient postern gate on the north side of the Castle should be 'stopped up . . . [for] the safetie of . . . [this] citty in theis tymes of danger'. The town governors' request met with a favourable reception at Whitehall. On 26 July it was recorded in the

Chamber act book that a letter had been received from the Privy Council ordering the Mayor to block up 'the posterne gate in the Castle & alsoe to make anie other place as defensible as . . . [he] can for the better safetie of this Cittie'.[11] The Chamber at once ordered that the gateway should be 'dammed upp & made stronge with a stone walle in the best sorte it may be done'.[12] The requisite work was swiftly put in hand and between 5 and 13 August almost £3 was spent on 'walling upp the posterne gat in the Castell'.[13]

At first sight, this episode appears perfectly straightforward. An order had been issued by the Crown; Exeter's local governors had hurried to obey. But were matters really so simple? Why had the Chamber raised the issue of the gateway in the first place, and why had the Privy Council's response been recorded with such careful precision? The answer emerges from a resolution made by the town governors at the same time as they agreed to block up the Castle postern, namely, 'that another posterne gate, latelie made through the walles of this cittie, by the late Lord Bishopp . . . shalbe in like manner dammed uppe soe soone as . . . may be'.[14] This second postern had been a bone of contention between the city and the bishops for some time. During the early 1620s Bishop Valentine Carey had begun to build a door through the town wall beside the Bishop's Palace so that he could pass directly from his garden into Southernhay.[15] Like the Earl of Bedford before him, Carey had clearly decided that the most convenient place to construct such a postern gate was through the outer wall of one of the mural towers. He had therefore begun to knock down the southernmost of the two towers which stood in his garden (the same structure which the citizens had repaired in 1612–14) [*see plate 11*]. The Chamber, outraged, had demanded that the bishop leave their property alone. Undaunted, Carey had petitioned James I, who considered the bishop's request 'very reasonable'. In March 1623 James had ordered the mayor to allow Carey 'to make a convenient doore through the . . . wall and to have the use of it from tyme to tyme, he beinge readie whensoever any publicq urgent necessity shall require for the good and safety of the citty to make it up againe'. The Chamber had responded with an indignant counter-petition, but to no avail: the postern was duly built. Carey had emerged triumphant—but there can be little doubt that the Chamber bitterly begrudged the postern gate to the bishop and his successors.[16]

Almost certainly it is this which explains the town governors' actions in 1626. The order which they had solicited from the Privy Council provided them with the perfect means of striking back at the bishop in the dispute over the postern. James' original decree had stipulated that the door might be blocked up again if 'any publicq urgent necessity' should threaten the city's safety. Now, with the Privy Council's letter in their hands, speaking as it did of 'these tymes of danger' and of the need to strengthen local defences, the town governors could claim that just such a state of emergency existed. Having pointedly obeyed the original order concerning the Castle gate, they swiftly moved on to secure their true objective: the blocking up of the bishop's postern. Workmen had already embarked on this task by 18 August.[17] A Chamber order that members of the Twenty-Four should 'directe the workemen in the doeinge thereof' hints at a desire to gloat over the bishop's defeat.[18] Certainly, it suggests that the Chamber was determined to assert its rights over the wall as conspicuously as possible. Whatever the case, by 8 September the bishop's postern had been firmly blocked up. Twice as much money had been spent on stopping up this gate as had been spent on the Castle postern, which had provided the original pretext for the work.

This complicated episode serves as a reminder that relations between the Chamber and the Cathedral—never particularly harmonious —were now becoming more strained than ever as zealous Protestants, or 'Puritans', grew increasingly influential among the civic elite.[19] At the same time, and for similar reasons, a certain *froideur* was growing up between the city authorities and the Crown. As early as 1623, James I had brusquely told a civic delegation that 'he understood the citizens were puritans'.[20] Matters did not improve with the accession of his son, whom many believed to have Catholic leanings. Within a decade of Charles I's coronation, if not well before, many Exeter people had come to mistrust the religious policies of their high-church monarch, to despise the King's equally high-church archbishop, William Laud, and to regard the Cathedral clergy as men who were disaffected to the true Protestant church. Such suspicions affected local attitudes towards the city defences, as they affected everything else. After 1625 the Chamber became increasingly determined to assert its authority over those sections of the enceinte which adjoined the property of the Dean and Chapter, and to inspect those parts of the wall to which the clergymen had access. Clear evidence of the citizens' growing distrust of the Chapter emerges from a document composed by an anonymous Exonian in *c*.1630. The writer observed that, although 'Exon is walled round about', the city's security was seriously compromised by the privileged jurisdiction of the Cathedral Close—and added that 'within the Close there are many . . . spacious howses wherein in tymes of trobles infinite multitudes of persons may be received without controlment, whearby the whole cittye may be surprized'.[21]

Rougemont Castle—which belonged to the Crown, and was thus the only other part of Exeter which lay outside the Chamber's jurisdiction—was also feared by some to be a potential threat to the city's security during the uneasy reign of Charles I. At the beginning of 1627 Giles Carpenter—who had served as Exeter's 'muster-master', or retained military expert, between 1588 and 1618—wrote an agitated letter to Alderman Ignatius Jurdain, the Puritan patriarch who was perhaps the most influential member of the early Stuart Chamber.[22] Carpenter's purpose was to warn Jurdain of 'a daungerous plot' centring upon the Castle, which had allegedly been hatched by various 'Londoners and decayed courtiers'.[23] Their aim, Carpenter averred, was to lease the Castle from the Crown. Once this had been achieved, he went on, the conspirators would cause 'all the old buildings to be reedyfied, together with the wals and gates [and] two dra[w]bridges: one into Northernhaye, the other into the City'.[24] In addition 'divers platformes for ordinance' would be built and a garrison of 100 soldiers installed: to be paid 'at the King's charge for 3 yeares' and afterwards at the expense of the plotters. Once the Castle had been garrisoned and provided with cannon, Carpenter alleged, trading was to be carried on within its precincts. Needless to say, this trading would proceed on terms very favourable to the plotters and, by inference, very unfavourable to the city merchants. It is hard to be sure if there was anything in all this, but the story is an intriguing one nevertheless. Particularly significant are the closing words of Carpenter's letter: 'the city of An[t]warpe was sacked by such a meanes of a Castell within ye walls [of] it within the memory of man'.[25] This statement is fascinating in its illustration of the citizens' worst fears concerning what might befall them if the Castle—or, indeed, the Cathedral Close—should fall into the wrong hands.

During the early 1630s there began a period of significant expenditure on the city defences: one which was to continue for the next seven years. In 1631–32 over £22 was spent on repairs to the walls.[26] This work does not seem to have been precipitated by any sudden collapse. On the contrary, the subsequent pattern of activity suggests that the Chamber had initiated a general overhaul of the city enceinte. Yet why should such a project have been considered necessary during the 'halcyon days' of Charles I's Personal Rule, when England basked at peace with all its neighbours? There are three possible answers to this question. First, it is conceivable that the repairs were carried out for their own sake; fifty years of relative neglect may have left the walls in such a dilapidated condition that they represented an affront to civic pride. Second, the defences may have been strengthened in order to counter the threat posed by Muslim pirates from North Africa, who were at this time becoming increasingly active around Devon's coasts.[27] As early as 1629 the citizens of Exeter had petitioned the Crown for protection against the corsairs. Similar pleas continued throughout 1630–33, but the royal fleet was unable to provide any adequate assistance.[28] The citizens may therefore have decided to look to their own defence. The 'Moors' had never yet assaulted an English town, but who could be sure that such an attempt might not one day be made?

The third possibility is that the work undertaken on the city walls of Exeter during the 1630s may have been initiated as the result of a legal dispute with the Crown. A little has already been said in this book about the so-called 'city wastes': the areas of open ground which lay directly beyond the town walls in Northernhay and Southernhay and which were used by the citizens for a multiplicity of purposes. What has not yet been made clear, perhaps, is that the Chamber's right to these lands was disputed. In 1617 John Norden—whom James I had appointed as surveyor of the lands of the Duchy of Cornwall—had visited Exeter and made a plan of the Castle and its environs [*see plate 10*]. After completing his survey, Norden had alleged that the Chamber had 'usurped' the banks and ditches in Northernhay, and that these lands—together with the city wastes in Southernhay—had once formed part of the Prince of Wales' demesne.[29] Within five years of Charles I's accession, the Prince's Council had begun a vigorous pursuit of this claim and the resultant lawsuit dragged on throughout the 1630s.[30] The Chamber was furious that its right to the city wastes had been cast in doubt: not only because these lands were profitable and useful in their own right, but also because they were of vital importance to the upkeep and security of the city enceinte. In their formal submissions to the court, the town governors laid great emphasis on the fact that the wastes had been used, time out of mind, in order to gain access to the town walls for the purposes of repair. Yet, as one witness was forced to concede, there had been little 'repayringe of the walles' over the past half century.[31] It seems at least possible, therefore, that the unusual amount of work carried out on the enceinte during the 1630s was a product of the Chamber's determination both to proclaim, and—by means of establishing fresh precedent—to reinforce, its continued right to the city wastes.

Whatever the cause, expenditure on the defences continued to rise. In 1633 the Chamber ordered the receiver to 'goe onwardes in the reperacions of the citties walles, where . . . [his predecessor] left of[f] . . . last yere'.[32] Over £30 was subsequently spent on repairs to Snayle Tower, West Gate and the walls nearby.[33] Still more money was laid out in 1633–34. During this year £42—the highest annual sum spent on the fortifications during the whole decade—went on repairs to the walls. The accounts suggest that most of this work took place on the barbican near North Gate, which had been presented as being in decay by the law jury in 1632.[34] During 1634–35 defensive disbursements fell, to just over £21. It may be significant that this was the year in which the navy at last took effective action against the corsairs.[35] Nevertheless, the money laid out on the defences in 1634–35 was still a very considerable sum. Most of it was spent on work behind the Bishop's Palace: at the 'citties walles & Bishops Tower'.[36]

The repairs in this area exacerbated still further the feud between the Chamber and the Cathedral. In October 1634 it was noted in the Chamber act book that the 'reperacion of the Citties walles . . . neare the Bishops Pallace . . . is somewhat opposed by the present Bishop'. The town governors were in no mood to make concessions and they defiantly agreed that 'the workmen shall goe on in the said work & . . . be defended by this house therein'.[37] Soon afterwards, Bishop Joseph Hall, Carey's successor, wrote to Archbishop Laud to complain that 'under pretence of mending their wall', the citizens had encroached upon 'an ancient castle of the . . . Bishops, now decayed, standing within . . . thirty paces of the Episcopal house, which . . . castle was of old the Bishops prison for clerks convict'. The structure to which Hall referred was clearly the 'Lollard's Prison': the larger of the two mural towers which adjoin the garden of the Bishop's Palace. Despite his express wishes to the contrary, Hall alleged, the Chamber had 'set workmen upon the said castle, to make a show of repairing the battlements of it for their own purposes'. The bishop asked Laud to remonstrate with the citizens—but, if the archbishop took any action, no record of it has survived.[38]

In addition to the work at the Palace, repairs were also carried out during 1634–35 to the 'garrets at ye steppes in Friernhay' and to the barbican between Water Gate and West Gate.[39] Next year, £10 was spent on repairs to 'Westgate & citties walles' and to 'the water passage under the pavement without Westgate'.[40] By now the dilapidated condition of West Gate itself was clearly causing concern. In October 1635 the Chamber ordered that, because the gate was 'much in decaye', it 'shalbe foorthwith amended or newe made, as shalbe thought best'.[41] To have rebuilt the gate from the ground up would have been prohibitively expensive, and the town governors clearly felt unable to embark on such a major project at this time. Instead, just £2 was spent on minor repairs to West Gate and to the 'water steps' there in 1636–37. In addition, some £3 went on repairs to East Gate, and over £5 on mending the city wall 'neare unto the Bishops Pallace with an arch, being the place of the passage of the water through the same for use of the cittizens'.[42] Next year, a structural collapse initiated more work on the fortifications. Almost £9 was laid out in 1638 for repairs to 'the barbican of the citties walles against St John's Hospital', which was in danger of falling.[43]

During 1638–39 the Crown's efforts against the pirates at last met with major success, so it may be significant that work on the defences of Exeter temporarily ceased in the same year. Unfortunately for the citizens, fears of attack from abroad were soon to be overshadowed by internal distractions at home. In 1637 Charles I's attempts to impose a new prayer book on Scotland—a prayer book which was popularly regarded as 'Popish'—had prompted a full-scale rebellion in that kingdom. By spring 1638 Charles was making ready to lead an English army against the Scots and rumours of war were causing ripples of apprehension in Exeter, as they were everywhere else. During July–October 1638 the Chamber went through the motions of preparing for trouble and ordered that various encroachments upon the city walls and the lanes leading up to them should be removed.[44] These orders were not followed up: perhaps because, like many English Puritans, the dominant party on the Chamber secretly sympathized with the Scots, perhaps because the town governors were confident that no Scottish army could ever penetrate so far south. Nothing seems to have been spent on the fortifications at Exeter during the First Scots War of 1638–39, although fifteen barrels of gunpowder were bought.[45] The Second Scots War of 1640 generated more of a reaction. No receiver's book survives for 1639–40, but the roll for this year records that over £31 was spent on 'diverse reparations on the city walls'.[46] This expenditure may well have been a reaction to the fighting in the North and to the general air of unease which was prevalent throughout the entire kingdom as the weakness of the royal regime became increasingly apparent. An entry in the Chamber act book indicates where the work was carried out. On 19 May 1640 the councillors agreed that the receiver should repair 'the defectes of the Citties Walles between Westgate & Snayle Tower, latelie presented by the Lawe Jury, and alsoe betweene Watergate & Helliars Garden'.[47]

The receiver's book for 1640–41—the year in which Charles I, unable to defeat the Scots, was forced to abandon the Personal Rule and to summon the assembly which would become known to posterity as 'the Long Parliament'—is also missing, but the roll shows that over £117 was laid out on Exeter's walls and gates in this year: the largest sum spent on the city fortifications since the 1580s.[48] Some of this money clearly went on furthering the repairs to the town walls begun during the previous year; in October 1640 the Chamber agreed that the receiver should 'goe on in the reperacion of the . . . walles . . . soe farr as the morter alreadie made will holde out'.[49] Yet the bulk of the expenditure, over £100, was occasioned by the construction of 'a certain house for keeping gunpowder on the walls of the city near East Gate'.[50] This new powder magazine, which the Chamber had ordered to be established in August 1640, was built within the shell of the eastern angle tower.[51] The decision to site the magazine here was probably taken in part because the civic artillery was stored in St John's Hospital next door, in part because—in this particular district of Exeter, where private houses were relatively thin on the ground—the consequences of an accidental explosion would be less catastrophic than they would be elsewhere.[52] Certainly, as tensions grew across the realm and as fear of 'powder plots'—never far below the surface of the seventeenth-century subconscious—began to stir, the town governors must have been mightily relieved to see the barrels of gun-powder removed from their previous storehouse above the Council Chamber in the Guildhall and taken away to the new magazine in the tower.

It is unfortunate that neither book nor roll survives for 1641–42—the critical year in which the already strained relationship between King and Parliament at last reached breaking point—but other sources make it clear that, by late 1641, Exeter's state of military preparedness had become a matter of pressing concern. On 14 October the Chamber ordered that the 'inclosures & incroachments' which had been built across Sticke Street (present-day Chapel Street) should be 'throwne downe & laid open, soe that the passage to the citties walles [may] be [made] open & free'. At the same time, it was noted that because many people—including Bishop Hall—had 'of late planted trees uppon the . . . walles, which it is feared wilbe verie prejudiciall to the said walles', they should be given 'speedie notice' to cut them down. Dr Lawrence Burnell, one of the Cathedral canons, was likewise told to dismantle a wooden fence which he had erected across the barbican between his garden and the city walls.[53]

A week after these orders were issued, a major rebellion broke out in Ireland. Hundreds, possibly thousands, of Protestants were massacred by the insurgents and rumours of imminent Irish invasion were soon sweeping across England. Exeter shared in the general panic. On 14 December the quality of the city's watchmen was upgraded and the citizens were reminded that it was their duty to provide themselves with clubs. Two days later the Chamber ordered that a new door should be made to the vault of the water pipes under East Gate because 'the old are decayed, & the lying open thereof may occasion danger to this cittie'.[54] By early 1642 fears of Irish invasion were becoming overshadowed by the increasingly alarming situation in London, where Charles I's abortive attempt to arrest the Five Members had brought open war between King and Parliament one step closer.[55] On 11 January the Chamber, obviously beginning to fear the worst, ordered three of its number to 'viewe the walles of this cittie & the defectes of the same and to certefie howe they fynde the[m]'. On the same day, it was agreed that a piece of wall 'which is of late follen neare the Eastgate shalbe with all convenient speede reedified . . . And that all other defectes shalbe repaired soe soone as . . . maybe'.[56] As the political situation continued to deteriorate, the Chamber took further measures to improve the city's defences. In March, permission was sought from the Earl of Bedford to block up the 'Bedford Postern', while in April 'a gutter through the walles' at the end of St Mary Arches Street was ordered to be 'stopte upp'.[57]

During the spring and early summer of 1642, as the kingdom fell apart into two armed camps, the dominant, Puritan faction on the Chamber strained every nerve to ensure that Exeter would eventually declare itself for the Parliament. By mid-August they had achieved their aim; for the first time in over 150 years the 'ever faithful' city had come out in rebellion against the Crown.[58] It would be absurd to suggest that it was concern for the integrity of the city enceinte which was chiefly responsible for this *volte face*. In Exeter, as across the country as a whole, it was clearly dislike of Charles I's religious policies which did more than anything else to persuade ordinary men and women to rally to his opponents.[59] Nevertheless, the frequency with which the Stuart kings and their servants had challenged, or at least appeared to challenge, the Chamber's accustomed control of the city defences—over Norden's survey in 1617, for example, over the bishop's postern in 1623, over the alleged plan to lease out the Castle in 1627, and above all over the city wastes during *c.*1630–40—may well have played its part in hardening the town governors' hearts against the royal regime and encouraging them to believe that a sinister clique centred on the Court was indeed bent on destroying 'English liberties'.

The story of Exeter's terrible experiences during the English Civil War has been told in detail elsewhere.[60] For the purposes of this book, it is enough to provide an overview of the unprecedented programme of work which took place on the city's fortifications between August 1642 and April 1646. On the eve of the conflict, the pro-Parliamentary authorities in Exeter—like town governors all over England—faced the challenge of converting, almost overnight, a crumbling medieval enceinte into a bastioned system of fortification capable of withstanding the fire of up-to-date artillery pieces.[61] They chose to meet this challenge not by constructing an entirely new defensive perimeter—a task which would have been almost impossibly expensive and time-consuming—but by adapting the ancient walls and gates, as far as was possible, to the requirements of 'the modern way of fortification'.[62] In September the Chamber hired a military engineer, one Peter Baxter, to oversee the city defences.[63] Baxter—the only expert in the art of fortification who is known to been employed at Exeter throughout the whole of the early modern period—swiftly got to work. Quite possibly it was he who recommended that the upper storeys of the ancient mural towers should be demolished and the lower storeys filled with rubble so that these now redundant structures might serve as primitive bastions (or batteries) upon which cannon could be mounted.[64]

Throughout the ensuing months, the receiver—presumably working, at least in part, under Baxter's direction—disbursed large sums of money on the city defences. Particularly intensive work was carried out on the walls at Northernhay. Repairs also took place on the section of the enceinte between East Gate and South Gate. New buttresses were constructed in this area; money was spent on 'posting upp the wales against Bedford House', and the blocked-up doorway in the Bishop's Postern Tower may have been reopened for use as a sally port.[65] A detailed set of instructions was issued for the defence of the city [*see document 7*]. In addition, South Gate was 'sufficientlie repaired with beames, planchinge & leadd' so that guns might be placed on top of the structure.[66] Hundreds of Parliamentarian troops were brought in from elsewhere to help garrison the city.[67] Finally, many new artillery pieces were procured. In September 1642 the city had possessed just six 'gunnes'. By October this figure had risen to twenty-five, and by September 1643 to forty-two.[68] The total cost of all the defensive works undertaken by the receiver between September 1642 and September 1643 (in which month Exeter was finally stormed and captured by a Royalist army) eventually came to £164.[69] This was the highest sum to be spent by any receiver on the enceinte since the mid-sixteenth century. When compared to the *total* amount spent on Exeter's defences during this year, though, the receiver's contribution pales into insignificance.

It is important to remember that the receivers were only responsible for the maintenance of those parts of the city fortifications which belonged to the Chamber, like the walls and gates. Additions to the existing defences—and, more especially, the construction of extensive defensive outworks of the type which had become so vital for the defence of a town by the mid-seventeenth century—did not fall within the receivers' brief. As a result, two sets of accounts were kept during the years 1642–43: the receiver's accounts proper, and the voluminous 'extraordinary accounts' which were drawn up by the Parliamentary authorities in Exeter. These detail the amounts which were spent on digging out the old city ditch, on excavating a new outer ditch from East Gate to South Gate in order to protect the city's vulnerable southern flank, on building earthworks, on laying batteries, on repairing the Castle, on demolishing houses in the suburbs, on paying labourers' wages and on a huge range of other tasks, which were vital to the city's security but which fell outside the jurisdiction of the receiver. By September 1643 the enormous sum of £4,374 had been spent on these extraordinary defensive measures.[70] Most of this money had been extracted from the citizens of Exeter themselves, by way of loans, levies and 'voluntary' contributions.[71] [*For the extent of the City defences in September 1643, see map 7.*]

Unfortunately, the accounts of 'extraordinary' work on the city's defences between September 1643 and April 1646 have not survived, so our knowledge of defensive activity at Exeter during the period of Royalist control rests on the receivers' accounts alone. Soon after the Royalist takeover in September 1643, the new receiver embarked on a fresh round of repairs to the walls and gates. A list of all the ordnance in the city was drawn up [*see document 8*], and almost £24 was spent on repairing 'the decayed Walle in Northenhay'.[72] Yet the main task, that of repairing the damage inflicted during the Royalist army's final attack, still remained to be done. On 2 January 1644 the Chamber finally took the plunge, ordering 'that the Cities walles that are now fallen downe or any other way defective . . . shalbe foorthwith builte upp againe & repaired'.[73] Accordingly, repairs to the city walls in Southernhay began on 6 January.[74] This work continued until November 1644, by which time the enormous sum of £345 had been spent. One of the most important tasks which the workmen carried out during this period may well have been to construct an entirely new sally port through the base of the 'Lollard's Tower': one which either complemented or entirely replaced the doorway through the adjoining Bishop's Postern Tower.[75] Total expenditure on the defences during this year eventually came to almost £370, a quite unprecedented figure.[76] A third of the city's total annual revenue had been expended on the upkeep of its fortifications.[77]

Despite the vast amounts expended in 1643–44, work on the defences showed no sign of stopping. In December 1644 it was ordered that the new receiver should 'repair the defects in the Westgate & the cities walles'.[78] This was clearly a retrospective instruction, for masons had been busy at West Gate since early November. Intensive repairs were carried out here until April 1645 and continued sporadically throughout the rest of the receiver's year. By the time the work was completed, West Gate had been effectively rebuilt and over £170 had been spent.[79] Again, this sum is a very considerable one. Even so, expenditure in 1644–45 was considerably less than in 1643–44. A decreased sense of urgency on the part of the defenders can hardly explain this, for, by the end of 1645, Parliament's New Model Army was advancing on Exeter. Instead, it seems probable that the proliferation of defensive works *outside* the walls had made the condition of the walls themselves less important in the general scheme of things. In addition, the sheer cost of the work during the previous years may at last have been starting to tell: the city was simply running out of money.

These two factors may explain why the Chamber did not order any fresh work to be undertaken on the walls during 1645–46. As the new receiver took office, in October 1645, the city was about to come under Parliamentary siege, and soon the defences were enduring heavy bombardment. Very little is known of events in Exeter during the closing months of the war. For the period between September 1645 and March 1646, even the receiver's accounts dry up, and as a result, there is simply

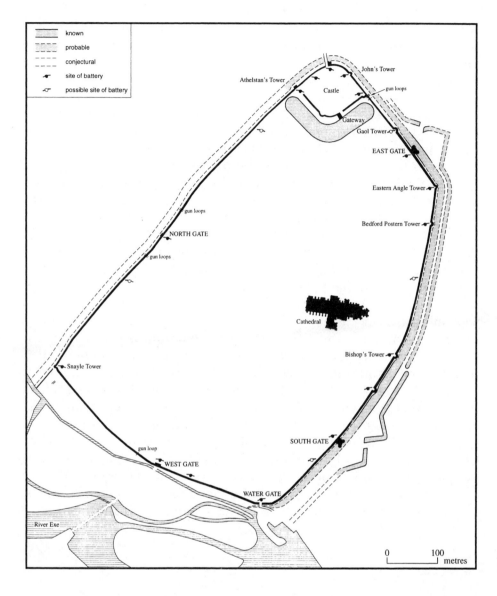

known
probable
conjectural
site of battery
possible site of battery

Athelstan's Tower
John's Tower
Castle
gun loops
Gateway
Gaol Tower
EAST GATE
Eastern Angle Tower
Bedford Postern Tower
gun loops
NORTH GATE
gun loops
Cathedral
Bishop's Tower
Snayle Tower
SOUTH GATE
gun loop
WEST GATE
WATER GATE
River Exe

0   100
                metres

Map 7 The city defences of
Exeter in 1643

no way of knowing how much was spent on the city walls during this
time. What *is* clear is that, by the time the victorious Parliamentary
troops finally entered Exeter in April 1646, the city's defences were
immeasurably stronger and more extensive than they had ever been
before. Not only had the Royalists continued to repair the city's walls and
gates and to maintain the new earthworks which had been thrown up
around Exeter by the Parliamentarians, but they had demolished the city
suburbs and built fresh outworks of their own upon the ruins [*see figure
16*].[80] By April 1646, Exeter was surrounded by a threefold ring of
fortifications, comprising first the ancient wall and 'dike'; second an
outer 'line', consisting of a deep-cut ditch and bank; and third a host of
satellite outworks, including four major forts at St David's Down, Mount
Radford, St Thomas and St Sidwells [*see map 8*].[81] To defend this mighty
fortress—considered by contemporary observers to have been one of the

strongest in the kingdom—the Royalists had amassed no fewer than seventy-five pieces of ordnance, while the strength of the garrison was put at some 3,000 men.[82] Exeter had reached the very apogee of its strength—but it was a strength which was swiftly to crumble.

During the sixteen years of restored Parliamentary rule in Exeter, spending on the city defences collapsed. In part, this was because the Chamber's financial resources had been utterly exhausted by the Civil War, in part because—with the installation of a garrison of Parliamentary soldiers in the Castle, and the establishment of a permanent standing army in England—the citizens were no longer primarily responsible for their own defence. Admittedly, some money was laid out on the fortifications in the immediate aftermath of the war. During 1646–47, for example, £7 was spent on 'mending the gates & locks of the cittie' (had the locks been changed after the expulsion of the Royalists?), while a mason was paid for mending Water Gate, which was 'fallen downe and so rotten and decayed that the wagons could not pass with merchants goods without great daunger'.[83] Even the walls received a little attention. In September 1647 it was noted that 'there are decayes in the citties walles against Southinghay and Northinghay by some works or fortifycacons that have byn of late made there, which nowe are become so ruinous that the passage from those places into the city is verie common & ordinary'.[84] The Chamber ordered that a cob wall should be built in those places to prevent people from entering the city in secret, and a few days later a mason was duly paid 'for the making upp of a clobb wall on the citties wall and stoppinge upp of som of the garrettes'.[85] That the Chamber decided to build these walls in cob, rather than in stone, is intriguing, for cob had never been incorporated in the fabric of the city wall before. Clearly, the repairs were intended merely to deter intruders, rather than to improve the state of Exeter's military preparedness.

Figure 16   The Civil War defences at East Gate

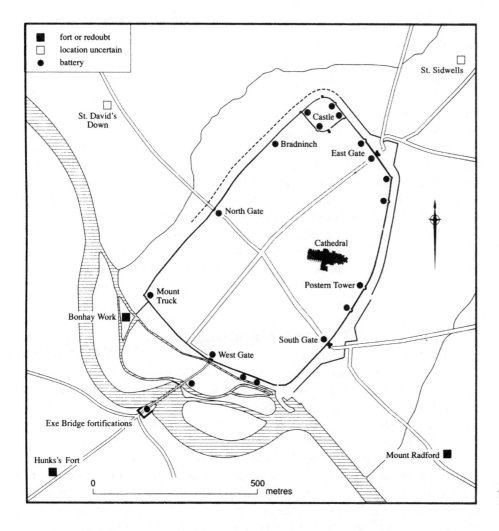

Map 8 The city defences of Exeter in 1646

During early 1648 serious popular disturbances took place in Exeter. The citizens had long resented the overweening behaviour of the soldiers in the Castle, and in May an unsuccessful attempt was made to prevent further Parliamentarian troops from entering the city.[86] As a result of this fracas, the weapons belonging to the city militia companies were confiscated.[87] A few days later, a pro-Royalist rising occurred in West Cornwall, and it may have been news of this insurrection which prompted the Chamber to order, on 6 June, that 'the defects in the citty walls' should be 'sufficiently repayred'.[88] If so, the panic was short-lived: less than £6 was laid out on the walls and gates over the following months. Expenditure fell lower still during the last two years of the 1640s: to under £4 in 1648–49 (the year of Charles I's execution) and to just £1 7 shillings in 1649–50. Over the next decade the Chamber spent more on demolishing fortifications than on building them. Between 1650 and 1660, well over £100 was paid to workmen and labourers for removing the temporary earthworks which had been thrown up around the city during the conflict of 1642–46.[89] Over the same period, less than £70 was spent on the walls and gates—and even some of this work was skimped, as can be seen from the repairs carried out on the town wall near Water Gate in 1654.

A large section of the wall here had fallen down, completely demolishing Helliar's Almshouses.[90] Further collapses were imminently expected, and in September 1653 the Chamber instructed two men 'to viewe that other parte of the citties walle neere the Keygate which is likely to fall alsoe, whereby the same may be timelie prevented'.[91] Ten months later, it was agreed that a certain Mr Prigge should take down the garrets on the city wall near Quay Gate, and arrange for 'soe much of the wall as is lately fallen downe [there] to bee made and raised upp with a mudd wall'.[92] Soon afterwards, a mason received £2 8 shillings for 'stopping upp the passage through the cittie walles neere Keygate'.[93] At first sight, this sequence of events appears to suggest that the Chamber was very concerned about the state of the defences—but it is important to note the precise nature of the 'repairs'. The garrets had not been mended, they had been removed: the city defences had been weakened, rather than strengthened, by the workmen's actions, in other words. More significant still is the fact that the breach in the city wall had not been repaired with stone, as was usual, but with cob, which was practically useless for defensive purposes.

Other pieces of evidence tend to confirm that the walls' defensive function was beginning to be disregarded during the Interregnum. By the early 1650s, for example, the law jury had begun to turn a blind eye to private gutters built through the town walls, so long as they were regularly cleaned out.[94] Before the Civil War, such water-channels had been banned because of the damage which they caused to the stonework [*see Chapter 3*]. Equally significant is the fact that several new 'tenements' were built on top of the city walls during the 1650s, thus impeding the fighting platform.[95] The Chamber's decision to have 'one of the garrets of the citty wall' near St John's Hospital removed in 1655 in order to provide more light 'for the hospitall chapple windowe' betrays a similar lack of concern for military imperatives.[96] During the same year, it was ordered that the sally port leading 'into the [Bishop's] Pallace from Southenhaye' should be 'walled upp'.[97] Again, this decision suggests that military considerations were going by the board. In December 1655, moreover, the Chamber agreed to let out a stretch of the city walls to a private individual for the purposes of drying cloth.[98] This decision was not as trivial as it sounds. Hanging cloth on the walls had been strictly forbidden since November 1640, when the Chamber had noted that the custom was 'verie prejudicial' to the fabric of the defences.[99] The decision to resume this practice in 1655 strongly suggests that the scrupulous preservation of the walls was no longer considered to be of prime importance.

Between 1654 and 1660, very little was laid out upon the city defences—and much of the money that *was* spent went on structures that did not have a military purpose. The large sums expended on 'the arch under Eastgate' during 1654–58, for example, went on repairs to the pipe-vault beneath the gate rather than to the gate itself.[100] Similarly, although the receiver recorded that over £8 had been expended on the city walls in 1655–56, most of this money went on repairing 'the howses on the wales nere Northgate', which served as a place of incarceration for lunatics.[101] Likewise almost all the money laid out in 1658–59 went on repairs to South Gate prison.[102] Once disbursements upon the prison, 'the madfolks house' and other non-defensive measures are discounted, the true insignificance of spending upon the fortifications during this period becomes clear. Only £1 12 shillings and 4 pence was laid out on repairs to the walls and gates in 1655–56 and only £1 7 shillings and 6 pence in 1656–57. Expenditure fell lower still in the next two years, to 5 shillings and 6 pence in 1658–59 and to just 3 shillings in 1657–58.

Only during the last year of the Interregnum did this situation change. In 1659–60 over £11 was spent, mainly on repairs to the North Gate and the town walls.[103] It is possible that this increase was a result of the disturbances which signalled the beginning of the end of the Commonwealth. In 1659 great riots had taken place in Exeter, the participants demanding an end to military despotism and the election of a 'free parliament'.[104] The Council of State had commanded an infantry regiment to occupy Exeter and the city was temporarily cowed.[105] Yet, nationally, the situation was turning against the government. In February 1660 General George Monk entered London with an army and a month later he forced the Rump Parliament to vote its own dissolution. This effected, Monk quickly summoned a new parliament, one whose pro-Royalist tendencies were clear. The restoration of the monarchy in England was now assured. A national settlement quickly followed and on 11 May 1660 King Charles II was at last proclaimed through the streets of Exeter.[106] With the King's Restoration, the citizens resumed control of their own defences. The trained bands were reconstituted, local captains were again chosen to lead them, and the militia companies played a major part in the festivities with which the citizens celebrated the monarch's return. While the conduits ran red with claret, the trained bands fired salutes, beat up their drums, and marched through the city streets behind their company colours.[107] Two years later the Chamber ordered that the city walls, so long neglected, should be thoroughly surveyed, and a year after that, a major programme of repairs was initiated.[108] For the ancient town defences of Exeter, as for the city government as a whole, the Restoration of the monarchy heralded a return to traditional ways after a twenty-year period of unprecedented flux and change.

CONCLUSION

The sudden burst of work which took place on Exeter's defences in the wake of the Restoration was prompted by ideological considerations, rather than military ones. By reversing the policy of near-total neglect which had been adopted by the 'rebel' Chamber during the 1650s, the members of the 'loyal' Chamber of the 1660s were demonstrating their principled opposition to the manner in which Exeter had been governed during the Interregnum, and underlining their determination to return to accustomed civic practice.[1] It seems probable that they were also reacting to Charles II's decree that a number of towns which had been especially prominent in resisting his father—including Coventry, Gloucester, Northampton and Taunton—should have their walls demolished.[2] If a dismantled enceinte was now to be regarded as the mark of a particularly disloyal town, the town governors may have reasoned, then a properly-maintained enceinte might equally well be regarded as the mark of a particularly loyal one.

In other words, the work which took place on the city defences during the 1660s was primarily intended to restore them to the condition in which they had been before the cataclysm of the 1640s, and to make a symbolic statement about the Chamber's political allegiance. What it was *not* intended to do was to update the city enceinte to meet the needs of modern warfare. Exeter's defences were already old-fashioned by 1660 and over the following decades advances in military technology were to render them wholly obsolete. On a visit to the city in *c.*1714, Daniel Defoe opined that warfare was now so different that Exeter at its strongest could not hold out five days against a siege. 'Nay', he added scornfully, 'it would hardly put an army to the trouble of opening trenches against it at all.'[3] So far had the military reputation of Exeter, once regarded as 'the most . . . defensible [town] of all . . . [the West]', declined in the seventy years since the Civil War—and the subsequent history of the city enceinte was to be one of piecemeal demolition and decay.[4]

Nevertheless, the town defences of Exeter had served their primary purpose. Thanks in large part to their looming presence, the city had been spared from foreign attack over the preceding centuries while, during periods of civic unrest, the inhabitants' lives and property had generally been kept safe from harm. Between 1485 and 1660, Exeter had only twice been compelled to open its gates to hostile forces—in 1643 and in 1646—and on both these occasions the strength of the fortifications had permitted the defenders to negotiate favourable surrender terms, thus preserving the citizens from the horrors of a storm. Exeter's experience contrasted markedly with that of many other, less fortunate, urban communities in Southern England—Plymouth, Dartmouth, Axminster, Weymouth, Taunton, Newport, Southampton, Portsmouth, Lewes, Winchelsea and Rye, for example—all of which suffered devastating attacks during the late medieval and early modern periods.[5] Yet, as the city's inhabitants knew only too well, Exeter's record of proud inviolability had come at a considerable cost.

The financial documents reproduced in the second part of this book show that, between 1485 and 1660, over £7,500 was laid out on Exeter's fortifications [*see Table, p.197*]. To put this figure into perspective, it may be observed that, during the 1540s, the city's average annual revenue was around £227, during the 1590s around £847 and during the 1630s around £1,082.[6] Thus the cost of maintaining Exeter's defences over the whole of the early modern period represented some seven times as much as the Chamber could hope to derive from all sources of income during an optimum year. The *total* amount spent on the city fortifications between 1485 and 1660 was undoubtedly far greater than the surviving records suggest, moreover. For many of the years covered by the present volume, the receivers' accounts are incomplete, while the loss of the 'extraordinary accounts' drawn up by the Royalist authorities in Exeter during the Civil War blurs the picture still further. The sums laid out on building the outer ring of earthwork defences with which Exeter was encircled during 1643–46 must have been enormous; the cost of constructing similar systems of fortification elsewhere is known to have run into many thousands of pounds.[7] Thus the total amount spent on the city's fortifications under the Tudor and early Stuart monarchs can hardly have been less than £10,000: indeed, it is perfectly conceivable that the true figure was closer to £20,000. Maintaining the town defences was clearly the single most expensive project which the inhabitants of early modern Exeter ever undertook.[8]

It comes as no surprise to find that the vast bulk of recorded expenditure on Exeter's fortifications took place during the Civil War. Of the £7,539 which is known to have been laid out on the city defences between 1485 and 1660, no less than £4,548 (60% of the total) was spent in the twelve-month period between September 1642 and September 1643. For the 1640s as a whole, the total was £5,259: a figure which represented nearly 70% of recorded expenditure on Exeter's defences over the entire early modern period. In this respect—as in so many others—the Civil War's impact on Exeter was quite unprecedented.[9] At no other time during the early modern period did the city undergo a remotely comparable period of crisis. The next most turbulent decade was probably the 1540s, when fears of invasion from abroad combined with popular rebellion at home to prompt the expenditure of over £320 on the defences. Yet, even allowing for inflation, this sum represents less than a fifth of that which is recorded to have been spent in the 1640s—and, as we have seen, *unrecorded* defensive expenditure during the Civil War was probably at least as great again! The shadow which the Prayer Book Rebellion cast over Exeter was fleeting indeed compared with that which was cast by the internecine conflict of the mid-seventeenth century.

No study of Exeter's defences during the early modern period can afford to neglect the dramatic developments of the Civil War, but it is important to recognize that the events of these years represent just one short chapter in a much longer story—and a wholly atypical chapter at that. The true story of the city enceinte at Exeter between 1485 and 1660 was not one of sudden innovation and change, but of deep-seated traditionalism and continuity. The inhabitants of medieval and early modern Exeter believed their town walls to date back to before the time of Christ[10] and, as late as the 1660s, they still displayed a stubborn, almost mystical sense of attachment to the familiar curves and contours of the ancient defensive circuit. Practical considerations—legal, political and, above all, financial—reinforced the citizens' innate aversion to change and ensured that, as far as the city's defences were concerned, renovation, rather than wholesale remodelling, would usually remain the order of the day. So it was that the ancient patterns endured. And if a resident of late medieval Exeter could have been transported forward in time to the days of Charles II, he or she would have found the basic lineaments of the city enceinte—like the methods by which that enceinte was repaired and maintained—virtually unaltered.[11] True, Exeter was now girdled by a ring of unfamiliar earthworks—but these were already crumbling away. True, some of the mural towers had been reduced in height—but these were already being rebuilt.[12] True, a fifth gateway now pierced the walls in the south-west corner of the city circuit, but even this entirely new structure had assumed the name of the ancient 'water-gate' which had stood on the same spot for centuries before, thus illustrating the enceinte's seemingly endless capacity to recreate itself in its former image. Like a living being, it might almost be said, the rich, red circle of stone which protected—and in many ways embodied—early modern Exeter was always changing, decaying and being renewed, but always, enduringly, the same.

SUGGESTIONS FOR FURTHER READING

Town walls have long been—in the words of the eminent castellologist, John Kenyon—'the poor relation as far as studies of medieval military architecture are concerned', and this is even more true when it comes to studies of military architecture during the early modern period. There is no single book devoted to town walls in England under the Tudor and Stuart monarchs, so anyone wishing to obtain a general overview of the subject is obliged to consult a wide range of secondary works. This appendix is designed to facilitate that task by indicating some of the sources which will be found most useful and stimulating by students of the early modern urban enceinte.

A good starting point is provided by Kenyon's own *Castles, Town Defences and Artillery Fortifications in Britain: A Bibliography* (CBA Research Reports, numbers 25 (1978); 53 (1983); and 72 (1990). These three volumes list all the books and articles published on English town defences between 1945 and 1990. Among the best general surveys of English town defences are: A.H. Harvey, *The Castles and Walled Towns of England* (1911, reprinted London, 1925); H.L. Turner, *Town Defences in England and Wales: An Architectural and Documentary Study, 900–1500* (London, 1970); M.W. Barley, 'Town Defences in England and Wales after 1066', in M.W. Barley (ed.), *The Plans and Topography of Medieval Towns in England and Wales* (CBA, Research Report 14, London, 1976), pp. 57–71; C.J. Bond, 'Anglo-Saxon and Medieval Defences', in J. Schofield and R. Leech (eds), *Urban Archaeology in Britain* (CBA Research Report, London, 1987), pp. 92–116; J.R. Kenyon, *Medieval Fortifications* (Leicester, 1990),

Chapter 10 ('Town Defences'), pp. 183–99; and D.M. Palliser, 'Town Defences in Medieval England and Wales', in A. Ayton and J.L. Price (eds), *The Medieval Military Revolution: State, Society and Military Change in Medieval and Early Modern Europe* (London, 1995), pp. 105–20. Many valuable insights will also be found in H.M. Colvin *et al.* (eds), *The History of the King's Works, Volume III, 1485–1660: Part 1* (London, 1975) and H.M. Colvin *et al.* (eds), *The History of the King's Works, Volume IV, 1485–1660: Part 2* (London, 1982).

The process by which English urban fortifications were gradually adapted to meet the demands of the gunpowder age is explored in B.H. O'Neil, *Castles and Cannon: A Study of Early Artillery Fortifications in England* (Oxford, 1960); J.R. Kenyon, 'Early Artillery Fortifications in England and Wales: A Preliminary Survey and Re-appraisal', *AJ*, 138 (1981), pp. 205–40; A.D. Saunders, 'The Cow Tower, Norwich: An East Anglian Bastille?', *MA*, 29 (1985), pp. 109–19; and A.D. Saunders, *Fortress Britain: Artillery Fortification in the British Isles and Ireland* (Liphook, 1989). Surveys of the defences of individual English cities are provided in E. Gooder, C. Woodfield and R.E. Chaplin, 'The Walls of Coventry', *Transactions of the Birmingham Archaeological Society*, 81 (Oxford, 1966), pp. 88–138; T.P. Smith, 'The Medieval Town Defences of King's Lynn', *Journal of the British Archaeological Association*, third series, 33 (1970), pp. 57–88; B.H. O'Neill, 'Southampton Town Wall', in W.F. Grimes (ed.), *Aspects of Archaeology in Britain and Beyond* (London, 1951), pp. 242–57; A.D. Saunders, 'The Defences of Southampton in the Late Middle

Ages', in L.A. Burgess (ed.), *The Southampton Terrier of 1454* (Southampton Record Series, 15, 1976), pp. 20–34; T.P. Cooper, *York: The Story of its Bars, Walls and Castles* (London, 1904); and—most detailed of all—RCHM, *An Inventory of the Historical Monuments in the City of York: Volume II, the Defences* (London, 1972).

For the remodelling of England's ancient town defences during the unprecedented military emergency of the mid-seventeenth century, see W.G. Ross, *Military Engineering during the Great Civil War, 1642–49* (1887, republished London, 1984); P. Harrington, *Archaeology of the English Civil War* (Princes Risborough, 1982); P. and Y. Courtenay, 'A Siege Examined: The Civil War Archaeology of Leicester', *PMA*, 26 (1992), pp. 47–90; M. Stoyle, *Plymouth in the Civil War* (*Devon Archaeology*, 7, 1998); and R. Hutton and W. Reeves, 'Sieges and Fortifications', in J. Kenyon and J. Ohlmeyer (eds), *The Civil Wars: A Military History of England, Scotland and Ireland* (Oxford, 1998).

For some interesting theoretical perspectives on the motives which underlay the construction and maintenance of urban fortifications, see C. Coulson, 'Hierarchism in Conventual Crenellation: An Essay in the Sociology and Metaphysics of Medieval Fortification', *MA*, 26 (1982), pp. 69–90; T.P. Smith, 'Why did Medieval Towns have Walls?', *Current Archaeology*, 8.12 (1985), pp. 376–79; and C. Coulson, 'Battlements and the Bourgeoisie: Municipal Status and the Apparatus of Urban Defence in Late Medieval England', in S. Church and R. Harvey (eds), *Medieval Knighthood V: Papers from the Strawberry Hill Conference, 1994* (Woodbridge, 1995), pp. 119–95. Finally, two recent collections of essays which help to set the English experience within a wider context are J.D. Tracy (ed.), *City Walls: The Urban Enceinte in Global Perspective* (Cambridge, 2000); and G. Perbellini (ed.), *Les Enceintes Urbaines au Moyen Age* (Europa Nostra Bulletin, 53, The Hague, 2000).

PART II

DOCUMENTS RELATING TO THE CITY WALLS

INTRODUCTION

The Exeter Receivers and their Accounts

The second part of this book is made up of detailed accounts of expenditure on the city defences between 1485 and 1660 which have been transcribed from original financial records kept in the city archives. As the previous chapters have made clear, the accounts were originally drawn up by the Exeter 'receivers', and in order to put the documents in context, it may be helpful to provide a short description of the receiver and his duties.

The receiver was one of early modern Exeter's most important civic officials. His position was, in essence, that of city treasurer and during his term of office he was expected to take care of all the city's financial affairs.[1] According to John Hooker—Exeter's Elizabethan chamberlain, and resident constitutional expert—the receiver had two main responsibilities. The first of these was to 'receve and gather upp all the rentes, revenewes and profyttes of the citie belonginge to his chardge'. The second was to pay 'all the fee fermes, annuyties, fees and pencions, as also to paye for all manner of other chardges belonginge to the citie'.[2] This latter duty could often be very onerous. The receiver was expected to pay for these various sums out of his own pocket, in the first instance. Only some time later would he be reimbursed by the city authorities. In certain cases, receivers had to wait for two, three or even four years before the money which they had laid out during their term of office was returned to them. As a result, even quite prosperous citizens were sometimes reluctant to accept the receivership.[3]

The office of receiver was held for one year. Because of the importance of the post, and its pecuniary responsibilities, the individual who held it was usually rich and influential in his own right. Indeed, it was laid down in the city statutes that the receiver could only be chosen from among the ranks of the Council of Twenty-Four.[4]

The manner of his election was simple. Every September the town councillors gathered together in order to select the civic officials for the forthcoming year. Nominations for the receivership were then put forward, each of the Twenty-Four made his choice, and the individual securing the greatest number of votes was duly declared receiver for the following accounting year (which ran from Michaelmas to Michaelmas).

Certain perquisites were attached to the post. The receiver was entitled to a yearly pension of £20, for instance. In addition, he was given 'canon bread' and 'wyne money' at Christmas and Easter: that is to say, eleven loaves and 2 shillings in cash at each feast.[5] Such privileges were little enough to compensate him for the great financial burdens which he would have to sustain, however, and the chief advantage of holding the post was clearly the civic advancement and prestige which it conferred. The receivership was a key position in the city's *cursus honorum*. By successfully carrying out the receiver's duties, an individual proved that he was worthy of the highest civic trust and, in the century between 1540 and 1640, most of those who had served as receiver eventually went on to become mayor.[6]

At the end of his year in office the receiver had to account for all the money he had spent. It was laid down in the city statutes that, upon receiving a formal summons, each receiver should 'come before the audytors apoynted'—usually the mayor, the aldermen and several of the more junior members of the Chamber—and 'before theym . . . make his accompte'.[7] To this final auditing session, which was always held in the Guildhall, the receiver brought the financial accounts which he had kept during the preceding year. Once these had been examined and pronounced satisfactory, the receiver's rough notes were formally engrossed by the town clerk.[8] In their final form, the accounts were written out on a large parchment roll, which consisted of several separate membranes roughly stitched together. The rolls were kept in Latin (except during the years 1599–1601 and 1653–60 when short-lived attempts were made by the city authorities to replace Latin with English).[9] The general presentation of the accounts tended to be the same from year to year. At the head of each roll appeared the receiver's name. Below this was an account of the money which he had collected during his year of office. The most important source of income was always derived from the city's rents. Until the beginning of the sixteenth century, the town clerk noted down the properties from which rent had been collected in no particular order, but after 1499–1500 the relevant sums were recorded parish by parish.[10] Below the list of rents came a note of any other sums of money which had been collected by the receiver in the form of fines, customs, fees and so forth. Below this again came a section entitled *Expensa Necessaria*, or necessary expenses. Under this heading were noted the precise sums which the receiver had laid out about the city's business during his year in office, and it is from this section of the accounts that most of the material reproduced in the following pages has been derived.

Towards the end of the fifteenth century, an important change took place in the format of the accounts. Before this time, the amounts spent by each receiver had been officially recorded only once: on the parchment roll. From 1497 onwards, references began to appear in the rolls to a second record of financial outlay—'the book of expenditure'—and, although the earliest of these 'books' have been lost, an example survives for 1505–6.[11] In that year, the sums of money collected and expended by the receiver were written down, in English, in a small paper booklet. At the end of the financial year, the booklet—which was made up of thin quires of writing paper—was sewn up inside the parchment roll and carefully stored away. Unfortunately, only one further book is extant for the next half century, but it is certain that they continued to be kept, for the rolls make frequent references to sums of money recorded in 'the book of expenditure', 'the book of account' or simply 'the paper boke'.[12] After 1556–57 the survival rate of the books improves markedly and—as the transcriptions make clear—they become far more informative than the rolls. Although the latter continued to be kept throughout the period covered by this volume, entries became increasingly brusque. Often, only the total amount spent on each particular project was noted down in the roll. For a detailed breakdown of expenditure, it was now necessary to consult the accompanying paper book.

From 1539 onwards, the rolls and individual books were supplemented by 'books of summary': rough work-books which recorded the total sums spent by the receivers year by year. [13] Entries in these volumes are usually very brief and, from the historian's point of view, uninformative. They add little to our knowledge of work on the fortifications and only a handful of extracts from the books of summary are included in the transcriptions. Considerably more useful are 'the receivers' vouchers': the original paper bills—or 'notes' as they were more usually termed—which were presented by the city's workmen to the receiver for payment. Examples of these survive from 1549 onwards, but such bills were not an innovation of the Tudor period.[14] As early as 1372–73, the then receiver had noted that a series of repairs at East Gate had cost over £1 'as appears by an itemized bill made by William Foterynghay' and similar references to bills now lost were made in 1393–34 and 1480–81.[15] (The fact that the earliest surviving bills date to the mid-sixteenth century perhaps reflects the fact that a combination of growing literacy among the city artisans and increasing availability of cheap paper had caused the number of bills submitted to swell.) Few relevant vouchers are extant for the Tudor period, but survival rates for the early Stuart period are a good deal better and the tradesmen's bills occasionally provide helpful amplification of the brief statements of expenditure which appear in the receivers' rolls and books. Once again, those vouchers which throw additional light on work on the fortifications have been transcribed below. By the mid-seventeenth century, if not before, some receivers were clearly demanding a 'note' for each and every payment which they made, and then filing the bills away for subsequent reference. Ralph Herman, receiver in 1648–49, amassed over 100 such notes, to each of which he allocated a number, and to each of which he later made specific reference in his 'book of account'.[16] Almost certainly, the bills which the receivers collected during their year of office were produced by them at the final audit as evidence of the various jobs on which money had been spent.

Once each receiver's account had been approved and written up, the roll, the book and sometimes the accompanying vouchers as well were 'carried into the Councell Chamber' in the Guildhall: a room which served, in the words of an early Stuart witness, as 'the common treasurie of the . . . cittie for such things'. Here they were 'putt amongst other such like accompts formerly made' and here they were left: 'preserved and kept' in case they should be needed again, and accumulating a thicker patina of dust and grime with each passing year.[17] The historical importance of the documents first began to be appreciated during the early nineteenth century,[18] but it was not until the 1860s that the City Council engaged an archivist, S.A. Moore, to sort through and catalogue the huge mass of ancient papers which lay piled, hugger-mugger, in the Council Chamber and elsewhere.[19] Under Moore's guidance, the records were removed from the presses, cupboards, little attic rooms and forgotten loft spaces in which they had slept out the intervening centuries and transferred to more suitable—but still very cramped and ramshackle—quarters in the 'record room' which the Council had ordered to be built in the upper storey of the 'Back Grate' (or temporary lock-up) behind the Guildhall in 1858.[20] Fears soon began to be expressed that this room was vulnerable to fire and in 1931 the civic archives were transferred to a 'fire-proof muniment room at the new City Library'.[21] From there, forty-three years later, the documents were moved once again, this time to the Devon Record Office in Castle Street, Exeter, just a few hundred yards from their original home. Once the documents had been established in this purpose-built repository, the wealth of information which they contain about almost every aspect of life in medieval and early modern Exeter could at last begin to be studied by scholars in depth, and it was at Castle Street between 1985 and 2002 that the transcriptions which appear in the present volume were made.

Editorial Conventions

(i) INCLUSIONS AND EXCLUSIONS

The text which appears as document 1 below includes full transcriptions of all references to expenditure on the city enceinte and the civic ordnance which occur in the Exeter receivers' accounts for the years 1485–1660. Accounts of expenditure on the prison at South Gate have not usually been transcribed but, for every year in which monies are known to have been laid out on this task, the total sum is given. Accounts of expenditure on paving the roadways beneath the gates, on organizing musters, on procuring gunpowder (which was used for a variety of purposes in early modern Exeter), on purchasing and repairing small arms and on supplying the porters with their winter coats have been excluded, on the grounds that such items are of only peripheral relevance to the book's main theme. The total sums of expenditure which appear in square brackets beneath the entries for each year do *not* include monies laid out on repairs to South Gate Prison. Very occasionally, receivers lumped expenditure on the walls and gates together with expenditure on other, unrelated items, making it impossible to calculate the precise sum of money which had been laid out on the enceinte during their year of office. In such cases, *two* total figures are given for expenditure over the year as a whole: one which includes the figure recorded for 'combined' expenses, and one which excludes it. The true amount laid out on the city defences during any such year will obviously fall somewhere between the two extremes.

(ii) EDITING AND TRANSLATING PRACTICE

The Exeter receivers' accounts are full of contractions and abbreviations; these have been expanded wherever possible. All roman numerals have been converted to arabic ones. All Christian names have been modernized, but all surnames have been left as they are spelt in the original. All passages of continuous Latin prose have been translated into English. Within such passages, words which are not conclusively in Latin are set in quotation marks. In cases where the interpretation of Latin words is in doubt, these are given in round brackets after the proposed translation. Foreign words and phrases which appear within passages of continuous English prose have been italicized. As much common form as possible has been omitted (for example, expressions such as 'Item, I (paid for)' which occur at the beginning of many entries). Words which have evidently been omitted by mistake appear within square brackets as do all other editorial interpolations. Uncertain transcriptions are followed by a question mark enclosed within square brackets. Illegible or missing words are indicated thus: '. . .'. The minimum of punctuation has been added. On the histograms, expenditure is shown to the nearest pound. Shillings and pence are denoted by the letters 's' and 'd'. The glossary on page 202 provides definitions of some of the more unfamiliar technical, archaic and dialect terms which appear in the documents.

EXTRACTS FROM THE CITY RECEIVERS' ACCOUNTS 1485–1660

1484–85

Receiver John Sterre.

Receiver's Roll

[*m.3*] Fees paid:
    To the 4 gatekeepers for their pensions: 12*s.*

Necessary expenses:
[*m.4*] Paid John Lake for 3 'plankys' bought to repair East
    Gate Bridge, with making of the same: 20*d.*
    Paid John Stevyn for repairing a tower in the City Wall
    outside East Gate at task: 40*s*.
    Paid for locks bought from William Osett for 'le Bolt' of
    each gate at 10*d* each: 3*s* 4*d.*
    Paid John Chafe for a 'bolte' for North Gate: 8*d.*
    For trestles, laths [?] and bars for the City Gates: 4*s* 8*d*.
    For making 4 'Gunstonys': 8*s.*
    For making a post for 'le Barris' at West Gate: 1*s* 5*d.*
    [Total: £2 19*s* 9*d.*]

[Total expenditure in this year: £3 11*s* 9*d.*]

1485–86

[The roll for this year is missing.]

1486–87

Receiver Thomas Pound.

Receiver's Roll

[*m.3*] Fees and pensions:
    To the 4 gatekeepers for their pensions: 12*s.*

[*m.4*] Necessary expenses:
    For repair of a lock at East Gate in a certain cistern
    there: 2*d.*
    For 1,000 slates with carriage: 2*s* 11*d.*
    For 1 'ewes bord': 2*d.*
    For 1 'stode' for the same: 2*d.*
    For 100 laths: 4*d.*
    For 500 'lathnayle[s]': 7*d.*

For sand for the same: 6*d.*
For slate-pins: 12*d.*
To William Dobyn and his servant for roofing there:
6*s* 8*d.*
For repair of a lock in South Gate: 12*d.*
[Total: 13*s* 6*d.*]

[Total expenditure in this year: £1 5*s* 6*d.*]

1487–88

Receiver John Hoker.

Receiver's Roll

[*m.2*] Fees and pensions:
    To the 4 gatekeepers for their pensions: 12*s* [crossed
    out].

[*m.3*] Necessary expenses:

[*m.3v.*] For repairing the City Wall (*parietis Civitatis*) at East
    Gate:
    Firstly for 1 sack of lime: 4*d*;
    For 2 loads of sand: 2*d*;
    For carriage of 8 loads of stones: 2*d*;
    For 2 masons for 1 day: 10*d*;
    For 3 masons for another day: 15*d.*
    [Total: 2*s* 9*d.*]
    For repairs in the tower over East Gate:
    Firstly 'for castyng of old lede': 18*s* 1*d*;
    For 4 *cwt* and 3 quarters of new lead at 6*s* the *cwt* for the
    same: 26*s* 8*d*;
    For slates, laths and sand: 2*s*;
    For boards bought from Mr Calwodeley: 2*s*;
    For 5 *lbs* of solder: 15*d*;
    For workmen's wages on the same: 2*s.*
    [Total: £2 12*s* 0*d.*]

[Total expenditure in this year: £3 6*s* 9*d.*]

1488–89

Receiver George Chepman.

Receiver's Roll

[*m.2*] Fees and pensions:
    To the 4 gatekeepers for their pensions: 12*s*.

Necessary expenses:
    In repairs to the bridge in East Gate:
        For 2 pieces of timber bought from William Whitelok: 12*s*;
        To 2 carpenters for 9 days at the same at 5*d* each a day: 7*s* 6*d*;
        To 3 carpenters for 6 days at the same at 5*d* each a day: 7*s* 6*d*;
        To 2 carpenters for 7 days at 5*d* each a day: 5*s* 10*d*;
        For carriage of the said timber: 7*d*;
        For 39 *lbs* 'of Spykys' at 2*d* the *lb* for the same: 6*s* 6*d*.
    For repair of the bridge of [South] Gate: 5*d*.
    [Total: £2 0*s* 4*d*.]

[Total expenditure in this year: £2 12*s* 4*d*.]

1489–90

Receiver Mathew Alyngton.

Receiver's Roll

[*m.2*] Fees and pensions:
    To the 4 gatekeepers for their pensions: 12*s*.

Necessary expenses:
    For repair of South Gate: 4*d*.

[*m.3*] To Robert Newton 'for the makyng of West yeate': 60*s*;
    For carriage of the said gate: 8*d*;
    To Robert Russell for 2 'brasis' weighing 34 *lbs* for the same: 11*s*;
    To 4 masons for 8 days at the same: 13*s* 3*d*;
    To Robert Saller for 1 day breaking down the wall of the same: 4*d*;
    For 17 seams of 'Pewmer' [Peamore] stones: 2*s* 11*d*;
    To John Michell for carriage of 4 cartloads of stones from Exe Bridge to the said gate: 20*d*;
    For 6½ quarters of lime: 4*s* 4*d*;
    For 14 seams of sand: 8*d*;
    For 100 quarters and 17 *lbs* of lead for the same: 9*s* 11*d*;
    For firewood for the same: 3½*d*;
    To John Whiteway for cleaning the said gate: 5*d*;
    To John Doke for carriage of 2 dozen of 'Robull' and stones: 12*d*;
    For ironwork for that gate, as appears by a bill: 26*s* 3*d*.
    [Total: £6 13*s* 0½*d*.]

[Total expenditure in this year: £7 5*s* 0½*d*.]

1490–91

Receiver John Calwodely.

Receiver's Roll

[*m.3*] [Fees and pensions:]
    To the 4 gatekeepers for their pensions: 12*s*.

[Necessary expenses:]
    For 1 piece of timber for making a 'rayle' outside South Gate: 6*d*;
    For making the same: 4*d*.
    For repair of West Gate: 12*d*.
    [Total: 1*s* 10*d*.]

[Total expenditure in this year: 13*s* 10*d*.]

1491–92

Receiver Nicholas Hamelyn.

Receiver's Roll

[*m.2*] Fees paid:
    To the 4 gatekeepers for their pensions: 12*s*.

[Total expenditure in this year: 12*s*.]

1492–93

Receiver Walter Champenez.

Receiver's Roll

[*m.2*] Fees paid:
    To the 4 gatekeepers for their pensions: 12*s*.

Necessary expenses:
    For repair of the locks of West Gate and South Gate: 10*d*.
    For 50 stones to repair the wall at 'Snayltore': 4*s* 6*d*.
    For 16 seams of 'Woneforde' stones to repair the wall next to 'Snayltoure': 18*d*;
    For 14 seams of sand for the same: 10*d*;
    For 5½ quarters of lime: 3*s* 8*d*;
    For 'Scafold tymber', 1 'Coffell' and 'Ropis' for the same: 6*d*;
    To 1 mason for 6 days at 6*d* a day: 3*s*;
    To another mason for 6 days: 2*s* 9*d*;
    To 1 boy for 6 days: 18*d*.
    For sand to repair the City Wall: 12*d*.
    [Total: £1 0*s* 1*d*.]

[Total expenditure in this year: £1 12*s* 1*d*.]

1493–94

Receiver Richard Unde.

Receiver's Roll

[*m.5*] Fees paid:
    To the 4 gatekeepers for their pensions: 12*s*.

[*m.8*] [Expenses:]
    For repair of a gutter at (*apud*) West Gate: 4*d*.

[Total expenditure in this year: 12*s* 4*d*.]

1494–95

Receiver John Slugge.

Receiver's Roll

[*m.2*] Fees paid:
　3*s* to each of the 4 gatekeepers for their pensions: 12*s*.

[*m.3*] Expenses this year:
　For 2 'plankes' bought and used about (*circa*) the bridge of the . . . South Gate: 8*d*;
　For 3 dozen of 'Gravyll' for the same at 5*d* the dozen: 15*d*.
　For repair of the lock of South Gate on 2 occasions this year: 13*d*.
　[Total: 3*s*.]

[Total expenditure in this year: 15*s*.]

1495–96

Receiver John Bonyfant.

Receiver's Roll

[*m.2*] Fees paid:
　3*s* to each of the 4 gatekeepers of the city for his pension: 12*s*.

[*m.3*] Necessary expenses:
　For expenses on bread, wine and other pleasant things [?; possibly *placenta* meaning 'cakes'] for the mayor and his fellows in John Burd's house at the inspection of the City Walls, as the custom is: 18*d*.
　For 2 iron hooks to hang chains from outside West Gate: 4*d*.
　For 3 'plankys' bought, *videlicet* 2 for South Gate and [1] used for the new conduit at Carfax (*in quadrivio*): 8*d*.
　[Total: *c*.2*s* 6*d*.]

Expenses on repairing East Gate and a 'vaulte' made there:
　For repairs to the foundation of East Gate and for a 'vault' there this year, *videlicet* stones, lime, sand and other materials necessary for that kind of work, with wages of the workmen hired at that work, as appears by a bill: £14 5*s* 7*d*.

Expenses on the City Wall:
　For renovation and rebuilding of a section (*parcella*) of the City Wall on the north side of the city, for stones, lime, sand and other materials necessary for that kind of work, with wages of workmen hired at that work, as appears by a bill: £14 6*s* 8½*d*.

[Total expenditure in this year: £29 6*s* 9½*d*.]

1496–97

Receiver Walter Yorke.

Receiver's Roll

[*m.2*] Fees paid:
　3*s* to each of the 4 gatekeepers of the city for his pension: 12*s*.

[*m.3*] Expenses on the King's commission:
　Paid 2 men for guarding (*ad Custodiendum*) East Gate for

1 day, by order of the commissioners: 8*d*;
　To men hired for watching (*ad vigilandum*) the city: 16*d*.

[*m.3v.*] Necessary expenses:
　For a piece of timber bought for South Gate: 14*d*;
　For 7 *lbs* of iron nails bought for that gate at 2*d* a *lb*: 14*d*;
　For 2 carpenters hired for 1 day at that work: 11*d*;
　For 1 'ovise borde' and nails bought for that work: 2*d*.
　For a new lock bought for 'le Wyket de Suth yate': 4*d*.
　For making the bridge at South Gate against [i.e. in advance of] the coming of the lord the King: 15*d*;
　And for the bridge at East Gate at that time: 12*d*.
　For carriage of timber to South Gate to make the bridge there: 10*d*;
　For 2 men to make that bridge: 14*d*;
　For 2 men hired there to throw 'robell': 10*d*.
　For carriage of timber to East Gate to make the bridge there: 2*s* 4*d*;
　For carriage of 'Robyll' within (*infra*) that gate: 3*s* 4*d*;
　Paid 2 carpenters hired at 'Rokysdon' [Rollestone] and Polsloe for 6 days: 5*s*;
　For 2 men to saw that timber for 2 days: 2*s*;
　For 2 dozen gravel placed on that bridge: 12*d*;
　For 1 carpenter hired for 4 days: 20*d*;
　To 2 carpenters for 7 days: 4*s*.

[*m.2v.*] For repairs to the house of master Henry Grymston this year, as appears by oath of the accountant: 21*s*.
　[Total: £2 11*s* 2*d*.]

[Total expenditure in this year: £3 3*s* 2*d*.]

1497–98

Receiver John Danaster.

Receiver's Roll

[*m.3*] Fees this year:
　3*s* to each of the 4 gatekeepers of the city for his pension: 12*s*.

[*m.4*] Expenses on remaking North Gate:
　To John Symon for 7 cartloads of timber for the said gate at 2*s* 8*d* a load: 18*s* 8*d*;
　For carriage of 7 loads of timber from 'Hethwode' Wood to North Gate at 2*s* 2*d* a load: 15*s* 2*d*;
　For carriage of 1 cartload of timber from 'Polslo' to North Gate: 14*d*;
　[? For carriage of] 2 seams of timber from 'Polslo' to the foresaid gate at 2½*d* a load: 5*d*;
　For 14 seams of timber for that gate at ½*d* each: 7*d*;
　To Simon Fayreman for 1 piece of timber: 18*d*;
　To Edward Rawe and Edward Taillour for carriage of 14 seams of timber for the foresaid gate at 2½*d* each: 2*s* 11*d*;
　To John Honyland, carpenter, and other workmen with him at 5*d* a day for diverse days making the said gate, as appears in the book of expenditure: £6 4*s* 2½*d*;
　For 2 men hired for 6 days to carry timber and do other work at 5*d* each a day: 5*s*;
　For 'Spekys', 'twysts', nails and other ironwork for the same gate, made by John Sengell, as by the receiver's oath: £4 9*s* 8*d*;

For 100 seams of stones bought for the said gate: 16s 5d;

For stones bought on another occasion to make 'le guttour' there: 4s 4d;

To John Maior, 'mason', and other workmen with him for diverse days on 'le guttour' at (ad) North Gate, as appears by a certain book thereof shown and examined: 29s 4d;

For 17 sacks of lime bought at 4d each: 5s 8d;

For laths used there: 7½d;

For 'lathnaylys': 7½d;

For 2 'ovysbordys': 3d;

For 3 workmen hired for 2 days to roof 'le pantys' there: 2s 4d;

For slates bought: 6s;

For pins called 'helyng pynnys': 3d;

To John Honyland for the said 'pantes': 6s;

For pitch, resin and tallow for the posts set outside the said gate: 8d;

For oil used when the gate was raised: 8d;

To 1 man called 'le quarryman' for 3 quarters of stones: 12s 2d;

Total: £17 4s 7½d.

Expenses on various houses and places:

[m.4] For 1 lock and 2 'hokes' for the door of 'Northyeate' prison: 8d;

To 'Masyns' to repair the said prison: 6d;

For stones, lime and sand for the same: 8d.

[m.4v.] Paid for a cart to carry 'lez Gonnez' as far as Topsham: 16d.

Paid 'a le barle berers' for carrying of 'lez gonnez' and timber: 16d.

[Total: 4s 6d.]

21s defected rent of the tenement lately of Henry Grymston, clerk, over East Gate, because it is allocated to him for diverse expenses and repairs undertaken by him to damage caused by the assault of Perkin Wosbek and others who rebelled against the King.

[Total expenditure in this year: £18 1s 1½d.]

1498–99

Receiver John Hull.

Receiver's Roll

[m.2v.] [Fees:]

3s to each of the 4 gatekeepers of the city for their pensions: 12s.

[m.1v.] Expenses on the City Walls outside West Gate:

To various workmen for lifting up stones fallen from the wall into the mill-leat and for breaking them up for the foundations (*fundamentum*) of the wall, so that men may cross there with their horses and loads, as is shown by the book of expenditure and the receiver's oath, together with 100 quarters of lime bought for the same work but not yet used: £4 14s;

Sum: £4 14s.

[Total expenditure in this year: £5 6s 0d.]

1499–1500

Receiver John Symon.

Receiver's Roll

[m.3v.] Fees:

3s to each of the 4 gatekeepers of the city for their pensions: 12s.

Necessary expenses:

To workmen hired to clean 'le gutter' at (*apud*) North Gate: 20d.

To workmen hired to repair the houses and chapel over (*ultra*) East Gate: 3s 8d.

[m.2v.] For monies given to Thomas Andrewe, receiver of the city, to help towards the repairs to the City Walls: £20.

Allocated to John Hull, late receiver, 27 quarters of lime, parcel of 100 quarters delivered to Thomas Andrew for re-edifying the City Walls aforesaid, which amounts to: 18s.

It is noted that the foresaid Thomas Andrew is charged in his account for the foresaid 27 quarters of lime. [Total: £21 3s 4d.]

[Total expenditure in this year: £21 15s 4d.]

1500–01

Receiver Thomas Andrewe.

Receiver's Roll

[m.3] Fees of the mayor and other officers:

3s to each of the 4 gatekeepers of the city for their pensions: 12s.

[m.3v.] Expenses on the City Walls:

To John Drake, 'mason', and other workmen for rebuilding the City Wall on the south side of West Gate and for stones, lime and other necessary materials, as appears by the book of expenditure, by agreement [i.e. contract] made between the mayor and bailiffs and the said John Drake: £31;

To Thomas Richeford and 2 other workmen with him hired for 4 days at 4d each a day to clean and prepare the foundation of the said wall: 4s;

To John Doke for taking away and carriage of 39 'dosyn' of 'Robyll' from the said wall at 2d a dozen: 6s 6d;

To the said John and other workmen there on diverse occasions: 20d;

To William Baker for rent of a house for the said John Drake and for making their food and storing materials during the building work on the wall: 4s;

For wine when the agreement was made: 4d;

Total: £31 16s 6d.

[Total expenditure in this year: £32 8s 6d.]

1501–2

Receiver William Crugge.

Receiver's Roll

[*m.4*] Fees of the mayor and other officers of the city:
3*s* to each of the 4 gatekeepers of the city for their pensions: 12*s*.

[*m.5*] Repair of the Great Conduit and West Gate:
For cleaning and renovation of the said conduit and the King's arms over West Gate, on the receiver's oath: 40*s*.

[Total expenditure in this year: £2 12*s* 0*d*.]

1502–3

[The roll for this year is missing.]

1503–4

Receiver John Guscote.

Receiver's Roll

[*m.3*] Fees of the mayor and other officers of the city:
3*s* to each of the 4 gatekeepers of the city for their pensions: 12*s*.

[*m.4v.*] Expenses at (*apud*) West Gate:
To John Lowton, hired for 3 days repairing 'le vawte' there: 18*d*;
To his servant hired for the same time: 15*d*.
[Total: 2*s* 9*d*.]

[*m.3v.*] Expenses on East Gate and next to the same and on Richard Underhay's house:
For stones called 'Tylestonys' used there: 14*d*;
To 1 workman for priming the same and for repairing a chimney there: 6*d*;
To Thomas Coyle for 400 slates used there: 15*d*;
To a slater hired for roofing a 'pentys' there: 8*d*;
For laths used there: 4*d*;
For nails and 'pynnys' bought for that work: 6*d*;
To 1 carpenter for 2 days there: 10*d*;
For 2 seams of stones bought: 4*d*;
For sand used there: 2*d*;
For lime used there: 8*d*;
For straw bought to repair Richard Underhay's house: 16*d*;
For 'Sparrys' used there: 2*d*;
For 'le Thacchers laber': 5*d*;
To his servant: 5*d*;
For 3 boards to make a door there: 12*d*;
[Total:] 9*s* 9*d*.

[*m.2v.*] Expenses on 2 leaves [of a folding-door; (*valvis*)] of East Gate:
To William Crugge for 1 piece of great timber (*magni maeremii*) bought for the same: 17*s*;
To workmen hired for sawing the same: 4*s* 8*d*;
To the said workmen for carriage of the same, once sawn: 2*s* 6*d*;
For carriage of 1 piece of timber to the bridge called 'le Wyenbrigge': 1½*d*;
For carriage thence of 1 other piece of timber to East Gate: 1*d*;
[Total:] 24*s* 4½*d*.

[*m.1v.*] [Necessary expenses:]
For wages of the workmen labouring at South Gate: 12½*d*.

[Total expenditure in this year: £2 9*s* 11*d*.]

1504–5

Receiver John Gomby.

Receiver's Roll

[*m.3*] Fees of the mayor and other officers:
3*s* to each of the 4 gatekeepers of the city for their pensions: 12*s*.

[*m.4*] Expenses of the Court and for the King's Subsidy:
For boards, nails and workmen's wages for the repair of East Gate: 6*d*.

[Total expenditure in this year: 12*s* 6*d*.]

1505–6

Receiver Robert Bonyfant.

Receiver's Roll

[*m.4*] Fees of the mayor and other officers:
3*s* to each of the 4 gatekeepers of the city for their pensions: 12*s*.

Receiver's Book

[*f.3*] 'Costes doon upon the house over Est yate & Yeldhall [i.e. the Guildhall] & Trobrigge is house
. . . 16 November paid to 2 Carpenters for makyng of a newe stayre at the house that my lady Ralegh dwellid in 2 dayes': 22*d*;
'[For] 6 Elmen Bordes to the same': 2*s* 1*d*;
'[For] naylls to the same': 6*d*;
'[For] 2 peces of Tymber for lyers for the same': 5*d*;
'[For] gutters of ledde to Trobrigge is house *ponderantia* (weighing) 68 *lbs* and for 4 pips over Est yate *ponderantia* 225 *lbs* and for 8 *lbs* of sawder to the same': 18*s*;
'The 27 day of January paid to helyers for 4 dayes upon the Yeld hall Wyse is house and over Est yate': 5*s*;
'For there servaunt': 12*d*;
'For a pek & half of pynnys': 4½*d*;
'For 9 semys of sond': 6*d*;
'For 3 sakkes of lyme': 13½*d*;
'For 600 of Stonys': 2*d*;
'To 2 helyers for Speke is house over Est yate for 4 dayes': 3*s* 4*d*;
'For 3 sakkes of lyme to the same': 12*d*;
'For 6 semys of sond': 4*d*;
'For a pek of helyng pynnys': 3*d*;
'For 500 of helyng stonys': 17*d*;
'For 5 Crestes': 6*d*;
'For 3 *lbs* of sauder for the gutters': 9*d*;
'For the plummer is labour': 7½*d*;
[Total: £1 19*s* 2½*d*.]

'Costes doon upon the housez at West yate
   . . . for 28 semys of stone': 4*s* 8*d*;
   'For 2 quarters of lyme and a half to the same': 20*d*;
   'For a dosen of sond': 9*d*;
   'To 2 masons for 4 dayes': 5*s* 4*d*;
   'For 200 of helyng stonys': 7*d*;
   'For 2 helyers for a day': 10*d*;
   'For 2 Crestes for the same': 3*d*;
   [Total: 14*s* 1*d*.]

'Costes doon upon the grate at Westyate & pavyng of the
same
   . . . for makyng of the grate *ponderantia* 51½ *lbs* at 1½*d*
   and settyng of the same': 6*s* 9*d*;
   'For 2 peces of Tymber for the same werk': 2*s* 4*d*;
   'For 4 sackes of lyme to the same': 16*d*;
   'For fifty of Peambere [i.e. Peamore] Stone to the same
   worke': 8*s* 5*d*;
   'For 6 Crampettes made to the same yate *ponderantia* 20
   lbs le lb 1½*d*': 2*s* 6*d*;
   'For pavyng of 34 yerdes': 2*s* 6*d*;
   'For 3 dosyn and 2 semys of stone and gravell to the
   same': 19*d*;
   Sum: 25*s* 5*d*.

[*f.*4] 'Costes doon uppon Southyate
   . . . for 5 plankes for planchyng of the Southyate': 5*s*;
   'For 2 dosen of Gravell': 18*d*;
   'To 2 men for layng of the plankes': 10*d*;
   'For 16 semys of stonys': 3*s*;
   'To the masons for there labor': 15*d*;
   'For 2 sakkes of lyme': 8*d*;
   Sum: 12*s* 3*d*.

[*f.*6] 'Diverse extraordinarie charges & expens . . .

[*f.*7] . . . for 2 lokks & 2 keys at Westgate': 10*d*.

[Total expenditure in this year: £5 3*s* 9½*d*.]

1506–7

Receiver John Lympyn.

Receiver's Roll

[*m.*3] Fees of the mayor and other officers:
   3*s* to each of the 4 gatekeepers of the city for his
   pension: 12*s*.

[*m.*2*v.*] Allocated for the repair of John Speke's tenement
   over East Gate: 2*s* 8*d*.

[Total expenditure in this year: 14*s* 8*d*.]

1507–8

Receiver John Bucknam.

Receiver's Roll

[*m.*3] Fees of the mayor and other officers:
   3*s* to each of the 4 gatekeepers of the city for his
   pension: 12*s*.

[This roll is incomplete; there are no necessary expenses
recorded.]

1508–9

Receiver William Wylford.

Receiver's Roll

[*m.*3] Fees of the mayor and other officers:
   3*s* to each of the 4 gatekeepers of the city for his
   pension: 12*s*.

[This roll is incomplete; there are no necessary expenses
recorded.]

1509–10

Receiver John Bradmore.

Receiver's Roll

[*m.*4] Fees of the mayor and other officers:
   3*s* to each of the 4 gatekeepers of the city: 12*s*.

[This roll is incomplete; there are no necessary expenses
recorded.]

1510–11

Receiver John Orenge.

Receiver's Roll

[*m.*4] Fees of the mayor and other officers:
   3*s* to each of the 4 gatekeepers of the city: 12*s*.

[This roll is incomplete; there are no necessary expenses
recorded.]

1511–12

Receiver Robert Broun.

Receiver's Roll

[*m.*4] Fees of the mayor and other officers:
   3*s* to each of the 4 gatekeepers of the city: 12*s*.

[This roll is incomplete; there are no necessary expenses
recorded.]

1512–13

Receiver John More.

Receiver's Roll

[*m.*3] Fees of the mayor and other officers:
   3*s* to each gatekeeper of the city: 12*s*.

[This roll is incomplete; there are no necessary expenses
recorded.]

1513–14

Receiver John Wynter.

Receiver's Roll

[*m.5*] Fees of the mayor and other officers:
3*s* to each of the gatekeepers of the city: 12*s*.

[*m.5v.*] Expenses . . .:
In monies paid both for diverse repairs to the mills in the manor of Duryard, on (*super*) the East Gate of the city, on diverse other tenements belonging to the city, and also for diverse other payments this year as appears by the book of expenditure annexed to this account [lost]: £75 19*s* 10*d*.

1514–15

Receiver Thomas Hunte.

Receiver's Roll

[*m.4*] Fees of the mayor and other officers:
3*s* to each gatekeeper of the city: 12*s*.

[*m.4v.*] Expenses . . .:
In monies paid both for diverse repairs to the mills in the manor of Duryard, on (*super*) the East Gate of the city, on diverse other tenements belonging to the city, and also for diverse other payments this year as appears by the book of expenditure annexed to this account [lost]: £61 11*s* 3*d*.

1515–16

Receiver Geoffrey Lewys.

Receiver's Roll

[*m.4*] Fees of the mayor and other officers:
3*s* to each gatekeeper of the city: 12*s*.

[*m.4v.*] Expenses . . .:
Expenses this year, as shown in the book of expenditure [lost; no mention of walls or gates]: £24 19*s* 11½*d*.

1516–17

Receiver John Noseworthi.

Receiver's Roll

[*m.3*] Fees of the mayor and other officers:
3*s* to each gatekeeper of the city: 12*s*.

[*m.4*] Expenses . . .:
For diverse expenses this year, as shown in the book of expenditure [lost; no mention of walls or gates]: £42 3*s* 2½*d*.

1517–18

[The roll for this year is missing.]

1518–19

Receiver Reginald Russell.

Receiver's Roll

[*m.5*] Fees of the mayor and other officers:
3*s* to each gatekeeper of the city: 12*s*.

[*m.5v.*] Expenses . . .:
For diverse expenses this year, as shown in the book of expenditure [lost; no mention of walls or gates]: £25 5*s* 10*d*.

1519–20

Receiver William Shapton.

Receiver's Roll

[*m.3v.*] Fees of the mayor and other officers:
3*s* to each gatekeeper of the city: 12*s*.

[*m.2v.*] Expenses . . .:
For diverse expenses this year as is clearly shown in the book of expenditure [lost; no mention of walls or gates]: [no sum total given.]

1520–21

Receiver Richard Russell.

Receiver's Roll

[*m.3v.*] Fees of the mayor and other officers:
3*s* to each gatekeeper of the city: 12*s*.

[*m.2v.*] Expenses . . .:
For diverse expenses this year as shown in the book of expenditure [lost; no mention of walls or gates]: £32 9*s* 7*d*.

1521–22

Receiver William Benett.

Receiver's Roll

[*m.4*] Fees of the mayor and other officers:
3*s* to each gatekeeper of the city: 12*s*.

[*m.4v.*] Expenses . . .:
For diverse expenses this year as shown in the book of expenditure [lost; no mention of walls or gates]: £26 17*s* 9½*d*.

1522–23

[The roll for this year is missing.]

1523–24

Receiver John Brycknall.

Receiver's Roll

[*m.4v.*] Fees of the mayor and other officers:
3*s* to each gatekeeper of the city: 12*s*.

[*m. 3v.*] Expenses . . .:
> For diverse expenses this year as shown in the book of expenditure [lost; no mention of walls or gates]: £30 6s 2d.

Receiver's Book [DRO, Box 214, Book 1]

[*f.4*] 'Item y paid morre to Rychard Smythe mason for myndyng of a wall at Synt John ys scherche yerde & for makyng of a brege of stone with awte Este yeatt under the grette there for all maner [of] stoff yt ys lyme & stonys & sonde a grette': 8s.

[Total expenditure in this year: £1.]

1524–25

Receiver Henry Hamlyng.

Receiver's Roll

[*m.4v.*] Fees of the mayor and other officers:
> 3s to each gatekeeper of the city: 12s.

Diverse expenses . . .:
[*m.2v.*] To a slater and his servant for 4 days on 4 tenements at (*apud*) West Gate: 3s 4d;
> For 1 quarter of lime for those tenements: 7d;
> For 200 laths: 8d;
> For 600 'lath naylys': 3d;
> For 600 slates: 2s;
> For 2 'Crestes': 3d;
> For 2 seams of sand: 1½d.
> For a new key for 'the vawte' at East Gate: 3d.
> [Total: 7s 5½d.]

[Total expenditure in this year: 19s 5½d.]

1525–26

Receiver Robert Buller.

Receiver's Roll

[*m.4v.*] Fees of the mayor and other officers:
> 3s to each gatekeeper of the city: 12s.

[*m.3v.*] [Necessary expenses:]
> For 1 pair of 'Gemys' and keys and for setting the same over (*ultra*) East Gate: 4d.
> For boards (*mensis*) called 'planckys' for the bridge at (*apud*) South Gate and for 1 man to set them: 12d.
> For solder for 3 gutters at (*apud*) West Gate: 7½d.
> Paid for 'Sawder' to amend a gutter over (*ultra*) West Gate and for the Great Conduit: 18d.

[*m.2v.*] To carriers for their labour about a tree outside East Gate: 5d.
> [Total: 3s 10½d.]

[Total expenditure in this year: 15s 10½d.]

1526–27

Receiver Robert Hoker.

Receiver's Roll

[*m.5v.*] Fees of the mayor and other officers:
> 3s to each gatekeeper of the city: 12s.

Expenses and payments . . .:
[*m.4v.*] [17 November] To John Jonys, 'helyer', and his servants for 1 day slating over (*ultra*) East Gate: 11d;
> 'A pecke de playster': 2d;
> For 2 small sacks (*saculis*) of lime: 8d;
> To a plumber for ½ day repairing the lead over the said gate: 4d;
> To the said plumber for 10 *lbs* of solder: 2s 6d;
> To Robert Dolle for 1 day's labour there: 4d.
> For gravel to cover the timber in South Gate: 4d.
> [12 April] To John Page, another man and 3 horses for 2 days carrying 'lee Robyll' to the City Wall by (*per*) 'Freren hay': 2s;
> To the said John for 1 day casting the said 'Robella' about (*erga*) the said wall: 5d.

[*m.2v.*] [3 August] To William Toloffe, 'smyth', for making 4 keys and repairing locks of the house over (*ultra*) East Gate, and for 1 key for the vault of the pipes (*vautum piparum*): 16d.
> [22 August] To the plumber for 4 *lbs* of solder used on John Martyn's house at (*apud*) West Gate: 12d;
> To the said plumber for half a day's work there: 3d;
> To Robert Dolle for carriage of 7 seams of firewood from 'Dureyurd Wode' for the plumber, including food and drink for him: 8d;
> For making the said firewood: 3d.
> To the said Robert Dolle for repairing a 'stall' of a tenement at East Gate: 4d.
> To Thomas Helyer for 3 days on the city's rents [(*redditus*); the source of these rents, i.e. the property, is meant] at West Gate at 6d a day: 18d;
> To his servant for 3 days: 12d;
> For 1 small sack (*sacculo*) of lime: 8d;
> For 100 laths: 5d.
> [Total: 15s 1d.]

[Total expenditure in this year: £1 7s 1d.]

1527–28

Receiver John Blakaller.

Receiver's Roll

[*m.4*] Fees of the mayor and other officers:
> 3s to each gatekeeper of the city: 12s.

[Expenses:]
[*m.4v.*] To Robert Talboytt for cleaning 'le gratte' at (*apud*) West Gate this year: 12d.

[*m.3v.*] For 4 seams of stones to make 'a dale' for the Wall at (*apud*) West Gate: 8d.
> To the carpenter who repaired 'lee lenye' at (*apud*) East Gate and in the house *quod sedebam* [meaningless], [and] to the mason for 5 days at 6d a day: 2s 6d;
> Paid Robert Doll for 2 days: 8d;
> Paid for carriage of timber from 'Dureyurd': 6d.
> Paid the mason 'that sett the pose to grate' at West Gate: 6d;
> For nails to set 'lee grate to the pose': 1d.

To John Whyte, 'carpenter', for ½ day making a door at 'Howe is house' at (*apud*) East Gate: 3*d*;
To 1 man for 1 day's labour: 6*d*;
To John Whyte's servant for 1 day: 5*d*;
To Robert Doll for ½ day: 2*d*;
For 5 locks (*sarris*) for 2 new doors and for 1 piece [of timber] to make legs (*tibias*): 20*d*;
For 1 pair of 'twystes & hokys': 3*d*;
For nails used on the said house: 6*d*.
For 1 lock to set on the door at East Gate: 7*d*.
To John Payge 'for redyng away of the robbell before the newe Walles': 2*s* 8*d*.
For 18 seams of 'borrys stonys' to repair the walls at (*apud*) 'Freryng hay': 2*s* 3*d*.
For 8 seams of sand: 6*d*.
For 1 dozen of small stones: 3*d*.
To John Mason and his 2 servants for 3 days' labour: 4*s*.
'For caryng a way of robell att yest [i.e. East] Gate': 8*d*.
For making a new key for a house at (*apud*) East Gate: 3*d*;
For another key for the same house: 3*d*;
For repair of 2 other locks: 3*d*.
'For a nother paire of twystis made of oure awne stuffe for the house att yest gate': 2*d*;
For 1 new key for the said house: 3*d*;
'For makyng of 3 hapsys & 6 stapellys to the same': 6*d*;
'For makyng of a newe kay for Este Gate for the dore': 3*d*.

[*m.2v.*] 'For redynge of the Ivee aboute the wallys': 6*s*.
For 10 quarters of lime which were used on the City's Jakes (*cloacas Civitatis*) and on the City Walls at 'Freren hay': 5*s* 10*d*.
'For makyng of a pice of Walle in the south parte of West Gate next to a pyce [*sc.* piece] of Walle that Thomas Androwe made conteynyng in lenght [*sic*] 61 fote & in height 18 fote to the garratte & the garctt upwardes 3 fote & 5 fote in thyknes by the fundacion with 2 botters to the same payng for the same unto Towte & he fyndyng all maner of stuffe': £24;
'More ther was geven hyme in rewarde for the same': £3.
[Total: £28 14*s* 4*d*.]

[Total expenditure in this year: £29 6*s* 4*d*.]

1528–29

Receiver Gilbert Kyrke.

Receiver's Roll

[*m.4*] Fees of the mayor and other officers:

[*m.4v.*] 3*s* to each gatekeeper of the city: 12*s*.

[*m.3v.*] [Necessary expenses:]
[On or after 18 December] '[For] Tuett & a nother man for 2 days Worke yn mendyng of the Gutter & the brygge at the Water Gate': 2*s*;
'[For] a quarter of hote lyme': 7*d*;
'[For] 14 horsse lode of Pemor Stone': 2*s* 4*d*.
[On or after 20 December] '[For] 6 *lbs* off Sawder with the Workeman Schepp to mend the goutters at Weste yate': 2*s*;

'30 day off Febryare to John Payge for Caryng of 24 Semys of Stokes [stakes] & tymber from Duryode [Duryard] hether [hither]': 3*s*.
'[To] the sayd Payge for Carryng a waye Robell from the broke at Est Gayte for 3 dayes Worke for hem & hys man & 2 horse': 2*s* 8*d*;
'[To] the said Payge for a dosyn of Sande': 9*d*;
'[To] the [said] Payge for 4 Semys of claye & for dabeng [*sc.* daubing] of a walle under the bryge': 6*d*;
'[To] the sayd Payge for a dossen & a half of clay to mende one of the howsyn that John Daye holdes at West yayte': 9*d*.
[On or after 18 February] '[For] 100 of Peymor stonys for the brygge & the pament that weryth the water over Water Gaytt': 9*s* 4*d*.
'[For] skabelyng at the quary' 18*d*;
'The same day to William Collyff [for] 40 *lbs* of Iron worke & workmanscheppe at 2*d* the *lb*': 6*s* 8*d*.
'[The] 3 day of Marche to Richard Smyth for Copyng of 13 Cresse apon the Towne Wallys by West Gaytt': 52*s*.

[*m.2v.*] [No date] 'To Robert Talbott one of the porters for Ryddyng of the gutter at Westgaytt': 41*d*.
[30 July] 'To John Plomer for 4 dayes Worke yn the vawett & att the Wylls hede & a pon the gutter at Estett . . .': 2*s*.
'6 day of October to Rychard Smyth Mason for makeyng of the butteras yn the south Syde of the West yaet and makeyng of 6 garrettes': £3.
[On or after 6 October] '[For] 3 menys labor 2 dayes for Castyng of Robyll apon the Wallys yn Savyng of the Walles': 12*d*.
[No date] 'To Richard Smyth masson for byllyng of a pece of a walle by the northe syde of the West Gate by the Counsell of the hole mastyres': £16.
[No date] 'For makeyng of a Steyr' & a aller' yn the howsse at Este yate that masteris Atkyns dwelleth yn': 2*s*.
[Total: £23 11*s* 6*d*.]

[Total expenditure in this year: £24 3*s* 6*d*.]

1529–30

Receiver William Peryham.

Receiver's Roll

[*m.5*] Fees of the mayor and other officers:
3*s* to each gatekeeper of the city: 12*s*.

[*m.5v.*] Expenses this year:
'. . . 5½ *lbs* Sauder for the Estgaytt': 16½*d*.
'For makeyn of a nowe dore & mendeng of 2 doresse of the hosses a pon the Walles': 17*d*;
'For 8 Semys of Klaye for the Same hosses & for a Workeman ys Wages': 7*d*.
'[For] a locke for a howese withyn Wested & also nayells for a Ster' [stair] for the Same': 5½*d*.
'[For] mendyng of a chyemley at Powglasse howsse withyn Westett': 6*d*.
'[For] more [nails] occapyed at Esget In tyem' [?]': 1*d*.
'[For] a locke & a kaye at Esgett for the Wayettes' [*sc.* waits]: 4*d*.
'[For] a kaye at a howesse at Estgett': 2*d*;
'[For] a locke & a kaye to the Same housse': 4*d*.

[*m.4v.*] '[To] William Robyns for Reddyng [i.e. clearing] of the gutter at Westget': 16*d*.
[Total: 6*s* 7*d*.]

[Total expenditure in this year: 18*s* 7*d*.]

1530–31
Receiver Richard Martyn.

Receiver's Roll

[*m.6*] Fees of the mayor and other officers:

[*m.6v.*] 3*s* paid each of the gatekeepers of the said city: 12*s*.

[*m.5v.*] Allocations for diverse expenses:
'. . . for Est Gate & Mr Fyz ys howse & Denys ys howse & 3 quarters of lyme': 2*s* ½*d*.
'To William Labbden mason for 2 days & ½ for makeyng off the draste yn Est Gate that Elizabeth Hoppkyns Dwellyth yn': 15½*d*;
'[For] 2 dayes & ½ for hys man to serve hym': 12½*d*;
'To Robert Doll for 3 dayes': 12*d*;
'To a Nother man to helpe Robert Doll': 7*d*;
'For Candelles for the same Worke': 7*d*.
'Paid Polyng for reparacions apone the brygge at Southgayt': 9*d*.
'For Ryddyng of the fondacion of the wall at Frerenhay': 20*d*.
'For rollyng away of Tymber': 4*d*.
'To John Whyte Carpynter for mendyng of the draw brygge withowte the Sowth Gate by the space of 3 dayes & ½': 21*d*;
'Payd Roger Gade for 3 dayes ½ at 6*d*': 21*d*;
'To William Lytell at 6*d*': 21*d*;
'To Thomas Gryll at 5*d* the daye *videlicet* 3 dayes & ½': 17½*d*;
'For Caryage off the tymber to South Gate': 5*d*.
'For Reparacions don uppon William Robyns howse for Settyng yn of 3 grett Corbylles yn to the Towne Walles to bere the Chymne & the flowre [i.e. floor]': 5*s* 1½*d*.
'For a key yn a tenement at West Gate': 3*d*.
'To John Whyte & to 2 men to sawe the plankeys for the vawte at Est Gate': 8*d*.
'To William Mason for pullyng Downe off the Ivys be enxt [i.e. betwixt] Snayle Towre & North Gate takeyng by the Weke for his labour 8*d*': 12*s* 8*d*.
'For Carryng off Sand & Stonys to the gattes as by a byll hyt Schall pere': 9*s* 6½*d*.

[*m.4v.*] 'To Richard Tute for the makeyng off 70 fotte off New Wall yn Freren haye & fendyng off [finding of] all Stuffe': £27 13*s* 4*d*;
'To the same Richard for makeyng off 6 fotte more ther off the same Walle': 48*s*.
'To Richard Tute for Ryddyng off Robyll from the same Walle': 10*d*.
[Total: £32 6*s* 10*d*.]

[Total expenditure in this year: £32 18*s* 10*d*.]

1531–32
[The roll for this year is missing.]

1532–33
Receiver Thomas Hoigge.

Receiver's Roll

[*m.4*] Fees of the mayor and other officers:

[*m.4v.*] 3*s* to each of the gatekeepers of the said city: 12*s*.

[*m.3v.*] Allocations for diverse expenses:
'For mendyng of a Chemney withyn Estyett': 17*d*;
'Payd for stonys': 6*d*.
'For a masson to mende the gutters at Westgate': 4*d*.
'For mendyng of a chymne & a dore of a howsse upon ye Towne Wall that John Day holdyth at Westgat': 2*s* 2*d*.
'To [a] helyer & hys man 4 dayes upon the howssys at West Gate apon 5 howsses': 3*s* 8*d*;
'For 4 cresses latnayles bordenayles & hach nayles': 9*d*;
'For 4 luppes of glasse' [*sic*; ? error for 'brasse', i.e. 4 loops of brass]: 2*s*.
'For bordys nayles & the carpynter ys labour to make the pentes at West Gate & for mendyng of dyvers fottes': 2*s*.
'To a smyth to mende the locke at Estgate': 4*d*.
'For 4 *lbs* of sauder for Gutters at Estgatt': 12*d*;
'For ye plummer ys labour': 6*d*.
'To Robert Dolle for mendyng of a wall withyn Estgatt': 4*d*.

[*m.2v.*] 'For a clamppe of yer' [iron] for Southgate': 2*d*.
'For makyng of a hooke of yer' for Northgate': 3*d*.
'Payed for making of ye tolehowsse at South Gate a marymaulynffayre': 3*d*.
'Payed to Mr Denys for hys labour to speake with the Juges for making of the Towne Walles': 6*s* 8*d*.
'For a loke for Mutton ys dore at Westgate': 2*s*.
'Payed for 4 men ys labour yt where [sc. were] working apon the bancke with owt Estgate 2 dayes labour 6[*d*] a daye': 4*s*;
'Payed to Robert Dolle for hys labour 2 dayes for the same Worke': 8*d*.
'To Robert Dole for paste to putt up the Kynges wretyng at every gatt': 1*d*.
'For mendyng of a dorth [?, *sic*] bare at Estgate': 3*d*.
[Total: £1 9*s* 4*d*.]

[Total expenditure in this year: £2 1*s* 4*d*.]

1533–34
Receiver John Thomas.

Receiver's Roll

[*m.4*] Fees of the mayor and other officers:
3*s* paid each gatekeeper of the city: 12*s*.

[*m.3v.*] Allocations for diverse expenses . . .:
'To the helyer for helynge of the housez over the Est Gate': 22*d*;
'For lyme at that tyme occupied': 15*d*;
'For a Crest & pyns then occupied': 4½*d*.
'For dyvers reparacions don aboute the Tenementes of John Polglase & Willyam Robyn at Westgate': 4*s* 4½*d*.

'For a locke & key for the Northyeate': 10*d*.
'Paid for making of a forlok for the grete Gon': 14*d*.
'Paid for Gonpowder to scowre the Gonnes withall': 18*s*.
'For a stapell for the Westgate': 2*d*.

[*m.2v.*] '[To] Downeman for coveryng of the Gutter at Estgate & brekyng upp of the same': 14*d*;
'For stones lyme & sande for the same with nayles': 10*d*.
'To John Mutton for ryddyng of the grates at Westgate': 16*d*.
[Total: £1 11*s* 4*d*.]

[Total expenditure in this year: £2 3*s* 4*d*.]

1534–35

Receiver Thomas Hunte.

Receiver's Roll

[*m.4*] Fees of the mayor and other officers:
3*s* to each of the gatekeepers of the said city: 12*s*.

[*m.4v.*] Necessary expenses this year:
'For the makyng of the Bryge att Est Gatt With other thyngges pertenyng therto as aperythe yn the paper boke [lost] of this accompt': [no sum given].
'Payd to Sir Thomas Denys for suyng of the Wallys': 20*s*.
'Payd to Sir John Fullford for suyng of the Wallys': 20*s*.

[*m.3v.*] 'To a helyer for 3 days Worke apon Northe Gatt att 6*d* the day': 18*d*;
'To a sarver [sc. an assistant] for the same': 15*d*;
'For a thousand of lathe nayllis': 9*d*;
'For 2 ovys bordes for the same gatt': 3*d*;
'For half a pecke of helyng pynnys for the same': 2*d*;
'For a rester for the same gatt': 3*d*.
'For vellyng [felling] & squaryng of a Elme that stode yn Freryn haye for the Southegatt for 3 men on day': 18*d*;
'Payde for Sayng [i.e. sawing] of the same Elme & setting uppe the same over Southegatt for 2 men 3 days att 7*d* the day': 3*s* 6*d*;
'For 2 hellyers & a sarver 2 days & a half apon the Southe Gatt': 3*s* 7*d*;
'For half a busshell of helyng pynnys': 6*d*;
'For 3 ovys bordes for the same gatt': 4½*d*;
'For 2 thowsand & a half of lathe naylys': 22*d*;
'For 6 thousand of helyng stonys price the thousand 3*s* 4*d*': 20*s*;
'For Carryng of the same stonys from Toppysham': 3*s* 9*d*.
[Total: £3 19*s* 2½*d*.]

[Total expenditure in this year: £4 11*s* 2½*d*.]

1535–36

Receiver Thomas Spurway.

Receiver's Roll

[*m.4*] Fees of the mayor and other officers:
3*s* paid each gatekeeper of the said city: 12*s*.

[*m.4v.*] Necessary expenses this year:
'[To] 2 men for Slattyng and dawbyng of the lytell howse under the brygge att Este Gate': 10*d*;
'To Page for 12 Semes of Claye haye and Naylys': 8*d*.

[*m.3v.*] 'For Candelles att the generall Wache': 2*d*.
'For mendyng of a locke uppon the Wekett att South Gate': 4*d*.
'For mendynge of a locke under the bregge att Estgate': 3*d*.
'For a newe locke over Este Gate': 4*d*.
'For a dosyn of gravelle att South Gate a yanst [i.e. in advance of] Lambmas [Lammas]': [no sum given].
[Total: 2*s* 7*d*.]

[*m.2v.*] [Allocations:]
16*d* allocated to John Mutton for cleansing 'le gratt' at West Gate.

[Total expenditure in this year: 15*s* 11*d*.]

1536–37

Receiver John Buller.

Receiver's Roll

[*m.4*] Fees of the mayor and other officers:
3*s* paid to each gatekeeper of the said city: 12*s*.

[This roll is incomplete; there are no necessary expenses recorded.]

1537–38

Receiver William Bucknam.

Receiver's Roll

[*m.5v.*] Fees of the mayor and other officers:
3*s* paid to each of the gatekeepers of the said city: 12*s*.

[*m.4v.*] Necessary expenses . . .:
'To Page for 2 dosen of gravyll for Estgate & Southgate': 14*d*.
'To Wyllyam Koke for a daye & half labor': 8*d*;
'To Morys the heller [sc. helyer] for 100 of lathes & 300 of lathe neylys': 8*d*;
'For 4 lityll stodes 3 krestes & bord neaylles': 10*d*;
'For 2 krestes and a owys bord att the Towne Sege': 4*d*;
'For a pecke of pynnys': 3*d*;
'To Morys & hys man for 6 Days Worke att the Est Gate & at the Towne Sege': 4*s* 2*d*.

[*m.3v.*] 'To Play & Thomas Trebell for keryng [carrying] of the stonys of the Towne Walles att Westgate': 16*d*.
'For Clensyng of the Garrites of ye Westyeate': 16*d*.
[Total: 10*s* 9*d*.]

[Total expenditure in this year: £1 2*s* 9*d*.]

1538–39

Receiver Robert Toker.

Receiver's Roll

[*m.4v.*] Fees of the mayor and other officers:
   3s paid to each of the gatekeepers of the said city: 12s.

[*m.3v.*] Necessary expenses:
   Firstly for repairing the City Wall, *videlicet*:
   'Paid John Wescott for 1 day and a half uppon Ryddyng the old Wallys there': 7½d;
   'To Gylbert Howenton for one day and a half': 7½d;
   'To Thomas Trebell for 1 day and a half': 9d;
   'To Willyam Geffrey for one day and a half': 9d;
   'To John Sandy for 5 day and a half': 2s 4d;
   'To Thomas German for 3 days and a half': 17½d;
   'To Willyam Anthoni & to John Wescott & to William Geffrey & to Thomas Trebell': 5s 7½d;
   'To Wyllyam Roger & to Willyam Mayne for 5 days and a half': 4s 7d;
   'To Thomas Stevyn & to Hugh Goodman for one day': 10d;
   'To 4 men for 2 days to make Wlakes [sc. 'flakes', scaffolding hurdles]': 4s;
   'To William Helyet & to Thomas Whythed & to Willyam Howper for 5 days and a half': 6s 6d;
   'To Willyam Frear for one day and a half': 7d;
   'To John Wescott & to Lewys Apryse & to William Anthony & to Thomas Howper & to Thomas Trebell & to Willyam Mayne & to Willyam Roger for 2 days and a half': 7s 3½d;
   'To 2 men for 2 days and a half': 2s 1d;
   'To Willyam Anthony & to John Geffrey for 3 days and a half': 2s 8d;
   'To William Roger for 4 days': 18d;
   'For 53 quarters off lyme': 26s 6d;
   'To Wyllyam Downeman the mason for one day and a half': 11d;
   'To Rychard Clase & to Thomas Talman for 2 days and a half': 2s 11d;
   'To Thomas Gesslyng & to Rychard Reddyll for 4 days and a half': 4s 8d;
   'To Wyllyam Cartor & to Symon Smott for one day and a half': 14d;
   'To John Hoper for 4 days and a half': 22½d;
   'To Richard Collyn & to Anthony for 2 days': 18d;
   'To John Ayscheton for half a day': 2½d;
   'To John Cornysh & to the Baylye for 3 days and a half': 2s 5d;
   'To Wyllyam Downeman for 2 days and a half': 17½d;
   'To Rychard Clase & to John Wyll & to Rychard Reddyll for 5 days': 8s 9d;
   'To Thomas Tallman & to Wat Hellecomb & to Robert Lye & to Thomas Joselyng & to William Carter for 6 days': 17s 6d;
   '[For] 100 semes off Stones to the same Wurke': 16s 5d;
   'To Pley for one day and a half': 10½d;
   'To the Baylye for 6 days': 2s;
   'To Anthony for 2 days': 12d;
   'For a dosen off peny Roopes for the makyng [*m.2v.*] off the Scaffottes': 12d;
   'For naylles': 2d;
   'For twyne': 1d;
   'For 31 quarters off lyme': 15s 6d;
   'To William Geffrey for 6 days': 2s 6d;
   'To the Seyd Willyam for a Cole [cowl] to cary Water [for] the Same Wurke': 6d;

'To John Cornysh & to John Upton for 5 days and a half': 3s 7d;
'To John Howper for 6 days': 2s 6d;
'To John Wyll the mason for 5 days': 2s 11d;
'[To] Rychard Clase & to Robert Lye & to Wat Hellyett & to Thomas Talman & to Thomas Joselyng & to Rychard Reddyll & to Wyllyam Carter & to John Cornysch & to William Geffrey & to John Howper for 6 days': 28s 6d;
'To Rychard Collyn for 2 days and a half': 14½d;
'[To] John Upton for 5 days and a half': 2s 3½d [?];
'For caryng off Scaffottes tymber & vlakes frome Derewode': 14d;
'To the Bayly for 6 days': 2s;
'To Anthony for 2 days': 12d;
'For Roopes': 3d;
'To Rychard Clase mason & to Thomas Talman & to Wat Hellecomb [*sic*] & to William Carter & to Willyam Geffrey & to John Cornysch & to Play & to the Baylye for 3 days and a half': 14s 5½d;
'To Robert Lye for one day': 7d;
'[For] 100 semes off Stones to the Same Wurke': 16s 5d;
'To John Payne for one day': 4d;
'To John Howper for 4 days': 20d;
'To Richard Classe for 5 days': 2s 11d;
'To Thomas Talman for 6 days': 3s 6d;
'To John Wyll & to Thomas Joselyng & to Richard Redyll & to William Carter & to Pley & to William Geffrey & to John Cornysch & to John Howper & to the Baylye for 5 days': 21s 10d;
'To Robert Lye for 4 days': 2s 4d;
'To Anthony for a day': 5d;
'For 3 Sackes off lyme': 9d;
'For naylles': 1d;
'To Rychard Classe & to Thomas Talman & to Robert Lye & to Thomas Joselyng & to Richard Redell & to William Carter & to William Geffrey & to John Cornysch for 6 days': 22s 6d;
'To Willyams for one day': 5d;
'To John Howper for 5 days': 2s 1d;
'For 50 off Scaple Stones & 50 off seme stones to the Same Wurke': 17s 4d;
'For 5 quarters off lyme': 2s 6d;
'To the Baylye for 6 days': 2s;
'To Rychard Classe & to Thomas Talman & to Robert Lye & to William Carter & to the Baylye & to John Howper for 6 days': 18s 6d;
'To John Cornysche for a day and a half': 7½d;
'To Ayscheton for 3 days': 15d;
'To Ball the lymer for a sacke off lyme': 6d;
'For mendyng off too pyckyses [i.e. 2 pick-axes]': 8d;
'To the quarymen for Stones': 10s;
'To Thomas Talman for 5 days': 2s 11d;
'To Rychard Classe for 3 days': 2s ½d [*sic*];
'To Willyam Carter & to Robert Lye & to Willyam Geffrey & to Thomas Trebell & to Thomas [*sic*] Howper for 4 days': 10s 5d;
'To John Cornysch for 6 days': 2s 6d;
'To the Baylye for 2 days': 10d;
'To Dounemans servant for 4 days': 2s;
'To the masons for 3 days': 7s;
'To a server for 2 days': 12d;
'To 2 men for dyggyng half a day': 6d;
'[For] led to Cast hokes yn Walles': 14d;
'To George Newhall for 6 days': 3s 6d;

'To Symon Schewet for 2 days and a half': 17½*d*;
'To Eslyng the mason for a day and a half': 10½*d*;
'To Robert Helyett a server for 2 days and a half': 15*d*;
'To a nother server for one day': 6*d*;
'To 3 masons & a server for 2 days': 4*s* 6*d*;
'For 6 quarters of lyme': 4*s*;
'[For] 52 Semes of Skaplyd Stones': 7*s* 10*d*;
'For a dosen off Sand': 9*d*;
'For a dosen off gravell': 9*d*.
'For anyron' ? [1 word illegible] for the Sowth Gayte':
14*d*.

[*m.2v.*] '[For] halff a dosen off Claye brougth to Estgayte':
2*d*.
'To a Carpynter for mendyng the enterclose under
Estgayte': 4*d*.
'For nayles': 4*d*.

[*m.1v.*] 'Payd for a locke for the Northegayte': 2*s* 4*d*.
[Total: £20 0*s* 6*d*.]

[Total expenditure in this year: £20 12*s* 6*d*.]

1539–40

Receiver Thomas Prestwoode.

Receiver's Roll

[*m.4v.*] Fees of the mayor and other officers:
3*s* to each of the gatekeepers of the said city: 12*s*.

[*m.3v.*] Necessary expenses . . .:
For various repairs on the City Walls next to the church
of All Hallows on-the-Walls this year: £170 4*d*.
Repairs on the wall next to the Bishop's Palace, in
addition to (*ultra*) £10 paid by the said Bishop towards
the repair of the said wall: £4 19*s* 10½*d*.
'Payd to Richerd Colwill & to Downeman for Seynt
Nicolas Tower': £5 10*s*.
'To Wolcote for pluckyng downe of yvys of the Wallys for
24 days at 5*d*': 10*s*.
'To Wylliam Downeman for the makyng of asmyche
Wall as he toke in taske to make in Fryrenhaye': £5.
'To John Hellyer for 10 quarters [of] lyme at 6½*d*': 5*s*
[*sic*].
'To Thomas Dyrham for 6 days Worke at Saynt Nycolas
to cast downe stons': 3*s*;
'For 2 mens wages 2 days halffe there also': 2*s* 6*d*;
'To Whithede and an other for 2 days halffe at Saynt
Nyclas': 2*s* 2*d*;
'[For] a cowle to put Watter yn and for mendynge of the
said Coule for that wall': 12*d*;
'For 4 poncent [posnets] to put watter yn for the wall in
Frernhay yn 2*s* 8*d* at Saynt Nycholas and walls in
Frerenhay': [*sic*];
'For a seve for to sefte sande': 4*d*;
'For a boket': 4*d*;
'For 10 quarters of lyme to John Hellyer at 7*d*': 5*s* 10*d*;
'To Hagyns for Carynge the walles [*sic*] with 4 horsses 1
daye': 18*d*;
'To Whythead for 1 days labor to the walle': 5*d*;
'To Upton for 5 days labor': 2*s* 1*d*;
'To Thomas Dyrham for 5 days at Saynt Nycholas': 2*s*
1*d*;

'To Heythfild for 1 daye at Saynt Nycolas': 6*d*;
'To John Gosse for 4 days at [blunder for 'and'] halffe
there': 22½*d*;
'To John Horither for 4 days there': 2*s*;
'To Thomas Whythed for 4 days and a half there':
22½*d*;
'To John Wescot for 4 days and a half there': 22½*d*;
'[To] Rycherd Huchyns for 4 days carynge 3*s* of stones
with 2 horsses at 9*d*': [*sic*];
'To Thomas Dyrham for 4 days wages at Saynt
Nicholas': 20*d*;
'To John Upton for 3 days labor there': 15*d*;
'[To] John Ashedon for 3 days labor there': 15*d*;
'To Bowdon for 3 mens wages 2 day To take downe the
frame at Saynt Nicholas': [no sum];
'To Heythfild for 6 days there [to] take downe stones at
Saynt Nicholas': 3*s*;
'To Gosse for 6 days at 5*d*': 2*s* 6*d*;
'To John Upton for 6 days at 5*d*': 2*s* 6*d*;
'To John Ashedon for 3 days and a half': 18*d*;
'To Thomas Whither for 6 days Worke': 2*s* 6*d*;
'To Rolston for 5 days at 5*d*': 2*s* 1*d*;
'To Mr Horssay for 6 days at 5*d*': 2*s* 6*d*;
'To John Hellyer John Whiting and Nycholas Hamlynge
for 49 quarters and 1 sack 26*s* 2*d* of lyme at the walles':
[*sic*];
'To Nycholas Ble for 18 quarters [*sic*] at 6*d* ½': 9*s* 9*d*;
'[To] hym more for 3 days caryage with 2 horsses':
2*s* 3*d*;
'To Sowdow [i.e. Sowdon] for 1 days carynge with 2
horses ? [illegible] also': 13*d*;
'To Sowdon for carynge stones to the Walles with 4
horse': 2*s* 8*d*;
'To Wylliam Dyvers for 8 days labour at The Walls in
Fryrenhaye': 3*s* 4*d*;
'To him for Caryage of stones with 1 horsse 4 days':
16*d*;
'To Ashdon for 5 days Wale [*sic*] at Saynt Nycholas':
2*s* 1*d*;
'To Myghell Tregen for 1 days Worke at Saynt Nycholas':
7*d*;
'To John Haydon for 5 days Worke there also': 2*s* 1*d*;
'For 2 poncovers [puncheons] to sett skaffoldes upon
for the Walles': 16*d*;
'To John Gosse for 1 days Worke at Saynt Nycholas': 5*d*;
'To John Upton for 1 days Worke at Saynt Nychlas': 5*d*;
'To Christofer Searll for 13 quarters & halffe of lyme at
7*d*': 8*s* 10*d*;
'To Nycholas Ball of Harcombe for 13 quarters and 1
sacke of lyme at 6*d*': 7*s* 6*d*;
'For a seve and a boket of the Walls': 6*d*;
'To Ashdon for 5 days Work att Saynt Nycholas': 2*s* 1*d*;
'To William Dyvers for 4 days Worke at Saynt Nycolas':
20*d*;
'To Cornyshe for 1 days Worke to take yves of the Walls':
7½*d*;
'To Huchins for the Caryage of Robbel with 2 horsys 1
day': 9*d*;
'To Boodbroke for 9 days [carrying] Watter for the
Walles': 3*s*;
'To Thomas Tyncombe for 6 days at Saynt Nycholas':
2*s* 6*d*;
'To John Cornyshe for 6 days at Saynt Nycholas': 2*s* 6*d*;
'To Hethfyld for 6 days at Saynt Nycholas': 3*s*;
'To Goosse for 6 days at Saynt Nycholas': 2*s* 7*d*;

'To John Parker for 2 days at Saynt Nycholas' 12½*d*.

'To William Quyntrell for 3 days at Saynt Nycholas': 15*d*;

'To Huchins for Caryage with 2 horses 6 days to the Walles': 4*s* 6*d*;

'To Lawrens for 2 days Worke & a half at the Walles': 15*d*;

'To Ynglond for 1 Baro Wages [? hire of 1 barrow] at Saynt Nycholas': 5*d*;

'To Thomas Dyrham for 2 days at Saynt Nycholas': 12½*d*;

'To Hethfyld for 1 day & a half at Saynt Nycholas': 9*d*;

'To John Parker for 1 day & a half at Saynt Nycholas': 13½*d*;

'To Thomas Treble for 2 days & halfe Worke at Saynt Nycholas': 13*d*;

'To Sawndor' for Caryage with 4 horsses 4 days to the Walles': 4*s*;

'To him for Caryage with 2 horses 1 daye from Saynt Nycholas': 18*d*;

'To hem for Caryage with 5 horses and 2 men halffe a daye': 13*d*;

'To Huchins for Carynge with 2 horsses & a man 2 days': 23*d*;

'To Upton for 2 days & halffe at Saynt Nycholas to pluck downe stones': 13*d*;

'To Ball for 46 quarters of hoott lyme to the Walles': 26*s* 10*d*;

'To Gosse for 3 days Worke & halfe at Saynt Nycholas': 18*d*;

'To William Quyntrell for 2 days Wark there': 10*d*;

'To the sayd Quyntrell for hys horsses laber to Cary sande to the Walles and for hys paynes to Ryde to Chydley [Chudleigh] to Causse that lyme myght be browght thether': 6*d*;

'To Nycholas Ball for 28 quarters of h[ot?] lyme at 6*d* the quarter': 16*s* 4*d*;

'To Edward Clement for 1 days Wark at Saynt Nycholas': 5*d*;

'To Sowden for 1 days Caryage': 18*d*;

'To Rychard Huchins for 1 days Wark with 2 horsses at the Walls': 9*d*;

'For 68 quarters of lyme [paid] to Craneborne': 34*s* 3*d*;

[*m.2v.*] 'For a slegg for the Workymen to Work With all Uppon the Towre of Saynt Nycholas [illegible; weighing] 11 *lbs* at 2*d*': 22*d*;

'To Hethfild for 3 days Work at Saynt Nycholas': 18*d*;

'To Thomas Treblle for 3 days Wark at Saynt Nycholas': 15*d*;

'To Edmond Clement for 3 days Work at Saynt Nycholas': 15*d*;

'To John Parker for 3 days Wark at Saynte Nycholas': 15*d*;

'To John Ashcote for 3 days Work at Saynt Nycholas': 15*d*;

'To Thomas Dyrham for 3 days Work at Saynt Nycholas': 15*d*;

'To William Quyntrell for 3 days Worke at Saynt Nycholas': 15*d*;

'To Rychard Huchins for Caryage of stones with 2 horsses 2 days & a half': 22½*d*;

'[To] Touett for 1 days Work at Saynt Nycholas': 7*d*;

'To Honyton for 49 quarters & 1 sack of lyme at 7*d*': 28*s* 10½*d*;

'To Hethfild for 6 days Work at Saynt Nycholas': 3*s*;

'To Laurence for 6 days Work there': 2*s* 6*d*;

'To Thomas Dyrham for 6 days Work at Saynt Nycholas': 2*s* 6*d*;

'To Huchins for 3 days Worke with horsses to Cary stones': 2*s* 3*d*;

'To John Ashdon for 2 days Work at Saynt Nycholas': 10*d*;

'To Page for 3 days labour to Cary stones and Claye with 2 horses': 3*s*;

'To Monstephin for Caryage with 2 horses 1 days [*sic*] to the Walles from Saynt Nycholas': 9*d*;

'To him more for 1 days labour with 4 horses to the Walles': 10*s* 3*d* [*sic*];

'To Marten Baybry for 36 seames of shyllyng for quarells to make crestes and batymentes [battlements] for the said Walles': 7*s* 6*d*;

'To Roger Monstephin for Carryage with 2 horsses of stones to the Walls': 22*d*;

'To Hethefyld for 6 days Work at Saynt Nycholas': 3*s*;

'Thomas Treblle for 6 days Work there': 2*s* 6*d*;

'To John Parker for 6 days Wark There': 2*s* 6*d*;

'To Thomas Dyrham for 6 days Worke': 2*s* 6*d*;

'To James Saunder for 6 days Warke at Saynt Nycholas': 2*s*;

'To Huchins for 6 days Carige with 2 horses': 4*s* 6*d*;

'To Myghell for 6 days Wark to pluck downe The Ivees yn The Towre of Saynt Nycholas': 3*s* 6*d*;

'To William Blage Carpenter for 6 days at Saynt Nycholas for the same': 3*s* 6*d*;

'To Edward Carpenter for 6 days at Saynt Nycholas for the same': 3*s* 6*d*;

'To Rychard Pewserer for the same wark': 2*s* 6*d*;

'To Morres for the same for 3 days and a half': 2*s* ½*d*;

'To Thomas Coosse for 2 days Worke at Saynt Nycholas': 14*d*;

'To William Pohyn Carpenter for 2 days and a half at Saynt Nycholas': 17½*d*;

'To Downeman for 3 days Wark at the Walles': 21*d*;

'To John Stephin for 2 days in ye Walles': 14*d*;

'To John Payne for 1 days Work there': 7*d*;

'To Paynes son for 3 days Work there': 15*d*;

'To Rychard Kychyn for 3 days there': 21*d*;

'To William Carter for 3 days Work at the Walles': 21*d*;

'To Robert Lye for 1 days Work there': 7*d*;

'To John Cornyshe for 3 days Worke': 15*d*;

'To John Ashdon for 3 days there': 15*d*;

'To John Stephyn for 6 days Worke at the quarey of Shyllyngford': 3*s* 6*d*;

'For 4 paniyers': 6*d*;

'For Ropes to make skafoldes': 10*d*;

'To Fryer for 4 days there at Walles': 20*d*;

'To Thomas Whyther for 4 days at Saynt Nycholas': 22½*d*;

'To James Sanderson for 4 days and a half at Saynt Nycholas': 18*d*;

'To John Grace for 4 days and a half there': 22½*d*;

'To John Parker for 4 days and a half there': 22½*d*;

'To Thomas Trebll for 1 day and a half at the Walles': 7½*d*;

'To Hethfyld for 4 days there': 2*s* 3*d*;

'To Thomas Trucomb for 4 days and a half': 22½*d*;

'For hopyng of Cosk to put Watter yn': 3*d*;

'To Downeman for 11 massons workyn at The Walles 51 days a mongest them in one wek as apperyth uppon hys byll': 25*s* 7½*d*;

'To him more for 2 Ropes': 7*d*;

'For a pannyre also': 1*d*;

'To Heythfyld for 3 days labour at Saynt Nycholas': 18*d*;

'To Thomas Treble for 4 days there': 20*d*;

'To Thomas Dyrham for 4 days there': 20*d*;

'To John Parker for 4 days there': 20*d*;

'To John Gosse for 4 days there': 20*d*;

'To William Downeman for 9 workmen at the Walles 34 days yn one weke betwen them as apperyth uppon hys byll': 17*s* 5*d*;

'To John Whany Nycholas Hamlyn and John Hellyen for 100 quarters of lyme at 6*d*': [no sum given; £2 10*s*];

'To Serell for 55 quarters of lyme at 7*d* paid to Hethefyld for 6 days at Saynt Nycholas': 32*s*;

'To Thomas Treble for 6 days there': 2*s* 6*d*;

'To Gosse for 6 days there': 2*s* 6*d*;

'To John Parker for 6 days': 2*s* 6*d*;

'To Thomas Dyrham for 6 days': 2*s* 6*d*;

'To Budbrocke for Carryage of 23 dosen of Watter': 7*s* 8*d*;

'To Thomas Locke for Carryage of stones unto the walles': 2*s* 6*d*;

'To William Downeman for 8 massons labor warkyng at the Walls 1 weke amonghest them 47 days as apperyghe uppon hys byll': 24*s* 5*d*;

'To James Sanders labor for 4 days there': 18*d*;

'To Ashedon for 2 days at Dyrwood [Duryard] for to make flackes': 10*d*;

'To Gylbert Ball and Nycholas Ball for 36 quarters of lyme': 18*s*;

'For 2 bolles to lade watter at ye walls': 2*d*;

'To Thomas Treble for 2 days at Saynt Nycholas': 12½*d*;

'Paid Thomas Gosse for 2 days at Saynt Nycholas': 12½*d*;

'To John Parker for 2 days at Saynt Nycholas': 12½*d*;

'To Thomas Tyncomb for 2 days': 12½*d*;

'To Heythfyld for 2 days there': 15*d*;

'To Monstephin for Cariage from Dyrwod [Duryard] of shkaffold Tymber to the walles': 9*d*;

'For Carryage of 2 dosen of Watter to the walles': 10*d*;

'To Hamlyn for 6 quarters & [*sic*] lyme': 3*s* 3*d*;

'To Clark for barowes & getheryng of Roddes': 12*d*;

'To Clark & 1 man for 3 days at Dyrwood': 18*d*;

'For a bokett to the walles': 6*d*;

'To Lawrens for 4 days and a half [at] Saynt Nycholas': 2*s* 3*d*;

'To Thomas Treble & hys feloys for 17 days': 7*s* 1*d*;

'To Downeman for 9 workmen 18 days': 9*s*;

'To Wylliam Downeman for 10 men 41 days and a half': 20*s* 8*d*;

'More to hem for 10 workemen 51 days and a half': 25*s* 4*d*;

'For halffe a dossen peny Ropes & a half dossen halfpenny Ropes': 9*d*;

'To Hethefyld & wother for worke': 32*s* 5*d*;

'To Fryer [for] 6 days worke': 2*s* 6*d*;

'To John Myddelton for 6 days': 2*s* 6*d*;

'To Downeman for 9 men': 23*s* 6*d*;

'To Thomas Trencomb & wother for worke': 22*s* 3*d*;

'To Downeman for 9 mens labor': 24*s* 2½*d*;

'For halffe a dossen 1*d* Ropes & a half dosen halpeny Ropes': 9*d*;

'To Fryer for worke': 2*s* 6*d*;

'To Nycholas Ball for lyme': 22*d*;

'To lens yvon [?] & Thomas Dyrham for Worke': 2*s* 1*d*;

'To Thomas Treble & for wother': 3*s* 5*d*;

'[Paid] unto Downeman & wother': 10*s* 7*d*;

'To Myddelton & wother': 22½*d*;

'To Monstephyn for 2 horsses at the walls': 22½*d*;

'To Serles son for lyme': 17*s* 6*d*;

'To John Upton & wother for worke': 7*s* 7*d*;

'To William Fryer & wother for worke': 4*s*;

'To John Smythe of Northgate for wedges sleges and pyksses [pick-axes] mendyng of them': 6*s*;

'To John Parker for 6 days at Saynt Nycholas': 2*s* 6*d*;

'To Myddelton for 6 days worke': 2*s* 6*d*;

'To Marten the smythe for mendyng of wedges sledges & pykesses': 2*s*;

'To Rychard Playe & wother for worke': 12*s* 6*d*;

'To Downeman for worke': 16*s*;

'To Downeman & wother': 27*s* 5½*d*;

'[Paid] unto Heythfyld for worke & wother': 12*s* 3½*d*;

'To Nycholas Ball for lyme': 6*s* 6*d*;

'To Thomas Tayncom & wother': 3*s* 11*d*;

'To Wylliam Cranefford for 8 quarters of lyme': 4*s*;

'To Wylliam Downeman for worke': [no sum given; the text dies off here].

[Total: £55 12*s* 2*d*.]

[*m.1v.*] £4 19*s* 10½*d* is charged above in necessary expenses and not allocated to the receiver because it was spent on the City Wall opposite (*ex opposite*) the Palace, being above £10 paid by John Vysy, then bishop, for repairs to the said wall, because repairs to that wall belong or appertain to the house of the bishop.

[Total expenditure in this year: £241 4*s* 4½*d*.]

1540–41

Receiver John Midwynter.

[Both the roll and the book for this year are missing.]

Book of Summary [DRO, Box 214, Book 2]

[*f.23*] [Illegible] the *pondfalda* [poundfold] at (*apud*) 'Northyeat': 16*s* 2*d*.

Cleaning the walls, as appears by the book of expenditure: [sum illegible].

1541–42

Receiver John Way.

Receiver's Roll

[*m.4v.*] Fees of the mayor and other officers:
3*s* to each gatekeeper of the city: 12*s*.

[*m.3v.*] [Expenses:]
Paid Barnard Doffyll for making and repairing the City Wall next to the Archdeacon of Cornwall's garden: £20.

[Total expenditure in this year: £20 12*s* 0*d*.]

1542–43

Receiver John Wolcott, merchant.

Receiver's Roll

[*m.3v.*] Fees of the mayor and other officers:
  3*s* to each gatekeeper of the said city: 12*s*.

[*m.2v.*] [Expenses:]
  [After 22 November; before 3 February] 'Payd for a new kye & mendeng of a lawke to the stor howsse at Est Gatt': 4*d*.
  'Payd Bauden the 3the day of Februariy for mendyng of the brege at Sothe Gatt': 16*d*.

[*m.1v.*] '[Paid] the 24 day of Marche for a quarter of borre stones for Ragland ys howsse att Northegatt': 3*s* 1½*d*;
  'Payd onto Gosse for 2 dayes Warke to Red the Wall at Ragland hosse': 10*d*;
  'Payd Bawden for to [2] of his men 3 dayes a pece to haw & Sa a nelme [*sc.* hew and saw an elm] for Raclands hosse at 7*d* the pece a day': 3*s* 6*d*;
  '[To] Rychard Kettell for 5 dayes labor to Wall att Raglands hosse att 7*d* the day': 2*s* 11*d*;
  'For hys lad 5 dayes': 20*d*;
  '[To] one Pawle a laborer 5 days': 20*d*;
  'For 4 mens labor 1 day to Wall att Raglands howsse': 2*s*;
  'Payd Payge for Carreng of stones Wyth 3 horses 2 dayes & halfe': 2*s* 7*d*;
  'Payd 3 laborers at Walleng a pon Raglonds hosse 1 day': 18*d*;
  'To John Bawden 4 days': 2*s* 4*d*;
  '[Paid] Rychard Deyr 5 dayes & a half': 3*s* 1*d*;
  'For 11 dayes labor': 6*s* 4*d*;
  '[Paid] Pewtener 5 dayes and a half': 2*s* 9*d*;
  '[Paid] the lad 4 dayes': 12*d*;
  'Payd 2 laborers for to Red the fondacyon & to Rep stones 4 dayes a pece': 3*s* 4*d*;
  'Payd onto Borrenton for 4 quarters of lyme': 2*s*;
  'Payd for Carreng home of tymber the 24 day of Aprill': 2*s* 6*d*;
  'To Wylyam Jeffere for 1 day to Rep stones att Sotheng hay': 5*d*;
  'Payd onto Rychard Mounstevynes servant for Carreng of stones att Sothenghay Wythe 2 horsys 2 dayes & a half at 9*d* the day': 22½*d*;
  'To John Bawden 24 day of Aprill for 3 dayes Worke': 21*d*;
  'Payd to Nott for 1 day': 7*d*;
  'Payd Thomas Coke 1 day': 7*d*;
  'To Rychard Dyer 4 dayes Worke': 2*s* 4*d*;
  'To Pewtener for 4 dayes': 2*s*;
  'To Bawdens lad for 3 dayes': 9*d*;
  'To Perwarden 2 dayes to draw stones': 10*d*;
  'Unto Wylyam Hoper 2 dayes & a half to Rep stones': 7½*d*;
  'Payd the 5the day of May to Wylyam Jeffere laborer to serve the massens 3 dayes & a half': 17½*d*;
  'To Pynvyll 1 day & a half': 7½*d*;
  'To Perwarden 1 day': 5*d*;
  'To Rychard Kettell masson the 5 day of May for 3 dayes & a half Worke': 2*s* ½*d*;
  'Payd hys lad 3 dayes & a half': 14*d*;
  'Payd Davy 3 dayes & a half att 7*d* the day': 2*s* ½*d*;
  'To Rychard Dyer kerpenter for 3 dayes & a half': 21*d*;
  'To Roger 3 dayes at 7*d* a daye': 21*d*;
  'Payd to Pewtener 3 days': 18*d*;

[No name given] '. . . for 2 days': 14*d*;
  'Payd to Nott for 2 days': 14*d*;
  'Payd to Bawdens lad for 3 dayes': 9*d*;
  'To Payge for Carreng of stones 3 dayes & a half Wythe 3 horsys at 4½*d* a horse': 3*s* 10½*d*;
  'For 8,000 of helyngstonys': 26*s* 4*d*;
  'To Bawdon & his men': 17*s* 6*d*;
  'To Bawdon & his men': 14*s*;
  'To Page': 7*s* 4*d*;
  'To Ketell and others as apperith by the recevers booke': 41*s* 5*d*;
  'To other Karpynters as apperith by the seid bucke': £4 4*s* 5*d*;
  'To Kettill & other lykewise apperith': £3 9*s* 8½*d*;
  'To Willyam Geffrey & other lykewise': £3 2*s* 10½*d*;
  'To William Geffry & other laborers': £4 2*s* 2*d*;
  'To the bayliffes & others': £3 14*s* 2*d*.
  [Total: £27 16*s* 0*d*.]

[Total expenditure in this year: £28 8*s* 0*d*.]

1543–44

Receiver John Helmore Junior.

Receiver's Roll

[*m.2v.*] Fees of the mayor and other officers:
  3*s* paid each gatekeeper of the city: 12*s*.

[This roll is incomplete; there are no necessary expenses recorded.]

1544–45

Receiver John Maynerd.

Receiver's Roll

[*m. 5v.*] Fees of the mayor and other officers:
  3*s* to each gatekeeper of the city: 12*s*.

[*m.4v.*] Expenses this year as appears in the book of account:
  £30 10*s* 2*d* paid for gunpowder, 'chambers, whelis' and other artillery for the city's ordnance this year, as appears by the account book.
  Repairs of the City Wall and 'le Coysy' [causey] next to 'Cowlegh Brigge' this year, as appears by the Book: £47 4*s* 10*d*.

[*m.1v.*] 6*s* 8*d* allocated for diverse 'Caskes' this year bought for keeping water for making mortar and lime for repairs to the City Walls.
  33*s* 11*d* paid for repairs to the tenement at (*apud*) 'Estgate' in which [blank] Upton now lives.
  [Total: £2 0*s* 7*d*.]

Book of Summary [DRO, Box 214, Book 2]

[*f.50*] 'For £4 that is to be payd to Mr Prestwode for the benevolens of the said John Maynard to the walls the which the said Thomas hath leyd oute as apperith by his accompte & ought to have the seid £4'.

[*f.51*] £4 paid 'Thomas Prestwode the which he hath leyd [out] for the walls which the seid John Maynard gave to the reparacion of the Ceties walls for his benevolens by cause he kept not his denner'.

[Total expenditure in this year: somewhere between £37 2*s* 9*d* and £84 7*s* 7*d*.]

1545–46

Receiver Nicholas Lymett.

Receiver's Roll

[*m.4v.*] Fees of the mayor and other officers:
   3*s* paid each gatekeeper of the said city: 12*s*.

[*m.3v.*] Expenses this year as appears by the book: [this section is blank apart from the sum £58 8*s* 2*d*; the roll is incomplete.]

1546–47

Receiver John Tuckefylde.

Receiver's Roll

[*m.4v.*] Fees of the mayor and other officers:
   3*s* to each gatekeeper of the said city: 12*s*.

[*m.2v.*] 10*s* paid John Prediaux [?], carpenter, for his labour and workmanship on the wheels and other ordnance for the city's artillery this year.

[Total expenditure in this year: £1 2*s* 0*d*.]

1547–48

Receiver John Drake.

Receiver's Roll

[*m.4v.*] Fees of the mayor and other officers:
   3*s* to each gatekeeper of the said city: 12*s*.

[*m.1v.*] 20*s* allocated from the fine levied for the admission [to the freedom] of a certain William Polyn, because the said William was slain at the time of the commotion, in the city's defence.
£62 18*s* 8*d* owing, of which £57 18*s* 8*d* is to be paid for the city's affairs at London, 'And the Residue £5 is alloyd uppon his bill of the Charges leyd oute duryng the Seyge in the last Comosion in parcell of the £15 as apperith by his bucke'.

[Total expenditure in this year: 12*s*.]

1548–49

Receiver William Totthyll.

Receiver's Roll

[*m.4v.*] Fees of the mayor and other officers:
   3*s* to each gatekeeper of the said city: 12*s*.

[*m.3v.*] Expenses this year, as appears in the account book:
Expenses at the time of the commotion and afterwards, for repelling the siege of the city: £78 16*s* 7*d*.

[*m.2v.*] 2*s* 6*d* defected rent of a garden and stable next North Gate which John Dier held, because they were destroyed at the time of the commotion.

[Total expenditure in this year: £79 8*s* 7*d*.]

1549–50

Receiver William Smyth.

Receiver's Roll

[*m.3v.*] Fees of the mayor and other officers:
   3*s* to each gatekeeper of the said city: 12*s*.

[*m.2v.*] Expenses this year, as appears in the book of account:
For repair and rebuilding of the City Wall[s] this year: £28 12*d*.
Paid for repairs to the ordnance, artillery and for gunpowder bought this year: [no sum given.]

Book of Summary [DRO, Box 214, Book 2]

[*f.80*] Necessary expenses:
£59 4*s* 6*d* paid for 'Gunnys & powder' this year.

[Total expenditure in this year: £87 17*s* 6*d*.]

1550–51

Receiver John Hurst.

Receiver's Roll

[*m.3v.*] Fees of the mayor and other officers:
   3*s* to each gatekeeper of the said city: 12*s*.

[*m.2v.*] Expenses there this year, as appears in the account book:
Repair of the City Wall[s]: £25 3*s* 3*d*.
Repairs at (*apud*) 'Westgate' and on the wall outside [*sic*] the said gate: £8 5½*d*.
Spent on the Wall and making 'le buttes' at 'Freerynghay' [Friernhay] this year: £8 11*s* 4*d*.
[Total: £41 15*s* 0½*d*.]

Book of Summary [DRO, Box 214, Book 2]

[*f.94*] Necessary expenses:
   £6 11*s* 9*d* paid for repairing 'le gonnys & ordnance artilary'.

[Total expenditure in this year: £48 18*s* 9½*d*.]

1551–52

Receiver Maurice Levermore.

Receiver's Roll

[*m.3v.*] Fees of the mayor and other officers:
   3*s* to each gatekeeper of the said city: 12*s*.

[*m.2v.*] Necessary expenses this year:
[Various city business and repairs on the houses, walls and tenements of the city, as appears by the book: no sum given.]

1552–53

Receiver John Periam.

[The roll for this year is missing.]

1553–54

Receiver Walter Staplehyll.

Receiver's Roll

[*m.3v.*] Fees of the mayor and other officers:
3*s* to each gatekeeper of the said city: 12*s*.

[*m.2v.*] Necessary expenses this year:
Paid for lead bought to roof (*ad cooperacionem*) West Gate, with money paid the plumber and his servant hired to make the said roof, and paid to various workmen for various days as appears by particulars in the account book: £11 13*s* 4*d*.
Paid Cornelius Paynter for making the Queen's Arms on the wall of the West Gate, with money paid for lime (*calcea*) bought for the same: 54*s* 2*d*.
Money paid for diverse repairs carried out on and about diverse guns (*petrariis*) of the city called 'the gunnes & ordynances', as appears by the book: £11 11*s* 5*d*.
Paid for necessary repairs to . . . the walls . . .: £61 7*s* ½*d*.

[Total expenditure in this year: £87 17*s* 11½*d*.]

1554–55

Receiver Griffin Amerydyth.

Receiver's Roll

[*m.3v.*] Fees of the mayor and other officers:
3*s* to each gatekeeper of the said city: 12*s*.

[Total expenditure in this year: 12*s*.]

1555–56

Receiver John Peter.

Receiver's Roll

[*m.3v.*] Fees of the mayor and other officers:
3*s* to each gatekeeper of the said city: 12*s*.

[*m.2v.*] Necessary expenses this year:
For repairs on the City Walls: 27*s* 11*d*.
For expenses at law against Robert Frye for 'le barbigan' of the City: £5 18*s* 9*d*.
For expenses at law against the inhabitants of 'Estgat' and John Midwynter: £4 16*s*.
Paid for amending and expenses on the ordnance and munitions of the city: £4 9*s* 1*d*.

16*d* defected rent of 'le Barbigan' near South Gate which John Wolcote lately held because it is the subject of a lawsuit between the City and John Frye and others, which lawsuit is undecided.

[Total expenditure in this year: £17 3*s* 9*d*.]

1556–57

Receiver Robert Mydwynter.

Receiver's Roll

[*m.3v.*] Fees of the mayor and other officers:
3*s* to each gatekeeper of the said city, in total: 12*s*.

[*m.2v.*] Necessary expenses this year:
For repairs to the City Walls this year: £20 6*s* 8*d*.

16*d* defected rent of 'le Barbigan' near South Gate because it is the subject of a lawsuit, which lawsuit is undecided.

Receiver's Book [DRO, Box 214, Book 5]

[*f.6v.*] 'Expenses in lawe . . .
Item to Mr Tothill for sewenge out of the *nisi prius* againe Mr Frie [concerning the barbican near South Gate] the 18 of Marche': 15*s* 8*d*.
'Item to Mr Prideouxe & to Mr Welshe for their fees at the same time': 20*s*.
[Total: £1 15*s* 8*d*.]
'The Cittie
Item for mendinge of the gate to the growned under the Snaile Towre': 4*d*.

[*f.9v.*] Expenses:
'St Johns November 21'. 'Item to 2 men for carieng of therle of Bedfords Armure from the New Inne to St Johns': 12*d*.

[*f.10*] [28 November] 'Item for 2 boltes for the Armure dore': 20*d*.
'For a key to the gonnehouse dore': 4*d*.
'December 4'. 'For a paier of twystes for tharmuirie dore': 16*d*.
Item to William Knolles the 23 of Juli for the chamber of a gonne': 4*s*.
[Total: 8*s* 4*d*.]

'The Towne Yates
To Nicholas Plomer the 24 of Aprill for 3 quarters & a 11 *lbs* of ledd [and] for sawder to the same for the leddes at Eastgate 14*s* 1½*d* & for 2 daies laboure 16*d* & to John Gilbert for 4 Iron cramps 11*d*';
'To William Monsedoune the 13 of November for carienge of cleye & bringing of a post without Northegate': 6*d*;
[Subtotal] 16*s* 10½*d*;
'To John Davie & his man the 30 of Maie for makinge of 2 new postes for the grat at the Westgate': 18*d*;
'For takinge up of the 2 old postes': 6*d*;
'To John Modeffilde & Robert the firste of October for eche of theime 2 daies to unhange & hange up the Weastgate [*sic*] and to amend the same': 4*s*;

'To John Gilbert for 82 *lbs* of Iron worke bestowed in the same gate & the grate there': 20*s* 6*d*;
[Subtotal] 26*s* 6*d*;
'To Robert Carpenter for one daies worke for makinge the 2 stooppes for Northegate grate': 12*d*;
'To John Gilbert for 42 *lbs* of Iron at 3*d* the *lb* for the same new grate': 10*s* 6*d*;
'To John Downe for bringinge of the 2 stoopes from Dyreherde [Duryard] woode': 4*d*;
[Subtotal] 11*s* 10*d*;

[*f.10v.*] 'To William Ungle for a daie to mende the stone worke of the same grate': 12*d*;
'To Thomas Dawe for one daie therre': 8*d*;
'To John Modeffilde for mending & settinge up of a dore at Northegate for kepinge of the Rike which is within the walles': 6*d*;
'For a new key for the same': 4*d*;
[Subtotal] 2*s* 6*d*;
Sum: 57*s* 8½*d*.

[*f.11*] 'The Citie Walles
The Water Gate
    Inprimis paied the 24 of October to Thomas Chapman for cariage of 12 dossen of stones from the new mylls unto the Water Gate at 8*d* ye dossen': 8*s*;
    'October 24: . . . to Thomas Lawman for 6 daies at 11*d* the daie': 5*s* 6*d*;
    'To his man for 6 daies at 10*d* the daie': 5*s*;
    'To William Carter for 5 daies at 12*d* the daie': 5*s*;
    'To Stephen Kettell for 6 daies at 11*d* the daie': 5*s* 6*d*;
    'To Richard Workeman for 4 daies & halfe': 3*s*;
    'To Thomas Dawe the yonger for 10 daies at 8*d* the daie': 6*s* 8*d*;
    'To William Mowsedowne for 6 daies at 7*d* the daie': 3*s* 6*d*;
    'To William Baylie for 6 daies at 6*d* the daie': 3*s*;
    [Subtotal] £2 5*s* 2*d*;
    '31 October: . . . to Thomas Dawe thelder for 4 daies': 16*d*;
    'To William Carter for 4 daies & halfe': 4*s* 6*d*;
    'To Stephen Ketell for 4 daies & halfe': 4*s* 2*d*;
    'To Thomas Lawman for 4 daies & halfe': 4*s* 2*d*;
    'To his man for 4 daies & halfe': 3*s* 9*d*;
    'To Thomas Dawe the yonger for 4 daies & halfe': 3*s*;
    'To William Baylie for 4 daies & halfe': 2*s* 3*d*;
    'To Chapman for cariage of 2 dossen seames of stones from St Johns at 10*d* the dossen': 19*d* [*sic*];
    [Subtotal] 24*s* 9*d*;
    '7 November: . . . to William Carter for 5 daies': 5*s*;
    'To Stephen Ketell for 4 daies': 2*s* 9*d*;
    'To William Bayliffe for 6 daies': 3*s*;
    'To Thomas Lawman for 5 daies': 4*s* 7*d*;
    '[To] Thomas Dawe the yonger for 6 daies': 4*s*;
    'To Lawmans man for 5 daies': 4*s* 2*d*;
    'To Chapman for cariage of 3 dossen & 4 seames': 22*d*;
    'To Laurans Oliver for 140 seames of stone from the quarie at 3½*d* the seame': 27*s* 11*d*;
    [Subtotal] 53*s* 3*d*;
    '13 November: . . . to William Mowsedoune for cariage of sand': 6*d*;
    'To William Carter for 2 daies': 2*s*;
    'To Stephen Ketell for 2 daies': 22*d*;

'To Thomas Dawe the yonger for 2 daies': 16*d*;
'To William Bayliffe for 3 daies': 18*d*;
'For a seve 4*d* [and] for a rope for the skaffold 4*d*': 7*d* [*sic*];
'To Chapman for 25 seames of stones cariage': 3*s* 10*d*;
'To Laurans Oliver for 26 seames of borroghes [burrs]': 4*s* 4*d*;
'To Burinton for 53 sackes of hote lyme at 7*d* the sacke': 29*s* 8*d*;
[Subtotal] 45*s* 7*d*;
Sum: £8 8*s* 9*d*.

'Crekepittmyll
Julie 3
Paid the 3 of Julie to William Carter for hewenge of stones at Crekepittmylle at 12*d* the daie': 3*s*;
'To Stephen Ketell the 18 of Julie for 3 daies to hew stones at 11*d* the daie': 2*s* 9*d*;
'To Thomas Dawe the 22 of Julie for a daie & halfe to ridd the grounde': 12*d*;
[Subtotal] 6*s* 9*d*;

[*f.11v.*] 'The 31 of Julie to William Carter for 3 daies': 3*s*;
'To Richard Ketell for 6 daies': 6*s*;
'To Stephen Ketell for 6 daies': 5*s* 6*d*;
'To William Turner for 6 daies': 5*s* 6*d*;
'To William Clerke for 4 daies at 10*d* the daie': 3*s* 4*d*;
'To John Ketell for 6 daies at 6*d* the daie': 3*s*;
'To to [*sic*] Thomas Dawe for 6 daies at 8*d* the daie': 4*s*;
'To William Bayliffe for 4 daies': 2*s*;
[Subtotal] 32*s* 4*d*;
'Paid the 27 of Auguste to John Moris for 9 dossen of stones caried form [*sic*] Exebridge to the walls at 4*d* the dossen': 3*s*;
'To him for 2 dossen of stones caried from the New Inne to the same walles at 6*d* the dossen': 12*d*;
[Subtotal] 4*s*;
'September 3: To William Carter for 6 daies': 6*s*;
'To Stephen Ketell for 7 daies': 6*s* 5*d*;
'To William Ungle for his 2 men eche of theyme 2 daies & half at 11*d* the daie': 4*s* 7*d*;
'To William Turner for 3 daies & halfe': 2*s* 11*d*;
'To Thomas Dawe for 3 daies & halfe': 2*s* 4*d*;
'To William Bayliffe for 4 daies': 2*s* 8*d*;
'To Laurans Oliver for 160 seame of seame stones & 80 seames of burres at 2*d* the seame': 40*s*;
[Subtotal] £3 4*s* 11*d*;
'11 [September]: . . . to William Ungle for 4 daies': 4*s*;
'To John Gardener for 3 daies & halfe': 3*s* 6*d*;
'To Henrie Combe for 3 daies & halfe': 3*s* 6*d*;
'To William Hew for 4 daies': 3*s* 8*d*;
'To Stephen Ketell for 4 daies': 3*s* 8*d*;
'To William Turner for 3 daies & halfe' 2*s* 11*d*;
'To William Bayle for 2 daies & half': 15*d*;
'To Thomas Dawe for 4 daies': 2*s* 8*d*;
[Subtotal] 25*s* 2*d*;
'17 [September]: . . . to Stephen Ketell for 4 daies': 3*s* 8*d*;
'To William Ungle for 4 daies': 4*s*;
'To John Gardiner for 4 daies': 4*s*;
'To Henrie Combe for 4 daies': 3*s* 8*d*;

'To William Hew for 4 daies': 3s 8d;
'To Thomas Dawe for 3 daies & halfe': 2s 4d;
'To William Turner for one daie': 11d;
'To John Baker for 2 daies': 18d;
[Subtotal] 23s 9d;
'25 [September]: . . . to William Ungle for 4 daies': 4s;
'To William Hew for 4 daies': 3s 8d;
'To Henrie Combe for 4 daies': 3s 8d;
'To Thomas Dawe for 4 daies': 2s 8d;
'To William Turner for 4 daies' 3s 8d;
'To Laurans Oliver for 171 seames of seame stones & 33 seames of burres': 34s;
[Subtotal] 51s 8d;
'October 1: . . . to William Ungle for 2 daies to finishe the same worke': 2s;
'To William Baylie for 10 daies': 5s;
'To Thomas Dawe for 2 daies': 16d;
[Subtotal] 8s 4d;

[f.12] 'To Peter Cokerham servaunte to Bartolomew Burrinton for 26 sackes of lime at 7d the sacke': 15s 2d;
'To Ball for 7 sackes of lime at 7d the sacke': 4s 1d;
'For twyne & new hoopinge of the lyme cole [cowl]': 5d;
'To John Morys for 3 dossen of sande & cariage of 6 seames of stones': 16d;
[Subtotal] 21s;
Sum: £11 17s 11d;
[Sum Total] 'of the wales': £20 6s 8d.

[f.13] 'Fees . . .
To William Mowsedon to kepe clen the Citie Walles' 20s;
'To John Scoble to kepe clene the grate at West Gate' 3s 4d.
[Total: £1 3s 4d.]

[Total expenditure in this year: £27 4s 0½d.]

1557–58

Receiver John Blackall.

[Both the roll and the book for this year are missing.]

1558–59

Receiver Richard Prestwode.

Receiver's Roll

[m.3v.] Fees of the mayor and other officers:
Paid the 4 gatekeepers for their fee: 12s.

[m.2v.] Necessary expenses this year:
Expenses at law: paid Geoffrey Tothill and others for diverse business and matters at law both against Robert Frye for 'le barbygan de Southgate Wall' and others: £14 2s 5d.

Expenses on building a tenement over (*supra*) North Gate:
Paid John Butler and other carpenters about building the tenement over North Gate this year: £6 15s 6d;
Paid on the wall and roofing the said tenement, for lime, lath nails and other necessaries: £48 8s 10d [*sic*; in fact £48 5s 6d];

For locks, keys and other ironwork of and for the foresaid tenement: £4 16s 2½d.

Receiver's Book

[f.10] 'Fees paid to the maior and other officers . . .
Paid to the 4 porters for their fee': 12s.

[f.14] 'Extra ordinary Charges . . .
Aprell 13 paid for shuttinge of the gonnes': 3s 6d.

[f.16] 'The buttes in Fryringhaye . . .
Paid to Gilbert the smythe for 4 claspes for the steares comminge in to Fryringe haye': 12d.

[f.18] 'Charges upon the howsse at Northe Gate
Carpenters
October 08 paid to Butler and his man for 6 dayes eche of them': 12s;
'Paid to Hunte for 6 dayes': 6s;
'Paid to 2 sawyers for 1 daye': 20d;
[Subtotal] 19s 8d;
'15 [October] paid to Butler for 6 dayes': 7s;
'Paid to him for his man for 1 daye': 10d;
'Paid to John Hunte for 6 dayes': 6s;
[Subtotal] 13s 10d;
'22 [October] paid to Butler for 5 dayes': 5s 10d;
'Paid to his man for 3 dayes and a halfe': 2s 11d;
'Paid to Hunte for 5 dayes': 5s;
[Subtotal] 13s 9d;
'29 [October] paid paid [*sic*] to Butler for 5 dayes': 5s 10d;
'Paid to his man for 5 dayes': 4s 2d;
'Paid to Hunte for 5 dayes': 5s;
[Subtotal] 15s;
'November 05 paid to Butler for 4 dayes and a half for him & his man': 9s;
'Paid to John Hunte for 4 dayes and a half': 4s 6d;
[Subtotal] 13s 6d;
'Aprell 22 paid to John Hunte for 6 dayes': 6s;
'Paid to Phillepp Sommerton for 6 dayes': 5s;
'Paid to Allexander Smyth for 6 dayes': 6s;
[Subtotal] 17s;
'29 [April] paid to Hunte for 9 dayes': 9s;
'Paid to Slee for 9 dayes': 6s 9d;
'Paid to Allexander Smyth for 6 dayes': 6s;
[Subtotal] 21s 9d;
'July 30 paid to John Hunte for 4 dayes': 4s;
'Paid to Petter Hunte for 4 dayes': 4s;
'Paid to Allexander for 1 daye': 1s;
[Subtotal] 9s;
'August 5 paid to John Hunte for 6 dayes': 6s;
'Paid to Petter Hunte for 6 dayes': 6s;
[Subtotal] 12s;
Sum: £6 15s 6d.

[f.19] 'Massonnes
October 08 paid to Harry Combe for 6 dayes': 5s 6d;
'Paid to William Hewe for 6 dayes': 5s;
'Paid to Nycollas Barter for 6 dayes': 5s;
'Paid to Elles Wheatton for 6 dayes': 4s 6d;
'Paid to William Backer for 6 dayes': 4s;
'Paid to Richard Hawckes for 6 dayes': 4s;
[Subtotal] 28s;
'15 [October] paid to Harry Combe for 6 dayes': 5s 6d;

'Paid to William Hewe for 6 dayes': 5s;
'Paid to Nycollas Bartor for 4 dayes': 3s 9d;
'Paid to Elles Whetton for 6 dayes': 4s 6d;
'Paid to William Backer for 6 dayes': 4s;
'Paid to Rychard Hawckes for 6 dayes': 4s;
'Paid to Clement Paine for 2 dayes': 1s 10d;
'Paid to Edmond Marten for 4 dayes and a half': 3s;
[Subtotal] 31s 7d;
'22 [October] paid to Harry Combe for 5 dayes': 4s 7d;
'Paid to Clement Payne for 4 dayes and a half': 4s 2d;
'Paid to William Hewe for 5 dayes': 4s 2d;
'Paid to Nycollas Barter for 5 dayes': 4s 2d;
'Paid to Elles Wheton for 5 dayes': 3s 9d;
'Paid to Richard Hawckes for 5 dayes': 3s 4d;
'Paid to William Backer for 5 dayes': 3s 4d;
[Subtotal] 27s 6d;
'29 [October] paid to Harry Combe for 5 dayes': 4s 7d;
'Paid to Clement Payne for 5 dayes': 4s 7d;
'Paid to Elles Wheaton for 1 daye': 9d;
'Paid to William Hew for 5 dayes': 4s 2d;
'Paid to Richard Kettell for 5 dayes': 4s 7d;
'Paid to Nycollas Barter for 5 dayes': 4s 2d;
'Paid to Kettelles Sonne for 5 dayes': 3s 4d;
'Paid to Rychard Hawckes for 5 dayes': 3s 4d;
'Paid to William Backer for 5 dayes': 3s 4d;
[Subtotal] 32s 10d;
'November 05 paid to Rychard Kettell for 4 dayes and a half': 4s 1½d;
'Paid to his sonne for 4 dayes and a half': 3s;
'Paid to Clement Paine for 4 dayes': 3s 8d;
'Paid to Nycollas Barter for 4 dayes and a half': 3s 9d;
'Paid to Rychard Hawckes for 4 dayes and a half': 3s;
'Paid to Harry Combe for 4 dayes and a half': 4s 1½d;
'Paid to Rychard Hawckes for 4 dayes and a half': 3s;
[Subtotal] 24s 8d;
'12 [November] paid to Kettell for 6 dayes': 5s 6d;
'Paid to his Sonne for 6 dayes': 4s;
'Paid to Harry Combe for 6 dayes': 5s 6d;
'Paid to Clement Paine for 6 dayes': 5s 6d;
'Paid to Nycollas Barter for 6 dayes': 5s;
'Paid to William Backer for 6 dayes': 4s;
'Paid to Rycharde Hawckes 6 dayes': 4s;
[Subtotal] 33s 6d;
Sum: £8 18s 1d.

[f.20] 'Massons
November 19 paid to Richard Kettell for 6 dayes: 5s 6d;
'Paid to his Sonne for 6 dayes': 4s;
'Paid to Clemet Paine for 6 dayes': 5s 6d;
'Paid to Harry Combe for 6 dayes': 5s 6d;
'Paid to Nycollas Bartor for 6 dayes': 5s;
'Paid to William Backer for 6 dayes': 4s;
'Paid to Rychard Hawckes for 5 dayes': 3s 4d;
'Paid to Mathew a Laborrer for 6 dayes': 2s 8d;
[Subtotal] 35s 6d;
'26 [November] paid to Clement Paine for 6 dayes': 5s 6d;
'Paid to Richard Kettell for 6 dayes': 5s 6d;
'Paid to his sonne for 6 dayes': 4s;
'Paid to Harry Combe for 6 dayes': 5s 6d;
'Paid to Rycharde [sic] Bartor for 6 dayes': 5s;
'Paid to Rychard Hawckes for 6 dayes': 4s;
'Paid to William Backer for 4 dayes and a half': 3s;
'Paid to a pore man for 4 dayes': 16d;

[Subtotal] 33s 10d;
'December 03 paid to Clement Paine for 5 dayes': 4s 7d;
'Paid to Rychard Kettell for 5 dayes': 4s 7d;
'Paid to his Sonne for 5 dayes': 3s 4d;
'Paid to Harry Combe for 5 dayes': 4s 7d;
'Paid to Nycollas Bartor for 5 dayes': 4s 2d;
'Paid to William Backer for 5 dayes': 3s 4d;
'Paid to Rychard Hawckes for 5 dayes': 3s 4d;
'Paid to a pore man for 4 dayes': 1s 4d;
[Subtotal] 29s 3d;
'[December] 07 paid to Rychard Kettell for 1 daye': 11d;
'Paid to his Sonne for 1 daye': 8d;
'Paid to Clement Payne for 1 daye': 11d;
'Paid to Harry Combe for 1 daye': 11d;
'Paid to William Backer for 1 daye': 8d;
'Paid to Rychard Hawckes for 1 daye': 8d;
[Subtotal] 4s 9d;
'September 09 [sic] paid Thomas Talman for 6 dayes': 5s 6d;
'Paid to Harry Combe for skoblyng [i.e. scappling] 6 semes [of stones]': 4d;
'Paid to Selleck for 2 dayes': 1s 10d;
'Paid William Baylly for 4 dayes and a half': 3s;
'Paid to Monsteven for carryaige 4 dayes and a half with too horsses': 6s;
[Subtotal] 16s 8d;
'16 [September] paid to Thomas Talman for 6 dayes': 5s 6d;
'Paid to William Bailly for 6 dayes': 4s;
[Subtotal] 9s 6d;
Sum: £6 9s 6d.

[f.21] 'Hellyers
October 08 paid to Thomas Derram for 6 dayes': 5s;
'Paid to his servant for 6 dayes': 3s;
[Subtotal] 8s;
'[October] 15 paid Thomas Derram for 6 dayes': 5s,
'Paid to his servant for 6 dayes': 3s;
[Subtotal] 8s;
'[October] 22 paid to Thomas Derram for 5 dayes': 4s 2d;
'Paid to his man for 5 dayes': 2s 6d;
[Subtotal] 6s 8d;
'[October] 29 paid to Thomas Derram for 5 dayes': 4s 2d;
'Paid to his man for 5 dayes': 2s 6d;
[Subtotal] 6s 8d;
'November 05 paid to Thomas Derram for 4 dayes and a half': 3s 9d;
'Paid to his man for 4 dayes and a half': 2s 3d;
[Subtotal] 6s;
'[November] 19 paid to Thomas Derram and his man for one daye eche of them': 16d;
'Aprell 22 paid to John Rossell for 6 dayes': 4s;
'Paid to Rychard Sergent for 6 dayes': 5s;
'Paid to Myghell Rossell for 6 dayes': 4s 6d;
[Subtotal] 13s 6d;
'Maye 03 paid to Rychard Sargent for 6 dayes': 5s;
'Paid to John his servant for 6 dayes': 4s;
'Paid to Myghell Rossell for 6 dayes': 4s 6d;
[Subtotal] 13s 6d;
'Auguste 05 paid to Richard Sargent for 6 dayes': 5s;
'Paid to his servant for 6 dayes': 4s;
'Paid to a Laborrer for 2 dayes': 1s 4d;
[Subtotal] 10s 4d;
Sum: £3 14s.

'Other charges for this howsse
18 of October paid for 1 dossen roppes for the skaffoldes': 10*d*;
'November 12 paid for a fyshe pott': 2*d*;
'[November] 19 paid for giltinge the vanne and payntinge the tabell': 5*s*;
'Janyver 14 paid William Bailly for 2 dayes': 12*d*;
'[January] 15 paid for carryaige of stoffe to ye work': 8*d*;
'Paid to Mowsdon for 4 dayes': 4*s*;
'Awgust 26 paid to Monsteven for carryaige 4 dayes and a half with 2 horsses': 6*s*;
'September 23 paid to Monsteven for carryaige 1 dossen roggell [*sic*]': 4*d*;
'[September] 23 paid to him for carryaige 1 day with 3 horses': 3*s*;
'Paid to Kinge for 2 dayes': 8*d*;
'Geven to Butler in recompence of his promes made for the buildinge of this howsse': 10*s*;
'Paid to Mowsdon for carryaige [of] 1 dossen sande': 8*d*;
[Total: £1 12*s* 4*d*.]

[*f.22*] 'Lead for that howsse
18 of October paid for the castinge of 2 *C* 1 quarter 7 *lbs* of Leade the wyche was for the gotter at farthinge and a half the *lb*': 8*s* 1*d*;
'November 12 paid for 1 quarter 15 *lbs* of Leade': 3*s* 1*d*;
'[November] 12 paid for the carryaige of 3 shettes led to the gaet [*sic*]': 8*d*;
'December 02 tacken for the coveringe of the Steare 17 *C* 2 quarters 6 *lbs* mor tacken for a gutter in too [2] angelles abowt the steare and chimle 2 *C* 1 quarter 7 *lbs* Some 19 *C* 3 quarters 13 *lbs* wher of was bowght new Leade 18 *C* 2 quarters 10 *lbs* at 10*s* 4*d* the *C*': £9 12*s* 1*d*;
'[December] 02 paid for the castinge of 17 *C* 2 quarters 6 *lbs* for the coveringe of the stare at 2*s* 4*d* [the] *C*': £2 10*d*;
Sum: £12 4*s* 9*d*.

'Bordes
November 05 paid to John Smithe [for] 3 quarter ½ elme borde': 4*s* 6*d*;
'[November] 05 paid to Pinson for 596 fote of bordes at 5*s* 4*d* [the] 100': 31*s* 9*d*;
'[November] 05 paid to him for 12 planckes beinge 98 fott . . .': 8*s* 10*d*;
'Aprell 13 paid to Mr Howcker for tymber [which] was bowght of one of Ashton': £2 6*s* 6*d*;
'[April] 13 paid to carryaige of the Same from thence': 6*s* 6*d*;
'Jully 13 paid to Tocker for 203 fowet borde': 15*s* 6*d*;
'Awgust 05 paid mor to him for 100 fowet of bordes': 7*s* 8*d*;
Sum: £6 15*d*.

'Lyeme
December 21 paid to Borrinton [for] 72 Sackes of Lyme wher of 31 sackes of hoot Lyme at 7*d*': £2 2*s*;
'[December] 21 paid to Ball for 29 sackes of hot lyme at 7*d*': 16*s* 11*d*;
'[December] 21 paid to him for 52 sackes of cold Lyme at 4½*d*': 20*s* 7*d*;
'Maye 14 paid to Borrington for 61 sackes Lyme at 7*d*': 28*s*;
'Awguste 20 paid for 6 sackes of Lyme': 3*s*;
'[August] 26 paid for 3 sackes hote Lyme': 16*d*;

'September 01 paid for 3 sackes Lyme': 16*d*;
'[September] 18 paid to Ball for 36 Sackes Lyme': 15*s*;
'[September] 18 paid to him for 2 hogshedes Lyme': 5*s* 5*d*;
Sum: £6 13*s* 7*d*.

[*f.23*] 'Heare [i.e. hair]
December 17 paid to Raw for 8 bowshelles': 2*s* 8*d*;
'June 20 paid by Mr Hocker for 15 bowshelles': 5*s*;
Sum: 7*s* 8*d*.

'Hellinge pines
October 15 paid for 1 peack of pines': 6*d*;
'[October] 22 paid for 3 pecke [paid] to Balles servant': 18*d*;
'November 16 paid for 2 bowshelles to Balles servant': 2*s* 8*d*;
'[November] 22 paid for 1 peck': 5*d*;
'Paid for 5 peckes': 1*s* 5*d*;
Sum: 6*s* 6*d*.

'Creasses [i.e. crests]
October 15 paid for 6 creasses': 16*d*;
'[October] 22 paid for 7 creasses': 18*d*;
'[October] 26 paid for 6 creasse': 17*d*;
Sum: 4*s* 3*d*.

'Lathes
Aprell 22 paid for 1,000 of Lathes': 3*s* 4*d*;
'08 of Awgust paid for 1,500': 5*s*;
'[August] 12 . . . paid for 1,500': 5*s*;
'16 of September paid 300 Lathes': 15*d*;
'[September] 16 . . . paid for 2,000': 6*s* 8*d*;
Sum: 21*s* 3*d*.

'Cleye & sande
12 of November paid to Monsteven for 2 dossen 9 semes from Hevetree': 4*s* 2*d*;
'[November] 12 paid to him for 1 dossen and a half from Exxe': 13*d*;
'[November] 12 paid to him for 1 daye and a half with 2 horsses to carry cley from the hall to Northgat': 3*s* 4*d*;
'[November] 19 paid to Mowsdon for the carryaige [of] ½ dossen sand': 4*d*;
'Paid to him for the caryaige of 1 dossen sande': 9*d*;
'07 of December paid to Monsteven for 1 daye and a half with 2 horsses': 2*s*;
'02 of October to Mowsdon for carryaige of 1 dossen of Sande': 8*d*;
[Total: 12*s* 4*d*.]

[*f.24*] 'Iron worcke
03 of November paid to Marten the smythe for a locke to the back dore in the garden': 15*d*;
'[November] 19 paid to Gilbert for 100 square naylles for the hall dore': 2*s*;
'Paid to him for gemowes for the said dore': 3*s*;
'Paid for 2 per of gemowes and 2 peires of twystes for a nother dore': 3*s* 9*d*;
'Paid for 2 boltes and twystes with stapelles weinge 6 *lbs* set uppon a dore above': 18*d*;
'Paid for 100 of leade naylles': 8*d*;
'Paid to him for a stapell for a dore': 2*d*;
'Paid to him for the spill of the vanne': 16*d*;
'[November] 26 . . . paid to him for a Locke for the hall

dore': 2s;
'Paid to him for 3 rodes of irron for the dyall': 2s;
'Paid for fowtinge of the irons for the vane': 8d;
'Paid for 2 crampes of iron': 4d;
'Paid for 60 Leaden naylles': 4d;
'06 [no month stated] paid for mackinge bares for the windowes': 6s 8d;
'10 of June paid for naylles by Mr Hocker': 3d;
'10 of September for 50 hache naylles [paid] by him': 4½d;
'Paid mor by him to Marten Phillepes for Lockes and gemowes for North Gatt': 14s 9d;
'Paid for 18,250 Lathe naylles at 1s 4d [the] 1,000': 24s 4d;
'Paid for 1,875 borde naylles at [blank]': 18s 9d;
'Paid for 145 ynglysh borde naylles': 3s 3d;
'Paid for 1,300 hache naylles and 300 tinckell naylles': 8s 10d;
Sum: £4 16s 2½d.

'Charges uppon stonnes from the quarry
15 of October paid to John Geill and William Walton for 6 dayes eche eche [sic] of them at the quary': 10s;
'12 of November paid to them for 13 dayes there': 10s 10d;
'[November] 26 . . . paid to Lawrence Ollyver for the carryaige of 192 seames stones': 32s;
'[November] 27 paid to Mr Howcker for freee [sic] stones set at St Marys Chirch': 7s;
'17 [no month stated] paid for a man at the quary for 4 dayes': 3s 4d;
'Paid to Lawrence Ollyver for caryaige [of] 4 semes': 15d;
'30 of December paid for breackings of 200 semes': 14s;
'10 of June paid to Lawrence Ollyver for 16 semes': 4s 4d;
'07 of September paid to Thomas Talman for 1 daye': 11d;
'23 of September paid to Lawrence Ollyver for carryaige 21 seames': 3s 6d;
'Paid to him for Elhes 21 seames': 2s 2d;
Sum: £4 9s 4d.

[f.25] 'Charges uppon a teniment with in the West Gatt
12 of November paid Butler for 4 dayes ½': 5s 3d;
'Paid to him for his servant': 3s 9d;
[Subtotal] 9s;
'19 of November paid Thomas Deram for 2 dayes for him and his man': 2s 8d;
'[November] 26 . . . to Thomas Derram for 6 dayes': 5s;
'Paid to his man for 6 dayes': 3s;
[Subtotal] 10s 8d;
[Margin: 'iron worcke'] '19 of November paid to Gelber for 9 haspes and 9 stapelles for the 2 howsses': 18d;
'Paid for a howcke and a twyste for a wyndow': 6d;
[Subtotal] 2s;
Sum: 21s 8d.

[f.27] 'Charges don uppon the brygge bye Westegate
Awgust 19 paid to Harry Combe and Thomas Talman for 6 dayes eche of them': 11s;
'Paid to Harry Combe for 1 daye at the quary': 11d;
'Paid to John Radmore for 6 dayes': 4s 6d;
[Subtotal] 16s 5d;
'[August] 26 paid to Thomas Talman for 5 dayes': 4s 7d;
'Paid to Harry Combe for 5 dayes': 4s 7d;

'Paid to John Radmore for 5 dayes': 3s 9d;
[Subtotal] 12s 11d;
'September 23 paid to John Ollyver for the carryaige of 44 seames to this worcke': 7s 4d;
'Paid to the quarry men for ther Labowre for thes 44 seames': 4s 7d.
[Total: £2 1s 3d.]

[Total expenditure in this year: between £68 5s 11½d and £82 8s 4½d.]

1559–60

Receivers John Paramore [who died in office] and John Wolcote.

Receiver's Roll

[m.3v.] Fees of the mayor and other officers:
Paid the 4 gatekeepers for their fee: 12s.

[The book for this year is missing.]

Book of Summary [DRO, Box 214, Book 2]

[John Paramore]

[f.195] Necessary expenses:
Expenses at 'le Water Gat': 53s 6½d.

[John Wolcote]

[f.226] 'Charges don upon Estyate': £4 18s 11d.

[f.227] 'Charges upon the Towne Walls' by John Paramore: 53s 6½d.

[Total expenditure in this year: £8 4s 5½d.]

1560–61

Receiver John Dyer Senior.

Receiver's Roll

[m.3v.] Fees of the mayor and other officers:

[m.2v.] Paid the 4 gatekeepers for their fee: 16s [altered from 12s].

[The book for this year is missing.]

Book of Summary [DRO, Box 214, Book 2]

[f.245] 40s paid Hugh Pope, now receiver, towards the building of a tenement over North Gate, by order of the Twenty-Four.
£10 paid that Hugh on another occasion for the use of the foresaid tenement.

[Total expenditure in this year: £12 16s 0d.]

1561–62

Receiver Hugh Pope.

Receiver's Roll

[*m.5v.*] Fees of the mayor and other officers:

[*m.4v.*] Paid the 4 gatekeepers for their fee: 16*s*.

[*m.3v.*] Monies paid out:
For the repair and building of a tenement on top of (*super*) North Gate: £70 17*s* 10½*d*.

[The book for this year is missing.]

[Total expenditure in this year: £71 13*s* 10½*d*.]

1562–63

Receiver Edward Bridgman.

Receiver's Roll

[*m.4v.*] Fees of the mayor and other officers:
Paid the 4 gatekeepers for their fee: 16*s*.

[*m.3v.*] Necessary expenses this year:
£27 18½*d* spent on repairs to North Gate [sic—in fact £22 8*s* 0½*d*].
£8 17*d* spent on repairs on (*super*) East Gate [sic—in fact £4 16*s* 2*d*].

Receiver's Book [DRO, Box 214, Book 11]

[*f.18*] 'Fees . . .
To William Mowsdone for his fee to clense the Citties Walls': £1.
'Also geven to William Knolls for his fee': £2.

[*f.23*] 'Northegate
Carpenters
The 6 of February to Roger Pytman & Robert Johnson eche of them 8 daies to halfe the bordes & to planche the howse': 16*s*;
'Them the 13 of February for 6 dayes': 12*s*;
'John Erland for 1,000 hatche nayles at 8*d*': 6*s* 8*d*;
'Roger Smythe for 300 bordnayles at 16*d* & 400 hatche nayles at 8*d*': 6*s* 8*d*;
'The 13 of Marche to Mychaell Frygons too servaunts for 6 daies': 12*s*;
'William Seager & his felow for eche too daies to sawe tymber at the Marshe for the leynye': 4*s*;
'The 20th of Marche to Mychaell Frigon & his too men for 6 daies to ende the lyney': 16*s* 2*d*;
'For 600 of bordenayles': 8*s*;

[*f.24*] 'The 28 of Marche to John Knight & his too men to fynyshe the whole carpentry worke at 6 daies the pece': 8*s*;
'For 800 of bordes to planche the said houses & to make the dores at 7*s* the hundreth': 56*s*;
[Total: £7 5*s* 6*d*.]

'Helyers
The 3 of Aprill to Rychard Helier to cover [1 word illegible] & playster the lyney & to cover the wall over the back dore for 6 daies at 11*d*': 5*s* 6*d*;
'John Newlond 6 daies at 10*d*': 5*s*;

'John Wyer 6 daies at 8*d*': 4*s*;
'Rychards boye 6 daies at 6*d*': 3*s*;
'For 16 sackes of lyme at 6*d*': 8*s*;
'For one bushell of pynnes': 2*s* 9*d*;
'For 1,000 & halfe of lathes': 7*s* 6*d*;
'For 3 dossen of cley to dawbe the walls': 4*s*;
'For hay to put amonge the claye': 14*d*;
'The 10th of Aprill to Rychard Helyer & his three men for one whole weke': 17*s* 6*d*;
'For 10 sackes of lyme': 5*s*;
'For 2 dossen of sand': 2*s* 8*d*;
[Total: £3 6*s* 1*d*.]

'Masons
The 19 of May to John Webber for 3 daies to make up the batlement over the gate at 12*d*': 3*s*;
'Robert Dacye for 3 daies at 12*d*': 3*s*;
'Rychard Prigge for 3 daies at 13*d* [sic]': 3*s*;
'For 2 dossen of scaffolde ropes': 2*s*;
'John Olyver for 100 of stones fetched from the New Mylles': 20*d*;
'For 14 sackes of lyme': 7*s*;
'The 10 of Julye to John Webber 4 daies': 4*s*;
'Robert Dacy 4 dayes': 4*s*;
'Water Marys 4 daies': 3*s* 4*d*;
'For 1 dossen & halfe of sand': 2*s*;
'For caridge of 1 dossen of stones': 10*d*;

[*f.25*] 'The 17 of July to John Webber 4 daies': 4*s*;
'Robert Dacy 4 daies': 4*s*;
'Rychard Poke 4 daies': 4*s*;
'Walter Morys 4 daies': 3*s* 4*d*;
'For 2 dossen of sand': 2*s* 8*d*;
'For caringe of a halfe dossen of flakes from Dyrehord [Duryard] wode': 12*d*;
'For 14 sackes of lyme': 7*s*;
'The 24 of Julye to John Webber 6 daies': 6*s*;
'Robert Dacye 6 daies': 6*s*;
'Walter Morys 6 daies': 5*s*;
'For 3 quarters of playster of Parys for the plat for the Kinges armes bought of Dacye': 20*d*;
'Mr Hurst for 2 *C* halfe of playster': 6*s* 8*d*;
'The 7 of August to John Webber & his too felowes for 6 dayes to laye the playster & poynt the whole gate': 17*s*;
'For 3 seames of hardwode to burne the playster': 18*d*;
'Rychard Keyser for 8 *lbs* of crampes for the fyllett of ledd at 3*d*': 2*s* 6*d*;
'John Broks yn part of payment to make & paynt the Quenes armes & Cities armes': 20*s*;
'Hym the 16 of August': 20*s*;
'Him the 21 of August': 5*s*;
'Hym the 29 day in full payment': 10*s*;
'Laurens Olyver for one halfe hundreth & one seame of stone to make the crests of the batlements ['& the stayers'—crossed out]': 14*s* 10½*d*;
'For pullynge downe of the scaffolds': 8*d*;
[Total: £8 16*s* 8½*d*.]

'Wallers
The 18th of Marche to Henry Benett & John Roberts for 2 dayes the peece to make the mudd wall next to William Langs garden at 11*d*': 3*s* 8*d*;
'Them for one daye at the Towne Jakes': 22*d*;
'For a seame of strawe': 16*d*;
'Also to them the [blank] of March': 8*s* 9*d*;

'Also the 6 of Aprill to the said Henry & John for ech of them too dayes at the same walle': 3s 8d;
'Also for a seame of strawe': 16d;
'Them the 10th of Maye for a day & halfe to fynyshe that wall as also the wall at the Towne Jakes': 2s 9d;
'For strawe': 9d;
[Total: £1 4s 1d.]

'Thatchers
The 12th of June to William Mager thatcher for 8 daies at 13d': 8s 8d;
'John Smerte & William Trenamey eche of them 4 daies to serve the thatcher at 10d': 6s 8d;
'For 2 C [and] 3 quarters of Rude at 6s 8d the C': 18s 4d;
'For the wateringe of the same rud': 8d;
'For gatheringe & bryngyng home of sparres': 16d.
[Total: £1 15s 8d.]

'Easte Gate . . .

[f.27] 'Masons
The 17 of September to Stephen Keroll 3 daies': 3s;
'John Keroll 3 daies': 3s;
'To their servitours 3 daies 2s 6d to make up walls of the brydge next without the gate': 8s 6d;
'The 25 of September to Stephen Keroll for 3 daies & halfe': 3s 6d;
'His serviture': 2s 11d;
'For 8 dossen of cley': 10s 8d;
'For 3 dossen of stones': 5s 6d;
'For caridge of 10 dossen out of the dytche': 4s 2d;
'For sand': 3s;
'For erthe': 3d;
'For the pavinge & paving for stuff': 3s;
[Total: £2 7s 6d.]

'Carpenters
The 11th of September paied to John Knight for 6 daies': 6s;
'John Pytman 6 daies': 6s;
'Yonge Knight 6 dayes 5s to make up the syed rayles & to new foote the same': 17s;
'William Seager & his felowes eche of them 4 daies to sawe & clyff [i.e. cleave] tymber for the same': 8s;
'The 15 of October to John Knight & his sone eche of them too daies to make the stoopes & to ende the worke': 3s 8d;
'John Bodyscombe for 2 fanes for the stoope': 2s;
'John Lokyer for too spylls of yron': 2s;
'John Brook for paynting of them': 4s.
[Total: £2 8s 8d.]

[Total expenditure in this year: £31 0s 2½d.]

1563–64
Receiver Thomas Richardson.

Receiver's Roll

[m.4v.] Fees of the mayor and other officers:
    Paid the 4 gatekeepers for their fee: 16s.

[The book for this year is missing.]

1564–65
Receiver John Smyth.

Receiver's Roll

[m.4v.] Fees of the mayor and other officers:

[m.3v.] Paid the 4 gatekeepers for their fee: 16s.

[m.2v.] For building the *machno* called the 'Key' and for the new gate called 'the Watergeate': £109 8s 9d.

Allocations:
    12d allocated for a garden next the Common Jakes because the new gate called 'the Water Geate' is now built there.

[The book for this year is missing.]

[Total expenditure in this year: between 16s 0d and £110 4s 9d.]

1565–66
Receiver Robert Chaffe.

Receiver's Roll

[m.5v.] Fees of the mayor and other officers:
    Paid the 5 gatekeepers for their fee: 20s.

[m.3v.] Necessary expenses this year:
    Paid for new building of 'le Key', purchasing land adjacent to 'le Kay' from Matthew Hull, and for the 'Water Gate': £104 15s 8d.

[The book for this year is missing.]

[Total expenditure in this year: between £1 and £105 15s 8d.]

1566–67
Receiver Simon Knight.

Receiver's Roll

[m.4v.] Fees of the mayor and other officers:
    Paid the 5 gatekeepers for their fee: 16s [sic].

[The book for this year is missing.]

1567–68
Receiver William Chapell.

Receiver's Roll

[m.3v.] Fees of the mayor and other officers:
    Paid the 5 gatekeepers for their fee: 16s [sic].

[The book for this year is missing.]

1568–69
Receiver Edward Limmett.

Receiver's Roll

[*m.4v.*] Fees of the mayor and other officers:
Paid the 4 gatekeepers for their fee: 16*s*;
Paid Thomas Rawlyns, porter of the gate called 'le Water Gate': 13*s* 4*d*.

[*m.2v.*] Necessary expenses:
Paid for amending and scouring the cannon (*bumbardo*) this year: £11 11*s* 5*d*.

[The book for this year is missing.]

[Total expenditure in this year: £13 0*s* 9*d*.]

1569–70

Receiver Thomas Brewarton.

Receiver's Roll

[*m.4v.*] Fees of the mayor and other officers:
Paid the 4 gatekeepers for their fee: 16*s*;
Paid Thomas Rawlyns, porter of the gate called 'le Water Gate' for ½ year [*sic*]: 13*s* 4*d*.

[The book for this year is missing.]

[Total expenditure in this year: £1 9*s* 4*d*.]

1570–71

Receiver William Tryvett.

Receiver's Roll

[*m.3v.*] Fees of the mayor and other officers:
Paid the 4 gatekeepers for their fee: 16*s*;
Paid John James, porter of the gate called 'le Water Gate', for his fee this year: 6*s* 8*d*.

[*m.1v.*] Necessary expenses:
For repair and making anew of a piece of the City Wall next to the Bishop's Palace, which piece of the wall had lately fallen down: £21 20*d*.

[The book for this year is missing.]

[Total expenditure in this year: £22 4*s* 4*d*.]

1571–72

Receiver Nicholas Martyn.

Receiver's Roll

[*m.6v.*] Fees of the mayor and other officers:
Paid the 4 gatekeepers for their fee: 16*s*;
Paid John Courtys, porter of the gate called 'le Water Gate', for his fee this year: 6*s* 8*d*.

[*m.4v.*] Necessary expenses:

[*m.2v.*] For erecting and building of a house called 'a pryvye' next to 'le Watergate': £10 17*s* 8½*d*.

Receiver's Book

[*f.5v.*] Charges laid out:
'To the 4 porters for there fye': 16*s*.

[*f.7*] 'Extra ordinary Charges as followyth . . .
Paid Honillond [?] for Clenseng part of ye Settys Walls':
1*s*.
'Paid for 7 quartes of wyn geven to ? [illegible] 2*s* 4*d* and paid for karyeng in and awt the ordynans to be shwt at hes comyng & goyng 6*s* 8*d*': 9*s*.

[*f.8*] 'Paid to Nycholas Tayller porter of Northe Get': 6*s* 8*d*.
'Paid to Waryn porter of ? [illegible] Get': 2*s*.
[Total: 18*s* 8*d*.]

[*f.10*] 'The newe beldyng of the prevy by ye Watar Gete
Paid Wyllym Barbour labouror for 22 dayes ½ at 8*d*':
15*s*;
'Paid John Miwall & John Davyd masons for there work in maikyng all the walles & foundasyons [2 words illegible; ? at task]': 43*s* 10*d*;
'Paid for 6 dosen of Claye at': 8*s*;
'Paid for 1 dosen 8 Sems of Sand at 18*d*': 2*s* 6*d*;
'Paid for 1 dosen sems of stones bought of Mr Hull': 2*s*;
'Paid for karyg of 18 sems of stones from ye Yearn Markyt': 8*d*;
'Paid for 30 stones from Pemar [i.e. Peamore] qwary':
9*s* 4*d*;
'Paid for 7 stones bought of Georg Peryman': 2*s* 3*d*;
'Paid for 11 hogsyds of lyme at 2*s* 6*d*': 27*s*;
'Paid for the gutter of led thruwe the house & the Cettys Wall beyng 6 *C* laid by the olde lee waye containing 2 *C* 56 [?] *lbs* so the newe led wese 3 *C* & 21 *lbs* at 8*s* 8*d* *C*? [illegible] ys 29*s* 8*d* paid the plumbour for kastyng ye hill [? whole] 12*s*': 41*s* 8*d*;
'Paid for 6 *lbs* ½ of Sauder for ye Same at *lb* 7*d*': 3*s* 9*d*;
'Paid for Iron howpyes abowt the Sam gottor beyng 17 *lbs* at 3*d* the *lb*': 4*s* 3*d*;
'For naylls to fasten the Sam': 18*d*;
'Paid to Salmon [the] Karpentor for 8 dayes to set upe the Rowff of the houes at 10*d* [the] daye': 6*s* 8*d*;
'Paid Parramor Karpenter for 2 dayes to planche ye lofte': 18*d*;
'Paid for 100 bord naylls': 14*d*;
'Paid Myghel Walker hellyer for hellyng of the Sam house at [illegible] he fyndyng all stoff': 46*s*;
'Sum of thes Charges for thes howes mounts to':
£10 17*s* 8½*d*.
[*f.11v.*] 'Paid Charges beldyng the toun prevey by ye Wattar Get': £10 17*s* 8½*d*.

[Total expenditure in this year: £12 19*s* 0½*d*.]

1572–73

Receiver Thomas Prestwode.

Receiver's Roll

[*m.4v.*] Fees of the mayor and other officers:
Paid the 4 gatekeepers for their fee: 16*s*;
Paid William Weare, porter of 'le Water Gate', for his fee this year: 6*s* 8*d*.
[Total: £1 2*s* 8*d*.]

Receiver's Book

[Three pieces of parchment attached to the end of the roll.]

[m.2] Fees:
'Paid to the porter of the West Gate for his fee': 3s 4d.
'Paid to the porter of ye Northe Gate for his fee': 6s 8d.
[Total: 10s 0d.]

[m.2v.] Monies paid out on various repairs and other necessaries:
'Paid for amendinge of East Gate staples for the Lockes therto with others': 10d.
'To ye prisoners of the Comon Gayle in breadd at the muralye walke': 2s 6d.
'Paid for clensing the said walles': 1s.
'Given the Scollers in peares the same tyme': 1s.
'For wyne at Wallers with fruyt the same tyme to Mr Maior & others': 2s.
[Total: 7s 4d.]

[Total expenditure in this year: £2 0s 0d.]

1573–74

Receiver George Perryman.

Receiver's Roll

[m.5v.] Fees of the mayor and other officers:

[m.4v.] Paid the 4 gatekeepers for their fee: 16s;
Paid William Weare, porter of the gate called 'le Water Gate', for his fee this year: 6s 8d.
[Total: £1 2s 8d.]

[m.3v.] Necessary expenses:

Expenses on the bridge at East Gate: £6 6s 2d.

Receiver's Book

[f.1.] [Expenses on the] 'Gyldhall [sic] . . .
[3 November] Paid unto the prysoners at the mural': 2s;
'Paid for apelles for the bouyes': 6d;
'Paid for maken Cleane of the mural way som amounts': 2s 8d.
[14 December] 'Paid for mendynge of a Lowcke at Estgatt the some of': 4d.
[Total: 5s 6d.]

[f.1v.] 'Charges paid for makeng of the bryge at Est Gatt
Paid unto Cal for Caryege of 4 Lodes of tymber from Derewod [Duryard] to Sowthenhaye': 12s;
'Paid unto Blachefford for 16 dayes at 10d the day som amounts': 13s 4d;
'Paid unto Thomas Geffery for Caryege of 3 dosen stackes from Derewod': 7s 6d;
'Paid for Caryege of 4 Lodes of tymber from Derewod to Sowthenhay': 10s;
'Paid unto Paramore for a days worke': 8d;
'Paid unto Trewman for a days worke': 1s;
'Paid unto Blachefford and his 2 men for 11 dayes at 10d the day som': 9s 2d;
'Paid hem for straw': 4d;

'Paid unto Thomas Geffery for Caryege of stacks from Derewode': 4s 3d;
'Paid for sawynge of 400 fowt of bord at 20d [the] 100 som': 6s 8d;
'Paid for sawyng of tymber for 2 men 1 daye and a half at 10d the day som': 2s 6d;
'Paid unto Knyght for Cuttynge of tymber for 2 days at [10d—crossed out] the day': 2s;
'Paid unto hem for his 2 men for 4 days at 10d the day som': 6s 8d;
'Paid unto Paramore for 4 days at 8d': 2s 8d;
'Paid unto Knyght for 1 daye and his man': 1s 10d;
'Paid unto Huntt for 6 days at 10d': 5s;
'Paid unto John Parker for 6 days': 5s;
'Paid unto Blacheford for 5 days and a half': 4s 4d;
'Paid unto Franses for 5 days at 10d': 4s 2d;
'Paid unto Wey [?] for 3 days at 10d': 2s 6d;
'Paid unto his sarvantt for 2 days': 1s 4d;
'Paid for 1 dosen Cle at': 1s 4d;
'Paid for Caryege of 1 dosen stonis from Thomas Loyntters to Estgat': 10d;
'Paid for Caryege of 4 seme stonis from Longebroke to Estgat': 4d;
'Paid for 6 semes gravell': 6d;
'Paid for 1 days [sic] unto 2 saers': 1s 8d;
'Paid for 13 semes of gravell': 1s;
'Paid unto Franses for 1 day and a half': 1s 4d;
'Paid unto Mighall Johnson for a day': 10d;

[f.2] 'Paid unto Walter Trychay for 1 day': 8d;
'Paid unto John Parker for 2 days': 1s 8d;
'Paid unto Hunt for 2 days at 10d': 1s 8d;
'Paid unto Tyller for bolttes and naylles': 1s 4d;
'Paid unto the pavore for 42 yardes pavyng at 1½d the yard': 5s 3d;
'Paid unto Henry Jube for 2 dosen stonis 1 dosen sande': 4s 6d;
'Paid for makeng Clenne of Estgatt': 6d;
Sum: £6 6s 2d.

'Charges extraordinarye
Paid for mendyng of the gat at Westgat': 4d.
'Paid for mendyng of a loke att Est Gatt and a staple for the Yarne Markett': 4d.
'Paid for 2 men at the Wattergat 1 day': 1s 8d.

[f.2v.] [10 January] 'Paid unto Ducke for makyng of a ke and a Locke at Estgatt': 6d.
'Paid unto Knolles and his 2 men for premyng and shutyng of the ordenans': 4s.

[f.3v.] [1 July] 'Paid unto John Seton for makeng Clenne of the walles betwyxt the Watter Gat and West Gatt': 1s.
[17 July] [Margin: 'Westgatt Sters'] 'Paid unto Chepman for 22 semis of stonis for the sters at West Gat': 5s 5d.
'Paid for 8 sackes [of] Lyme': 3s 4d.
'Paid unto Nycholas Bartter for 6 days at 12d the day som': 6s.
'Paid unto his man for 6 days at 8d': 4s.
'Paid unto Franses for a day and a half': 1s 2d.

[f.4] [4 October] 'Paid for maken Clenne of the walles': 15s.

[f.4v.] [3 October] 'Paid unto Russell for mendyng of the glaishe [?] wyndows at Estgate and new quarelles the some of': £1 2s.

'Paid unto Rychard Coffell for maken Clenne of the walles': 15s.
'Paid unto hem for kyping Clenne of the walles': 3s 4d.
[Total: £4 2s 1d.]

[f.7] 'Petye fyes . . .
Paid to the portter of Northegatt': 6s 8d.
'Paid to the portter of Westgatt': 3s 4d.
[Total: 10s 0d.]

[Total expenditure in this year: £12 6s 5d.]

1574–75

Receiver John Pope.

Receiver's Roll

[m.5v.] Fees of the mayor and other officers:

[m.4v.] Paid the 4 gatekeepers for their fees: 16s;
Paid William Weare, porter of the gate called 'le Water Gate', for his fee this year: 6s 8d.

[The book for this year is missing.]

1575–76

Receiver Richard Prouze.

Receiver's Roll

[m.5v.] Fees of the mayor and other officers:
Paid the 4 gatekeepers for their fees: 16s.

Receiver's Book

[f.2] 'Extraordinary Charges

[f.2v.] 'Paid to hyme that maketh clene the walles for the whole year': 16s.

[Total expenditure in this year: £1 12s 0d.]

1576–77

Receiver Thomas Martyn.

Receiver's Roll

[m.5v.] Fees of the mayor and other officers:
Paid the 4 gatekeepers for their fees: 16s;
Paid John Curtis, porter of the gate called 'le Watergat', for his fee this year: 6s 8d.
[Total: £1 2s 8d.]

Receiver's Book

[f.4v.] [Expenses:]
'Item for mendinge the benche at Eastegate': 5d.
'Item for stoppinge a hole at the Castell Bayley which wente thorrowe the walles': 16d.
'Item for amendinge the bridge at Eastegat': 10d;
'Item for carrienge awaie of the Rubbell': 18d.
[Total: 4s 1d.]

'Southinghey
Paid for mendinge the walles in Southinghey': 3s 6d;
'Item paid for a sacke of lyme': 4d.
[Total: 3s 10d.]

[f.5v.] 'Charges bestowed upon the previes at the Watergate'.
[This section has been deleted.]

[f.8] 'Charges bestowed against my lordes comyng into the Cittie
Paid for 35 lbs of powder at 14d the pounde': 40s 10d;
'Paid for 10 lbs of matche at 4d the pounde': 3s 4d.
[Total: £2 4s 2d.]

[f.9] 'Charges extraordinary . . . as followeth . . .

[f.9v.] Paid to Coffeilde to make cleane the walles the whole year': 13s 4d.

[f.10] 'Paid to the prisoners of Southgate in reward': 12d;
'Paid to the prisoners at the Quens Gaole': 2s;
'Paid for pears and nuttes to geve the boies': 10d;
'Paid for clensinge of the muralle walk': 2s.
[Total: 19s 2d.]

[Total expenditure in this year: £4 13s 11d.]

1577–78

Receiver Nicholas Germyn.

Receiver's Roll

[m.7v.] Fees of the mayor and other officers:

[m.6v.] Paid the 4 gatekeepers for their fees: 16s;
Paid John Courtis, porter of the gate called 'le Watergate', for his fee this year: 6s 8d.
[Total: £1 2s 8d.]

Necessary expenses:
[m.5v.] Money paid for repairs to 'le grat' at West Gate this year: £3 2s 4d.

Receiver's Book

[f.1] 'Extraordinary charges . . .
Paid to a Carpenter for makinge of Quynes for the great Gonne at my lords first comyng': 12d;
'Paid for bringinge home the great Gonne frome Northinghey to the stoare howse': 6d.
'Paid unto Mr Waller at the mewralley walk for wyne and money geven to the prisoners': 2s 6d;
'Paid for Apples which were geven to the boyes the same tyme': 6d;
'Paid unto the prisoners ? [illegible] of the Quens Gaole at the tyme of the said walke': 2s 6d.

[f.1v.] 'Paid for setting upp againe of the bridg for the arches to pas over in Northinghey': 6d.
'Paid for clensing of the walls against the mewralley walk': 12d.

[f.2] 'Paid to hyme that beganne to builde a howse at the Watergat in recompenc of his graunt & towards his Charges bestowed': 20s.
[Total: £1 8s 6d.]

[*f.5*] 'Charges bestowed in repairing of the grat at Westgat as followeth
Inprimis paid for 2 newe postes for the grat at the Westgat': 4s;
'Paid for mending and scowringe of the same vawt': [blank];
'Paid a mason for a daies woork to ripp the vawt': 12d;
'Paid a workeman to serve hyme': 8d;
'Paid for 3 sacks of lyme': 15d;
'Payd for 6 sacks of lyme': 2s 6d;
'Paid for 4 seames of Claye': 6d;
'Paid for a dossen of quary stones to mende and Cover the vawt': 4s 4d;
'Paid a poor labourer for ridding the vawt': 12d;
'Paid for 2 seames of sand': 3d;
'Paid for 5 seames of sande for the pavier': 6d;
'Paid for 3 seames of stones to pave aboute the sides and hedd of the vawte': 6d;
'Paid to John Davie mason for working there three daies at 12d *per diem*': 3s 6d;
'Paid a labourer to serve hyme 2 daies': 20d;

[*f.5v.*] 'Paid unto the pavier for paving about the vawt': 8d;
'Paid unto Gilbert the Smith for a new grat waieng 41 *lbs* at 4d the *lb* besides the olde': 10s;
Sum: [blank].

[*f.6*] 'Charges laied oute for musters as ['followeth'—crossed out] & receaving of my lorde of Cumberlande as followeth . . . [extracts only:]
Inprimis paid unto Laurence Seldon for 50 *lbs* of gonne pooder spent in receaving of my lorde of Comberlande & for 8 *lbs* of matches': £3 2s 6d;
'Paid for a 100 of gonners wages at 6d the pece': 50s;
'Paid for paper to putt there powder in': 6d;
[Total: £5 13s 0d.]

[Total expenditure in this year: £11 6s 6d.]

1578–79

Receiver Geoffrey Thomas.

Receiver's Roll

[*m.6v.*] Fees of the mayor and other officers:
Paid the 4 gatekeepers for their fees: 16s;
Paid John Courtis, keeper of the gate of 'le Watergate', for his fee this year: 6s 8d.
[Total: £1 2s 8d.]

[*m.5v.*] Necessary expenses:
Paid for a new structure (*nova Structura*) on the walls of the city next 'le Water Gate': £41 13s 4d.

[The book for this year is missing.]

[Total expenditure in this year: £42 16s 0d.]

1579–80

Receiver Thomas Reymonde.

Receiver's Roll

[*m.5v.*] Fees of the mayor and other officers:
Paid the 4 gatekeepers for their fees: 16s;
Paid John Courtys, keeper of the Watergate, for his fee this year: 6s 8d.
[Total: £1 2s 8d.]

[*m.4v.*] Necessary expenses:
Paid for repairs to the walls at Watergate: £40 11s 5d.

Receiver's Book

[*f.1*] 'Charges bestowed aboute the Cytties Wales neare Watergate from the 17th day of October 1579 as followethe
17th October *Inprimis* paid Antony Maunder for 2 dayes worke at 12d a daye': 2s;
'Paid to William Rogers for one daye': 10d;
'Paid John Bagwill for one daye': 8d;
'Paid Henry Dally for 3 daies and halfe at 8d a daye': 2s 4d;
'Paid Water Norrishe for 3 daies and halfe at 8d [a] daye': 2s 4d;
'24th October . . . paid Antony Maunder for 6 daies at 12d a daie': 6s;
'Paid George Pitts for 3 daies and halfe at 10d a daie': 2s 11d;
'Paid Thomas Comon for 5 dayes and halfe at 10d a daye': 4s 7d;
'Paid William Rogers for 3 daies and halfe at 10d a daye': 2s 11d;
'Paid John Bagwill for 6 dayes at 8d a daie': 4s;
'Paid Water Morrishe for 6 daies at 8d a daie': 4s;
'Paid Henry Dally for 6 daies at 8d a daye': 4s;
'Paid Newalls man for 3 daies and halfe at 8d [a] daie': 2s 4d;
'Paid for a pott to Cary stones': 2d;
'31th [*sic*] October . . . paid Water Morishe for 2 daies at 8d a daye': 16d;
'Paid John Bagwill for 2 dayes at 8d a daye': 16d;
'7 November . . . paid Antony Maunder for 2 daies worke at 12d [a] daye': 2s;
'Paid William Rogers for 4 dayes at 10d a daye': 3s 4d;
[Subtotal] 47s 1d;

[*f.1v.*] 'Paid John Newall for one dayes worke': 12d;
'Paid John Pytts for 6 dayes at 10d [a] day': 5s;
'Paid Thomas Comon for 9 dayes at 10d [a] day': 6s 6d;
'Paid Ambrose Newall for 2 daies at 10d [a] day': 20d;
'Paid Henry Dallye for 7 daies at 8d [a] day': 4s 8d;
'Paid Water Morishe for 5 dayes at 8d [a] day': 3s 4d;
'Paid John Bennett for 7 dayes at 8d [a] day': 4s 8d;
'Paid Henry Hunt for 2 dayes worke at 8d [a] daye': 16d;
'Paid for twyne': 2d;
'10th November . . . paid Antony Maunder for 2 dayes at 12d [a] day': 2s;
'Paid William Rogers for one dayes worke at 10d': 10d;
'Paid John Pitts for 2 dayes at 10d': 20d;
'Paid Thomas Comon for 2 dayes at 10d': 20d;
'Paid John Bennett for 2 dayes at 8d': 16d;
'14th November . . . paid Henry Dally for 4 daies at 8d': 2s 8d;
'Paid Water Morishe for 4 dayes at 8d': 2s 8d;
'21th [*sic*] November . . . paid Water Morishe for 6 dayes at 8d': 4s;

'Paid Henry Dally for one day': 8*d*;
'28th November . . . paid Walter Morishe for 6 dayes at 8*d*': 4*s*;
'Paid Thomas Comon for 16 dayes at 10*d*': 13*s* 4*d*;
'7th Maye . . . paid Michael Frygins for 2 dayes for makinge the morter howse': 2*s*;
'Paid to Chaunt for Thychinge said howse': 6*d*;
'Paid Thomas Comon for 6 dayes at 11*d*': 5*s* 6*d*;
'Paid Water Morishe for 5 dayes at 8*d*': 3*s* 4*d*;
'Paid Zachary Dyer for 2 dayes at 8*d*': 16*d*;
'Paid for 2 pottes': 4*d*;
'Paid for twyne': 2*d*;
'Paid for a dosen of scaffell ropes': 8*d*;
'14th May . . . paid William Hewishe for 5 daies at 12*d*': 5*s*;
'Paid Thomas Comon for 5 dayes at 11*d*': 4*s* 7*d*;
'Paid William Bargery for 3 dayes and halfe at 11*d*': 3*s* 3*d*;
'Paid Water Morishe for 5 daies at 8*d*': 3*s* 4*d*;
'Paid Zachary Dyer for 5 daies at 8*d*': 3*s* 4*d*;
'Paid Robert Hodder for 5 daies at 8*d*': 3*s* 4*d*;
'Paid for a tole to prime the wall': 3*d*;
[Subtotal] £5 1*s* 1*d*;

[*f.2*] '21 May . . . [paid] William Hewishe for 6 dayes at 12*d* a daye': 6*s*;
'Paid William Bargery for 6 dayes at 11*d* a daye': 5*s* 6*d*;
'Paid Robert Hodder for 6 dayes at 8*d*': 4*s*;
'Paid Thomas Comon for 6 dayes at 11*d*': 5*s* 6*d*;
'Paid Zachary Dyer for 6 daies at 8*d*': 4*s*;
'Paid William Hewishe for scobling a 100 of stones at 5*s* [the] 100': 5*s*;
'Paid John Bagwill for 6 daies at 9*d*': 4*s* 6*d*;
'Paid Water Morishe for 6 daies at 8*d*': 4*s*;
'Paid for a buckett for to dipp water': 2*d*;
'28th May . . . paid Thomas Comon for 4 dayes at 11*d*': 3*s* 8*d*;
'Paid William Bargery for 4 daies at 11*d*': 3*s* 8*d*;
'Paid Water Morishe for 4 daies at 8*d*': 2*s* 8*d*;
'Paid Robert Hodder for 4 daies at 8*d*': 2*s* 8*d*;
'4 June . . . paid Thomas Comon for 6 dayes at 11*d*': 5*s* 6*d*;
'Paid William Bargery for 3 dayes and halfe at 11*d*': 3*s* 2*d*;
'Paid Water Morishe for 6 dayes at 8*d*': 4*s* 2*d*;
'Paid Robert Hodder for 3 daies and halfe at 8*d*': 2*s* 4*d*;
'11 June . . . paid William Bargery for 6 dayes at 11*d*': 5*s* 6*d*;
'Paid Robert Hodder for 6 daies at 8*d*': 4*s*;
'Paid Thomas Comon for 6 daies at 11*d*': 5*s* 6*d*;
'Paid Zachary Dyer for 6 dayes and halfe at 8*d*': 4*s* 4*d*;
'Paid Water Morishe for 6 dayes at 8*d*': 4*s*;
'17 June . . . paid William Hewishe for 4 dayes & halfe at 12*d*': 4*s* 6*d*;
'Paid William Bargery for 4 daies at 11*d*': 3*s* 8*d*;
'Paid William Hewishe for scobling 50 stones': 2*s* 6*d*;
'Paid Robert Hodder for 5 daies at 8*d*': 3*s* 4*d*;
'Paid Water Morishe for 5 daies at 8*d*': 3*s* 4*d*;
'Paid Zachary Dyer for 4 daies at 8*d*': 2*s* 8*d*;
'Paid Thomas Comon for 5 dayes and halfe at 11*d*': 5*s* 1*d*;
'25 June . . . paid William Hewishe for 6 daies at 12*d*': 6*s*;
'Paid Thomas Comon for 5 dayes at 11*d*': 4*s* 7*d*;
'Paid William Bargery for 5 daies at 11*d*': 4*s* 7*d*;

'Paid Water Morishe for 2 daies at 8*d*': 16*d*;
'Paid Robert Hodder for 5 daies at 8*d*': 3*s* 4*d*;
'Paid John Crapp for 5 daies at 8*d*': 3*s* 4*d*;
'Paid William Hewishe for 6 daies at 12*d*': 6*s*;
'Paid William Bargery for 4 daies at 11*d*': 3*s* 8*d*;
'Paid Thomas Comon for 5 daies at 11*d*': 4*s* 7*d*;
'Paid Robert Hodder for 5 daies at 8*d*': 3*s* 4*d*;
'Paid Water Morishe for 4 daies at 8*d*': 2*s* 8*d*;
'Paid John Crapp for 5 daies at 8*d*': 3*s* 4*d*;
[Subtotal] £8 1*s* 8*d*;

[*f.2v.*] '9 July . . . paid William Hewish for 2 dayes at 12*d*': 2*s*;
'Paid Thomas Comon for 6 daies at 11*d*': 5*s* 6*d*;
'Paid Robert Hodder for 6 daies at 8*d*': 4*s*;
'[Paid] Water Morishe for 4 dayes & halfe at 8*d*': 3*s*;
'12 July . . . paid Thomas Comon for 2 dayes at 11*d*': 22*d*;
'Paid Water Morishe for one daie & halfe at 8*d*': 12*d*;

'Wonford stones
14 October . . . paid John Chapman for 6 dosen of stones at 3*s* 4*d* [the] dosen': 20*s*;
'10 November . . . paid John Chapman for 9 dosen of stones & 3 semes': 30*s* 10*d*;
'28 November . . . him for 6 dosen & 9 semes': 22*s* 6*d*;
'21 May . . . paid him for 5 dosen': 16*s* 8*d*;
'17 June . . . paid him for 10 dosen': 33*s* 4*d*;
'15 June . . . paid him for 2 dosen': 6*s* 8*d*;
'17 July . . . paid him for 2 dosen': 6*s* 8*d*;

'Shillingford stones
5 December paid George Backer for 100 semes of stones at 4*d* quarter a seme': 35*s* 5*d*;
'Paid for scobling of the said stones': 5*s*;
'21 May paid George Backer for 100 semes of stones at 4*d* quarter a seme': 35*s* 5*d*;
'24 June paid George Backer for 50 stones at 4*d* quarter a seme': 17*s* 5*d*;
'6 July paid the said George for 21 semes of stones at 4*d* quarter a seme': 7*s* 5*d*;
[Subtotal] £13 4*s* 11*d*;

[*f.3*] 'Lyme
30 November paid Christopher Serell for 29 hogesydes at 3*s per* hogesyde': £4 7*s*;
'9 June paid him for 20 hogesydes at 3*s per* hogesyde': £3;
'25 July paid him for 20 other hogesydes': £3;

'Sande
24 October paid Thomas Bicknoll for 11 dossen of sande at 12*d* [the] dosen': 11*s*;
'14 November paid him for one dosen 12*d*': 12*d*;
'28 November paid him for 8 semes of sande': 8*d*;
'21 May paid Francis Geffry for 8 dosen of sande at 12*d* [the] dosen': 8*s*;
'4 June paid him for 4 dosen': 4*s*;
'17 June paid him for 3 dosen': 3*s*;
'25 June paid him for 2 dosen': 2*s*;
[Subtotal] £11 16*s* 8*d*;
Sum: £40 11*s* 5*d*.

'The reparacion of the Geale at Southgate 1580 . . .

[*f.3v.*] Sum: £4 9*s* 1*d*.

'Extraordinary Charges

[*f.5v.*] [6 October] 'Paid to the Quenes Geale by Mr Maiers Commandement at the Murally': 2*s* 6*d*.

[*f.6*] '19 October paid to Wallers at Southgate for wyne': 2*s* 6*d*;
'Paid to the prisoners there': 12*d*;
'Paid for appels': 8*d*;
'Paid for makeinge Clene of the murally walke': 16*d*.
'30 November paid Simon Blackmore and his man for 4 dayes work for Rolinge of the bridge at Eastgate': 7*s* 8*d*;
'Paid for bord nayles': 6*d*.

[*f.6v.*] [3 May] 'Paid the smyth for mendinge of Eastegate': 2*s*.

[*f.7*] '4 September paid for mendinge of the locke att Eastgate': 4*d*.
'Paid for 4 *C* of peares': 12*d*.
[Total: 19*s* 6*d*.]

[Total expenditure in this year: £42 13*s* 7*d*.]

1580–81

Receiver John Davye.

Receiver's Roll

[*m.5v.*] Fees of the mayor and other officers:
Paid the 4 gatekeepers for their fee: 16*s*;
Paid John Curtys, porter of 'le Watergate', for his fee this year: 6*s* 8*d*.
[Total: £1 2*s* 8*d*.]

[*m.4v.*] Necessary expenses:
Paid for repairs to the City Walls this year: 22*s* 6*d*.

Receiver's Book

[*f.2v.*] 'Charges payd upon the Gayle at Southgate & keeping of the same . . .'
Sum: £6 3*s* 8*d*.

[*f.5*] 'Extraordinary Charges bestowed this yere as foloweth . . .
Paid for payers at Mr Maiers going in the murally walke': 6*d*;
'Paid at the Kyngesgaole the same tyme': 3*s* 4*d*;
'Paid at Wallers the same tyme for wyne & beare': 2*s* 4*d*;
'Paid the prisoners at South Gate': 12*d*.

[*f.5v.*] 'Paid for mending of the locke at Eastgate': 8*d*.
'Paid for zawying of palls & other stuffe for the pale under the walls': 5*s* 6*d*.
'Paid for caryadge of 14 Seames for the pale & posses with Westgate from Duryord [Duryard]': 3*s* 2*d*.
'Paid Edward Secke for makinge of 2 palls & 2 styles without Westgate being 7 dayes worke': 7*s*.
'Paid for 200 of bordenales aboute the same': 2*s* 8*d*.

[*f.6*] 'Paid a man for 7 dayes to helpe make the pale under the walls at 11*d* [a] day': 6*s* 5*d*.
[Total: £1 12*s* 7*d*.]

[*f.7*] 'Charges bestowed upon reparacion of the walles this yeare in Frerenhay
Paid Dayman for 5 dayes to mende the garretts in Frerenhay': 5*s*;
'Paid his man for 5 dayes at 10*d* [a] day': 4*s* 2*d*;
'Paid for Scabling of 19 stones': 10*d*;
'Paid Serell for a hogshed & sacke of lyme': 3*s*;
'Paid for half a dossen of Sande': 9*d*;
'Paid a quaryman for 19 stones at 4*d* [a] peece': 6*s* 4*d*;
'Paid for a wylly to cary rubble in': 10*d*;
'Paid for caryadge of stones from Bridzewell': 4*d*;
'Paid for Scubling of Stones for the walls in Frerenhay': 8*d*;
'Paid for a mason for half a dayes worke': 6*d*;
Sum: 22*s* 5*d*.

[Total expenditure in this year: £3 17*s* 8*d*.]

1581–82

Receiver John Peryam, gentleman.

Receiver's Roll

[*m.3v.*] Fees of the mayor and other officers:
Paid the 4 gatekeepers of the city for their fee this year: 16*s*;
Paid John Courtys, keeper of 'le Watergate', for his fee this year: 6*s* 8*d*.
[Total: £1 2*s* 8*d*.]

Necessary expenses:
Paid for repairs to the City Walls this year: £31 1*s* 1*d*.

Receiver's Book

[*f.1*] 'Expences bestowed upon the repayrynge of the Towne Walls without Southegate nere the Key
Paid to John Ryve for 26 hogseds and a half of lyme at 2*s* 6*d* hogsed': £3 6*d*;
'Paid to Christofer Serell for 48 hogseds of lyme at 3*s* per hogsed': £7 4*d* [*sic*];

[*f.1v.*] 'Paid to Baker of Shillingford for 4 dossen and a half of Burres at 2*s* 8*d* per dossen': 12*s*;
'Paid to him for 50 Seame Stones at 4*d* [a] pece': 16*s* 8*d*;
'Paid to Chapman for 30 dossen of Brares at 3*s* 4*d* dossen': £5;
'Paid to Bicknell for 26 dossen and a half of Sande at 16*d* dossen': 35*s* 4*d*;
'Paid to Deyman for pullyng downe the wall & makyng the fundacion': 40*s*;
'Paid to him for Scablyng of Stones & for a cowle': 3*s*;
'Paid to him for 65 perches of wall at 2*s* 6*d* perche': £8 2*s*;
'Paid to him for makyng of flakes': 9*s* 9*d*;
'Paid to Thomas Jeffry for caryage of Stuffe': 2*s* 8*d*;
'Paid for Scaffolde ropes': 4*s*;
'Paid for Iron worke to Gilbert the Smythe': 19*d*;
'Paid Walden for takyng thaccompte of lyme & Sande': 3*s* 4*d*;
'Paid for 6 Seames of Quary Stones for the Barbygan at Northegate': 18*d*;
'Paid for caryage of a dossen of Stones from the Guihald': 12*d*;

'For half a dossen sande for the same': 9*d*;
'Paid for 3 hogsheds of lyme for the same': 9*s*;
'Paid for 4 dossen of hard gravell & for Syftynge': 4*s*;
'Paid for the masons worke aboute the same': 4*s* 6*d*;
£31 1*s* 1*d*.

[*f.4*] 'Reparacions upon the Guihald & St Johns . . .
Paid William Knolls for 3 dayes worke aboute the ordynance & others with him': 4*s* 2*d*.

[*f.4v.*] 'Extraordinary expences layde out as folowethe . . .
Geven to the Gayle at the murally walke': 2*s* 6*d*;
'Paid the Beedells for Clensing the walles then': 2*s*.

[*f.5*] 'Paid for raylyng of Snayletower': 11*s* 8*d*.
[Total: 16*s* 2*d*.]

[Total expenditure in this year: £33 4*s* 1*d*.]

1582–83

Receiver George Smythe, gentleman.

Receiver's Roll

[*m.5v.*] Fees of the mayor and other officers:

[*m.4v.*] Paid the 4 gatekeepers of the city for their fee this year: 16*s*;
Paid John Courtys, keeper of 'le Water Gate', for his fee this year: 6*s* 8*d*.
[Total: £1 2*s* 8*d*.]

Necessary expenses:
Paid for repairs to the City Walls this year: £88 16*s* 8½*d*.

Receiver's Book

[*f.1*] 'Extraordinary charges . . .
October 1582 paid to the Gaiell at the muralie walke': 2*s* 6*d*;
'Paid to the poor [of] Mr Hurstes Almshouses the same time': 12*d*;
'Paid for appells the same time': 12*d*;
'Paid to the Bedels for macking clene of the walles agaynst the muraly': 2*s*.

[*f.2v.*] [June 1583] 'Paid for Caryadge of 2 trees to the Towne Walls': 2*s*.
'Auguste 1583 . . . paid to William Russell for worke done at Eastgate as apperes by his bill': 3*s*.

[*f.3*] 'Paid William Knolls for his fee for kepenge the Ordinance': 26*s* 8*d*.
[Total: £1 18*s* 2*d*.]

[Total expenditure in this year: £91 17*s* 6½*d*.]

1583–84

Receiver William Martyne, gentleman.

Receiver's Roll

[*m.7v.*] Fees of the mayor and other officers:

Paid the 4 gatekeepers of the city for their fee this year: 16*s*;
Paid Robert Gaydon, keeper of 'le Water Gate', for his fee this year: 6*s* 8*d*.
[Total: £1 2*s* 8*d*.]

[*m.5v.*] Necessary expenses:
Paid for diverse reparations at West Gate and Water Gate: £7 8*s* 8*d*.

Receiver's Book

[*f.1v.*] 'Extraordinary Chardges . . .
Paid the two Beedells for Clensinge of the walls at the mewralye': 16*d*;
'Paid and geven to the High Gaole': 2*s* 6*d*;
'Paid to the gaole at Southgate': 12*d*;

[*f.2*] 'Paid for Appells for the schollers': 8*d*;
'Paid and geven to the poore of the Ame houses': 12*d*.
[Total: 6*s* 6*d*.]

[*f.4v.*] 'Reparacions upon the walls of Southgate
Paide for 3 dosen of Stones from Hevitree': 9*s*;
'Paid for 7 hogsheds of Lyme': 21*s*;
'Paid for 3 dosen of Sande': 4*s*;
'Paid Richard Deymond for 4 daies': 4*s*;
'Paid John Ellacom for 4 daies': 3*s* 8*d*;
'Paid Walter Morris for 4 daies': 3*s*;

[*f.5*] 'Paid for one laboure man one daie': 8*d*;
'Paid one Bowie for 4 daies': 2*s* 8*d*;
[Sum:] 48*s*.

'Reparacions upon the walles at Estgate
Paide for 9 hoggsheds of hote lyme': 27*s*;
'Paid for 5 dosen of Sande': 6*s* 8*d*;
'Paid for 9 dosen of Seame stones from Hevitree': 27*s*;
'Paid for 3 dosen of Seme stones': 10*s*;
'Paid for 2 basketts to Carry Stones': 6*d*;
'Paid for one Skeyne of Twyne': 2*d*;
'Paid to Richard Deymond for 7 daies': 7*s*;
'Paid John Deymond for 3 daies': 3*s*;
'Paid William Laurens for 2 daies': 2*s*;
'Paid John Ellecom for 7 daies': 6*s* 5*d*;
'Paid Richard Deymonds man for 5 daies': 3*s* 4*d*;
'Paid Walter Morris for 7 daies': 5*s* 3*d*;
'Paid John Deymond for 2 daies': 16*d*;
[Sum:] £4 19*s* 8*d*.

'Reparacions upon the walls at Northgate
Paide for 4 hogsheds of Lyme': 12*s*;
'Paid for Caryinge of 9 Seemes of Lyme & Sande from Estgate to Northgate & 3 Seemes of Stones': 12*d*;

[*f.5v.*] 'Paid for Caryinge of one dosen and halfe of Stones from the Guihald to Northgate': 9*d*;
'Paid for 26 Seemes of Sande': 2*s* 11*d*;
'Paid for 8 Semes of Seme stones': 2*s* 8*d*;
'Paid for 21 Semes of Stones': 5*s* 3*d*;
'Paid Richard Deymond for 3 daies & halfe': 3*s* 6*d*;
'Paid William Laurens for 3 daies & halfe': 3*s* 6*d*;
'Paid John Ellecom for 3 daies': 2*s* 9*d*;
'Paid John Deymonds man for 3 daies': 2*s* 4*d*;
'Paid Walter Morris for 4 daies & halfe': 3*s* 4*d*;

'Paid for a Coole and a buckett for to cary Water & bordes & Cordes to make a Scaffolde': 2s 6d;
[Sum:] 42s 6d.

'Reparacions at the Westegate & Watergate
Paid for 2 seemes of Silferton [Silverton] Stones': 2s 8d;
'Paid for more Stones Lyme & Sande which comes in the Compte of the Kaie: [is therefore blank];
'Paid Brocke for 1 dosen of hewen seeme Stones': 5s;
'Paid for 9 dosen & halfe of Seeme stones': 34s 10d;
'Paid George Cooke for 7 dosen of Seeme stones': 28s;
'Paid hym for two dosens & halfe of Burres': 7s 6d;
'Paid for 2 hoggshedds & 21 sackes of Lyme': 13s 2d;
'Paid for 8 seemes of Sande': 22d;
'Paid for Scablinge of 83 Stones': 4s;

[f.6] 'Paid two laboure men for 9 daies': 6s 9d;
'Paid William Laurens William Deymond Roberte Lake masons for 27 daies': 27s;
'Paid John Ellacom for 9 daies': 8s 3d;
'Paid to John Robinson mason for 14 daies & halfe': 9s 8d;
[Sum:] £7 8s 8d.

[Total expenditure in this year: £18 8s 0d.]

1584–85

Receiver John Levermore, gentleman.

Receiver's Roll

[m.5v.] Fees of the mayor and other officers:

[m.4v.] Paid the 4 gatekeepers of the city for their fee this year: 16s;
Paid Robert Gaidon, keeper of 'le Watergate', for his fee this year: 6s 8d.
[Total: £1 2s 8d.]

Receiver's Book

[f.1] 'Extraordinarie Charges paid by Mr Receyver . . .
Paid for Appells at Mr Maiors going the murale': 12d;
'Geven to the Kinges Gaole 2s & to the Citties Gaole the same tyme 12d': 3s;
'Paid for making Cleane of the walles': 16d.

[f.1v.] 'Paid to Wilcocks for gravell put upon the Barbigans at Freerenhay': 13d.

[f.2] 'Paid for mendinge of the Iron Work of the Estegate to Gilberte the Smyth': 16d.

[f.2v.] 'Paid the Twentith of Februarie towardes the rudinge of the Vate at Westgate': 20d;
'Paid by Mr Maiors appointement to three men 4d a peece for the same worke & unto 2 men 6d a peece for the same worke': 2s.

[f.3v.] 'Paid for the amending of the Iron worke of Estegate beinge broken': 18d.
'Paid for a lock for Westegate': 8d.

[f.4] 'Paid for 3 longe Staves for the ordynaunce of St

Johns': 2s.
'Item for so much Brasse Plate': 20d;
'Paid Newall for the makinge of them': 16d.

[f.4v.] 'Paid Hunte the Chandeler for Candells for charging the watch and for examinge [sic] at sundry tymes': 20d.
[Total: £1 0s 3d.]

[Total expenditure in this year: £2 2s 11d.]

1585–86

Receiver Thomas Chapell, gentleman.

Receiver's Roll

[m.3v.] Fees of the mayor and other officers:
Paid the 4 gatekeepers of the city for their fee this year: 16s;
Paid John [sic] Gaydon, porter of 'le Watergate', for his fee this year: 6s 8d.
[Total: £1 2s 8d.]

Necessary expenses:
[m.2v.] For new making the bridge near East Gate and the walls there on either side of that bridge [?], as appears: £17 4s 10d.

Receiver's Book [DRO, Box 214, Book 13]

[f.1] 'Extraordynary Chardges . . .
Paid for Appells when the Maior went a Murale': 2s;
'Geven to the two Gaoles': 8s 7d;
'Paid for beating of the Beare the same tyme by Mr Maiors order': 12d;
'Paide for making Cleane of the Towne Walls': 12d.
'For mending of the grate at Westegate the 17th of November': 3s 4d.

[f.3] 'For amending of Westegate': 16d.
'For amending of the Grate at Westegate the 28th of July': 10s 10d.
[Total: £1 8s 1d.]

[f.6] 'Chardges Laide out for ['amending' crossed out] new buildinge of the Bridge of the Eastegate
'For 4 seames of stones': 13s 4d;
'For 2 men for 3 daies at 12d the daye': 12s;
'For one man for 3 daies at 12d the daie': 3s;
'For 8 seames of sand & 20 seames of Claye & 2 seames of stones': 3s 6d;
'For a Labour Man for 6 dayes at 9d the daye': 4s 6d;
'For 8 dosen of Seame stones at 3s 4d the dosen': 26s 8d;

[f.7] 'For one man for 5 daies at 12d the daye': 5s;
'For 12 stones the 24th of September': 4s;
'For 80 stones the 27th of August': 26s 8d;
'John Davye mason for him & his men for 24 daies at 12d the day': 24s;
'For a man to serve him 2 daies': 2s;
'For stones to helpe the great stones': 18d;
'For 3 men for 6 dayes at 12d the day': 18s;
'For a man to serve hym 6 daies': 4s;
'For Carryage of a pece of Tymber at Eastegate': 16d;
'For 6 dosen of stones at Eastegate': 20s;

'For sand claye 2 dosen & 8 seames': 6s;
'For a man to serve hym 5 dayes': 3s 4d;
'For one day & half for a Labor man': 12d;
'For 4 men for 5 dayes at 12d the daye': 20s;
'For a Labour man for 5 daies at 9d the daye': 3s 9d;
'For one dosen of stones': 3s 4d;
'For 2 men for 6 dayes at 12d the daye': 12s;
'For one man for 3 daies at 12d the daye': 3s;
'For Silferton [Silverton] stones': 20s;
'For one dosen of Sande': 18d;
'For 3 daies unto John Davy': 3s;
'For the paving of Eastegate': 12d;
'For a man for 6 dayes at 9d the daye': 4s 6d;
'For dressing of the Vanes & the stones at Eastegate': 5s 6d;

[f.8] 'For tenne hoggshedds of Lyme at 3s the hoggshedd': 30s;
'John Davy for 5 daies': 5s;
'John Davye for engraving of the stone': 6s;
'For Ledd for Eastegate': 11d;
'For Iron for the spill of the Pillers': 2s 6d;
'For Silferton stones 74 foote at 3d the foote': 18s;
'For the Pillers': 6s;
'John Davy for 7 daies': 7s.
'Sum': £17 4s 10d.

[Total expenditure in this year: £19 15s 7d.]

1586–87

Receiver Nicholas Spycer.

Receiver's Roll

[m.4v.] Fees of the mayor and other officers:
Paid the 4 gatekeepers of the city for their fee this year: 16s;
Paid Robert Gaydon, keeper of 'le Watergate', for his fee this year: 6s 8d;
Paid the keeper of West Gate for cleansing [the grates at] that gate: 3s 4d;
Paid the keeper of North Gate for cleansing [the grates at] that gate: 6s 8d.
[Total: £1 12s 8d.]

Receiver's Book

[f.1] 'Reparacions . . . upon the . . . Eastgate Westgate Northgate & Southgat . . .

[f.1v.] . . . paid for mendinge the Loacke at Northgate': 15d.
'Paid for amendinge the Iron worke at Kaye Gate': 2s 6d.
'Westgat
. . . paid [for] 12 lbs of Iron Worke at West Gate': 3s;
'Paid to a Carpenter for amendinge that Gate': 6d.

[f.2] 'Paid for Candellight & Tallow for the ordynaunce': 4s 4d.

[f.2v.] 'Paid for 4 lbs half of ledd for the windowes at Southgat': 6d.
[Total: 12s 1d.]

[f.3] 'Expenses extraordinarie laide out this yere by Mr

Receyver as foloweth . . .
Paid for 13 lbs of Iron Worke for the Ordynaunce': 3s 8d.
'Paid to the 4 poore of Palmers Almes house & to the prisoners at Southgat': 22d;
'Paid for one pott of Apples at the murale': 3s;
'Geven then to the Quenes Gaole': 3s 4d;
'Paid for Wyne & else at Edmond Clerkes the same tyme': 5s;
'Paid to the beedells for making Cleane the walls': 2s.

[f.4] 'Paid Pope the Constable for candells at the watchinge at Westgat': 10d.

[f.4v.] 'Paid for 4 men to watch one night in Freerenhaye': 12d.

[f.5] 'Paid to one to gravell the walls': 12d.
[Total: £1 1s 8d.]

[Total expenditure in this year: £3 7s 5d.]

1587–88

Receiver Philip Yarde, gentleman.

Receiver's Roll

[m.5v.] Fees of the mayor and other officers:

[m.4v.] Paid the 4 gatekeepers of the city for their fee this year: 16s;
Paid Robert Gaydon, keeper of 'le Watergate', for his fee this year: 6s 8d;
Paid the keeper of West Gate for cleansing [the grates of] that gate: 3s 4d;
Paid the porter of North Gate for cleansing [the grates of] that gate: 6s 8d.
[Total: £1 12s 8d.]

Necessary expenses:
Paid for reparations on the Guildhall, West Gate, East Gate, New Inn, South Gate and North Gate, and for other necessary reparations: £9 15s 4d.

Receiver's Book

Extraordinary Charges:
[f.4v.] 'To the prysoners of the geale goinge of the Murallye': 2s 6d;
'To beddells for makinge clene of the walls': 1s 6d;
'For Appells for the Chyldren Cominge from the Muralye at Mr Brewtons doore': 2s.
'For mendinge a breche in the brige at Eastgate': 2s.
[Total: 8s 0d.]

[Total expenditure in this year: somewhere between £2 0s 8d and £11 16s 0d.]

1588–89

Receiver Thomas Spycer.

Receiver's Roll

[m.5v.] Fees of the mayor and other officers:

Paid the 4 gatekeepers of the city for their fee this year: 16s;
Paid Robert Gaydon, keeper of 'le Watergate', for his fee this year: 6s 8d;
Paid the keeper of West Gate for cleansing [the grates of] that gate: 3s 4d;
Paid the keeper of North Gate for cleansing [the grates of] that gate: 6s 8d.
[Total: £1 12s 8d.]

Receiver's Book

[*f.1*] 'Extraordinarie Charges
Inprimis paid in the Muralia Walke to the Geale': 1s 8d;
'Paid to Southgate Counter & prison': 2s;
'Paid to Quintens for the banquetts': 5s.
'Paid for reparacions & mendinge upon the Key Gate & Southgate and Westgate': £5 11s 2d.
'Paid for pavinge at Westgate and for led bestowed about the gates': 14s 4d.
'Paid for a locke and a barre upon Southgate': 2s 6d.

[*f.1v.*] 'Paid for Apples cast to the boyes': 2s 6d;
'Paid to the Beedells to Clens the walls of the Citie': 1s 3d.

[*f.3*] 'Paid to Blackmore and his man for 4 dayes worke about the pillory and the Key Gate': 6s 8d.
[Total: £7 7s 1d.]

[Total expenditure in this year: £8 19s 9d.]

1589–90

Receiver John Chappell.

Receiver's Roll

[*m.3v.*] Fees of the mayor and other officers:
Paid the 4 gatekeepers of the city for their fee this year: 16s;
Paid Robert Gaydon, keeper of 'le Watergate', for his fee this year: 6s 8d;
Paid the keeper of West Gate for cleansing [the grates of] that gate: 3s 4d;
Paid the keeper of North Gate for cleansing [the grates of] that gate: 6s 8d.
[Total: £1 12s 8d.]

Receiver's Book

[*f.1*] 'Extraordinary Charges
Inprimis paid for a banket at the Muralye Walke': 6s 8d;
'Payd for Apples at the Muraly Walke': 3s 4d.

[*f.1v.*] 'To John Davye for Clensinge the Citye Walls for one quarter': 5s.

[*f.2*] 'Payd to Wilcoxe for sand to mend the wall at Northgate': 11d.
'Payd to Leonerd Roche for Clensinge the Citye Walls one quarter': 5s.
[Total: £1 0s 11d.]

[Total expenditure in this year: £2 13s 7d.]

1590–91

Receivers Richard Sweete and John Howell.

Receiver's Roll

[*m.4v.*] Fees of the mayor and other officers:

[*m.3v.*] Paid the 4 gatekeepers, *videlicet* to each of them 4s: 16s;
Paid Robert Gaydon, keeper of 'le Watergate', for his fee this year: 6s 8d;
Paid the keeper of West Gate for cleansing [the grates of] that gate: 4s;
Paid the keeper of North Gate for cleansing [the grates of] that gate: 6s 8d.
[Total: £1 13s 4d.]

[*m.3v.*] Necessary expenses:
For various items of expenditure, including building the house on the walls called 'the madfolkes house': £119 8s 7½d.

Receiver's Book

[*f.3*] 'Charges layd out upon the Littell house upon the walls by Mr Mors house within Northgate
Inprimis paid for two hoggesheds of Lyme': 4s 8d;
'Payd for two dosens of Claye': 3s;
'Payd for carryage of 20 seames of stones from the Lyttell Conducte [Little Conduit] to the walls': 15d;
'Payd to Richard Comer for sawynge 5 dayes': 9s 2d;
'Payd for a hoggeshed of lyme': 2s 6d;
'Payd to Deymond for wallynge': 18s;
'Payd for 9 sacks of Lyme': 16d;
'Payd for two workmen one daye': 18d;
'Payd for stones from the quary': 8s 6d;
'Payd to Deymonde for the Masons': 20s;
'Payd to a labor man for 7 dayes': 3s 6d;
'Payd to Marks for Iron Worke for hooks Twists and staples': 6s 3d;
'Payd for one hundred & halfe of hatche nailes': 12d;
'Payd for halfe a hundred of borde nailes': 8d;
'Payd for two dosen of Claye': 3s;
'Payd for Carryage of one dosen of stones from Mr Maiors': 6d;
'Payd for two seames of gravell': 2d;
'Payd for stones that lay by the Cocke': 8d;
'Payd for 1,600 of lathes at 3s 8d the 100': 5s 11d;
'Payd for Lyme': 7d;
'Payd to George Cocke for one dosen & two seames of bursesles [?]': 5s 9d;
'Payd for 6 seames of stones': 2s;
'Payd to the Plumber for *CCC* three quarters two poundes & halfe of ledd at 11s the *C*': 38s 3d;

[*f.3v.*] 'Payd for 4 *lbs* of sawder': 2s 4d;
'Payd to the Masons': 26s 4d;
'Payd for 100 Nayles lackinge 7 [sc. ninety-three]': 15d;
'Payd for one 100 & halfe of hatch nailes': 12d;
'Payd for two payre of hooks & twists & one odde hooke': 21d;
'Payd for one dosen & 8 seames of Claye': 2s 6d;
'Payd for Carryage of heylinge stones from the Keye': 6d;

'Payd for carriage 1,800 stones of the helliers': 6*d*;
'Payd for Carryage of 6 seames of stones of John Smyths and 3 seames of Mr Maiores': 4*d*;
'Payd for woode & Coales to sawder the gutter': 1*d*;
'Payd to Richard Darke to Clense the walls': 4*d*;
'Payd to Mr Maior for 15 seames of stones': 3*s* 1*d*;
'Payd to John Smyth for 6 seames of stones': 2*d*;
'Payd for 700 & halfe of hellinge stones': 4*s* 3*d*;
'Payd for greate hard woode to make slate with [?]': 14*d*;
'Payd for 6 seames of stones from the quary': 2*s*;
'Payd to Marks for 400 & halfe of hatche nayles': 2*s* 10*d*;
'Payd for 25 borde nayles': 4*d*;
'Payd for hookes': 4*d*;
'Payd for three staples': 6*d*;
'Payd for a payre of gemmes & hooks': 18*d*;
'Payd to a laber man for 6 dayes': 3*s*;
'Payd for 10 seames & for the hellyers': 20*d*;
'Payd for 11 seames of Claye': 16*d*;
'Payd for Carriage of 5 thousand stones from Mr Bridgemans': 20*d*;
'Payd for two thousand hellinge stones': 11*s* 2*d*;
'Payd for one thousand of stones': 4*s* 4*d*;
'Payd for one bushell of pynes': 2*s* 6*d*;
'Payd to Mr Bridgemans man for 5 thousand stones': 31*s* 8*d*;
'Payd for two thousand of lathe nayles': 2*s* 8*d*;
'Payd for three hoggesheds of Lyme': 7*s* 6*d*;

[*f.4*] 'Payd for two locks two staples & nayles': 2*s* 9*d*;
'Payd to John Trosse for three Cresses': 7½*d*;
'Payd to him for 6 ovis bordes': 18*d*;
'Payd for halfe a thousand of lathe nayles': 8*d*;
'Payd to John Clavell for Tymber & his worke as appeareth by two bylls': £4;
'Payd to Mr Prow for 23 resters and one blade & for 1,600 of hellinge stones': 31*s*;
'Payd to Wilcoxe for carryage of 3 thousand of stones': 11*d*;
'Payd to the hellyers for layenge 12 thousand 3 hundred & halfe of stones': 24*s* 9*d*;
'Payd for a pecke of hellinge pynes': 5*d*;
'Payd for two lockes for the two Inner doores': 14*d*;
'Payd to a labor man one daye': 6*d*;
'Payd for a Lettice [lattice] for the Chamber wyndowe': 12*d*;
'Payd to the helliers for dabinge and for endinge of the worke': 4*s*;
'Payd to Wilcocks for Carryenge away the Rubbell': 2*s* 6*d*;
'Payd for two thousand of stones': 11*s* 4*d*;
[Sum:] £21 22½*d*.

[*f.5*] 'Charges layd out for [miscellaneous] reparacions . . . Payd for a locke for a doore of the new house upon the walls': 6*d*.
'Payd for Charges layd out upon the house for mad folkes': 26*s* 2*d*.

[*f.5v.*] 'Payd for mendinge the walls of the City by West Gate': 11*s* 2*d*.
[Total: £1 17*s* 10*d*.]

Book of Summary [DRO, Box 214, Book 3]

[*f.99*] [Necessary expenses:]

'Paid for building a house on the City Wall next St Mary Arches Lane and near the garden now in the tenure of R. Moore' [crossed out.]

Receiver's Vouchers [Box 1]

Voucher No. 28
'31 July 1591 for the Cities Walls
First due to Buryngton for 4 hogshedds of lyme at 3*s*': 12*s*;
'Also 6 dossen & half of burrestones & seames stones': 20*s*;
'Also a dossen & half of same at 16*d*': 2*s*;
'Also to Dymon & for his man for 7 dayes at 20*d*': 11*s* 8*d*;
'Also for one man a daye & half': 16*d*;
'Jo Hooker'.
'Payd the last daye of August 1591 in . . . [illegible] of thys byll'.
[Total: £2 7*s* 0*d*.]

Voucher No. 30
'Payd for Mr Recever att Mydsomer 1591'.
[Includes:]
'Paid James Gaydon for makynge clene of the walles': 1*s*.
[Total: 1*s* 0*d*.]

Voucher No. 40
'Payd for . . . [the] . . . Recever of the cittie of Exeter at the feast of St Mychell Th'archangell 1591'.
[Includes:]
'Paid James Gaydon for makynge cleane of the walles': 10*s* 3*d*.
'To the 4 porters': 10*s* 1*d*.
'To the porter of the Water Gate': 6*s* 8*d*.
'To the porter of Southgate for keepynge cleine of the grates': 6*s* 8*d*.
'To the porter of Westgate for keepynge clene of the grates': 4*s*.
'To William Knolles for hys fee': 26*s* 8*d*.
[Total: £3 4*s* 4*d*.]

[Total expenditure in this year: £30 6*s* 7½*d*.]

1591–92

Receiver Thomas Walker.

Receiver's Roll

[*m.3v.*] Fees of the mayor and other officers:
Paid the 4 gatekeepers, *videlicet* to each of them 4*s*: 16*s*;
Paid Robert Gaydon, keeper of 'le Watergate', for his fee this year: 6*s* 8*d*;
Paid the keeper of West Gate for cleansing [the grates of] that gate: 4*s*;
Paid the keeper of North Gate for cleansing [the grates of] that gate: 6*s* 8*d*.
[Total: £1 13*s* 4*d*.]

Receiver's Book

[*f.1*] 'Extraordynary Charges
Inprimis payd to Richard Darke & Thomas Ferrett for

Clensinge the walls 2*s* 6*d* & for whippinge 8*d* which in the whole is': 3*s* 2*d*.
'For worke done at Southgate': 11*s*.

[*f.1v.*] 'Item for amendinge of Thest [the East] Gate': 3*s* 8*d*.

[*f.2*] 'Payd for new makinge of the twists of Thestgate with nayles and hookes': 10*s*.

[*f.2v.*] 'Geven to the two Gaoles at the muraly walke': 8*s*.
[Total: £1 15*s* 10*d*.]

[Total expenditure in this year: £3 9*s* 2*d*.]

1592–93

Receiver Richard Bevys.

Receiver's Roll

[This roll is headed '33–(blank) Elizabeth' (i.e. 1591–92), but in fact appears to be the account for 1592–93.]

[*m.2v.*] Fees of the mayor and other officers:
Paid the 4 gatekeepers, *videlicet* to each of them 4*s*: 16*s*;
Paid John Hundaler, keeper of 'le Watergate', for his fee this year: 6*s* 8*d*;
Paid the keeper of West Gate for cleansing [the grates of] that gate: 4*s*;
Paid the keeper of North Gate for cleansing [the grates of] that gate: 6*s* 8*d*.
[Total: £1 13*s* 4*d*.]

Receiver's Book

[*f.1*] 'Extraordinarye Charges . . .
Item to the poore of Palmers Almeshouses and to the pryssners at Southgate': 16*d*;
'Item for Clensynge of the muraly walke': 2*s*;

[*f.1v.*] 'Item for Apples for the boyes at the Muraly Walke': 2*s*;
'Item to the Quenes Pryson and to Southgate Pryson': 8*s*.
'Item for pavynge and mendynge a locke at Northgate': 20*d*.
'Item for two crampes of Iron at Watergate and for settyng of the same': 2*s* 3*d*.
[Total: 17*s* 3*d*.]

[*f.2v.*] 'Extraordinary Charges layd out for reparacions at Southgate
Inprimis for one hoggeshed of Lyme for Southgate and a mans labour': 4*s* 4*d*;
'Item for 3 seames of sand & Claye & 2 seames of stones': 15*d*;
'Item for 4 seames of stones and rounde woode coales': 2*s* 2*d*;
'Item for 62 *lbs* of lead at 1½*d* the *lb*': 6*s* 6*d*;
'Item to Deymond for 3 dayes and a man and a boye': 7*s* 9*d*;
'Item for sand and stones': 21*d*;
'Item for one hoggeshed and halfe of Lyme and 98 *lbs* of Iron worke': 27*s* 4*d*;
'Item to Deymond & 2 men for 2 dayes & halfe': 6*s* 5*d*;

'Item to John Clavell for a plancke and 2 Lynternes and nayles': 5*s* 4*d*;
'Item for 33 *lbs* of Iron worke for the prison at Southgate': 2*s* 7*d*;
'Item for mendynge of the arche at Estgate': 18*d*;
'Item for a locke and for settynge of the same and for Twistes and spukes at Estgate': 2*s* 7*d*;
[Sum: £3 6*s* 11*d*].

[Total expenditure in this year: £5 17*s* 6*d*.]

1593–94

Receiver Henry Hull.

Receiver's Roll

[*m.4v.*] Fees of the mayor and other officers:

[*m.3v.*] Paid the 4 gatekeepers, *videlicet* to each of them 4*s*: 16*s*;
Paid John Hundaller, keeper of 'le Watergate', for his fee this year: 6*s* 8*d*;
Paid the keeper of West Gate for cleansing [the grates of] that gate: 4*s*;
Paid the keeper of North Gate for cleansing [the grates of] that gate: 6*s* 8*d*.
[Total: £1 13*s* 4*d*.]

Receiver's Book

[*f.1*] 'Extraordinarye Charges . . .
Item geven to the knitsters at the Muraly Walke by Mr Maiors appoyntmente': 6*d*;
'Item to the pryseners at Southgate the same tyme by Mr Maiors order': 2*s* 6*d*;
'Item to Edmond Clarke towards his bankett for Mr Maier and the officers': 5*s*;
'Item to the Prysoners at the Castell Gaole': 2*s* 6*d*;
'Item for Apples geven to the boyes at Mr Maiors doore the same tyme': 2*s* 6*d*;
'Item to the Beedells for makynge Cleane the Cittye Walls': 2*s*.

[*f.1v.*] 'Item for mendynge of the gutter at Westgate with Lyme and stones': 2*s* 8*d*.
[Total: 17*s* 8*d*.]

[*f.5*] 'Reparacions upon Eastgate . . .
Item to Richard Deymond for mendynge of the walls behynd Brogans house at Eastgate': 9*s* 3*d*.

[Total expenditure in this year: £3 0*s* 3*d*.]

1594–95

Receiver Richard Dorchester.

Receiver's Roll

[*m.2v.*] Fees of the mayor and other officers:
Paid the 4 gatekeepers, *videlicet* to each of them 4*s*: 16*s*;
Paid John Hundaller, keeper of 'le Watergate', for his fee this year: 6*s* 8*d*;
Paid the keeper of West Gate for cleansing [the grates of] that gate: 4*s*;

Paid the keeper of North Gate for cleansing [the grates of] that gate: 6s 8d.
[Total: £1 13s 4d.]

Receiver's Book

[*f.1*] 'Extraordinary Payments . . .
Item given to Twentye poore Children of St Paules parishe walkinge about the Murallye Walke': 12d;
'Item to Quyntyns for his Banquet': 10s;
'Item to the Bedells for makinge cleane the Murallye Walke': 20d;
'Item for Apples given to the Boyes': 3s 8d.

[*f.2*] 'Item for mendinge the Barbigans before Mr Moors dore': 7s 5d.
Total: £1 3s 9d.]

[Total expenditure in this year: £2 17s 1d.]

1595–96

Receiver Christopher Spycer.

Receiver's Roll

[*m.2*] Fees of the mayor and other officers:
Paid the 4 gatekeepers, *videlicet* to each of them 4s: 16s;
Paid John Hundaller, 'Porter de le Watergat', for his fee this year: 6s 8d;
Paid the keeper of West Gate for cleansing [the grates of] that gate: 4s;
Paid the keeper of North Gate for cleansing [the grates of] that gate: 6s 8d.
[Total: £1 13s 4d.]

Receiver's Book

[*f.1*] 'Extraordynary Charges . . .
Paide at the Murally for clensinge the walls twise': 2s 6d;
'Geven by Mr Maiors order to the poore woork maydes': 2s;
'Moore to the Prisoners of the Hye Goale': 2s 6d;
'More to the Prisoners of Southgat': 2s;
'More to a poore woman that hade a sore legge': 12d;
'More to Edmond Clarke for the banquett': 6s 8d;
'Paid for Aples at the Muraly walke': 2s 4d.

[*f.1v.*] 'Paid John Clavell for a planke for the vawte of one of the sesterns & a peece of Tymber used at Southgat': 12d.
'Paid John Sanders for mendinge of a geve [i.e. a leg-iron] & the grate of the Wyndowe at Southgat': 2s.
[Total: £1 2s 0d.]

[*f.4v.*] 'Charges bestowed at South Gate & in the Prison . . . paid Hellyer to helpe ride the Water there': 6d;
'More to Gibbyns for the same worke': 12d;
'More paid for an iron hope with a Chayne of 8 *lbs*': 2s 8d;
[Subtotal] 4s 2d;

[*f.5*] 'More payd for two basketts to ride the pryvie': 6d;
'More paide Henry Smythe to helpe there two daies': 16d;

'More paid Gibbyns for three daies in the Privye': 3s;
'More payde John Saunders for 29 *lbs* of iron worke for a grate at Southgate at 3d [the] *lb*': 7s 3d;
'More paid Hethman for two dayes worke there & a Stone': 2s 6d;
'More paid Michaell Gibbyns for two daies in the Privye': 2s 4d;
'More paid William Lawrence for six daies & his boye fower daies': 11s 4d;
'More paid Hethman & Gibbyns for eche a daie': 2s 2d;
'Paid John Saunders for a Gratt for the gutter there': 18s 9d;
'More paid for fower hogshedds of lyme to use there': 12s;
'More paid John Saunders for 37 *lbs* of iron worke there': 9s 3d;
'Paid William Lawrence for himselfe & his boye one daye in the vawte of the privy there': 2s;
'More paide for riddinge of the bancke before the grate to make the wall in at Southgat': 18d;
'More paid William Lawrence for 7 perche of wall there after 18d the perche': 10s 6d;
'More paid Hamlyn for Carriadge of 8 dozens of stones from the Quarry to Southgat & the Yarnemarkett': 6s 8d;
'Moore paid for 24 *lbs* of leade used to sett in the Grattes at Southgat': 2s;
'More paid for three men three daies & one man a daie at Southgat': 10s 6d;
[Subtotal] £5 3s 7d;

[*f.5v.*] 'More for Strawe & sifting the same there': 8d;
'More paid for Lyme used at Southgate': 2s 2d;
'Paid for 44 *lbs* of iron for a grate for the Chamber at Southgate in the Prison Wyndowe at 3d *per lb*': 11s;
'More paid Richard Deymonde for three daies for himselfe & his boye for this worke': 5s;
'More for Carriadge of six seame Stones thither': 6d;
'More for Lyme, heare [hair] & Morter to this': 4s 1d;
'Paid for a grate at Northgate wayinge fortye nyne *lbs*': 12s 4d;
Sum: £7 3s 5d.

[*f.6*] 'Extraordynary Charges by buildings & Reparacions upon St Johns the Guihald & the Walls at Thestgate . . .
Paide for half a hogshed of Lyme for the Wall at Estgate': 15d;
'More payde for Carriadge of fower dozen of Stones thither': 3s;
'More to the Carryer for two seames of sande': 4d;
'More to Richard Deymond for 5 daies for himselfe & two daies for an other Mason': 7s;
'More to a laborman there for thre dayes & a halfe': 2s 8d;
'More payd John Wilcoxe for 18 seames of sande for this worke': 2s 9d;
'More paid for fower hogshedds of lyme for this worke': 12s;
'Paid for three hogshedds & halfe of lyme for the walles': 9s 10d;
'Paid Richard Deymonde for hyme & his boye six daies': 10s;
'More paid for Tenne seames of sande to this worke': 20d;
'More paid for Carriadge of eight seame stones thither': 8d;

'Paid for 20,000 helling stones at the Quary': £3 10s.
[Total: £6 1s 2d.]

[f.7] 'Extraordinary Charges in buildings & Reparacions . . .
Item for filling & squaringe six Trees for Southgate Bridge': 11s;
'More payd John Vitrye for two dayes worke there': 20d;
'More to Piddesley Lewes Horwell & Wheaton eche of them a daye': 2s 8d;
'More to John Clavell with three menn there': 3s 6d;
'More to two Sawyers for two dayes worke & half a peece': 5s;
'More for Carriadge of 5 load of Tymber for this bridge': 20s.
'More for a Stone for Northgate grate': 6d.
'More paid Richard Deymond for two daies worke for hime & his boye': 3s 4d;
'More paid for Morter to Thomas Brenocke for this worke': 10d;
'More paid for Carriadge of Stones to this worke': 3d.
[Total: £2 8s 9d.]

[Total expenditure in this year: £18 8s 8d.]

1596–97

Receiver Alexander Mayne.

Receiver's Roll

[m.3] Fees of the mayor and other officers:
    Paid the 4 gatekeepers: 16s;
    Paid John Hundaler, 'porter de le Watergate', for his fee this year: 6s 8d;
    Paid the porter of West Gate for cleansing [the grates of] the same: 4s;
    Paid the porter of North Gate for cleansing [the grates of] the same: 6s 8d.
    [Total: £1 13s 4d.]

Receiver's Book

[f.1] 'Extraordinary Payments . . .
For makinge cleane of the Murallye & mending the bushell': 2s 10d.
'For mendinge a hole in Estgate': 20d.
'For setting of the grate at Northgat': 8s 3d.
'More unto Quyntyns for his banquett': 6s.

[f.3] 'Rychard Deymond for clensyng the wals': 6s 8d.

[f.4] 'Wylcoxe for 5 dossen of clay for the Wals': 3s;
'Hyme for 18 semes of sannd for the Wale': 2s 2d;
'For 4 dossen of stones for the same': 12s;
'For 7 hogsheds of lyme for the Wals at 2s 10d': 19s 10d;
'Demond for hym & his thre men a Wyke [week]': 20s 6d.
'For mendyng a Cheyn at Sothgate': 10d.

[f.6] 'Wylcoxe & Erell for carying of 4 dossen of sand & stones for the Wals': 6d.
[Total: £4 4s 3d.]

[Total expenditure in this year: £5 17s 7d.]

1597–98

Receiver William Spycer.

Receiver's Roll

[m.2v.] Fees of the mayor and other officers:
    Paid the 4 porters, *videlicet* 4s to each of them: 16s;
    Paid John Hundaller 'porter de le Water Gate', for his fee this year: 6s 8d;
    Paid the porter of West Gate for cleansing [the grates of] the same: 4s;
    Paid the porter of North Gate for cleansing [the grates of] the same gate: 6s 8d.
    [Total: £1 13s 4d.]

Receiver's Book

[f.1v.] 'Extraordynary payments payd out for the Cittie
For mendinge of a locke for the Southe Gatte wickett': 10d.
'The 4 beadells for Clensinge the Muralie Walke': 1s.
'For a watcheman att Southgatt the 17th of November': 4d.
[Total: 2s 2d.]

[f.2v.] 'Charges paid out uppon the Bridewell St Johns & other Charges as maye apere followinge . . .
Deamond for 1 dayes worke for mendinge of a holle att Estgatt': 1s.
'For makinge of 2 dores att Northgatt': 2s;
'For settinge in of a greatt bar for the greatt gatt': 1s;
'For hockes & twistes & haspes for the 2 dores containing 13 lbs ½ att 3d lb': 3s 4d;
'For 2,000 of hatch naylles for the dores & mendinge of olde Iron': 1s 10d.
[Total: 9s 2d.]

Receiver's Vouchers [Box 1]

[Undated part of an account book; clearly a copy of the receiver's book for 1597–98.]

[f.1] 'Extraordynary Paymentes . . .
More payd for 14 C of payres when Mr Maior went amuralling': 2s 6d;
'More paid when Mr Maior went amurallinge to Quintance for a banckett 10s to the Pryson 2s, to almes houses 1s 6d, to the Greatt Gealle: 3s 4d, to knetsters 2s, all is': 18s [illegible; 10d].
[Total: £1 1s 4d.]

[Total expenditure in this year: £3 6s 0d.]

1598–99

Receiver John Prouz.

Receiver's Roll

[m.3v.] Fees of the mayor and other officers:
    Paid the 4 porters, *videlicet* 4s to each of them: 16s;

[m.2v.] Paid [blank], porter of the Water Gate, for his fee this year: 6s 8d;

Paid the porter of the Water [*sic*] Gate for cleansing [the grates of] that gate: 4*s*;
Paid the porter of North Gate for cleansing [the grates of] that gate: 6*s* 8*d*.
[Total: £1 13*s* 4*d*.]

Receiver's Book

[*f.1*] 'Extraodenarie Payements . . .
The Beadells for Clensinge the Wales': 16*d*;
'The 7th of October 1598 geven to the Comter and Guyole [Gaol] at Southgate by Mr Maiors order': 2*s* 4*d*;
'More geven to dyvers Maids in the Meweralie Walke by Mr Mayors order': 5*s* 2*d*;
'To the Highe Gayole the same time': 2*s* 6*d*;
'Then to Quenten for his Banquett': 6*s* 8*d*;
'Then to the Comter & Gayole at Southgeate': 1*s* 7*d*;
'To the poore by the Keye Geate': 4*d*;
'Paide for Appels for the Boyes': 1*s* 8*d*.

[*f.2v.*] 'For 3 dozen & half of burres for the wales': 11*s* 6*d*.
[Total: £1 13*s* 1*d*.]

[Total expenditure in this year: £3 6*s* 5*d*.]

1599–1600

Receiver Thomas Edwards, gentleman.

Receiver's Roll [N.B. This roll is in English]

[*m.3v.*] [Fees of the mayor and other officers:]
'To the 4 porters every of theym 4*s*': 16*s*;

[*m.2v.*] '[To] [blank] Slingsby porter of the Water Gate': 6*s* 8*d*;
'To the porter of Westgate for clensinge of the streetes at the grate their': 4*s*;
'To the porter of Northgate for keepinge Cleene of that gate': 6*s* 8*d*.
[Total: £1 13*s* 4*d*.]

Receiver's Book

[*f.2*] [Extraordinary expenses:]
'Richard Darke for clensing the walls': 21*d*.
'Richard Deymond for mending Estgat & for three stones & sand': 3*s* 5*d*.
'Mr Borowe for planks for Estgat': 4*s*.
'For Apples at the Murally Walke': 16*d*;
'Paid then by Mr Maiors order unto fowre companies of poore Maides': 2*s*;
'To an other companie of poore': 3*d*;
'To the Prisoners at the Queens Geale': 2*s*;
'To the Prisoners of the Citties Geale': 2*s*;
'Paid Quyntens for his banquett': 6*s*.
[Total: £1 2*s* 9*d*.]

[*f.3v.*] 'Reparacions uppon the Bridge at Estgate the Walls St Johns Newe Inne and other places . . .
A workman for two halfe daies worke at Estgate Bridge': 12*d*;
'Elliott & Symons for two whole dayes there': 4*s*;

[*f.4*] 'Deymond the Mason & his fowre men for working uppon the same one daie': 5*s*;
'Weeks & his felowe for workinge there two daies & a halfe': 4*s*;
'Deymond & his man for working uppon the same bridge 5 daies': 10*s*;
'Richard Deymond & John Deymond for working fowr daies there': 8*s*;
'Deymonds man for one other daies worke there': 12*d*;
'Shapster & his man for one daies worke': 2*s*;
'Willes for two daies worke there': 2*s*;
'For Lyme for the bridge': 11*s*;
'For fowre dozen & two seames of pavinge stones': 8*s* 4*d*;
'Wilcocks for sande & cley for Estgat Bridge': 3*s* 4*d*.
'Deymond the Mason for worke upon the Cities Wall': 10*s* 8*d*.
'Wilcocks for 15 dozen of sande for the Citties Wall': 17*s*.
'Hime for thre dozen of Rubble at Estgat': 3*s*;
'For 3 dozen of paving stones there': 6*s*.
'The Pavier for Estgat Bridge': 11*s* 3*d*;
'For Nailes for the same bridge': 6*d*;
'For pavinge the Streat bye Estgatbridge': 4*s* 6*d*;
'For two hogshedds of Lyme': 5*s* 4*d*.
[Total: £5 17*s* 11*d*.]

[Total expenditure in this year: £8 14*s* 0*d*.]

1600–01

Receiver John Ellacott.

Receiver's Roll [N.B. This roll is in English]

[*m.6v.*] 'Fees of the Maior & other Officers . . .
To the fower Porters everie of them 4*s*': 16*s*;
'To the Porter of the Watergate': 6*s* 8*d*;
'To the Porter of the Westgate for Clensinge of the Streate at the Grates there': 4*s*;
'To the Porter of Northgate for keeping clene of the Gate': 6*s* 8*d*.
[Total: £1 13*s* 4*d*.]

[*m.5v.*] [Necessary expenses:]
'For the Porters Lodge': £10 10*s* 2*d*.

Receiver's Book

[*f.1*] [Extraordinary expenses:]
Paid for 'mending of the Counter': 7*s* 9*d* [not included in sub-total below, or in figure for total expenditure in this year].
'Mending the Towne Walles with stone & lime': 17*s* 9*d*.
'Mending the South Gate with Ire worke': 5*s* 9*d*.
'For pavinge by the Towne Walles': 2*s* 6*d*.
'Mending the Towne Walles also': 9*s* 3½*d*.
'Mending the barbican by Madocks howse': £3 14*s* 5*d*.
[Total: £5 9*s* 8½*d*.]

[*f.1v.*] 'Geven out by Mr Maiors order
Apells & Peares for boies in Murallye': 3*s* 8*d*;
'To Quentence in the Murallye': 8*s*;
'To the prisoners in Quenes Gaille': 2*s*;
'To divers knitsters': 3*s* 10*d*;

'To the bedells for clensing the Walles': 2s.
[Total: 19s 6d.]

[f.2] 'Charges on the Porters lodg' . . .
£10 10s 2d.

[Total expenditure in this year: £18 12s 8½d.]

1601–2

Receiver Walter Borrowe.

Receiver's Roll

[m.3v.] Fees of the mayor and other officers:
Paid the 4 porters, *videlicet* to each of them 4s: 16s;
Paid the porter of 'le Watergat' for his fee this year:
6s 8d;
Paid the porter of West Gate for cleansing [the grates
of] that gate: 4s;
Paid the porter of North Gate for cleansing [the grates
of] that gate: 6s 8d.
[Total: £1 13s 4d.]

Receiver's Book

[f.1] [Extraordinary expenses:]
'Appells provided & geven the boyes at the Retorne of
Mr Maior from the Mewerawly walcke': 1s 3d;
'More geven unto dyvars companys of poure maydens
that weare knyttinge': 2s;
'The Prysoners of the Hye Gaylle': 2s 9d;
'The Beedells for makinge cleane the walls at the
Mewrally walcke': 1s 8d;
'The Prysoners at Southgatte': 6d;
'Paid to Qwintance for the Bankkett': 6s 8d.

[f.2] 'January 4' [paid Saunders] 'for Iron work to mend the
Cay Gat': 6d.
'Paid Demond mason for mending the stonework at
Eastgat': 4d.
'October 28th Paide to Saunders smith for makinge a
new Iron grate at Westgate of 28 *lbs* & 20 *lbs* old Iron &
for a new hamer att the Westgate': 5s 2d.
'Paide William Bargery for pavinge som holes in the
West Gate & for mendinge the greate stones at the
grates': 7d.

[f.2v.] 'Paid Peter Mogridge for two dossen of gravell which
was laid upon the barbagan by the stepes in Frenhay':
3s.
[Total: £1 4s 5d.]

[f.6v.] 'Chargs paid owt . . . upon the Counter & gaylle': £1
10s [not included in figure for total annual expenditure].

[Total expenditure in this year: £2 17s 9d.]

1602–3

Receiver Alexander Germyn.

Receiver's Roll

[m.2v.] Fees of the mayor and other officers:

Paid to the 4 porters, *videlicet* to each of them 4s: 16s;
Paid the porter of 'le Watergate' for his fee this year:
6s 8d;
Paid the porter of the West Gate for cleansing [the
grates of] that gate: 4s;
Paid the porter of the North Gate for cleansing [the
grates of] that gate: 6s 8d.
[Total: £1 13s 4d.]

Receiver's Book

[f.1] [Extraordinary expenses:]
'Paid the 12th of October, by Mr Maiors order, when
hee went in the Murall Walke, which was geeven unto
divers persons is': 18s 6d.
'Paid the 16th of October, unto the three Biddells, for
clensing the Murall Walkes, and for whipping of one is':
1s 8d.
'Paid the 17th of October, unto certain carryers with 9
horses to carry rubbell and sand from Exe, to mend the
waye by the walls is': 6s 9d.
'The 27th of October unto a workman, which cast upp
the dung by the Cittyes Waell is': 6d.

[f.1v.] 'Paid the 23th of Januarye, for a key for North Gaet':
6d.
'Paid the 24th of March for the mending of ye
Southgaet of this Citty': 8d.
'Paid Trewman the Carpenter, for 3 dayes wages, and
for a peec of Timber for to mend the North Gaet, is':
3s 6d.
'Paid John Waye for 3 dayes wages, and Timber at the
West Gact and is': 3s 9d.
'Paid unto Mr John Chappell, for his boettes hier and
10 mens wages, which brought upp ordinaunce for the
use of the citty, March 29th 1603': 14s.
'Paid the same tyme for one hodgsett of lime to mend
the waells of the Citty, neer the Snealltower in Fryerhey
is': 3s 6d.
'Paid for stones to mend the walls, and carryadg of
them, and for sand & the masons wages, which did the
wourcke': 6s.
'Paid the first of Aprill 1603 unto Mr Avery, of
Thapsham [Topsham], Gunner for clensing & trimming
the great ordinaunce, at St Johns is': 7s 6d.
'For a peec of Elme to make a baer for West Gaet':
1s 8d.
'Paid the 4th of Maye 1603 for Iron Twists for West Gaet
. . . & for Iron work upon South Gaet . . . & for other
Iron': £1 9s.
'For one pound and a halfe of gunpowder, to clense the
great ordynaunce with, uppon the death of our laet
most vertuous Queen': 1s 6d.
Paid for horse hire and for 'roomedging ye great
ordinaunce at ye Keye' [no sum].
'Paid unto Hugh Crout . . . towards ye building of a
chimneye in ye Porters lodge at Eastgaet': 10s.

[f.3] 'Paid for two boetts which brought ordynaunce from
Mr John Chappells ship to the Citty, and for cranadge
of the same': 6s.
[Total: £5 15s 0d.]

[Total expenditure in this year: £7 8s 4d.]

1603–4

Receiver Hugh Crossinge.

Receiver's Roll

[*m.3v.*] Fees of the mayor and other officers:
Paid the 4 porters, *videlicet* 4*s* to each of them: 16*s*;

[*m.2v.*] Paid the porter of 'le Watergate' this year for his fee:
6*s* 8*d*;
Paid the porter of West Gate for cleansing [the grates
of] that gate: 4*s*;
Paid the porter of North Gate for cleansing [the grates
of] that gate: 6*s* 8*d*.
[Total: £1 13*s* 4*d*.]

[*m.1v.*] Allocations:
10*s* allocated Jeremy Hilliard for making a stair (*gradum*)
and a gutter next 'le Keygate'.

Receiver's Book

[*f.1*] 'Worke in the Counter at Southgate': £2 3*s* 11*d* [not
included in figure for total expenditure in this year].

[*f.3*] Extraordinary expenses:
'Geven to dyvers poore children at the High Gaiole &
spent at Quintins in the Muraillie Walke': 16*s* 10*d*;
'For Appels for the boyes then': 1*s* 6*d*.
'For mending the caie of Thestgat': 2*d*.
'The bedels for clensing the wals': 1*s* 6*d*.
'Paid Mr Poope for the cariadg of 4 peeces of ordnance
to Apsam [Topsham]': 8*s*.
'Paid Mr John Chapple for porters to help lade that
ordnance here at ye Caie': 4*s* 6*d*.

[*f.3v.*] 'Paid for candell light at the gates this yere': 6*s* 11*d*.
[Total: £1 19*s* 5*d*.]

[Total expenditure in this year: £4 2*s* 9*d*.]

1604–5

Receiver William Newcombe.

Receiver's Roll

[*m.2v.*] Fees of the mayor and other officers:
Paid the 4 porters, *videlicet* 4*s* to each: 16*s*;
Paid the porter of 'le Watergat' for his fee: 6*s* 8*d*;
Paid the porter of West Gate for cleansing [the grates
of] that gate: 4*s*;
Paid the porter of North Gate for cleansing [the grates
of] that gate: 6*s* 8*d*.
[Total: £1 13*s* 4*d*.]

Receiver's Book

[*f.1*] Extraordinary payments:
'*Inprimis* payed by the appointement of Mr Maior at the
Murallye to spinsters': 2*s*;
'Item to the Kinges Gaol': 3*s* 4*d*;
'Item to Quintances for his Bankett': 6*s* 8*d*;
'Item to the prisoners in Southgate': 12*d*;

'For Appells when Mr Maior came from the Murallye':
10*d*;
'For clensinge of the walls': 1*s* 2*d*.
'For a newe grate of stone for the Westgate': 7*s* 6*d*.

[*f.2*] 'For mendinge of the Loke at West Gate': 4*d*.
'For nayles for the seate at Westgate': 5*d*.
'Paid to Duke for wallinge uppe of Snell Tower as
appereth': 15*s* 10*d*.
[Total: £1 19*s* 1*d*.]

[*f.4.*] 'Mony Layed out in Reparacions at the Guihald the
Counter [i.e. Southgate Prison] Newe Inne, Estgate &
ellswher
Item for the amendinge of the Barbegan in my Lord
Bishopps & Mr Leaches garden': 21*s*.
'For the amending of the Counter': £1 12*s* 2*d* [not
included in figure for total expenditure].

[Total expenditure in this year: £4 13*s* 5*d*.]

1605–6

Receiver John Lante.

Receiver's Roll

[*m.2v.*] Fees of the mayor and other officers:
Paid the 4 porters, *videlicet* 4*s* to each: 16*s*;
Paid the porter of 'le Watergat' for his fee: 6*s* 8*d*;
Paid the porter of West Gate for cleansing [the grates
of] the same: 4*s*;
Paid the porter of North Gate for cleansing [the grates
of] the same: 6*s* 8*d*.
[Total: £1 13*s* 4*d*.]

Receiver's Book

[*f.5*] 'Extra ordyneryes Charges layd out sence the 29th of
September 1605 . . .
Paid Demond the masson for Lyme & worke over the
walles at the Bishopes Palic': 2*s*.
'Paid att Palmers Almeshouses & Jeale & Counter
according to Mr Mayors orders': 1*s* 8*d*;
'Paid to Quintens for a banquitt att Murally': 6*s* 8*d*;
'Paid to the Kings Jeale & to knitsters': 3*s* 10*d*;
'Paid for apelles for the boyes': 2*s* 8*d*;
'Paid to the Bedelles for clension [i.e. cleansing] of the
waye': 2*s*.
'Paid for Candells when watche was at the gats': 6*d*.
[Total: 19*s* 4*d*.]

[Total expenditure in this year: £2 12*s* 8*d*.]

1606–7

Receiver Gilbert Smythe.

Receiver's Roll

[*m.2v.*] Fees of the mayor and other officers:
Paid the 4 porters, *videlicet* 4*s* to each: 16*s*;
Paid the porter of 'le Watergate' for his fee: 6*s* 8*d*;
Paid the porter of West Gate for cleansing [the grates
of] that gate: 4*s*;

Paid the porter of North Gate for cleansing [the grates of] that gate: 6s 8d.
[Total: £1 13s 4d.]

Receiver's Book

[*f.3*] 'Payementes & expences extraordinarie . . .
[13 October] Geven to the poore when Mr Maior went the murale walke': 7s 6d;
'Paide to James Clarke for the banquett the same time': 6s 8d;
'Paide the same daye for apples': 2s.
[28 November] '. . . paide for mendinge of the Water Gate': 6d;
'Paide to one that did watche att the Water Gate before the same was mended': 8d.

[*f.3v.*] [9 February] 'Paide for mendinge the Barbygan within Westgate': 17s 7d.

[*f.4*] [18 April] 'Paide to the smyth for Iron worke done for the Watergate & for crookes att the Shambells': 2s 6½d.

[*f.4v.*] [3 June] 'To too men that served the mason one day . . . [at the Water Gate]': 20d.

[*f.5*] [7 June] 'Paide for 28 seames of sande for the Barbygan by Northgate': 2s 4d;
'For 16 seames of stones for the same Barbygan': 2s 8d;
[8 June] 'For carriage of 8 seames of claye & earthe': 20d;

[*f.6v.*] [3 June] 'Paide for two hoggesheddes of lyme for the Barbygon by Nothgate': 6s 8d.
[Total: £2 12s 5½d.]

[*ff.9v–10.*] 'Reparacions done uppon the Counter': £37 17s 8½d [not included in figure for total expenditure].

[Total expenditure in this year: £4 5s 9½d.]

1607–8
Receiver Geoffrey Waltam.

Receiver's Roll

[*m.4v.*] Fees of the mayor and other officers:
Paid the 4 porters, *videlicet* 4s to each: 16s;
Paid the porter of 'le Watergate' for his fee: 6s 8d;
Paid the porter of West Gate for cleansing [the grates of] that gate: 4s;
Paid the porter of North Gate for cleansing [the grates of] that gate: 6s 8d.
[Total: £1 13s 4d.]

[The book for this year is missing.]

[Total expenditure in this year: £1 13s 4d.]

1608–9
Receiver John Marshall.

Receiver's Roll

[*m.5v.*] Fees of the mayor and other officers:
Paid the 4 porters, *videlicet* 4s to each: 16s;
Paid the porter of North Gate for cleansing [the grates of] that gate: 6s 8d;
Paid the porter of 'le Watergat' for his fee: 6s 8d;
Paid the porter of West Gate for cleansing [the grates of] that gate: 4s.
[Total: £1 13s 4d.]

[*m.4v.*] Necessary expenses:
For repairs to the City Wall [?; part illegible]: £8 17s 7d.

[The book for this year is missing.]

[Total expenditure in this year: £10 10s 11d.]

1609–10
Receiver John Sheer.

Receiver's Roll

[*m.7*] Fees of the mayor and other officers:
Paid the 4 porters, *videlicet* 4s to each: 16s;
Paid the porter of North Gate for cleansing [the grates of] that gate: 6s 8d;
Paid the porter of 'le Watergate' for his fee: 6s 8d;
Paid the porter of West Gate for cleansing [the grates of] that gate: 4s.
[Total: £1 13s 4d.]

[*m.7v.*] Necessary expenses:
For repairs to the City Wall—*nihil.*

Receiver's Book

[*f.1*] [Extraordinary expenses:]
[9 October 1609] 'For apples for the boyes when Mr Maior went aboute the wales': 8s;
'Given to certaine poore Children by order of Mr Maior the same time': 7s 2d;
'To the prisoners of the Gaole the same time': 2s;
'To three Biddles for makinge cleane the walles the same time': 1s 6d;
'To James Clarke for a banket the same time': 5s.

[*f.1v.*] [20 October 1609] 'Paide for a newe Key for the Northgate': 9d.

[*f.2v.*] [19 May] 'To Deman the mason for reparations done upon the Citties Walles': 7s 6d.
'Paide for mendinge of the Key Gate and reparinge of the Countrey Shambles . . .' £1 4d;
'Paide Saunders the smyth for ireworke for the same': 7s 5d.
[Total: £2 19s 8d.]

[Total expenditure in this year: £4 13s 0d.]

1610–11
Receiver Ignatius Jurden.

Receiver's Roll

[*m.4*] Fees of the mayor and other officers:
Paid the 4 porters, *videlicet* 4s to each: 16s;
Paid the porter of North Gate for cleansing [the grates of] that gate: 6s 8d;
Paid the porter of 'le Watergate' for his fee: 6s 8d;
Paid the porter of West Gate for cleansing [the grates of] that gate: 4s.
[Total: £1 13s 4d.]

[*m.4v.*] Necessary expenses:
For repairs to the City Wall—*nihil*.

Receiver's Book

[*f.1*] [Extraordinary expenses:]
[8 October 1610] 'Given the poore goinge the Muraile and for aples': 11s 11d.
[16 October] 'Paid the Bedells for making Cleane the walles': 1s 6d.
[18 December] 'For mendinge of Slingesbyes howse & on the wales': 2s 10d.

[*f.1v.*] [7 February 1610] 'Paid for mendinge the Cittyes Wales in Mr Lambals garden': 4s 6d.

[*f.2*] [27 April] 'For riddinge the trench under Southgate': 1s 4d.

[*f.2v.*] [31 August] 'Paid for mendinge the Wall & gutter at Eastgate': 5s 7d.

[*f.3*] [21 September] 'Paid for mendinge the Walls in Frerenhaye': 5s 9d.
'For 3 seame stones for Eastgate': 1s.
[Total: £1 14s 5d.]

[*f.13*] 'Charges paid out in repayreing the Counter': £1 6s 5d [not included in figure for total expenditure].

[Total expenditure in this year: £3 7s 9d.]

1611–12

Receiver Thomas Martyne.

Receiver's Roll

[*m.5*] Fees of the mayor and other officers:
Paid the 4 porters, *videlicet* 4s to each: 16s;
Paid the porter of North Gate for cleansing [the grates of] that gate: 6s 8d;
Paid the porter of 'le Watergate' for his fee: 6s 8d;
Paid the porter of West Gate for cleansing 'le grates' of the same: 4s.
[Total: £1 13s 4d.]

Receiver's Book

[*f.1*] [Extraordinary expenses:]
[12 October] 'For paires & Apples': 5s 2d.
[13 October] 'To the poore *per* Mr Mayors order goinge the Muraulye walke': 13s 3d.
[15 October] 'Paid the Beadles for bowes and makinge clene of the walls': 1s 6d.

[*f.1v.*] [30 November] 'For mendinge the gutter *per* Northgate': 6s.
[30 January] 'Paid James Clarke for the banquet at Muralye': 6s 8d.

[*f.3*] [26 October] 'Paid for watchinge at Southgate at the time of the Porters death which Mr Lane paid': 2s.
[Total: £1 14s 7d.]

[*f.18v.*] '. . . Other Reparacions *Videlicet*
[11 November] Northgate
Paid Richard Daymond & Barnard Squire for 12 daies': 12s;
'Paid Cazely for 4 daies at 10d': 3s 4d;
'Paid John Jarman for 30 Seame stones': 10s;
'Paid for 3 bags of Lime': 2s 8d;
'Paid for 6 Seames of Sand & Clay': 1s;
'Paid for Scablinge 30 stones': 1s 6d;
'Paid Mr Bridgman for this weeke': 6s;
'Paid Colmer for 1 day': 1s;
[Subtotal] 37s 6d.
[20 April] 'For Northgate
Paid John Kinge & Lawrence Hew for 3 daies': 3s;
'Paid for drillinge the post heals': 1s;
'Paid for a pec of Tymber': 8d;
'Paid Lawrence & Robins 1 day': 11d;
'Paid for Lime stones & Sand and for mendinge the grate of Iron': 2s 5d.
[Total: £2 5s 6d.]

[Total expenditure in this year: £5 13s 5d.]

1612–13

Receiver John Modiforde.

Receiver's Roll

[*m.5*] Fees of the mayor and other officers:
Paid the 4 porters, *videlicet* 4s to each: 16s;
Paid the porter of North Gate for cleansing [the grates of] that gate: 6s 8d;
Paid the porter of 'le Watergate' for his fee: 6s 8d;
Paid the porter of West Gate for cleansing 'le grates' [of the same]: 4s.
[Total: £1 13s 4d.]

Receiver's Book

[*f.1*] Extraordinary payments:
[12 October 1612] 'Paid James Clarke for the bankett at the Muraley walke': 10s;
'Plus given the same time to diverse poor folke *per* Mr Mayors order': 6s 10d;
[13 October] 'Paid the Beedles for Clensinge of the walles': 1s 6d;
[13 October] 'For 2 hundred of apples at 2d *per* C': 1s 10d.
[Total: £1 0s 2d.]

[*f.17*] 'Reparacions about the walls in Fryeren hay . . .

[24 December] Paid Mogridge for Carridge of 48 seames of sand to the walls in Fryeren haye': 4s;
'Plus paid Ellis for spreadinge of sand': 1s 2d;
'7 January Paid Ellis for spreadinge of sand': 6d.
[Total: 5s 8d.]

[*f.18*] '1613 Reparacion of a tower in the Bishoppes Pallace
[23 August] Paid John Paine for 3 dozen of barres': 10*s*;
'William Laurence 4 daies att 14*d*': 4*s* 8*d*;
'John Peecke 3 dayes at 13*d*': 3*s* 3*d*;
'John Robines 4 dayes': 4*s*;
'John Rumson a daie': 1*s* 2*d*;
'John Rumson Junior 4 daies': 4*s*;
'Nicholas Casley 3 daies': 2*s* 6*d*;
'Paid Mr Sheeres for 6 hogdsheads of lyme att 4*s* 6*d per*
hogshead is': £1 7*s*;
'Paid John Glanfeild for 18 seames of burres att 3*s* 4*d*
per dozen is': 5*s*;
'Paid for 7 seames of stones at 4*d per* seame': 2*s* 4*d*;
'To Mogridge for 24 seames of Walling sand': 4*s*;
[30 August] 'William Lawrence 3 daies': 3*s* 6*d*;
'John Rumson 6 dayes att 14*d*': 7*s*;
'John Peecke 2 daies att 13*d*': 2*s* 2*d*;
'John Rumson Junior 6 daies': 6*s*;
'Nicholas Casley 2 daies': 1*s* 8*d*;
'Paid John Glanfeild for 2 dozen & 2 seames of burres
att 3*s* 4*d per* dozen': 9*s* 9*d*;
'Paid for 11 seames of stones at 4*d*': 3*s* 8*d*;
'Paid for 18 seames of stones from Plimouth att 5*s* 4*d*
per dozen': 8*s*;
'To Mr Sheeres for 2 hogsheads of Lyme': 9*s*;
'To Mogridge for 2 dozen of sand': 4*s*;
'To Mr Bridgman overseer of this & other woorks': 5*s*;
[8 September] 'William Lawrence a daie': 1*s* 2*d*;
'John Rumson 2 daies': 2*s* 4*d*;
'John Rumson Junior 2 daies': 2*s*;
'Nicholas Casley a daie': 1*s*;
'Thomas Bridgman overseer': 3*s*;
[18 September] 'William Lawrence 3 daies': 3*s* 6*d*;
'John Rumson 3 daies': 3*s* 6*d*;
'John Rumson Junior 2 dayes ½': 2*s* 6*d*;
'John Robbines a daie': 1*s*;
'Nicholas Casley 3 daies': 2*s* 6*d*;
'To Mr Sheares for 2 hogsheads of lime': 9*s*;
'£7 19*s* 2*d*'.

[*f.19*] [25 September] 'Paid John Rumson for 4 daies ½':
5*s* 4*d*;
'Paid John Rumson Junior 3 daies ½': 3*s* 6*d*;
'Nicholas Casley 5 daies': 4*s* 2*d*;
'To Mr Sheeres for 3 hogsheads of lime at 4*s* 6*d*': 13*s* 6*d*;
'To Modgridge for 18 seames of sand': 3*s*;
[27 September] 'William Lawrence 4 daies att 14*d*':
4*s* 8*d*;
'John Rumson 4 daies att 14*d*': 4*s* 8*d*;
'John Rumson Junior 4 daies ½': 4*s* 6*d*;
'John Peecke a daie': 1*s* 1*d*;
'John Robbines 2 daies': 2*s*;
'Nicholas Casley 4 daies ½ att 10*d per* daie': 3*s* 9*d*;
'William Lawrence for Scablinge of 64 seames of stones
att 5*s* 4*d per Centum*': 3*s* 2*d*;
'To Mr Sheeres for 5 hogsheads of Lime at 4*s* 6*d*':
£1 2*s* 6*d*;
'To Mogridge for 24 seames of sand': 4*s*;
'To John Whitt for 46 seames of stones att 5*d per* pece':
19*s* 2*d*;
'To Mr Bridgman overseer': 5*s*;
'Paid John Rumson the elder & the Younger for ½ a
dayes woorke each': 1*s* 1*d*;
'£5 5*s* 1*d*'.
'Some ys': £14 4*s* 3*d* [*sic*, in fact £13 4*s* 3*d*].

[*f.25*] 'Reparacions on Southgat and the prisson *videlicet*
Some ys': £11 10*s* 8½*d* [not included in figure for total
expenditure in this year].

[*f.37*] 1613 'Reparacions of Westgate *videlicet*
[21 August] Paid John Way & Company for 4 dayes
worke';
'Paid Saunders for three crampes wayeing 52 *lbs* at 4*d*
lb': 17*s* 4*d*;
'Plus for 3 bolts with ther keyes weyinge 6 *lbs* ½ att 4*d*
per lb': 2*s* 2*d*;
'Plus for 22 *lbs* in the new twiste': 7*s* 4*d*;
'Plus for 26 *lbs* ½ spewkes & a forlocke ½ *lb*': 2*s* 4*d*;
'Plus for a broad plat conttaining 3 *lbs* & nealles 3*d*':
1*s* 3*d*;
'£1 14*s* 5*d*'.

[Total expenditure in this year: £17 17*s* 10*d*.]

1613–14

Receiver John Gupwell, gentleman.

Receiver's Roll

[*m.8*] Fees of the mayor and other officers:
Paid the 4 porters, *videlicet* 4*s* to each: 16*s*;
Paid the porter of North Gate for cleansing [the grates
of] that gate: 6*s* 8*d*;
Paid the porter of 'le Watergate' for his fee: 6*s* 8*d*;
Paid the porter of West Gate for cleansing 'le grates' of
the same: 4*s*.
[Total: £1 13*s* 4*d*.]

Necessary expenses:
Paid for repairs to the City Wall: £6 9*s* 4½*d* [*sic*].

Receiver's Book [DRO, Box 214, Book 14]

[*f.1*] 'Extraordinary Charges . . .
[25 October] Paid to severall pooer att the Mureally
Walke 6*s* 9*d*, and to the keeper of the Pryson for the
Banquett 13*s* 6*d*, and to the prysoners 2*s* 6*d*, and for
Apples 3*s* 6*d*, ye whole is': £1 6*s* 3*d*.

[*ff.7–8.*] Expenses on South Gate Prison: £1 19*s* 8½*d* [not
included in figure for total expenditure in this year].

[*f.8*] 'Westgate
Payd for 4 seame stones att 5*d per* peece': 20*d*;
[2 May] 'Payd John Moody and his sonne for one dayes
worke': 2*s* 2*d*;
'Payd for drillinge of the heads of ye 2 Posts': 12*d*;
'Payd to Nicholas Saunders for a new Iron grate wayeng
28 *lbs* and half att 4*d per* pound les for 14 *lbs* of old Iron
att 1*d* ½ *per lb*': 7*s* 9*d*;
'Payd for Nayles to fasten the same': 2*d*;
[Total: 12*s* 9*d*.]

[*f.9*] 'Reperacions upon the walls in the Bishopps Pallace
[4 October] *Inprimis* payd to Willyam Lawrence and
John Rumsdon for 9 dayes and half att 14*d per* day: 11*s*;
'Payd to John Rumsdon the younger and John Robbyns
for 9 dayes and [illegible] att 12*d per* day': 9*s* 4*d*;
'Payd to John Peeke for 2 dayes att 13*d per* day': 2*s* 2*d*;

'Payd to Nicholas Caseley for 4 dayes and 3 quarters att 10*d*': 3*s* 6*d*;

'Payd to John Whyte of Exmister for one dosen of seame stones and half att 5*s per* dosen': 7*s* 6*d*;

[11 May] 'Payd to John Rumsdon for 4 dayes worke att 14*d per* day': 4*s* 8*d*;

'Payd to his sonne for 4 dayes worke att 12*d per* day': 4*s*;

'Payd to John Peeke for a half day': 6½*d*;

'Payd to Nicholas Caseley for 5 dayes att 10*d per* day': 4*s* 2*d*;

'Payd to Mr Thomas Bridgman overseer of the worke': 5*s*;

[18 May] 'Payd William Lawrence and John Rumsdon for 8 dayes att 14*d*': 9*s* 4*d*;

'Payd to John Rumsdon the younger and John Robyns for 8 dayes att 12*d per* day': 8*s*;

'Payd to John Peeke for 2 dayes att 13*d per* Daie': 2*s* 2*d*;

'Payd to Nicholas Caseley for 4 dayes and half att 10*d*': 3*s* 9*d*;

'Payd to John Sheere for 2 Hoggsheads of stone lyme att 4*s* 6*d*': 9*s*;

'Payd to Halstaffe for one Hoggshead of lyme att 4*s* 4*d*': 4*s* 4*d*;

'Payd to Peter Moggridge for a dosen of Sand att 2*s*': 2*s*;

'Payd to Whyte for 2 dosen of seame stones att 5*s* dozen': 10*s*;

'Payd to William Lawrence for scavelinge the same': 14*d*;

'Payd to William Lawrence and John Rumsdon for 4 dayes att 14*d per* day': 4*s* 8*d*;

[25 May] 'Payd to John Peeke for 3 dayes att 13*d per* day': 3*s* 3*d*;

'Payd to John Rumsdon ye younger and John Robyns for 6 dayes att 12*d*': 6*s*;

'Payd to Nicholas Caseley for 3 dayes at 10*d per* day': 2*s* 6*d*;

'Payd for amendinge a Cowle and Buckett': 5*d*;

'Payd to John Sheere for 2 hoggsheads of stone lyme att 4*s* 6*d*': 9*s*;

'Payd to Peter Moggridge for 9 seames of Sande': 18*d*;
[Total: £6 8*s* 11½*d*.]

[Total expenditure in this year: £10 1*s* 3½*d*.]

1614–15

Receiver Thomas Crossinge, gentleman.

Receiver's Roll

[*m.4*] Fees of the mayor and other officers:
Paid the 4 porters, *videlicet* 4*s* to each: 16*s*;
Paid the porter of North Gate for cleansing [the grates of] that gate: 6*s* 8*d*;
Paid the porter of 'le Watergate' for his fee: 6*s* 8*d*;
Paid the porter of West Gate for cleansing 'le grates' there: 4*s*.
[Total: £1 13*s* 4*d*.]

Receiver's Book

[*f.1*] 'Extraordinary Charges . . .
[10 October] Paid at the Mureally walke given to the prisoners & poore is 8*s*, paid & gave the keeper for a banquet 13*s* 4*d*, for apples 2*s* 8*d*, to the stavebearers the same time for clensinge the walles 2*s*, all is': £1 6*s*.

[*f.2*] [6 June] 'Paid for 2 men to watch at Southgate William Marckes his Chimney beeinge on fire': 1*s*.
[Total: £1 7*s* 0*d*.]

[*f.5*] Expenses on South Gate Prison: £20 8*s* 10*d* [not included in figure for total expenditure in this year].

[*f.5v.*] 'Westgate Rocklane & Northgate . . .
[30 September 1615] Paid Massons & others for mendinge the Channell at & without Northgate & for lime & sand & althings necessarye as *per* Mr Burrowes note appers': 17*s* 10*d*.
'Paid Nicholas Saunders for a hooke for Northgate is': 12*d*.
[Total: 18*s* 10*d*.]

[Total expenditure in this year: £3 19*s* 2*d*.]

1615–16

Receiver John Taylor, gentleman.

Receiver's Roll

[*m.4*] Fees of the mayor and other officers:
Paid the 4 porters, *videlicet* 4*s* to each: 16*s*;
Paid the porter of North Gate for his fee this year: 6*s* 8*d*;
Paid the porter of 'le Watergate' for his fee this year: 6*s* 8*d*;
Paid the porter of West Gate for cleansing [the grates of] the same: 4*s*.
[Total: £1 13*s* 4*d*.]

Receiver's Book

[*f.1*] 'Extraordinary Chargs . . .
[9 October] Paid out in the Murale walk by order of Mr Maior': £1 10*s*;
[13 October] 'Paid to 4 bedells for clensinge the Murall walke': 2*s*;
'For apples at the Murale walke': 2*s* 6*d*.
[28 February] 'To two men appointed to wayt for victualls at East Gatte for 5 daies & half ech in the Lent': 9*s* 2*d*.
'To two men for waytinge for victualls at West Gatte by Mr Maiors order for three dayes ech in Lent': 5*s*.
[Total: £2 8*s* 8*d*.]

[*f.8*] [Paving:]
[12 November] 'Paid Richard Menifie for 8 daies work with his servaunt in mendinge the staires at Norgatt & laying of the stons in the Cannell': 8*s*;
'Paid for a peck of lyme to sett the stonns': 4*d*.
[Total: 8*s* 4*d*.]

[*f.11v.*] 'Reperacions on East Gatte walls & upon the bridge . . .
[2 December] Paid for the exchange of 2 *lbs* of old lead': 1*d*;
'Paid workmen their wages in mending the Wall': 4*s* 6*d*;
'Paid for lyme for the same': 14*d*;
[4 March] 'Paid William Lawrence for settinge of a stonne without East Gatte on the bridge & for mendinge the Wall with lyme & sand is': 6*s*;
[Subtotal] '11*s* 9*d*'.

[Total expenditure in this year: £5 2*s* 1*d*.]

1616–17

Receiver Thomas Amey.

Receiver's Roll

[*m.4*] Fees of the mayor and other officers:
  Paid the 4 porters, *videlicet* 4*s* to each: 16*s*;
  Paid the porter of North Gate for his fee this year: 6*s* 8*d*;
  Paid the porter of 'le Watergate' for his fee this year: 6*s* 8*d*;
  Paid the porter of West Gate for cleansing [the grates of] the same: 4*s*.
  [Total: £1 13*s* 4*d*.]

[*m.4v.*] Necessary expenses:
  Paid for repairs to the City Wall outside West Gate: £12 5*s* 9*d*.

Receiver's Book

[*f.11*] 'Charge for worke donne in making of a newe stone banke under the walls without Westgate
  [22 December] Paid Moody the mason and company for their worke at the said banke and for 1 dosen ½ of clay': 13*s* 2*d*;
  'Paid for 208 seames of Heavitree stones': £1 16*s*;
  'Paid for 14 seames of Milbery stones at 5*d* and for skabling of 20 seames': 11*s* 4*d*;
  [29 December] 'Paid masons wages & passage at Kay': 7*s* 6*d*;
  [5 January] 'Paid masons wages for the said worke': £1 7*s* 8*d*;
  'Paid 4 dosen ½ of burres & 1 hogshed of lyme': £1 4*d*;
  [12 January] 'Paid for 90 seames of quary stones, and skabling, and for 6 seames of burres': £1 16*s* 2*d*;
  [19 January] 'Paid for 2 dosen ½ of seame stones, & skabling, and for 25 seames of burres': £1 3*s* 1*d*;
  'Paid masons wages in the same worke': £1 10*s* 6*d*;
  [26 January] 'Paid for 20 seame stones & skabling, and for 1 hogshed ½ of lyme, & cariage of gravell': 18*s* 3*d*;
  'Paid masons wages for worke there, and for footing the walls without West Gate': £1 1*s* 9*d*;
  £12 5*s* 9*d*.

[*f.12*] 'Charge in extraordinaryes . . .
  Paid by Mr Maiors order at the Murall walke to the poore & High Gaile': 9*s* 9*d*;
  'Paid for apples in a largesse': 4*s*;
  'Paid Stabb and consorts for clensing ye lane': 1*s* 6*d*;
  'Paid William Marks for the banquet at the Murall walke' 15*s*.
  'Thomas Russell for mending the windowes at Markes his howse': 5*s*.
  'For setting 2 newe posts within Westgate, 1 seame stone & ½ a bushell of lyme': 5*s*.
  'Paid 3 masons wages for worke at Kay Gate and seame stones for the worke': 10*s* 11*d*.
  'Labourers wages about the water course stopped at Southgate': 10*s* 7*d*.
  'Paid the cityes laborers for one other weeks worke in clensing the water course of Southgate': 10*s*.

[*f.14v.*] 'Paid Jasper Robins & 2 more 3 dayes worke in

clensing the water passage at Southgate for candles and 6*s* for exterordinary': 15*s* 8*d*.
  'For 2 newe skene [?] pinnes for the Key Gate': 1*s*.
  'Paid for 30 seames of quary stones & skablinge for repairing the breach at Southgate made to open the water course': 13*s* 2*d*.
  'Paid masons wages and candle light': 15*s* 2*d*.
  'For lyme & claye for the worke': 5*s* 4*d*.
  'Paid setting up the bridge in Minsons garden': 3*s* 4*d*.

[*f.15*] 'Paid masons wages for worke at Southgate': 3*s* 1*d*.
  [Total: £6 8*s* 6*d*.]

[*f.16*] For 'repairing the prison': 10*s* 4*d* [not included in figure for total expenditure].

[Total expenditure in this year: £20 7*s* 7*d*.]

1617–18

Receiver Peter Coleton.

Receiver's Roll

[*m.4*] Fees of the mayor and other officers:
  Paid the 4 porters, *videlicet* 4*s* to each: 16*s*;

[*m.5*] Paid the porter of North Gate for his fee: 6*s* 8*d*;
  Paid the porter of 'le Watergate' for his fee: 6*s* 8*d*;
  Paid the porter of West Gate for cleansing [the grates of] the same: 4*s*.
  [Total: £1 13*s* 4*d*.]

[*m.5v.*] Allocations:
  10*s* allocated for defected rent of 'le Porters Lodge' at West Gate.

Receiver's Book

[*f.1*] 'Extraordynarye Paymenttes. . .
  [13 October] Gave to the poore and to the prisoners in the gaoles ye muralia walke': 10*s*;
  Gave William Markes for our bancket their, then': 15*s*;
  'For apples at Mr Maiors howse from the muralia walke': 3*s*;
  [24 October] 'Clensing the walles agaynst the muralia walke': 6*d*.
  [3 November] 'For mending of a locke of ye wicket att Southgate': 4*d*.
  [12 March] 'Paid two watchmen to watch the gate for victualls': 2*s*.
  [27 March] 'Paid ye biddells for one yeers stipent for clensing the Towne Walles': 4*s*.
  [31 March] 'For removyng the traytor his quarter from Snail Tower to North Gate': 2*s* 6*d*.

[*f.2*] [27 August] 'Paid for mending of the wickett locke att Westgate': 10*d*.
  [Total: £1 18*s* 2*d*.]

[*f.5*] 'For mending of the prison at Southgate': £4 4*s* 10*d* [not included in figure for total expenditure].

[Total expenditure in this year: £3 11*s* 6*d*.]

1618–19

Receiver John Aclande.

Receiver's Roll

[m.6] Fees of the mayor and other officers:
Paid the 4 porters, *videlicet* 4s to each: 16s;

[m.6v.] Paid the porter of North Gate for his fee: 6s 8d;
Paid the porter of 'le Watergate' for his fee: 6s 8d;
Paid the porter of West Gate for cleansing [the grates of] the same: 4s.
[Total: £1 13s 4d.]
Allocations:

[m.4v.] Paid the beadles for cleansing the walls: 4s.

Receiver's Book

[f.1] 'Exter ordenary Paymentes . . .
[21 November] Unto divers poore att the muraly walke *per* Mr Mayors Apoyntment is': 11s;
'Paide Markes for his Bankate . . .': 15s;
'For Appells for the Boyes the same tyme is . . .': 2s 6d.

[f.1v.] [10 October] 'For repayringe of Bures lodg att West Gate': 6s.
'Payd Markes att Southgat for Reperations about his howse': 7s.
[Total: £2 1s 6d.]

[f.2] 'Reperasions one the walles the brudge att Estgate and stepes at Westgatte
Payd for Repering the Walles for 7 seme stones for that worke be twext Estgate & g[aol]': 2s 4d;
'Payd Mudey & his Compenye for Repering the walls be twext Est Gat & the gelle': 12s 6d;
'Payd for 8 semes of sand and 3 of Claye for sayd worke is the some': 1s 10d;
'Pay for a hocsed and hallfe of lyme for sayd worke is the some': 6s;
[9 January] 'Payd for 2 dossen of Bures for Reperinge sayd walles is the some': 6s 8d;
'Payd for halfe a hocsed of lyme and 2 semes of sand is the some': 2s 4d;
'Payd Mudey and his Compeny for worke one sayd walles is the [sum]': 4s;
'Payd Cumans and his Company for worke one the brudg att Est Gate is': £1;
[31 January] 'Payd to sayers 6 dayes to sawe plankes for sayd brudg is the some of': 14s;
'Payd Blachford for passinges att the Caye is the some of': 10d;
'Payd for worke mens wages att the brudge att Est Gat as by Mr Sherods note aperes': £2 14s;
'Payd for 2 dosen & ½ of Claye 1 dosen & ½ of paven stones 2 dosen ½ of gravell 12 forse fagots': 11s 5d;
'Payd for pych and tar to pych the plankes of sayd brudge as [by] Mr Sherods note apperes': 16s;
'Payd for 2 watch men att the gat be for the brudge was upe & Candells': 2s 6d;
'Payd Saunders the smyth for Ireworke for the brudge . . .': 8s 6d;
'Payd for a worke mans wages there is the some of': 1s 2d;

[13 February] 'Payd Williams the plumer for nue castinge the led over the kings picter at Est Gat & for nue led and soder unto it as by his note appereth is the some': £1 8s 11d;
'Payd for Caridge of 5 bemes and all the plankes from the Cay to Est Gate is': 6s 6d;
'Payd for mending of Mr Caryes garden Wall which was brocken by our workemen in [illegible]': 1s 6d;
'Payd the paver for 50 yeards of pavement over the brudg att Est Gate is': 8s 6d;
'Payd for 4 dosen of sand and stones for sayd pament is the some of': 8s 8d;
'Payd for worke mens wages att Est Gat & other places as by Mr Sherods note apperes': 10s 3d;
[3 October] 'Payd Mudey and his Compeny for worke one the walles by Mr Sherods note': 17s 6d;
'Payd for a hocsed of lyme and sand for sayd wales is the some of': 4s 8d;
'Payd for quarye stones and skabling of them for sayd worke is the [sum of]': 3s 8d;
'Payd Mudey and his Compeny for worke one the stepes att West Gate is': 5s 11d;
'Payd for 18 seme stones for sayd stepes is 4d *per* stone is the some': 6s;
'Payd Mudey and his Compeny for worke one sayd stepes is the [sum of]': 10s;
'Payd for hallfe a hocsed of lyme and 3 semes of sand is the some': 2s 6d;
'Payd for Repering the porters lodge att West Gate is the some': 8s 11d.
'Payd for Refreshing the Collors of the stone att Est Gate and Collering 9 band stones, I me[a]n the letters, with the word Exon is the some of': 5s 4d;
[Total: £14 12s 11d.]

[Total expenditure in this year: £18 11s 9d.]

1619–20

Receiver George Pyle.

Receiver's Roll

[m.4] Fees of the mayor and other officers:
Paid the 4 porters, *videlicet* 4s to each: 16s;

[m.4v.] Paid the porter of North Gate for his fee: 6s 8d;
Paid the porter of 'le Watergate' for his fee: 6s 8d;
Paid the porter of West Gate for cleansing [the grates of] the same: 4s.
[Total: £1 13s 4d.]

[Necessary expenses:]
[m.3v.] Paid for repairs to the City Walls: 42s 10d.

Receiver's Book

[f.1] 'Extraordinary Payments . . .
[9 October] Paid William Markes for the Banquett': 16s;
'Gyven the prisoners & spinsters when muraling day was': 8s 7d;
'Paid for Apples for the boyes for that daye': 4s.
[8 November] 'Paid Scues the hellier for amending a fault att Guyhall [Guildhall] & repayringe the darke house by the walles being much torren with the winde & for stones, lyme & sand & his labour, is': 3s 9d.

[18 December] 'Paid the Bedles for Clensinge the Towne Walles is': 4s.

[f.3] [23 June] 'For wier nayles & flax for the dyoll att Norgate is': 5d;

[f.4] [16 October] 'Paid Holwell & others to take downe the scaffold att Norgate & for carrenge of it at court': 1s 6d; 'Paid Commings painter for the dioll att Norgate': £1 2s.
[Total: £3 3d.]

[f.6] 'Repairinge the Towne Walles
Paied for cleansinge the Walles of ivey & Brembelles': 12s;
'Paied for Lyme & sand for that worke is': 2s 6d;
'Paid Moody for repayringe in Doctor Gouches garden & Bishop Gren': 5s 10d;
'His boye 5 daies att 10d a daye is': 4s 2d;
[24 September] 'Wiatt 5 daies & Gowdwyn 3 daies both is': 8s 3d;
'2 hogsides of stone lyme is': 8s;
'Paied for 10 seames of sand is': 2s 1d.
[Total: £2 2s 10d.]

[f.11] 'Charges bestowed uppn Southgate & Bridewell': £3 18s 1d [not included in figure for total expenditure].

[Total expenditure in this year: £6 16s 5d.]

1620–21

Receiver John Lynne.

Receiver's Roll

[This roll is much decayed.]
[m.4] Fees of the mayor and other officers:
Paid the 4 porters: 16s.
[Rest lost.]

[The book for this year is missing.]

Book of Summary [DRO, Box 214, Book 3]

[f.486] Allocations:
Paid the beadles for cleansing the walls at the time of the mural walk: 4s.

[Total expenditure in this year: £1 0s 0d.]

1621–22

Receiver Thomas Wakeman.

Receiver's Roll

[m.4] Fees of the mayor and other officers:
Paid the 4 porters, *videlicet* 4s to each of them: 16s;
Paid the porter of North Gate for his fee: 6s 8d;
Paid the porter of 'le Watergate' for his fee: 6s 8d;
Paid the porter of West Gate for cleansing [the grates of] the same: 4s.

[The book for this year is missing.]

[Total expenditure in this year: £1 13s 4d.]

1622–23

Receiver John Jurdaine.

Receiver's Roll

[m.3v.] Fees of the mayor and other officers:
Paid the 4 porters for their fee, *videlicet* 4s to each of them: 16s;
Paid the porter of North Gate for his fee: 6s 8d;
Paid the porter of 'le Watergate' for his fee: 6s 8d;
Paid the porter of West Gate for cleansing [the grates of] the same: 4s.
[Total: £1 13s 4d.]

[Extraordinary charges:]
For reparations on the City Walls: 37s 1d.

[The book for this year is missing.]

[Total expenditure in this year: £3 10s 5d.]

1623–24

Receiver Nicholas Spicer.

Receiver's Roll

[m.3v.] Fees of the mayor and other officers:
Paid the 4 porters for their fee this year, *videlicet* 4s to each of them: 16s;
Paid the porter of 'le Watergate' for his fee: 6s 8d;
Paid the porter of West Gate for cleansing [the grates of] the same: 4s.
[Total: £1 6s 8d.]

[m.2v.] [Extraordinary charges:]
Paid for reparations on the walls: *nihil*.
Paid for diverse reparations on 'le Southgate': £4 3s 11d.

Receiver's Book

[f.2] 'Worke done att Sought Gatte [prison]': £4 3s 11d [not included in figure for total expenditure in this year].

[f.5] 'Exetterordinarye payments [*sic*] . . .
Given in the muralia walke': 11s 10d.
'For carrnge the mach and powder to the store howse': 1s.

[f.7] 'For mendinge the Key Gate': 4s 4d.

[Total expenditure in this year: £2 3s 10d.]

1624–25

Receiver Thomas Flaye.

Receiver's Roll

[m.3v.] Fees of the mayor and other officers:
Paid the 4 porters for their fee this year, *videlicet* 4s to each of them: 16s;
Paid the porter of 'le Watergate' for his fee: 6s 8d;
Paid the porter of West Gate for cleansing [the grates of] the same: 4s;

Paid the porter of North Gate for cleansing the step
(*gradus*) there: 6s 8d.
[Total: £1 13s 4d.]

Necessary expenses:
[*m.2v.*] Paid for diverse reparations on South Gate and the
City Walls: £2 16s 8d.

Allocations:
Paid the 4 beadles for scouring the City Walls against
the mural walk: 4s.

[The book for this year is missing.]

[Total expenditure in this year: £4 14s 0d.]

1625–26

Receiver Nicholas Martin, gentleman.

Receiver's Roll

[*m.2v.*] Fees of the mayor and other officers:
Paid the 4 porters for their fee this year, *videlicet* 4s to
each of them: 16s;
Paid the porter of 'le Watergate' for his fee: 6s 8d;
Paid the porter of West Gate for cleansing [the grates
of] the same: 4s;
Paid the porter of North Gate for cleansing the step
(*gradus*) there: 6s 8d.
[Total: £1 13s 4d.]

Extraordinary expenses:
For closing up 'le posterne gate' of Exeter Castle: £2 14s.
Paid for closing up the Bishop's gate towards Southernhay:
£4 9s 10d.

Allocations:
Paid the 4 beadles for scouring the City Walls against
the mural walk: 4s.

Receiver's Book

[*f.2*] 'The 5 of August 1626
Chardges bestowed in walling upp the posterne gat in
the Castell the day and yeare above writtin *videlicet*
Paid for 11 dozen of quary stones and for scobling of
them': 9s 2d;
'Paid Thomas Dowdell for 20 seames of sand at 2s *per*
dozen': 3s 4d;
'Paid for 5 hogsheads and on bushell of stone lyme at 3s
8d *per* hoghead': 19s 3d;
'Paid for on hogshead from John Gyles of stone lyme':
4s;
'Paid Courtes & another man for didggine of stones on
day at ye Castell': 2s;
'Paid Lawrence and 2 more at 14d *per* day for 2 dayes':
7s;
[13 August] 'Paid 2 men for macking of morter 2 dayes
½ of a day at 12d *per* day': 5s 6d;
'Paid 2 men mor on[e] at 12d a day the other at 10d is':
3s 8d;
'Paid for lent of a rope to draw water in the Castell': 2d.
£2 14s 1d.

'The 18 of August 1626
Charges on the posterne gate att the Bishopps Palace:
Paid for 2 hogshead of stone lyme at 2s 8d *per* hogshead':
5s 4d;
'Paid for ½ dozen of sand carryed into the Pallace':
1s 3d;
[28 August] 'Paid for 4 hogsheads of lyme more att 3s
8d *per* hogshead': 14s 8d;
[3 September] 'Paid to Moody Puttley and Kenneck for
6 dayes work at the doore and macking a new garrett as
per Sherwoods noat': £1;
'Paid 5 other labourr men as *per* the same noate
appears for filling upp the trench carrying of stones &
macking morter': 18s;
'Paid for 1 dozan ½ of morter, sand, at 2s 6d dozen':
3s 9d;
'Paid for carridg of 5 seames of morter from the Castell
to the Pallice': 10d;
'Paid for a baskett to carry stones & repayring a Croock
borrowed': 8d;
'Paid 2 men to mack morter in the Pallace before hand':
2s;
'Paid Maunder and his sonn for watching the door to
keep in ye deere': 2s 6d;
[7 September] 'Paid for carrying of 4 great stones from
the posterne gate to St Johns within Eastgate': 6s;
[8 September] 'Paid 2 Worckmen for 3 dayes ½':
6s 6d;
'Paid the old Maunder for damage don to his garden':
1s 6d;
'Paid Moody and 3 men more for walling there': 4s 4d;
'Paid Courtes and King for 1 dayes worck at the
Pallace': 2s;
'Paid for sand to mack morter with all': 6d;
£4 9s 10d.

[*f.4*] 'Charges laid out on the prison at Southgate': £2 6s
[not included in figure for total expenditure in this
year].

[*f.6*] 'Exterordenary Chardges . . .
[15 July] 'Paid for paving of the Westgate to make the
gates goe easy': 6d.
[16 July] 'Paid Saunders the smyth for hoocks & twists
and other Ironn worck to new hang the Westgate as by a
noat appears': £1 11s 10d.
[16 July] 'Paid Comings and Moody and other masons
for ther worck to hang the West Gate and for lyme and
stone as *per* the noat appers': 12s.

[*f.7*] [13 August] 'For a seame stone to putt over the grates
at Northgate': 1s.
[17 September] 'Paid Oxenbury for helping the
Carpenter to mend the Westgate': 1s.

[*f.8*] 'Paid for mending the Lock of the Little Dore in ye
Sowthgate': 4d.
[Total: £2 6s 10d.]

[Total expenditure in this year: £11 8s 1d.]

1626–27

Receiver John Hakewill.

Receiver's Roll

[*m.2v.*] Fees of the mayor and other officers:
Paid the 4 porters for their fee this year, *videlicet* 4*s* to each of them: 16*s*;
Paid the porter of 'le Watergate' for his fee: 6*s* 8*d*;
Paid the porter of West Gate for cleansing [the grates of] the same: 4*s*.
Paid the porter of North Gate for cleansing the step (*gradus*) there: 6*s* 8*d*.

[The book for this year is missing.]

[Total expenditure in this year: £1 13*s* 4*d*.]

1627–28

Receiver Gilbert Sweete.

Receiver's Roll

[*m.2v.*] Fees of the mayor and other officers:
Paid the 4 porters for their pension this year, *videlicet* 4*s* to each of them: 16*s*;
Paid the porter of West Gate for cleansing [the grates of] the same: 4*s*;
Paid the porter of North Gate for cleansing the step (*gradus*) there: 6*s* 8*d*;
Paid the porter of 'le Watergate' for his pension: 6*s* 8*d*.
[Total: £1 13*s* 4*d*.]

Receiver's Book

[*f.7*] 'Reparacions on the Citties Walles
Paid for a locke for Southgate Wickett': 2*s*;
'Paid the Mason for worke att Northgate 2*s* 2*d* with Stones': 4*s* 5*d*;
'Paid for a Hamer att Eastgate': 1*s* 6*d*;
'Paid Moodie & Nicholas Thomas for mendinge a breach under Southgate': 1*s* 10*d*;
'Paid Ambrose Dodge for nayles for Northgate': 2*d*;
'Paid for mendinge the Locke att Westgate': 1*s*;
'Paid Saunders for Iron worke att Westgate': 5*d*;
'Paid for a Locke and Key att the Porters Lodge': 2*s* 6*d*;
'Paid Saunders for mendinge the barr att Keygate—beinge broken': 5*s*;
'Paid Comyns & others for 3 dayes worke on the Keygate': 10*s* 6*d*;
'Paid William Searle for Timber': 4*s*;
'Paid for men to helpe unhange the gate': 3*s* 3*d*;
'Paid William Reede for a pole sheed': 3*s* 8*d*;
'Paid William Reede for a peece of Timber': 3*s* 8*d*;
'Paid the Smith for Iron Worke': £1 10*s*;
'Paid Carpenters & Masons & for a plancke & placinge it': 12*s* 3*d*;
'Paid the Smith for Iron Worke': 7*s*;
'Paid the Smiths men for helpinge to hang the gate': 1*s*;
[Total: £4 14*s* 0*d*.]

[*ff.8–9*] 'Reparacions on the prison': £41 18*s* [not included in figure for total expenditure in this year].

[*f.11*] 'Extraordinarie Charges . . .
Paid in the Murallie Walke and to the prisoners': 3*s*.

[Total expenditure in this year: £6 10*s* 4*d*.]

1628–29

Receiver Francis Crossinge.

Receiver's Roll

[*m.2v.*] Fees of the mayor and other officers:
Paid the 4 porters for their pension this year, *videlicet* 4*s* to each of them: 16*s*;
Paid the porter of West Gate for cleansing [the grates of] the same: 4*s*;
Paid the porter of North Gate for cleansing the step (*gradus*) there: 6*s* 8*d*;
Paid the porter of 'le Watergate' for his pension: 6*s* 8*d*.
[Total: £1 13*s* 4*d*.]

Receiver's Book

[*ff.2–4*] 'Reparacions on the prison': £87 1*s* [not included in figure for total expenditure in this year].

[*f.12*] 'Extraordenary Payments . . .
[17 October] Paid unto Sible and at the Murallie Walke': 19*s* 7*d*.
[14 November] 'Paid Hoppinge for a locke & key for Southgate': 10*s*.
[31 January] 'Paid for repairinge the howses upon the walls at the end of Mr Birdalls garden as *per* a noate': £1 10*s*.

[*f.14*] [9 August] 'Paid for repayringe the Porters lodge at Southgate': 9*s*.
'Paid for repairinge the Porters lodge at Westgate': 7*s* 5*d*.
[22 September] 'Paid for worke done at Northgate as *per* a noate': 18*s* 8*d*.
[Total: £4 14*s* 8*d*.]

[Total expenditure in this year: £6 8*s* 0*d*.]

1629–30

Receiver Adam Bennett.

Receiver's Roll

[*m.2v.*] Fees of the mayor and other officers:
Paid the 4 porters for their pension this year, *videlicet* 4*s* to each of them: 16*s*;
Paid the porter of West Gate for cleansing [the grates of] the same: 4*s*;
Paid the porter of North Gate for cleansing the step (*gradus*) there: 6*s* 8*d*;
Paid the porter of 'le Watergate' for his pension: 6*s* 8*d*.
[Total: £1 13*s* 4*d*.]

Receiver's Book

[*f.4*] 'Reparacions on the prison': £13 17*s* 8*d* [not included in figure for total expenditure in this year].

[*f.7*] 'Extraordinarie Charges . . .
Paid for planchinge the Wooll Markett, repairinge a Floer in the New Inne, for Masons work att Northgate, & for cleiveing Stakes & makinge wood att Duriurd': £5 18*s* 9*d*.
'Paid in the murallie walke and to the prisoners': 2*s*;

'Paid Siblies wife towards a banquett': 10*s*;
'Paid for apples att the murallie walke': 5*s*.
'Paid for clensinge fower peeces of ordinance & other charges thereabout': 8*s* 8*d*.

[*f.9*] 'Paid for a locke for the Keygate': 2*s* 6*d*.
[Total: between £1 8*s* 2*d* and £7 6*s* 11*d*.]

[Total expenditure in this year: between £3 1*s* 6*d* and £9 0*s* 3*d*.]

1630–31
Receiver Roger Mallacke.

Receiver's Roll

[*m.2v.*] Fees of the mayor and other officers:
    Paid the 4 porters for their pension this year, *videlicet* 4*s* to each of them: 16*s*;
    Paid the porter of West Gate for cleansing [the grates of] the same: 4*s*;
    Paid the porter of North Gate for cleansing the step (*gradus*) there: 6*s* 8*d*;
    Paid the porter of 'Watergate' for his pension: 6*s* 8*d*.
    [Total: £1 13*s* 4*d*.]

Receiver's Book

[*f.5*] 'Reparations one the Prison': 15*s* 3*d* [not included in figure for total expenditure in this year].

[*f.8*] 'Extraordinary Charges . . .
    [11 October] Paid for Apples when Mr Maior went about the walls': 3*s* 4*d*;
    'Paid for & towards a banquitt at Siblies house in ye Southgate': 15*s*;
    'Paid to the prisoners in the South Gaille': 2*s* 6*d*.
    [25 January] 'Paid for a new plate locke upon the West Gate': 3*s* 4*d*.
    [2 April] 'Plus paid the poore in veisiting the High Gaille at the muralia walke': 5*s*.
    [Total: £1 9*s* 2*d*.]

[Total expenditure in this year: £3 2*s* 6*d*.]

1631–32
Receiver John Crocker.

Receiver's Roll

[*m.2v.*] Fees of the mayor and other officers:
    Paid the 4 porters for their pension this year, *videlicet* 4*s* to each of them: 16*s*;
    Paid the porter of West Gate for cleansing [the grates of] the same: 4*s*;
    Paid the porter of North Gate for cleansing the step (*gradus*) there: 6*s* 8*d*;
    Paid the porter of 'Watergate' for his pension: 6*s* 8*d*.
    [Total: £1 13*s* 4*d*.]

[*m.1v.*] Necessary expenses:
    Paid for diverse reparations on the City Walls this year: £22 11*d*.

[The book for this year is missing.]

[Total expenditure in this year: £23 14*s* 3*d*.]

1632–33
Receiver James Tucker.

Receiver's Roll

[*m.2v.*] Fees of the mayor and other officers:
    Paid the 4 porters for their pension this year, *videlicet* 4*s* to each of them: 16*s*;
    Paid the porter of West Gate for cleansing [the grates of] the same: 4*s*;
    Paid the porter of North Gate for cleansing the step (*gradus*) there: 6*s* 8*d*;
    Paid the porter of the Watergate for his pension: 6*s* 8*d*.
    [Total: £1 13*s* 4*d*.]

Necessary expenses:
[*m.1v.*] Paid for diverse reparations on the walls of the city this year: £30 12*d* [*sic*].

Receiver's Book

[*f.6*] 'Reparations on the Towne Walles
    [23 March] Payde William Laraunce for reparinge walles without Westgate': £1 2*s* 6*d*;
    '30 [March] Payde William Larance for repairinge the south sade of Westgate': 6*s* 10*d*;
    'Julye 20th payde Arther Wines for 14 Dayes worke & stons & sande': £1 5*s*;
    'August 3 payde for 6 dozen of stonns & for Caredge as ye Bille': 10*s*;
    '10 [August] payde John Romsen for 36 Dayes Worcke for Caredge & sande': £2 18*s* 3*d*;
    '17 [August] payde John Romsen for 39 Dayes Worke for Carridge Lyme & sande': £1 19*s* 2*d*;
    '24 [August] payde John Romsen for 24 Dayes Worke & Caridge of Lyme & sand': £1 14*s* 5*d*;
    'Payde For 2 dozen ½ of sems stonns from Heavytree': 11*s* 3*d*;
    '31 [August] payde John Romsen for 31 Dayes ½ worke & Caridge of Lyme & sand': £2 2*s* 7*d*;
    'September 7 payde John Romsen for 16 Dayes Worke & for sand & stonns': £1 2*s* 7*d*;
    '14 [September] payde Arther Wines for 34 Dayes worke & for Caridge sand Lyme': £2 3*s*;
    '21 [September] payde John Romsen for 33 Dayes & for stoons & scablen': £3 3*s* 8*d*;
    '28 [September] payde Arther Wine 37 Dayes Worke & 12 dozen ½ of stons & scablen & Carridge off Lyme and sande for the way by Snayle Tower': £5 4*s* 2*d*;
    'Payde Arther Wines for finnishinge this worke': 6*s* 11*d*;
    'Payde Mr Nicholas Boulte for 31 hodghidse & 2 Bushell of Lyme': £5 15*s* 3*d*;
    '£30 5*s* 7*d*'.

[*f.7*] 'Exterordenare Charges . . .
    [8 October] Payde 2*s* 6*d* and 1*s* to the poore by the prison, the 2*s* 6*d* was given to the poore in the Heaye Gayle [High Gaol] as appeares': 3*s* 6*d*;
    '2*s* 9*d* was given to my Ladye Smiths servants at the Bancket': 2*s* 9*d*;
    'Paid Sybleys wife . . . at the Bankett by order': 10*s*;
    'Payde 2*s* to the prisoners in South Gatte & 6*d* to the Key Gatt': 2*s* 6*d*;
    'Payde for Applles for the boayes at the same tyme': 6*s*.

[*f.9*] [12 November] 'Payde Mr Herman for 8 dozen of stoans for the walles': 4*s*.

[11 May] 'Paid John Pyttman, John Guye, Homperye Locke for mending a place under South Gatte as ye bill payde, I saye': 11*s* 4*d*.

[Total: £2 0*s* 1*d*.]

[Total expenditure in this year: £33 19*s* 0*d*.]

1633–34

Receiver Robert Walker.

Receiver's Roll

[*m.2v.*] Fees of the mayor and other officers:

Paid the 4 porters for their pension this year, *videlicet* 4*s* to each of them: 16*s*;

Paid the porter of West Gate for cleansing [the grates of] the same: 4*s*;

Paid the porter of North Gate for cleansing the step (*gradus*) there: 6*s* 8*d*;

Paid the porter of the Watergate for his pension: 6*s* 8*d*.

[Total: £1 13*s* 4*d*.]

Necessary expenses:

[*m.1v.*] Paid for diverse reparations on the walls of the city this year: £41 19*s* 5*d*.

Receiver's Book

[*f.4*] 'Reparations on the pryson': £1 16*s* 3*d* [not included in figure for total expenditure in this year].

[*f.6*] 'Reparations on the Cityes Walls

1633

[25 October] Paid Roger Wills for seame stones': £1 16*s* 3*d*;

[16 November] 'Paid William Laurence mason for repairinge the barbican at Northegate & is': £1 4*s* 6*d*;

'16 [November] paid Humphrey Locke for carridge of Lyme': 1*s* 6*d*;

'16 [November] paid for 16 seames of sand from Heavietree': 4*s*;

'23 [November] paid William Laurence mason *per* his note': 19*s* 2*d*.

'23 [November] paid Humphrey Locke for carridge of Lyme & sand': 2*s*;

'23 [November] paid for 3 dozen of seame stones & is': 15*s*;

'1634

03 [June] paid William Laurence mason *per* his note is': 15*s* 6*d*;

'03 [June] paid for carriege of Lyme & sand': 3*s* 2*d*;

'07 [June] paid Roger Wils for seame stones & burrs': 11*s* 1*d*;

'August 02 paid the masons *per* their worke & scabling stons': 8*s* 9*d*;

'02 [August] paid for seame stones from Heavietree': £1;

'02 [August] paid for carridge of Lyme & sand': 4*s* 10*d*;

'09 [August] paid William Laurence mason *per* his, & his companies worke 4 dozen of stones and scrablinge them as *per* his note is': £2 14*s* 7*d*;

'16 [August] paid William Laurence mason for his & his companies worke seame stones & scabling them': 19*s* 4*d*;

'16 [August] paid for carridge of Lyme & sand': 3*s* 4*d*;

'23 [August] paid for 6 dozen of seame stones': £1 10*s*;

'23 [August] paid William Laurence mason for his companyes wages omitted last weike & is': 8*s*;

'23 [August] paid *per* this weiks worke & scablin stones': £2 2*s* 5*d*;

'23 [August] paid for carridge of Lyme & sand is': 8*s* 10*d*;

'29 [August] paid William Laurence Mason for his companyes wages, a sive & basket & is': £1 16*s* 2*d*;

'29 [August] paid for carridge of Lyme & sand': 7*s* 4*d*;

'06 [September] paid for carridge of Lyme & sand': 9*s* 2*d*;

'06 [September] paid William Laurence mason for his wages': £1 15*s* 4*d*;

'13 [September] paid him more for wages & scaffold ropes': £2 13*s* 4*d*;

'13 [September] paid John Griffin for 2 dozen of stones': 16*s*;

'13 [September] for one dozen & ½ more from Heavietree': 7*s* 6*d*;

'13 [September] paid for carridge of Lyme & sand': 7*s* 4*d*;

'20 [September] paid William Laurence mason for his companys wages': £2 5*s* 1*d*;

'20 [September] paid him more for slings & scaffold ropes': 6*s* 4*d*;

'20 [September] paid for 7 dozen of stones is 35*s*': £1 15*s*;

'20 [September] paid for carridge of Lyme & sand': 8*s*;

'27 [September] paid William Laurence mason for his wages & scabling stones as *per* his note & is': £2 14*s* 8*d*;

'27 [September] paid Mr Tothil for stones 12*s*': 12*s*;

'27 [September] paid for stones from Heavietree & is': £1 5*s*;

'27 [September] paid for carridge of Lyme & sand': 14*s* 2*d*;

'Paid Mr Bolt for 38 hogsheads & ½ of Lyme at 3*s* 6*d* a [hogshead] delivered at sevrall tymes': £6 14*s* 9*d*;

'£41 19*s* 5*d*'.

[*f.9*] 'Extraordynarie Chargs . . .

[7 October] Given the poore 4*s*, the Ladye Smithes servants 3*s*, Mistris Sibley 10*s* when Mr Maior went the mural walke': 17*s*.

[*f.10*] [3 May] 'Paid for makeinge a seate under Eastgate': 7*d*.

[*f.11*] [5 July] 'Paid Sanders for naylles & staples at Westgate': 1*s* 10*d*.

[*f.12*] 'Paid the porter of Southgate for riddinge out the dirt under the pryson & is': 2*s* 6*d*.

[Total: £1 1*s* 11*d*.]

[Total expenditure in this year: £44 14*s* 8*d*.]

1634–35

Receiver John Hayne.

Receiver's Roll

[*m.2v.*] Fees of the mayor and other officers:
Paid the 4 porters for their pension this year, *videlicet* 4*s* to each of them: 16*s*;
Paid the porter of West Gate for cleansing [the grates of] the same: 4*s*;
Paid the porter of North Gate for cleansing the step (*gradus*) there: 6*s* 8*d*;
Paid the porter of the Watergate for his pension: 6*s* 8*d*.
[Total: £1 13*s* 4*d*.]

Necessary expenses:
[*m.1v.*] Paid for diverse reparations to the City Walls this year: £21 18*d*.

Receiver's Book

[*f.5*] 'Reparacions on ye Gaole': £1 11*s* 8*d* [not included in figure for total expenditure in this year].

'Reparacions on ye Cittie Walles
1634
October 4 paid Masons wages for worke done in ye Pallace by a note': £1 13*s* 6*d*;
[11 October] 'For Masons wages, lime & sand, as by a note': £1 11*s* 8*d*;
[18 October] 'For Masons wages, & materialls, as by a note': £2 7*s* 8*d*;
[25 October] 'For Masons wages, & materialls, as by a note': £2 11*s* 11*d*;
[31 October] 'For Masons wages, lime & sand, as by a note': £2 1*s* 10*d*;
'November 8 for Masons wages, lime & sand, & seame stones, as by a note': 13*s* 8*d*;
'December 13 for repairing two coines of a wall, in ye Pallace, in ye note': 3*s* 1*d*;
'February 14 for repairing ye Garrets at ye Steppes in Friernhay, in ye note': 5*s* 8*d*;
[21 February] 'For repairing the Barbican neere Westgate, by a note': 3*s* 6*d*;
'March 7 for Masons wages to repaire said Barbican, & materialls, in ye note': £2 19*s* 5*d*;
[14 March] 'For repairing ye said Barbican, & materialls, in ye note': £1 8*s* 6*d*;
[21 March] 'For carying ye ruble hereof into Southenhay, in ye note': 15*s*;
'1635
[28 March] For carying more of this rubble into Southenhay, in ye note': 11*s* 8*d*;
'Aprill 4 for Masons wages & materialls to repaire said Barbican, & carying away more of the rubble into Southenhay, in the note': £3 5*s* 1*d*;
[11 April] 'For Masons wages, & carying away more of ye rubble, in ye note': 9*s* 4*d*;
'£21 1*s* 6*d*'.

[*f.6*] [Extraordinary expenses:]
[13 October] 'Paid in going ye Muraille walke with Mr Maior, *videlicet*: to ye poore at High Gaole 1*s* 6*d*, to a scholer of ye Freeschoole which made an oration 5*s*, to ye prisoners of Southgate 1*s* 10*d*, to Siblies wife for a banket 15*s* is': £1 3*s* 4*d*;
'For Apples at ye Muraille walke at Keye, & at Mr Maiors house': 8*s* 4*d*.
[25 October 1634] 'For cleansing ye Lock of Northgate': 1*s*.

'Paid John Wittenall for cleansing grates under Southgate prison, 18*d* & for clearing ye Lock of Watergate 6*d* is': 2*s*.
[*f.7*] [3 July] 'Paid a Smith for a newe Lock & Keye for the Northgate': 4*s* 6*d*.
'Paid for mending the Locke of the Keygate dore': 10*d*.
[Total: £2.]

[Total expenditure in this year: £24 14*s* 10*d*.]

1635–36

Receiver John Pennye.

Receiver's Roll

[*m.2v.*] Fees of the mayor and other officers:
Paid the 4 porters for their pension this year, *videlicet* 4*s* to each of them: 16*s*;
Paid the porter of West Gate for cleansing [the grates of] the same: 4*s*;
Paid the porter of North Gate for cleansing the step (*gradus*) there: 6*s* 8*d*;
Paid the porter of the Watergate for his pension: 6*s* 8*d*.
[Total: £1 13*s* 4*d*.]

Necessary expenses:
Paid for diverse reparations to West Gate and the City Walls this year: £10 10*s* 6*d*.

Receiver's Book

[*f.3*] 'Reparacions on the Gaole': £5 1*s* 5*d* [not included in figure for total expenditure in this year].

[*f.10*] 'Reparacions on the Westgate & Cittie Walles
1636
September 10th to Humfrie Locke for carriage of 4 hogsheads of Lyme': 2*s*;
'For 26 seames of Sand att 2*d*': 6*s* 6*d*;
'To William Laurence for 5 dayes worke about the repairinge of Westgate': 5*s* 10*d*;
'To Phillipp Robyns for the like': 5*s* 10*d*;
'To George Creamer for the like': 5*s* 10*d*;
'To Christopher Rey for fower dayes': 4*s* 8*d*;
'To John Honicombe for 5 dayes': 5*s* 10*d*;
'To John Reede for 5 dayes': 5*s* 10*d*;
'To Nicholas Wyott for 5 dayes': 5*s*;
'17th [September]: To Humfrie Locke for 1 dozen & ½ of Sand': 4*s* 6*d*;
'For carriage of 2 hogsheads of Lyme': 1*s*;
'To William Laurence for one dayes worke done att Westgate & the Cities Walles': 1*s* 2*d*;
'To Phillipp Robyns for 2 dayes worke there': 2*s* 4*d*;
'To George Creamer for 4 dayes worke there': 4*s* 8*d*;
'To Nicholas Wyatt for 5 dayes & a halfe': 5*s* 6*d*;
'To John Reed for 5 dayes & a halfe': 6*s* 5*d*;
'For one dozen of burrs for Westgate': 4*s*;
'For one halfe dozen of Peamour stones': 4*s* 4*d*;
'24th [September]: To Humfrie Locke for carriage of 2 hogsheads of Lyme': 1*s*;
'For one dozen of Sand': 3*s*;
'To William Laurence for one dayes worke done att Westgate and on the Walles': 1*s* 2*d*;
'To George Creamer for 5 dayes worke there': 5*s* 10*d*;

'To Phillipp Robyns for 5 dayes': 5s 10d;
'To John Reede for 5 dayes': 5s 10d;
'For 1 dozen & ½ of Ropes for the Scaffolds': 6s;
'For one stirrupp of iron with bolts and nailes waighing 33 [lbs]': 11s;
'October 1 to William Laurence for 5 dayes worke att Westgate & on the Citties Walles': 5s 10d;
'To George Creamer for the like': 5s 10d;
'To Phillipp Robyns for the like': 5s 10d;
'To John Honicombe for 4 dayes': 4s 8d;
'To Christopher Rey for 4 dayes': 4s 8d;
'To John Reede for 5 dayes': 5s 10d;
'To Nicholas Wyott for 5 dayes': 5s;
'For 15 seames of Peamour stones': 10s 8d;
'To Humfrie Locke for carriage of Lyme & sand to Westgate': 2s;
'£8 14s 8d';

[f.11] '1635 December 19th: Paid William Laurence & John Honicombe either of them for one dayes worke for repairinge the water passage under the pavement without Westgate': 2s 4d;
'For 4 seame stones lyme & sand': 2s;
'For 9 hogsheads of lime from Mr Bolt at 3s 6d per hogshead': £1 11s 6d;
'*Summa Totalis*: £10 10s 6d'.

[f.14] 'Other Extraordinarie payments . . .
[10 October 1635] To severall poore people in the murall walke by Mr Maiors order': 7s 6d;
'To the 2 schollers in the Free Schoole which made orations to Mr Maior & the Aldermen': 10s;
'To Robert Siblies wife for a banquett': 16s;
'For aples att the murall walke att the Key and att Mr Maiors house': 7s.
[14 October 1635] 'To John Saunders for a newe Key and repairing the locks of the two great gates att Westgate': 1s 4d.

[f.15] 'Februarie 1 For mending the locke of the Key Gate': 1s 2d.

[f.16] 'June 24th For mendinge the locke of the Key Gate': 6d.
'To Constable Maunder for candlelight att Westgate': 3s 6d.
1s 6d each given to the porters of the North, South and East Gates 'for candlelight'.
[Total: £2 11s 6d.]

[Total expenditure in this year: £14 15s 4d.]

1636–37
Receiver Richard Saunders.

Receiver's Roll
[m.2v.] Fees of the mayor and other officers:
Paid the 4 porters for their pension this year, *videlicet* 4s each: 16s;
Paid the porter of West Gate for cleansing [the grates of] the same: 4s;
Paid the porter of North Gate for cleansing the step (*gradus*) there: 6s 8d;

Paid the porter of the Watergate for his pension: 6s 8d;
Paid the porter of South Gate for his pension as warden of the door (*ostii*) leading towards 'le Key': 10s.
[Total: £2 3s 4d.]

[m.1v.] Necessary expenses:
Paid for diverse reparations on the West Gate and the City Wall: £5 8s 1d.

Receiver's Book
[f.21] 'Reparacions upon the Cittye Walles
December 15th
Inprimis to Edmond Hoppyn for mendinge & settinge a lock on the Cityes Walles on the dore bettweene Bedford Garden & St Johns Garden & for nayles all': 5d;
'January 14th
To Roger Willes of Heavitree for 2 dozen stones at 5s a dozen': 10s;
'To Him for skavellinge of those stones': 1s 2d;
'To Joseph Jerman Robert Battyn & Nicholas Wyett every of them on[e] dayes worke at 12d a day is': 3s;
[21 January] 'To William Laurance & George Cremer each 2 dayes ½ worke about the Arch in the Cittye Wall leadinge into the Palace': 5s 10d;
'To John Reed masson 2 dayes worke there at 14d a day is': 2s 4d;
'To Nicholas Wyett 3 dayes worke at 12d a day is': 3s;
'To John Rumpson 2 dayes Worke 20d & for a new baskett 5d': 2s 1d;
'To Humphery Lock for carriage of 3 hodgesides ½ of Lyme from the Cay to the walles in Southenhay': 1s 9d;
'To him for 20 seames of sand at 3d a seame': 5s;
'To Nicholas Bolt for 5 hodgesides ½ of Lyme for this worke at 3s 6d a hodgeside': 19s 3d;
[28 January] 'To William Laurance & George Cremer every of them 6 dayes worke about the Arch under the Cittyes Walles leadinge to the Bishopes Palace at 14d a day is': 14s;
'To John Reed the like wages for 4 dayes worke there': 4s 8d;
'To Nicholas Wyett 6 dayes Worke at 12d a day is': 6s;
'To John Rumpson 6 dayes worke at 10d a day is': 5s;
'To John Jerman of Heavitree for 3 dozen & 5 seames of stones for the building of the Arch leadinge into the Bishops Palace at 5s a dozen is': 17s 1d;
'To Humphery Lock for carriage of 2 hodgesides of Lyme from the Cay to the Walles in Southenhay': 1s;
'To him for Carriage of 6 seames of sand': 1s 6d;
'To him for carriage of 20 seames of Wallinge stuffe from St Johns to Southenhay': 3s;
[17 February] 'To Benedick Stukeley for some wronge done in his garden in Southenhay where the Arch under the Wall was made by stone Rubble & other matterialls paid him': 2s;
'£5 8s 1d'.

[f.24] 'Extraordinarye Expences
Reparacions about Westgate & the water steps there
October 8th *inprimis* to William Laurance John Honnicombe & John Reed massons one dayes worke each about the West Gate at 14d a day': 3s 6d;
'To Phillipe Robbins George Cremer & Christopher Rey every of them 2 dayes worke at 14d a day is': 7s;
'To Nicholas Wyett 2 dayes worke at 12d a day is': 2s;

'For Hoopinge of a Cowle': 2d;
'November 17th to John Bennett for carriage of 56 seames of Rubble from the West Gate at 8d a dozen is': 3s 1d;
'December 10th To William Laurance for 2 Peymouth [Peamore] stones one over the grate th'other at the Glovers dore cost 8d a piece is': 1s 4d;
'15th To Nicholas Saunders for Iron worke about the gate & the grates that lett passe the Channel water under the gate & for nayles paide him': 15s 8d;
'31th To Nicholas Saunders for nayles for the West Gate & Repaireinge of the grate neare adjoyneing paide': 5s 11d;
'March 18th To Christopher Commyns & his man each on[e] dayes worke about the West Gate at 14d a day is': 2s 4d;
'Aprill 24th To Nicholas Saunders for a plate for Wesgate wayinge 3 lbs': 1s;
'June 24th To John Rumpson masson 4 dayes worke about the water steps neere Westgate at 14d a day': 4s 8d;
'To Humphery Lock for 3 seames of Clay': 9d;
'Jully 1st To John Row Carpenter 2 dayes worke about the Water steps neere Westgate at 14d a daye is': 2s 4d;
'22th To Edward Cockle for 22 foote of planke for the water steps neere Westgate': 5s 6d;
'September 30th To John Guy for paveinge over the gutter without West Gate & for matterialls for the worke paide': 3s 6d;
[Total: £2 18s 9d.]

[ff.24–25] 'Reparacions on the porters lodge neer Westgate': £4 12s 9d.

[f.25] 'Reparacions within & withoute Eastgate Northgate & Southgate about the Channells & streets . . .
To John Whittenall for clensinge of the grats under the prison at Southgate at severall tymes': 4s.
[20 December] To William Cole of Salcombe for 2 thousand of healinge stones bought for the coveringe of Eastgate at 10s a thousand': £1;
'To Byott masson 2 dayes worke about coveringe of the East Gate at 14d a day': 2s 4d;
'To Mathew Robinson the like for on[e] dayes worke': 1s 2d;
'To a boy 2 dayes worke there at 6d a day': 1s;
'For pynnes & lath nayles': 6d;
[31 December] 'To a Carpenter for setting up a dore over East Gate & for nayles there about spent': 1s 6d;

[f.26] 'February 18th To Nicholas Saunders for 1 lb ½ of Hatch nayles for East Gate': 1s 3d;
'To him for a new hooke for a dore & mendinge of others there': 5d;
'Aprill 17th To Nicholas Saunders Blacksmith for Ireworke for the new hanginge of East Gate the old beinge consumed wayinge 61 [lbs] at 4d a [lb] is': £1 4d;
'May 19th To William Laurance mason & his man on[e] dayes worke each for setting of a new hooke & workinge of him into the stone Wall at Eastgate': 2s 4d;
'To Lewes Grinslade John Gerfoote & William Williams every of them on[e] day & ½ worke for hanginge &

mendinge of Eastgate at 14d a day is': 5s 3d;
'27th To Nicholas Saunders for mendinge of the Ireworke for East Gate & for Spukes & orlake nayles the old Iron beinge deducted I paide but': 10s 10d;
'Jully 21th To James Willes for 29 [lbs] of lead for fastinge the hooke at Eastgate': 4s 3d;
'22th To Edward Cockle for 2 pieces of tymber 16 foote ½ for Eastgate': 3s 2d;
[Total: £3 18s 6d.]

[f.27] 'Reparacions on the Cay Gate & the Cay Lane . . .
December 24th To Mr Hoppyn for mendinge of the Cay of the Cay Gate': 6d;
'April 1th To a lockier for mendinge the Lock of the Cay Gate & for a new Cay & for spooks to sett the lock againe paide all': 1s 6d;
'24th To Nicholas Saunders for mendinge the Ireworke of the Cay Gate': 1s;
[Total: 3s.]

[Expenses:]
'10th [October] To Mr Mallack Major [mayor] for his purse for the poore that pase ye city given by Mr Majors order the day he made the Muralla walke, to the Common Gaole 4s, to 3 Frenchmen then prisoners 3s, to the boy that made the oration in the Free Schole 5s, to the other Schollers 5s, To Sibley for his Banqett 15s, to the dore keeper in Southgate prison 12d, & to the poore in Severall places 4s 6d, all given was': £1 17s 6d;
'8th [October] For 18 lbs of Apples to give the boyes the day Mr Major [mayor] made the Muralla Walke at 3d per lb is': 4s 6d.

[f.28] '7th [November] To the 4 porters of the gates payd them for Candlelight by order from Mr Major': 8s.
'11th [March] To Roger Walker for watchinge at Southgate for victuals brought in that way in the lent given him per Mr Majors order': 4s.

[f.29] 'To Alice Smyth for keepinge the watch over East Gate': 5s.
'To the 4 porters of the gates for Candlelight delivered them by Glide the winter Season paid him per Mr Majors order': £1 15s 10d.
[Total: £4 14s 10d.]

[Total expenditure in this year: £23 19s 3d.]

1637–38

Receiver Thomas Tooker.

Receiver's Roll

[m.2v.] Fees of the mayor and other officers:
Paid the 4 porters for their pension this year, *videlicet* 4s each: 16s;
Paid the porter of West Gate for cleansing [the grates of] the same: 4s;
Paid the porter of North Gate for cleansing the step (*gradus*) there: 6s 8d;
Paid the porter of the Watergate for his pension: 6s 8d;
Paid the porter of South Gate for his pension as warden of the door (*ostii*) leading towards the Quay: 10s.
[Total: £2 3s 4d.]

Receiver's Book

[*f.23*] 'Reparacions on the Citties Walles Barbicans Cannells & Porters lodges . . .
[3 February 1637] Paid William Laurence for one dayes Worke done uppon the Barbican of the Citties Walles behinde the Chapple of St Johns': 1s 2d;
'Paid George Creamer for one day for the like': 1s 2d;
'Paid John Reede for one day for the like': 1s 2d;
[Subtotal] '3s 6d';

[*f.24*] 'Paid John Rumson for one day for the like': 1s 2d.
'Paid Nicholas Wyott for one day for the like': 1s;
'Paid 2 men for halfe a day each for worke done by them': 1s 2d;
'Paid for a Peymouth [Peamore] stone & for Lyme': 11½d;
[10 February] 'Paid Humfrie Locke for carriage of 4 hogsheads & ½ of Lyme from the Key to St Johns for th'amendinge of the Barbican': 2s 3d;
'Paid for carriage of 18 seames of Claye from Southenhay to the Barbican': 1s 6d;
'More paid for carriage of one hogshead of Lyme': 6d;
'Paid William Laurence & George Creamer for 6 dayes worke each for Worke done on the Barbican behinde St Johns Hospitall': 14s;
'Paid John Reede & John Rumson to each for 5 dayes for the like': 11s 8d;
'Paid Nicholas Wyott for 6 dayes for the like att 12d a day': 6s;
'Paid Joseph Jarman for the like for 3 dayes': 3s;
[13 February] 'Paid for 2 dozen & halfe of Heavitree stones for the Barbican of the Citties Walles att 5s a dozen': 12s 6d;
[24 February] 'Paid George Creamer for 4 dayes on the Barbican': 4s 8d;
'Paid John Hunnycombe for 3 dayes for the like': 3s 6d;
'Paid John Rumson for 4 dayes for the like': 4s 8d;
'Paid for 2 dozen & halfe of Burrs from Heavitree att 4s a dozen': 10s;
'Paid for carriage of one hogshead of Lyme from Mr Bolts & for 3 seames of sand': 1s 3d;
[31 (*sic*) February] 'Paid William Laurence for halfe a day': 7d;
'Paid John Hunnycombe for 3 dayes uppon the Barbican behinde St Johns att 14d a day': 3s 6d;
'Paid John Rumson for 3 dayes for the like': 3s 6d;
'Paid George Creamer for one daye': 1s 2d;
'Paid Nicholas Wyott for one day for the like': 1s;
'Paid for 10 seames of stones': 4s 2d;
'Paid for 3 seames of Burrs for the same Worke': 1s;
'Aprill 7th Paid Humfrie Locke for the carriage of two hogsheads of lyme from the Barbican of the Citties Walls att the hospitall of St Johns': 1s;
'Paid for 8 seames of sand att 3d a seame': 2s;
'Paid William Laurence for 3 dayes Worke on the Barbican of the Citties Walles against St Johns Hospitall at 14d a day': 3s 6d;
'Paid George Creamer for the like 6 dayes': 7s;
'Paid John Hunnycombe for 5 dayes & halfe': 6s 5d;
'Paid John Reede for the like 3 dayes': 3s 6d;

[*f.25*] 'Paid John Rumson for the like 4 dayes': 4s 8d;
'Paid Nicholas Wyott for the like 6 dayes': 6s;
'Paid Humfrie Locke for carriage of 2 hogsheads & halfe of Lyme for the Citties use': 1s 3d;

'Paid for 3 seames of sand for the Citties Walles': 9d;
'Paid for carriage of 22 seames of Claye from Southenhaye to the Citties Walles': 1s 10d;
'Paid Mr Bolt for 11 hogsheads of Lyme for the Barbican of the Citties Walles att 3s 6d a hogshead': £1 18s 6d.
[13 October 1637: £1 16s 4½d spent on] 'the Porters Lodge'.
[18 October] 'Paid James Symons for 2 dayes worke att Southgate in the vault under the prison & att other places': 2s 4d.
'Paid for candles': 1d.

[*f.26*] [March 1638: Total of 15s spent on] 'the Porters lodge att Eastgate'.
[Total of 10s 8d spent on] 'the Porters lodge att Westgate'.
'March 17th paid for clensinge of a watercourse under Southgate': 1s 0s 6d.
[Total: £12 0s 7d.]
'Other Extraordinarye expences . . .
[30 October] Paid for mendinge of a Locke & a newe Key att Kaygate': 1s 4d.

[*f.30*] [16 October] 'Given by Mr Maiors order the day he went the murally walke unto the prisoners att the High Gaole': 6s;
'Given to the prisoners att Southgate, to the porter and to the poore on the walls att the Keygate att the same time': 4s 5d;
'Paid to the boy that made the oracion att the Free Schoole 5s & 5s more to bee given amongst the schollers & to the usher—5s in all': 15s;
'Paid Robert Siblye for a banquett att the same time': 13s 4d;
'Paid to the poore of St Lawrence the same time': 2s;
'Paid for 12 *lbs* of Apples to give the boyes the day Mr Maior made the Murallic walke': 4s.
[Total: £2 6s 1d.]

[Total expenditure in this year: £16 10s 0d.]

1638–39

Receiver Christopher Clarke.

Receiver's Roll

[*m.2v.*] Fees of the mayor and other officers:
Paid the 4 porters for their pension this year, *videlicet* 4s each: 16s;
Paid the porter of West Gate for cleansing [the grates of] the same: 4s;
Paid the porter of North Gate for cleansing the step (*gradus*) there: 6s 8d;
Paid the porter of the Watergate for his pension: 6s 8d;
Paid the porter of South Gate for his pension as warden of the door (*ostii*) leading towards 'le Key': 10s.

[The book for this year is missing.]

[Total expenditure in this year: £2 3s 4d.]

1639–40

Receiver Henry Battishill.

Receiver's Roll

[*m.2v.*] Fees of the mayor and other officers:
    Paid the 4 porters for their pension this year, *videlicet* 4*s*
    each: 16*s*;
    Paid the porter of West Gate for cleansing [the grates
    of] the same: 4*s*;
    Paid the porter of North Gate for cleansing the step
    (*gradus*) there: 6*s* 8*d*;
    Paid the porter of the Watergate for his pension:
    6*s* 8*d*;
    Paid the porter of South Gate for his pension and for
    keeping the door (*ostii*) leading towards 'le Keygate'
    [superscript: 'lane' inserted between 'Key' and 'gate']:
    10*s*.
    [Total: £2 3*s* 4*d*.]

[*m.1v.*] Necessary expenses:
    Paid for diverse reparations on the City Walls:
    £31 5*s* 3*d*.

[The book for this year is missing.]

[Total expenditure in this year: £33 8*s* 7*d*.]

1640–41

Receiver Walter White.

Receiver's Roll

[*m.2v.*] Fees of the mayor and other officers:
    Paid the 4 porters for their pension this year: 16*s*;
    Paid the porter of West Gate for cleansing the *gradus* for
    the passage of rainwater near the said gate: 4*s*;
    Paid the porter of North Gate for cleansing the step
    (*gradus*) there: 6*s* 8*d*;
    Paid the porter of the Watergate for keeping and
    closing that gate: 6*s* 8*d*;
    Paid the porter of South Gate for closing the gate at
    (*apud*) 'le Key Lane end': 10*s*.
    [Total: £2 3*s* 4*d*.]

Necessary expenses:
    Paid for diverse reparations this year on the walls and
    gates of the city: £16 18*s* 5*d*.
    Paid for the erection of a certain house for keeping
    gunpowder on the walls of the city near East Gate:
    £100 3*s* 8*d*.
    Paid for reparations to the porter of North Gate's roof
    this year: nothing as it is included with the charges on
    the walls.

[The book for this year is missing.]

[Total expenditure in this year: £119 5*s* 5*d*.]

1641–42

[Both the roll and the book for this year are missing.]

1642–43

Receiver J. Cupper [?].

Receiver's Roll

[*m.2v.*] Fees of the mayor and other officers:
    Paid the 4 porters for their pension this year, *videlicet* to
    each of them 4*s*: 16*s*;
    Paid the porter of West Gate for cleansing [the grates
    of] the same: 3*s* [*sic*];
    Paid the porter of North Gate for cleansing the step
    (*gradus*) there: 6*s* 8*d*;
    Paid the porter of the Watergate for his pension: 5*s*;
    Paid the porter of South Gate for closing the gate of the
    lane called 'Key Lane': 10*s*.
    [Total: £2 0*s* 8*d*.]

Receiver's Book

[*f.4*] 'Disbursements about the Citties gates [&] walls *videlicet*:
    October 1642 8 Paid John Lawrence [&] others for 11
    dayes worke at 16*d* a day for 3 dayes at 14*d* a day for 21
    dayes at 12*d* a daye all is': £3 18*s* 4*d*;
    'Paid Humphrey Locke for 2 dozen sand 8*s* [&] ½
    dozen clay 12*d* all is': 9*s*;
    'Paid John Jerman for 7 dozen of seame stones at 5*s* a
    dozen is': £1 15*s*;
    '15 [October] paid Roger Wills for 3 dozen seame
    stones at 5*s* a dozen is': 15*s*;
    'Paid John Jerman for 2 dozen seame stones at 5*s* a
    dozen is': 10*s*;
    'Paid Arthur Willing [&] others for 7 dayes worke ½ at
    14*d* a day for 5 dayes at 12*d* a day 2 dayes ½ at 8*d* a day
    [&] 4*s* for a hogshead of lyme all is': £1 1*s* 5*d*;
    'Paid John Laurence & others for 5 dayes ½ worke at
    16*d* a day for 29 days at 14*d* a day & for 14 dayes at 12*d*
    a day all is': £2 15*s* 2*d*;
    'Paid Humphrey Locke for 16 seames sand for ye
    Masons morter at 4*d* a seame': 5*s* 4*d*;
    '22 [October] paid John Lawrence & others for 12 dayes
    worke at 16*d* a day for 40 dayes ½ at 14*d* a day & for 12
    dayes at 12*d* a day all is': £3 15*s* 3*d*;
    'Paid John Jerman for 4 dozen seame stones at 5*s* a
    dozen is': £1;
    'Paid Arthur Willing & others for 2 dayes worke at 14*d* a
    day for 2 dayes at 12*d* a day and for one daye at 8*d* a
    day all is': 5*s*;
    'Paid Humphrey Locke for 2 dozen sand from St
    Thomas at 6*d* a seame & 6 seames of Ex sand at 4*d* a
    seame all is': 14*s*;
    'Paid Roger Wills for 7 dozen & 5 seame stones at 5*s* a
    dozen is': £1 17*s*;
    'Paid John Alford for 16 hogsheads ½ Chidly lyme at 4*s*
    a hogshead is': £3 6*s*;
    '29 [October] paid John Lawrence & others for 5 dayes
    worke at 16*d* a day for 29 days at 14*d* a day & for 10
    dayes at 12*d* a daye all is': £2 10*s* 6*d*;
    'Paid Humphrey Locke for carridg of 6 seames clay
    from Southenhay to Northenhay & for 14 seames sand
    from St Thomas at 6*d* a seame all is': 8*s*;
    'Paid Roger Wills for 5 dozen seame stones at 5*s* a
    dozen is': £1 5*s*;
    'Paid Peter Halstaff for mending the locke at Eastgat &
    an other lock': 2*s* 6*d*;
    'Paid Arthur Willing & others for 3 dayes worke at 14*d* a
    day and for 3 dayes worke at 12*d* a day all is': 6*s* 6*d*;
    'Paid John Jerman for 15 seames stones at 5*s* a dozen
    is': 6*s* 3*d*;

'5 [November] paid Lewes Greenslade & others for postinge upp the wales against Bedford House for 6 dayes worke ½ at 14*d* a day all is': 7*s* 7*d*;

'Paid Roger Wills for 2 dozen 3 seames burrs at 4*s* a dozen & for 2 dozen and one seame stone at 5*s* a dozen all is': 19*s* 5*d*;

'Paid Humphrey Locke for carridge of 2 dozen 8 seames claye at 2*s* a dozen & for 16 seames sand at 4*d* a seame all is': 10*s* 8*d*;

'Paid John Lawrence & others for 12 dayes worke at 16*d* a day for 41 dayes at 14*d* a day & for 17 dayes at 12*d* a day all is': £4 10*d*;

'Paid John Griffen for 1 dozen ½ Pamouth [Peamore] stones at 9*s* a dozen is': 13*s* 6*d*;

'Paid Arthur Willing & others for 6 dayes work at 14*d* a day & for 6 dayes at 12*d* a day is': 13*s*;

'Paid John Jerman for 2 dozen 3 seames burrs at 4*s* dozen & for 1 dozen seame at 5*s* is': 14*s*;

[Subtotal] '£35 4*s* 3*d*';

[*f.5*] '1642 12 [November] paid John Laurence & others for 11 dayes worke at 16*d* a day for 23 dayes ½ at 14*d* a day for 13 dayes at 12[*d*] a daye & for 3 planks to stopp up Leaches well 3*s* all is': £2 15*s*;

'Paid Arthur Willinge & others for 22 dayes at 4*d* a day for 28 dayes at 12*d* a day for a seeve & baskett to carry stones 8*d* all is': £2 4*s* 4*d*;

'Paid Edward Avery for 4 days work at 12*d* a day': 4*s*;

'Paid Roger Wills for 6 dozen less one seame stones at 3*s* a dozen & 4 dozen burrs at 4*s* a dozen all is': £2 3*s* 7*d*;

'Paid John Griffen for 5 dozen 3 seames of Paymouth stones at 9*s* dozen': £2 7*s* 3*d*;

'Paid John German for 11 dozen seame stones at 3*s* dozen and for 2 dozen ½ burrs at 4*s* dozen all is': £3 5*s*;

'Paid Humphrey Locke for 2 dozen ½ morter sand at 4*s* dozen for the carridge 2 dozen clay 2*s* & for 2 seames of smooth stones to pyn the walls is': 13*s*;

'Paid John Alford for 10 hogsheads & 10 pecks of lime at 4*s* a hogshead is': £2 2*s* 6*d*;

'19 [November] paid Arthur Willinge & others for 22 days worke at 14*d* a day, & for 16 days ½ at 12*d* a day': £2 2*s* 2*d*;

'Paid John Laurence & others for 10 days work & ½ at 16*d* a day for 13 days at 14*d* a day & for 19 days ½ at 12*d* a day': £2 9*s* 8*d*;

'Paid Humphrey Lock for 20 seams Morter sand from St Thomas parish at 6*s* a seame': 10*s*;

'Paid William Hellier for 2 hogshead Lyme at 4*s* a hoghead': 8*s*;

'26 [November] paid Arthur Willinge & others for 29 days worke at 14*d* a daye, & 21 days at 12[*d*] a daye': £2 12*s* 6*d*;

'Paid John Laurence & others, for 8 dayes worke at 16*d* a day for 13 dayes at 14*d* a day & for 17 dayes at 12*d* a day is': £2 8*d*;

'Paid Humphrey Locke for a dozen sand, & for carridg of 18 seames morter from Helliers Garden against Bedford Hous': 6*s* 3*d*;

'Paid John Jerman for 2 dozen ½ seame stones at 5*s* a dozen & for carridge of 15 seame stones from the sayd garden to the place 20*d*—all is': 14*s* 4*d*;

'Paid Roger Wills for 19 seames Heavitree stones at 3*s* a dozen & for carridg of 18 seames as aforesyd 2*s* 3*d*': 10*s* 2*d*;

'Paid William Hellier for 2 hogshead ½ lym at 4*s* a hogshead': 10*s*;

'3 [December] paid Arthur Willinge & others for 18 days Worke at 14*d* a day, & for 12 days worke at 12*d* a day is': £1 13*s* [illegible]*d*;

'Paid for carridg of 12 seames lime & sand from Minsons garden against Bedfor House': 2*s* [illegible]*d*;

'Paid Roger Wills for 6 seames of seamston at 5*s* a doz' is': 2*s* [illegible]*d*;

'10 paid John Laurence & others for 4 days ½ at 16*d* a daye for 26 dayes ½ at 14*d* a day & for 18 days at 12*d* a day': £2 14*s* 9*d*;

[Subtotal] '£32 12*s* [illegible]*d*';

[*f.6*] '1642 17 [December] paid John Laurence & others for 6 days worke at 16*d* a day for 34 dayes at 14*d* a day & for 23 dayes at 12*d* a day': £3 9*s* 8*d*;

'Paid Humphrey Locke for carridge of Lyme & sand': 4*s* 4*d*;

'Paid Zacharye Sanders for Ironworke for the prison at South Gate, *videlicet*: 13 barrs containing 163 *lbs* at 4*d* a C, 1 barr of 23 *lbs*, 4 bolts, 15 staples, containing 26 *lbs* at 4*d* a pound, 200 Orely Nayls at 3*s* 4*d* a 100, 3 plats, containing 39 *lbs* at 4*d* a pound, 2 payre of hooks and twists 6*s* 9*d*': £4;

'20 [December] paid Peter Halstaff for mendinge a broken lock at Eastgate': 2*s* 6*d*;

'24 [December] paid George Creemer & others for 3 dayes worke at 16*d* a day for 23 dayes at 14*d* a day & for 17 days at 12*d* a day': £1 16*s*;

'January 7 paid Humphry Locke for 18 seames of clay & carridge': 1*s* 6*d*;

'Paid Arthur Willinge & others for 10 dayes worke at 14*d* a day for 13 dayes at 12*d* a day & for laths & nails for a ratch to sift the old sand': £1 5*s* 2*d*;

'Paid Roger Wills for 1 dozen ½ seame stones at 5*s* a dozen': 7*s* 6*d*;

'14 [January] paid Arthur Willinge & others for 39 days ½ worke at 14*d* a day, for 31 days ½ at 12*d* a day, & for 5 days at 9*d* a day': £3 13*s* 6*d*;

'Paid Humphrey Locke for 2 dozen sand at 5*s* a dozen & for carridge of 26 seames of clay at 1*d* a seam': 12*s* 2*d*;

'Paid Roger Wills for 9 dozen of seame stones at 5*s* a dozen': £2 5*s*;

'21 [January] paid Lewes Greenslade & others for 31 days worke at South Gate at 14*d* a day, & for 8 days at 10*d* a day, is': £2 2*s* 10*d*;

'Paid Humphrey Locke for 26 seams of Ex sand at 5*s* a dozen': 10*s* 10*d*;

'Paid John Ramson & others for 5 dayes work at 14*d* a day & 2 days at 12*d* a day': 7*s* 10*d*;

'Paid John Jerman for 4 dozen of seame stons at 5*s* a dozen': £1;

'Paid Roger Wills for 3 dozen & one seame stons at 5*s* a dozen': 15*s* 5*d*;

'Paid Arthur Willinge & others for 31 dayes work at 14*d* a day & for 19 days at 12*d* a day, & for 5 days at 9*d* a day': £2 18*s* 11*d*;

'Paid Gilbert Cleare for 12 hogshead of Lyme at 4*s* a hogshead': £2 8*s*;

'Paid for 60 deale boards for the planchinge at South Gate at £5 10*s* a 100 & for 5 days to William Furs': £3;

'28 [January] paid John Jerman for 6 dozen & 9 seam stons at 5*s* a dozen': £1 13*s* 9*d*;

'Paid Lewes Greenslade & others for 7 dayes worke at

South Gate, for planchinge at 14*d* a day & 4 days for 10*d* a day': 11*s* 6*d*;
'Paid George Gibbs for 20 hogsheads of Lyme at 4*s* a hogshead': £4;
'Paid Roger Wills for 4 dozen & 8 seam stons at 5*s* a dozen': £1 3*s* 4*d*;
'Paid Humphrey Locke for 18 seams of sand at 5*s* a dozen for 6 seams at 4*s* a dozen and for carridge of 22 seams of clay at 1*d* a seame': 11*s* 6*d*;
'Paid Arthur Willinge & others for 35 days ½ work at 14*d* a day for 42 days ½ at 12*d* a day & for 6 days at 9*d* a day': £4 8*s* 5*d*;
[Subtotal] '£43 9*s* 8*d*';

[*f.*7] 'February 1642 4 paid John Jerman for 3 dozen seam stons at 5*s* a dozen': 15*s*;
'Paid Humphrey Locke for 1 dozen ½ of sand at 5*s* a dozen': 7*s* 6*d*;
'Paid Arthur Willinge & others for 20 days ½ worke at 14*d* a day for 21 days at 12*d* a day for 7 days at 9*d* a day': £2 10*s* 2*d*;
'Paid Roger Wills for 2 dozen sand at 5*s* a dozen': 10*s*;
'11 [February] paid Humphrey Locke for carridge of Six thousand healiage [*sic*] stones, to South Gate & the Guildhall, 3*s* for dozen 3 seams of sand at 5*s* a dozen & for carridg of 6 seams of clay 6*d* all is': 9*s* 8*d*;
'Paid John Jerman for 1 dozen seame stons at 5*s* a dozen': 5*s*;
'Paid Roger Wills for 22 seams of seame stone at 5*s* a dozen': 9*s* 2*d*;
'Paid William Heard & others for 2 dayes to make morter at 12*d* a day, & 2*s* for pitching & ladinge 6,000 Healinge stones': 4*s*;
'Paid for 6,000 healinge stons at 5*s* 2*d* a *Millena*': £1 11*s*;
'Paid Arthur Willinge & others for 26 days ½ worke at 14*d* a daye, for 21 days at 12*d* a day, for 4 days ½ at 9*d* a day & 18*d* for cuttinge of datestons in the Walls is': £2 16*s* 9*d*;
'18 [February] paid William Heard & others for 3 days work over South Gate at 14*d* a day, for 3 days at 12*d* a day for 1 dozen of Crests 3*s* & for ½ peck of pins 6*d* is': 10*s*;
'Paid John Alford for 1 hogshead & a busshell of lime': 5*s* [illegible]*d*;
'25 [February] paid John Gibbs for 6 hogsheads of Lyme': £1 4*s* [illegible]*d*;
'March 22 paid James Wills for 5,325 *lbs* new Ledd to cover the house at South Gate, at 17*s* a *C* abating for 900 of old Ledds £5 at 13*s* a *C* neate is': £39 7*s* 6*d*;
'March 27 paid James Wills for 92 *lbs* Ledd at 15*s* a *C* & for wood for heatinge his irons, for fastninge the Iron barrs at South Gate 6*d* all is': 12*s* 9*d*;
'Maye 1643 20 paid William Heard & others for 6 days worke over South Gate at 14*d* a daye for 3 days at 12*d* a day for a pecke of pins 12*d* for 300 of Laths & 1000 nayles 3*s* 2*d* all is': 14*s* 2*d*;
'June 10 paid Peter Halstaff for mendinge of the Locks at ye Eastgate, & at Westgate 3*s* 4*d*': 3*s* 4*d*;
[Subtotal] '£52 14*s* 6*d*';
[Total] '£164 1*s* 1*d*'.

[*f.*9] 'Disbursments Called Extraordinary Charges . . .
December 1642 paid 16 watchmenn by . . . order [of the Mayor] att Eastgate 4 one the fast dayes to each 12*d* for 3 fast dayes paid in all butt': £1 16*s*;

'Paid the 4 porters by sayd order for Candle light att each gate for 20 weekes att 12*d* a weeke to each of them is': £4.
'To the Master and boy that made the Oration att the Freeschoole att the tyme of the Murally walke': 15*s*;
'To the prisoners in the High Gaole by Mr Maiors directions': 5*s*;
'To Mr Hockwell for the Collection att Southgate': 16*s*;
'To the Prisoners there': 3*s*.
[Total: £7 15*s* 0*d*.]

[Total expenditure in this year: £173 16*s* 9*d*.]

1643–44

Receiver Richard Yeo, merchant.

Receiver's Roll

[*m.*2*v.*] Fees of the mayor and other officers:
Paid the 4 porters for their pension this year: 3*s* [*sic*];
Paid the porter of North Gate for his fee and for cleansing the step (*gradus*) near that gate: 6*s* 8*d*.
[Total: 9*s* 8*d*.]

Necessary expenses:
Paid for diverse reparations to the walls of the city by the book thereof: £369 1*s* 10*d*.

Receiver's Book

[*f.*4] 'Monies disbursed about the Reparacions on the Citties Walles & Gates &c
November 4th 1643 paid for 12 seames of sand and for 18 seames of Claye for the decayed Walle in Northenhay': 5*s*;
[11 November] 'Paid for 6 hogsheads of Lyme 27*s* and for sand 2*s* 8*d*': £1 9*s* 8*d*;
'Paid for 4 dozen of seame stones from Heavitree att 5*s*': £1;
'Paid John Laurence Mason & his Companye for their Worke': £2 1*s* 8*d*;
[18 November] 'Paid for 3 dozen & 9 seame stones from Heavitree': 18*s* 9*d*;
'Paid for 4 seames of Sand att 5*d*': 1*s* 8*d*;
'Paid John Laurence & his Companie for their Worke': £1 14*s* 10*d*;
[25 November] 'Paid for 7 hogshedds & ½ of Chudleigh Lime at 4*s* 6*d*': £1 13*s* 9*d*;
'Paid for 3 dozen & ½ of Heavitree seame stones att 5*s*': 17*s* 6*d*;
'Paid for 2 dozen & 4 seames of Sand att 5*d* a seame': 11*s* 8*d*;
'Paid John Laurence & his Companie for their Worke': £2 19*s* 4*d*;
'December 2: paid for 4 dozen and 5 seames of Heavitree Stones att 5*s*': £1 2*s* 1*d*;
'Paid for 18 seames of Sand att 5*d*': 7*s* 6*d*;
'Paid John Laurence & Companie for their Worke': £2 2*s* 6*d*;
[9 December] 'Paid for 3 dozen of Seame stones from Heavitree att 5*s*': 15*s*;
[26 December] 'Paid John Laurence & his Companie for their Worke & for a date stone': £2 10*s* 10*d*;
'Paid them more for their Worke': £2 16*s* 10*d*;

'Paid Peter Martyn of Teingmouth a Master Workman Mason over and above his pay: 5s;

[18 May (?)] 'Paid unto William Plumer of Thorverton for [the] like': 4s;

'June 22th paid the Ropemaker for 3 dozen of Scaffold Ropes 2 paire of sling Ropes & 4[illegible] worth of Cord': 11s 4d;

'July 11th paid the plumer for 6 *lbs* of ledd for the inscripcion of the date stone': 11d;

'November 20th paid the Widdow Kelly for 26 delbords for making of Scaffolds att 12d': £1 6s;

'£345 8s 2d'.

'The disbursements about the reparacions of the Walles in Northenhay amounts as in folio 4: £23 13s 8d;

'£369 1s 10d'.

[Total expenditure in this year: £369 17s 10½d].

1644–45

Receiver John Martin.

Receiver's Roll

[*m.2v.*] Fees and pensions of the mayor and other officers:
Paid the porter of West Gate for cleansing the *gradus* for conducting rainwater there for the foresaid gate: 4s;
Paid the porter of North Gate for similar labour there: 6s 8d.

[Total: 10s 8d.]

Payments and necessary expenses:
Paid for diverse reparations on the gates and walls of the city this year: £170 16d.

Receiver's Book

[*f.3*] 'Monies laid out for Reparacions on the Westgate & the Citties Walles neere thereunto
October 30th 1644 *Inprimis* paid John Guy pavier & others for worke done as appeares by a note of the particulars': £1 7d;

'November 9th paid John Jarman for 1 dozen of Heavitree stone for the same worke': 5s;

'Paid John Laurence Mason and his Company for the like': 18s 8d;

'Paid William Saunders for 2 dayes Worke': 2s;

'Paid Humfrie Locke for 2 dozen & 4 seames of sand': 10s 7d;

'Paid Zacharie Saunders Blacksmith for iron Worke about the Westgate & other places *parut*': £4 13s;

[16 November] 'Paid John Jarman & George Allyn for 3 dozen & 10 seames of Heavitree stones': 19s 2d;

'Paid the Quarriemen of Peymouth [Peamore] for 17 seame stones': 12s 9d;

'Paid John Laurence Mason & his Company about the same work': £3 2s 4d;

[23 November] 'Paid George Pottell for 6 dozen of Peymouth stones': £2 14s;

'Paid Humfrie Lock for sand': 4s 8d;

'Paid John Alford for 12 hogsheads of Chidleigh Lime': £2 14s;

'Paid John Jerman & George Allyn for 3 dozen & ½ of Heavitree stones': 17s 6d;

'Paid John Laurence & his Company about the same work *parut*': £5 2d;

[30 November] 'Paid George Pottell for 6 dozen & halfe of Peymouth stones': £2 18s 6d;

'Paid Humfrie Locke for 2 dozen & 4 seame stones': 9s 4d;

'Paid John Laurence Mason & his Company about the same worke': £4 14s 2d;

'Paid Mr Cristofer Parr for 1 dozen & ½ of Peymouth stones': 6s;

'December 7th paid Thomas Pottell for 4 dozen & halfe of Peymouth stones': £2 6d;

'Paid John Alford for 4 hogsheads & one Bushell of Lime': 19s 2d;

'Paid John Jerman for 2 dozen & one seame of seame stones and for a dozen & halfe more bought of Mr Cristofer Parr': 13s 5d;

'Paid John Laurence Mason & his Company for work done *parut*': £5 8s 10d;

[14 December] 'Paid them more for the same worke *parut*': £4 19s 8d;

'Paid them more for the like': 6s;

'Paid Humfrie Lock for 2 dozen of sand': 8s;

'Paid George Pottell for 3 dozen of seame stones': £1 7s;

'Paid him for 4 dozen & halfe more': £2 6d;

[21 December] 'Paid John Jarman & George Allyn for 5 dozen of Heavitree stones': £1 5s;

'Paid John Alford for 13 hogsheads of Lime': £2 18s 6d;

[Subtotal] '£54 9s';

[*f.4*] 'Paid George Pottell for 8 dozen & 8 seame stones': £3 18s;

'Paid John Laurence Mason & Company for work done *parut*': 19s;

'Paid them more for the like *parut*': £5 10s;

'Paid Humfrie Locke for 22 seames of sand': 7s 4d;

[24 December] 'Paid John Jerman & George Allyn for 2 dozen of seame stones': 10s;

'Paid George Pottell for 2 dozen & 8 seame stones': £1 4s;

'Paid Humfrie Lock for 24 seames of sand': 8s;

'Paid John Laurence & his Company for worke done *parut*': £2 4s 8d;

'Paid George Paddon for cutting & engraving the stone on Westgat': 6s 3d;

'January 4 paid George Pottell for 2 dozen & 10 Peymouth [Peamore] stones': £1 5s 6d;

'Paid Lewes Grenslade & his Company for work done *parut*': 7s 8d;

[11 January] 'Paid George Pottell for 5 dozen & 10 seame stones': £2 12s 6d;

'Paid Humfrie Lock for 8 seames of sand': 2s 8d;

'Paid John Laurence & his Company for work done *parut*': £4 2s 3d;

[28 January; *sic*] 'Paid John Alford for 9 hogsheads & ½ of Lime': £2 2s 9d;

'Paid Humfrie Lock for 14 seames of sand': 4s 8d;

'Paid George Pottell for 7 dozen & ½ of Peymouth [Peamore] stones': £3 7s 6d;

'18th [January] paid John Laurence & his Companie for worke done *parut*': £5 11s;

[25 January] 'Paid George Pottell for 8 dozen & 7 seame stones': £3 17s 3d;

'Paid Humfrie Lock for 10 seames of sand': 3s 4d;

'Paid John Laurence & his Company for worke done *parut*': £6 18s 1d;

'February 1 paid them more for the like *parut*': £7 8s;

South Gate, for planchinge at 14*d* a day & 4 days for 10*d* a day': 11*s* 6*d*;

'Paid George Gibbs for 20 hogsheads of Lyme at 4*s* a hogshead': £4;

'Paid Roger Wills for 4 dozen & 8 seam stons at 5*s* a dozen': £1 3*s* 4*d*;

'Paid Humphrey Locke for 18 seams of sand at 5*s* a dozen for 6 seams at 4*s* a dozen and for carridge of 22 seams of clay at 1*d* a seame': 11*s* 6*d*;

'Paid Arthur Willinge & others for 35 days ½ work at 14*d* a day for 42 days ½ at 12*d* a day & for 6 days at 9*d* a day': £4 8*s* 5*d*;

[Subtotal] '£43 9*s* 8*d*';

[*f.*7] 'February 1642 4 paid John Jerman for 3 dozen seam stons at 5*s* a dozen': 15*s*;

'Paid Humphrey Locke for 1 dozen ½ of sand at 5*s* a dozen': 7*s* 6*d*;

'Paid Arthur Willinge & others for 20 days ½ worke at 14*d* a day for 21 days at 12*d* a day for 7 days at 9*d* a day': £2 10*s* 2*d*;

'Paid Roger Wills for 2 dozen sand at 5*s* a dozen': 10*s*;

'11 [February] paid Humphrey Locke for carridge of Six thousand healiage [*sic*] stones, to South Gate & the Guildhall, 3*s* for dozen 3 seams of sand at 5*s* a dozen & for carridg of 6 seams of clay 6*d* all is': 9*s* 8*d*;

'Paid John Jerman for 1 dozen seame stons at 5*s* a dozen': 5*s*;

'Paid Roger Wills for 22 seams of seame stone at 5*s* a dozen': 9*s* 2*d*;

'Paid William Heard & others for 2 dayes to make morter at 12*d* a day, & 2*s* for pitching & ladinge 6,000 Healinge stones': 4*s*;

'Paid for 6,000 healinge stons at 5*s* 2*d* a *Millena*': £1 11*s*;

'Paid Arthur Willinge & others for 26 days ½ worke at 14*d* a daye, for 21 days at 12*d* a day, for 4 days ½ at 9*d* a day & 18*d* for cuttinge of datestons in the Walls is': £2 16*s* 9*d*;

'18 [February] paid William Heard & others for 3 days work over South Gate at 14*d* a day, for 3 days at 12*d* a day for 1 dozen of Crests 3*s* & for ½ peck of pins 6*d* is': 10*s*;

'Paid John Alford for 1 hogshead & a busshell of lime': 5*s* [illegible]*d*;

'25 [February] paid John Gibbs for 6 hogsheads of Lyme': £1 4*s* [illegible]*d*;

'March 22 paid James Wills for 5,325 *lbs* new Ledd to cover the house at South Gate, at 17*s* a C abating for 900 of old Ledds £5 at 13*s* a C neate is': £39 7*s* 6*d*;

'March 27 paid James Wills for 92 *lbs* Ledd at 15*s* a C & for wood for heatinge his irons, for fastninge the Iron barrs at South Gate 6*d* all is': 12*s* 9*d*;

'Maye 1643 20 paid William Heard & others for 6 days worke over South Gate at 14*d* a daye for 3 days at 12*d* a day for a pecke of pins 12*d* for 300 of Laths & 1000 nayles 3*s* 2*d* all is': 14*s* 2*d*;

'June 10 paid Peter Halstaff for mendinge of the Locks at ye Eastgate, & at Westgate 3*s* 4*d*': 3*s* 4*d*;

[Subtotal] '£52 14*s* 6*d*';

[Total] '£164 1*s* 1*d*'.

[*f.*9] 'Disbursments Called Extraordinary Charges . . .

December 1642 paid 16 watchmenn by . . . order [of the Mayor] att Eastgate 4 one the fast dayes to each 12*d* for 3 fast dayes paid in all butt': £1 16*s*;

'Paid the 4 porters by sayd order for Candle light att each gate for 20 weekes att 12*d* a weeke to each of them is': £4.

'To the Master and boy that made the Oration att the Freeschoole att the tyme of the Murally walke': 15*s*;

'To the prisoners in the High Gaole by Mr Maiors directions': 5*s*;

'To Mr Hockwell for the Collection att Southgate': 16*s*;

'To the Prisoners there': 3*s*.

[Total: £7 15*s* 0*d*.]

[Total expenditure in this year: £173 16*s* 9*d*.]

1643–44

Receiver Richard Yeo, merchant.

Receiver's Roll

[*m.2v.*] Fees of the mayor and other officers:
  Paid the 4 porters for their pension this year: 3*s* [*sic*];
  Paid the porter of North Gate for his fee and for cleansing the step (*gradus*) near that gate: 6*s* 8*d*.
  [Total: 9*s* 8*d*.]

Necessary expenses:
  Paid for diverse reparations to the walls of the city by the book thereof: £369 1*s* 10*d*.

Receiver's Book

[*f.*4] 'Monies disbursed about the Reparacions on the Citties Walles & Gates &c

November 4th 1643 paid for 12 seames of sand and for 18 seames of Claye for the decayed Walle in Northenhay': 5*s*;

[11 November] 'Paid for 6 hogsheads of Lyme 27*s* and for sand 2*s* 8*d*': £1 9*s* 8*d*;

'Paid for 4 dozen of seame stones from Heavitree att 5*s*': £1;

'Paid John Laurence Mason & his Companye for their Worke': £2 1*s* 8*d*;

[18 November] 'Paid for 3 dozen & 9 seame stones from Heavitree': 18*s* 9*d*;

'Paid for 4 seames of Sand att 5*d*': 1*s* 8*d*;

'Paid John Laurence & his Companie for their Worke': £1 14*s* 10*d*;

[25 November] 'Paid for 7 hogshedds & ½ of Chudleigh Lime at 4*s* 6*d*': £1 13*s* 9*d*;

'Paid for 3 dozen & ½ of Heavitree seame stones att 5*s*': 17*s* 6*d*;

'Paid for 2 dozen & 4 seames of Sand att 5*d* a seame': 11*s* 8*d*;

'Paid John Laurence & his Companie for their Worke': £2 19*s* 4*d*;

'December 2: paid for 4 dozen and 5 seames of Heavitree Stones att 5*s*': £1 2*s* 1*d*;

'Paid for 18 seames of Sand att 5*d*': 7*s* 6*d*;

'Paid John Laurence & Companie for their Worke': £2 2*s* 6*d*;

[9 December] 'Paid for 3 dozen of Seame stones from Heavitree att 5*s*': 15*s*;

[26 December] 'Paid John Laurence & his Companie for their Worke & for a date stone': £2 10*s* 10*d*;

'Paid them more for their Worke': £2 16*s* 10*d*;

[23 December] 'Paid for a newe Kay for the Kaygate & for altering the Wards the other Kay being lost': 2s 1d;
'January 6th paid for filling of a hole under Southgate and for 2 plancks to lye under the earth': 3s;
[Subtotal: £23 13s 8d;]
'May 4th 1644 paid for one dozen of seame stones from Peymouth [Peamore]': 9s [sum crossed out];
'Paid for 5 seame stones from Heavitree': 12s 1d [sum crossed out];
'Paid John Laurence Mason & Companie & other labouring men': £5 6s 1d [sum crossed out];
[11 May (?)] 'Paid for 3 dozen & ½ of Peymouth stones att 9s': £1 11s 6d [sum crossed out];
'Paid for bottoming of the Citties Coole & for 4 hoopes &c': 1s 3d [sum crossed out];
'Paid John Laurence Mason & Companie & other labouring men': £4 11s 5d [sum crossed out];
'Paid for a quart & ½ a pinte of Lynseed oyle & for 2 lbs of colours for the date stone sett upp in the Walle': 2s 6d [sum crossed out];
[18 May (?)] 'Paid for 4 Peymouth seame stones': 3s [sum crossed out];
'Paid John Laurence & his Companie of Masons & other laboring men': £2 4s [sum crossed out];
[25 May (?)] 'Paid for mens labour for leavelling of the barbican & carrying away of the bords and stakes of the staples to the storehouse': 6s [sum crossed out];
'Charged in folio 20': £23 13s 8d;
'The Tenn somes raised out are charged in folio 20';
[f.5] 'The 19th of Aprill paid Peter Martin of Teingmouth a Maister workman over & above his ordinary pay for the time hee wrought in the Citties worke': 5s [sum crossed out];
'18th paid William Plumer of Thorverton Mason another Maister Workeman over and above his ordinarie pay': 4s [sum crossed out];
'June 22th paid the Ropemaker for 3 dozen of Scaffold Roopes att 3s & 2 paire of sling Ropes & 4d worth of Candall is': 11s 1d [sum crossed out];
'July 11th paid the Plumer for 6 pounds of Leadd for the inscripcion of the date stone': 11d [sum crossed out];
'November 20th paid the Widdow Kelly for 26 delebords bought of her husbond the 16th March 1643 for the makeing of Scaffolds att 12d each bord': £1 6s [sum crossed out];
'The five somes abovesaid being raised are charged in folio 20';
'Sum total' [blank].
[f.9] 'Monies disbursed about the Reparacions on the Citties Walle in Southenhay &c
January 6th 1643 paid for 7 dozen and 4 seame stones from Heavitree att 5s': £1 16s 8d;
'Paid for 20 Seames of Sand att 4d': 6s 8d;
'Paid for mens labour for Clensing of the foundacion': £1 6d;
[Subtotal] '£3 3s 10d';
[f.10] [13 January] 'Paid for 7 dozen and ½ of Seames of Sand att 4d': £1 10s;
'Paid for 3 dozen & ½ of Peymouth [Peamore] stones': £1 11s 6d;
'Paid for 7 dozen of Heavitree stones att 5s': £1 15s;
'Paid for 6 hogsheads & ½ of Chudleigh Lime att 4s 6d': £1 9s 3d;

'Paid for 12 hogsheads of Lime from Weare att 4s 2d': £2 10d;
'Paid John Laurence Mason and Companie for their worke': £2 12s 2d;
'Paid a Laboring man for ridding the foundacion of the Walle': £6 7d 2d;
'Paid for a hogshead to measure Lyme with for a Seeve & a Buckett': 3s 8d;
[20 January] 'Paid for the carriage of 12 seames of Claye': 12s;
'Paid for 17 hogshedds of Chudleigh Lime att 4s 6d': £3 16s 6d;
'Paid for 6 dozen & ½ of Heavitree stones att 5s': £1 11s 8d;
'Paid for 8 dozen of Peymouth [Peamore] stones att 9s': £3 12s;
'Paid John Laurence & his Companie for their Worke': £9 14s 4d;
'Paid Ames Burgesse & his Companye of Laboring men': £3 3s;
'Paid for the sharpening of Stakes & for the makeing of a Rake for siftinge of Earth': 2s 11d;
'Paid for 4 lbs of Spukes for the bridge over the dike': 1s 4d;
'Paid for mending of one of the Citties Wheelebarrows': 6d;
[27 January] 'Paid John Laurence and his Companie for their Worke': £7 2s;
'More paid to other laboring men of his Companie': £5 1s 2d;
'Paid Ames Burgesse and his Company of Laboring men': £2 3s 6d;
'Paid for 10 dozen & 8 seame stones from Heavitree att 5s': £2 13s 4d;
'Paid for 6 dozen of Peymouth [Peamore] stones att 9s': £2 14s;
'Paid for 2 newe Wheelebarrowes bought for this worke cost': 11s 8d;
'Paid for 4 dozen & 2 seames of Sand att 4d': 16s 8d;
'Paid for a mans Labour to sawe and sharpen stakes': 2s 4d;
'February 3rd paid John Laurence and his Companie of Masons & other laboring men': £13 17s 9d;
'Paid Ames Burgesse & his Companie of Laboring men': £2 8s 6d;
'Paid for 4 dozen Seames of sand att 14d': 16s;
'Paid for 15 dozen and 10 seame stones from Heavitree att 5s': £3 19s 2d;
'Paid for 12 dozen of Peymouth stones att 9s': £5 8s;
'Paid for cutting & sharpening of Stakes': 1s 2d;
[5 February] 'Paid Nicholas Woolcott for 90 stakes for piling of the foundacion of the Walle containing 738 foote att 1½d a foote': £4 12s 3d;
[Subtotal] '£92 15s 6d';
'The charges disbursed on the other side belonging to this Accompt is: £3 3s 10d';
'£95 19s 4d';

[f.11] [10 February] 'Paid for 17 hogshedds of Chudleigh Lime att 4s 6d': £3 16s 6d;
'Paid Reymond Wislake for 17 hogsheads of Lime att 4s 2d': £3 10s 10d;
'Paid for 14 dozen & ½ of Heavitree seame stones att 5s': £3 12s 6d;
'Paid for 11 dozen seames of stones from Peymouth [Peamore] att 9s': £4 19s;

'Paid for 4 dozen seames of sand att 4*d*': 16*s*;
'Paid John Laurence & his Companye of Masons for their Worke': £5 12*s* 2*d*;
'Paid him for other laboring men of his Companye': £4 2*s* 9*d*;
[17 February] 'Paid for 20 dozen & 3 stones from Heavitree att 5*s*': £5 1*s* 3*d*;
'Paid for 12 dozen & 2 seame stones from Peymouth att 9*s*': £5 9*s* 6*d*;
'Paid John Laurence & his Company of Masons & for other Laboring men for their Worke': £12 2*s* 6*d*;
[17 February] 'Paid for 3 dozen & ½ of Sand att 4*d*': 14*s*;
'Paid for 26 dozen & ½ of Heavitree stones att 5*s*': £6 12*s* 6*d*;
'Paid for 8 dozen & ½ of seame stones from Peymouth att 9*s*': £3 16*s* 6*d*;
'Paid for 6 Basketts for the carrying of materialls': 3*s*;
'Paid for 12 hogsheads & halfe of Chudley [Chudleigh] Lime att 4*s* 6*d*': £2 16*s* 3*d*;
'Paid for 5 dozen seames of sand att 4*d*': £1;
'Paid John Laurence and his Companye for Worke done by them this Weeke': £13 13*s*;
'Paid George Follett for 3 studes and for lasts for makeing of a Ratch for the sifting of sand for morter': 2*s*;
'More paid him for 100 foote of stakes att 1½*d*': 10*s* 5*d*;
'March 2 paid John Laurence for himselfe & Companye of Masons & for other labouring men of his Companye': £11 19*s* 11*d*;
'Paid for 40 hogsheads of Chudleigh Lime att 4*s* 6*d*': £4 10*s*;
'Paid for 6 dozen seames of Sand att 4*d*': £1 4*s*;
'Paid for 15 dozen of Heavitree stones att 5*s*': £3 15*s*;
[9 March] 'Paid John Laurence & his Companye of Masons & others': £9 17*s* 6*d*;
'Paid for 17 dozen of Heavitree stones att 5*s*': £4 5*s*;
'Paid for 4 dozen seames of Sand att 4*d* a seame': 16*s*;
'Paid for 17 hogsheads & ½ of Chudleigh Lime att 4*s* 6*d*': £3 18*s* 9*d*;
'Paid for 5 dozen of Peymouth [Peamore] stones att 9*s*': £2 5*s*;
[16 March] 'Paid John Laurence & his Company of Masons & other labouring men': £11 4*s* 2*d*;
'Paid for 20 dozen & 7 seame stones from Heavitree att 5*s*': £5 2*s* 11*d*;
'Paid for 7 dozen & 8 seame stones from Peymouth att 9*s*': £3 9*s*;
'Paid Zacharie Saunders for 20 delbords': £1;
'Paid for 6 dozen & ½ of seames of sand att 4*d*': £1 6*s*;
[Subtotal] '£143 3*s* 11*d*';
'The charges disbursed as appeares on the other side is': £95 19*s* 4*d*;
'£239 3*s* 3*d*';

[*f.12*] [23 March] 'Paid John Laurence & his Company of Masons & other laboring men': £10 19*s* 2*d*;
'Paid for 7 dozen & 9 seame stones from Peymouth att 9*s*': £3 9*s* 9*d*;
'Paid for 17 dozen & 8 seame stones from Heavitree att 5*s*': £4 8*s* 4*d*;
'Paid for 3 dozen & ½ of Sand att 4*d*': 14*s*;
'[30 March] 1644 paid John Laurence & his Companie of Masons & other Laboring men': £9 1*d*;
'Paid for 12 dozen & 10 seame stones from Peymouth [Peamore] att 9*s*': £5 15*s* 6*d*;

'Paid for 6 dozen & 4 seame stones from Heavitree att 5*s*': £1 11*s* 8*d*;
'Paid for 12 hogsheads & ½ of Chudleigh Lime att 4*s* 6*d*': £2 16*s* 3*d*;
'Paid Thomas Somerton for a date stone for the Walle': 6*s*;
'Aprill 6th paid for 3 dozen & ½ of Heavitree seame stones att 5*s*': 17*s* 6*d*;
'Paid for 12 dozen & 2 seame stones from Peymouth att 9*s*': £5 16*s* 3*d*;
'Paid John Laurence & Company of Masons & other Labouring men': £11 9*s* 3*d*;
'Paid Ames Burgesse & one other Workeman for 1 dayes labor for takeing upp of the Stakes & bridg over the ditch & other Worke': 2*s* 4*d*;
[13 April] 'Paid for 6 dozen of Heavitree stones att 5*s*': £1 10*s*;
'Paid for skabling of 114 seame stones att the Quarry at 1*s* a score': 5*s* 6*d*;
'Paid for 13 dozen & ½ of Peymouth stones att 9*s*': £6 1*s* 6*d*;
'Paid John Laurence & his Companie of Masons & other laboring men': £6 2*s*;
'20th [April] paid for 11 dozen & 9 Peymouth seame stones att 9*s*': £5 5*s* 9*d*;
'Paid for a hogshead of Chudley Lime': 4*s* 6*d*;
'Paid for 6 seames of sand att 4*d*': 2*s*;
'Paid John Laurence & Companie of Masons & other Labouring men': £7 7*s* 8*d*;
[27 April] 'Paid for 3 dozen & ½ of Heavitree seame stones att 5*s*': 17*s* 6*d*;
'Paid for 3 dozen & halfe of Peymouth seame stones att 9*s*': £1 11*s* 6*d*;
'Paid John Laurence & his Companie of Masons & other laboring men': £2 13*s* 10*d*;
[Subtotal] '£88 17*s* 10*d*';
'The charges disbursed on the other side belonging to this Accompt is': £239 3*s* 3*d*;
'Past this same to Account in folio 20: £328 1*s* 1*d*'.

'Monies disbursed for the Cittie called Extraordinary Charges &c . . .
1644 [?] October 2 paid for 17 *lbs* of Candells for the Guildhall & Gates': 6*s* 4½*d*.

[*f.20*] 'The reparacions of the Citties Walles in Southenhaye amounts as it appeareth in folio 12
1644 May 4th paid for 1 dozen of seame stones from Peymouth [Peamore] ': 9*s*;
'Paid for 5 seame stones from Heavitree': 2*s* 1*d*;
'Paid John Laurence Mason & Companie & other labouring men': £5 6*s* 1*d*;
[11 May] 'Paid for 3 dozen & ½ of Peymouth stones att 9*s*': £1 11*s* 6*d*;
'Paid for bottoming of the Citties Coole & for hoopes': 1*s* 3*d*;
'Paid John Laurence Mason & his Companie & other Labouring men': £4 14*s* 5*d*;
'Paid for a quart & halfe a pinte of Linseed oyle & for 2 *lbs* of colours for the date stone sett on the Walle': 2*s* 6*d*;
[18 May] 'Paid for 4 Peymouth seame stones': 3*s*;
'Paid John Laurence Mason & Companie & other labouring men': £2 4*s*;
[25 May] 'Paid for mens labour for leavelling of the Barb[ican &] other Worke: 6*s*;

'Paid Peter Martyn of Teingmouth a Master Workman Mason over and above his pay: 5s;

[18 May (?)] 'Paid unto William Plumer of Thorverton for [the] like': 4s;

'June 22th paid the Ropemaker for 3 dozen of Scaffold Ropes 2 paire of sling Ropes & 4[illegible] worth of Cord': 11s 4d;

'July 11th paid the plumer for 6 *lbs* of ledd for the inscripcion of the date stone': 11d;

'November 20th paid the Widdow Kelly for 26 delbords for making of Scaffolds att 12d': £1 6s;

'£345 8s 2d'.

The disbursements about the reparacions of the Walles in Northenhay amounts as in folio 4: £23 13s 8d;

'£369 1s 10d'.

[Total expenditure in this year: £369 17s 10½d].

1644–45

Receiver John Martin.

Receiver's Roll

[*m.2v.*] Fees and pensions of the mayor and other officers:
Paid the porter of West Gate for cleansing the *gradus* for conducting rainwater there for the foresaid gate: 4s;
Paid the porter of North Gate for similar labour there: 6s 8d.
[Total: 10s 8d.]

Payments and necessary expenses:
Paid for diverse reparations on the gates and walls of the city this year: £170 16d.

Receiver's Book

[*f.3*] 'Monies laid out for Reparacions on the Westgate & the Citties Walles neere thereunto
October 30th 1644 *Inprimis* paid John Guy pavier & others for worke done as appeares by a note of the particulars': £1 7d;

'November 9th   paid John Jarman for 1 dozen of Heavitree stone for the same worke': 5s;

'Paid John Laurence Mason and his Company for the like': 18s 8d;

'Paid William Saunders for 2 dayes Worke': 2s;

'Paid Humfrie Locke for 2 dozen & 4 seames of sand': 10s 7d;

'Paid Zacharie Saunders Blacksmith for iron Worke about the Westgate & other places *parut*': £4 13s;

[16 November] 'Paid John Jarman & George Allyn for 3 dozen & 10 seames of Heavitree stones': 19s 2d;

'Paid the Quarriemen of Peymouth [Peamore] for 17 seame stones': 12s 9d;

'Paid John Laurence Mason & his Company about the same work': £3 2s 4d;

[23 November] 'Paid George Pottell for 6 dozen of Peymouth stones': £2 14s;

'Paid Humfrie Lock for sand': 4s 8d;

'Paid John Alford for 12 hogsheads of Chidleigh Lime': £2 14s;

'Paid John Jerman & George Allyn for 3 dozen & ½ of Heavitree stones': 17s 6d;

'Paid John Laurence & his Company about the same work *parut*': £5 2d;

[30 November] 'Paid George Pottell for 6 dozen & halfe of Peymouth stones': £2 18s 6d;

'Paid Humfrie Locke for 2 dozen & 4 seame stones': 9s 4d;

'Paid John Laurence Mason & his Company about the same worke': £4 14s 2d;

'Paid Mr Cristofer Parr for 1 dozen & ½ of Peymouth stones': 6s;

'December 7th paid Thomas Pottell for 4 dozen & halfe of Peymouth stones': £2 6d;

'Paid John Alford for 4 hogsheads & one Bushell of Lime': 19s 2d;

'Paid John Jerman for 2 dozen & one seame of seame stones and for a dozen & halfe more bought of Mr Cristofer Parr': 13s 5d;

'Paid John Laurence Mason & his Company for work done *parut*': £5 8s 10d;

[14 December] 'Paid them more for the same worke *parut*': £4 19s 8d;

'Paid them more for the like': 6s;

'Paid Humfrie Lock for 2 dozen of sand': 8s;

'Paid George Pottell for 3 dozen of seame stones': £1 7s;

'Paid him for 4 dozen & halfe more': £2 6d;

[21 December] 'Paid John Jarman & George Allyn for 5 dozen of Heavitree stones': £1 5s;

'Paid John Alford for 13 hogsheads of Lime': £2 18s 6d;

[Subtotal] '£54 9s';

[*f.4*] 'Paid George Pottell for 8 dozen & 8 seame stones': £3 18s;

'Paid John Laurence Mason & Company for work done *parut*': 19s;

'Paid them more for the like *parut*': £5 10s;

'Paid Humfrie Locke for 22 seames of sand': 7s 4d;

[24 December] 'Paid John Jerman & George Allyn for 2 dozen of seame stones': 10s;

'Paid George Pottell for 2 dozen & 8 seame stones': £1 4s;

'Paid Humfrie Lock for 24 seames of sand': 8s;

'Paid John Laurence & his Company for worke done *parut*': £2 4s 8d;

'Paid George Paddon for cutting & engraving the stone on Westgat': 6s 3d;

'January 4 paid George Pottell for 2 dozen & 10 Peymouth [Peamore] stones': £1 5s 6d;

'Paid Lewes Grenslade & his Company for work done *parut*': 7s 8d;

[11 January] 'Paid George Pottell for 5 dozen & 10 seame stones': £2 12s 6d;

'Paid Humfrie Lock for 8 seames of sand': 2s 8d;

'Paid John Laurence & his Company for work done *parut*': £4 2s 3d;

[28 January; *sic*] 'Paid John Alford for 9 hogsheads & ½ of Lime': £2 2s 9d;

'Paid Humfrie Lock for 14 seames of sand': 4s 8d;

'Paid George Pottell for 7 dozen & ½ of Peymouth [Peamore] stones': £3 7s 6d;

'18th [January] paid John Laurence & his Companie for worke done *parut*': £5 11s;

[25 January] 'Paid George Pottell for 8 dozen & 7 seame stones': £3 17s 3d;

'Paid Humfrie Lock for 10 seames of sand': 3s 4d;

'Paid John Laurence & his Company for worke done *parut*': £6 18s 1d;

'February 1 paid them more for the like *parut*': £7 8s;

'Paid Lewes Grenslade & another mans Labour about the same work': 2s 4d;

'Paid Humfrie Lock for 9 seames of sand': 3s;

'Paid George Pottell for 8 dozen & ½ of Peymouth stones': £3 16s 6d;

[8 February] 'Paid Humfry Lock for sand': 8s;

'Paid John Laurence & his Companie for work done *parut*': £4 2s;

'Paid James Bennett for a parcell of Walling stones': £1;

'Paid John Alford for 12 hogsheads of Lime': £2 14s;

'Paid John Laurence & his Company for work done *parut*': £2 7s 8d;

'Paid Lewes Grenslade & others about the same Work': 6s 2d;

'Paid John Laurence & his Companie for work done *parut*': £3 13s 6d;

'Paid Humfrie Lock for Sand': 4s;

'15th [February] paid him more for sand': 4s;

'Paid John Laurence & his Company for ridding of John Turners seller': £1 1s 8d;

22 February] 'Paid them more for work done there': £4 14s 9d;

'Paid Humfrie Locke for halfe a dozen of Sand': 2s;

[Subtotal] '£78 10s';

[*f.5*] 'Paid George Pottell for 2 dozen & 2 seame stones': 19s 6d;

'March 1 paid John Alford for 7 hogsheads of Lime': £1 15s;

'Paid George Pottell for 3 dozen of Peymouth [Peamore] stones': £1 7s;

'Paid Lewes Grenslade & his Company for work done *parut*': 4s 8d;

'Paid Humfrie Lock for 10 seames of Sand': 3s 4d;

'Paid John Laurence & his Company for work done *parut*': £5 4s 4d;

[8 March] 'Paid them more for the like': £3 14s 10d;

'Paid George Pottell for 22 seames of Peymouth stones': 16s 6d;

[22 March] 'Paid John Laurence & his Companie for work done att Westgate & other places': £1 7s 4d;

'29th [March] paid Humfrie Lock for carriage of 2 dozen of sand': 8s;

'Paid George Pottell for stones for the Barbicans of the Citties Walls': £1 10s;

'Paid John Laurence & his Company about that work *parut*': £3 8s 6d;

'Aprill 5th 1645 paid Humfrie Lock for Sand': 2s 6d;

'Paid George Pottell for a dozen of choice Burrs': 7s;

'Paid John Laurence & his Company for work done *parut*': £3 17s;

'Paid John Alford for 9 hogsheads & ½ of Lime': £2 12s 3d;

'May 10th paid him for 1 hogshead & halfe more': 8s 3d;

[16 May (?)] 'Paid John Guy & Humfrie Lock for paving sand & stones': £1 6s 11d;

'September 17th paid Lewes Grenslade & his Company for work done *parut*': 14s 8d;

[27 September (?)] 'Paid John Laurence & his Company for the like *parut*': 5s 8d;

[Subtotal] '£30 13s 3d';

'Other chargs after *parut*': £6 9s 1d';

[Total:] '£170 1s 4d'.

[*f.9*] 'Reparacions on the Northgate

November 23th paid John Bennett for 2 dozen of Gravell & stones': 8s;

'Paid Humfry Lock John Guy & others for sand and stones': £2 16s 11d;

'Paid George Pottell for one dozen of Peymouth [Peamore] stones': 9s;

[30 November (?)] 'Paid Humfrie Lock & others for sand and stones': £1 16s 2d;

'March 22th paid John Greedy & his Company for 15 foote of oake planck to lay over the gutter & for worke done *parut*': 19s;

'Sum £6 9s 1d'.

[*f.10*] 'Other disbursements called Extraordinary payments . . .

Paid Humfrie Lock for 2 dozen of sand for the Citties Walles': 8s.

[7 October 1644] 'Paid the lazer people & for Apples att the Murallia Walke': 2s 2d.

[8 February 1645] 'Paid Phillipp Harris for mending of the ladder goeing upp to the Tower against the hospitall garden': 1s 6d.

[Total: 11s 8d.]

[Total expenditure in this year: £171 3s 8d.]

1645–46

Receivers John Colleton and James Gould.

[The roll for this year is missing.]

Receiver's Book [DRO, Box 214, Book 15]

[*f.1v.*] [City Walls:]

[29 March] To 'Richard Glanvill Chanler for Candles for the Guards as *per* Chambers order': £5.

[1646 March] '29 . . . paid Humphry Lock for 5 dozen of Cley for the Citty Walls att 4s a dozen': £1;

'Paid John Larrance for worke done by him & Company about ye Citty Walls': £3 14s 4d;

[4 April] 'Paid John Larrance & Company for more worke done about ye Citty Walls': £2 11s;

'Paid Humphry Lock for 24 seames of Clay for ye Citty Walls': 8s;

[5 April] 'Paid for cleansing the Gutter under the Westgate': 1s;

[11 April] 'Paid John Larrance more for worke done about ye Citty Walls & for 2½ dozen of Clay': £4 3s 6d;

[18 April] 'Paid Thomas King for flatt stones used about the Citty Walls': 7s 6d;

'2 [May] . . . paid John Larrance & Company for finnishing ye Citty Walls as by Mr Passemers bill': £3 6s 11d;

[30 May] 'Paid Lewes Greenslade for framing poasts for ye Iron grate at Northgate': 6s 2d;

[*f.2v.*] '20 [March] . . . paid Humphry Lock for 4 dozen and 8 seames of Clay for ye Citty Walls att 4d *per* seam': 18s 8d;

'Paid John Larrance Mason for worke done by him & Company about ye Citty Walls': £3 1s 6d.

[Total expenditure in this year: £24 18s 7d.]

1646–47

Receiver Richard Crossing.

[The roll for this year is missing.]

Receiver's Book [DRO, Box 214, Book 17]

[*f.2*] [Extraordinary expenses:]
[12 October] 'Given by order goeing the Maralia Walke to the prisoners of the High Geole': 4s;
'To Thomas his wife towards the Banquett at ye prison at Southgate': 15s;
'Paid for Apples at Mr Maior his house given ye boyes': 2s 2d.
[19 November 1646] 'For 4 Keys of the Gates of ye Citty & for mending ye Locks to John Branscombe as by his note is': 11s.

[*f.4*] [6 January 1646] '1s [paid] Gilbert Tothill for clearing ye earth yt stopt ye gutters att Northgate': 1s.

[*f.10*] '15th [May 1647] . . . paid Richard Dare for worke done about East Gate by note': 1s 6d.

[*f.13*] [25 September 1647] 'Paid Richard Dare porter of Eastgate for mending a broken Key as by note': 8d.

[*f.14*] [2 October 1647] 'Paid ye Porter of Westgate for Cleansing ye grates of Westgate for ½ a yeare 2s & for Clensing ye grates of Key Gate for ½ yeare 3s 4d': 5s 4d.
'Paid ye Porter of Northgate for cleansing ye grates for halfe yeare': 3s 4d.
[Total: £2 4s 0d.]

Receiver's Book A

[There are two books for this year].
[*f.2a*] [Extraordinary expenses]:
[19 September 1647] 'By £7 18s payd unto severall persons for mending the Gates & locks of the Cittie': £7 18s.

[*f.3a*] [24 September] 'By £1 07s payd for repairing the walls of ye Cittie': £1 7s.
[Total: £9 5s 0d.]

Receiver's Vouchers [Box 2]

Receiver's Vouchers, 1646–47

'A note for worke done for the cittye of Exon by Joshua Branscombe as followeth
Inprimis for one key for Southgate & mending ye locke & nayles to sett him': 3s;
'For a key for Keygate & one staple & nayles': 2s 6d;
'For a key for Eastgate & nayles to sett him': 2s 6d;
'For a key for Westgate & new staples & nayles to sett him & for righting the locke of the greate gate': 3s;
'Some totall is': 11s.
'Paid this noate 19th November 1646 Robert Ridler Captain.'

'The 17th of January 1646 [i.e. 1647]
To John Larrance mason and company for worke don without the Kay Gate which was fallen downe and so

rotten and decayed that the wagons could not pass with merchants goodes without great daunger.
John Larrance master workeman one day 18d': 1s 6d;
'Christopher Kennicke 2 dayes att 14d': 2s 4d;
Thomas Pole 2 dayes att 14d': 2s 4d;
'George Passemer: 6s 2d'.
[Total: 6s 2d.]

'The 23th of January 1646 . . . [i.e. 1647]
To John Gove the wagoner . . . for drawinge of 3 beames from Southgate battery to the Kaye . . .': 2s.

'The 13th of February 1646 [i.e. 1647]
To John Larrance mason and company for worke don without the gate without the Kay Gate for puttinge in of seame stones and for castinge upp of much earth which was rused downe from the banke of the Kay garden which caused the downfall of the water that came from Southgate to diverte the water out of his course and so spoyled the waye.
John Larrance cheefe mason one day': 1s 6d;
'Christopher Kennick, John Robins and Thomas Pole ech of them one daye at 14d': 3s 6d;
'George Passemer: 5s 0d'.
[Total: 5s.]

'The 13th of February 1646 [i.e. 1647]
To Lewes Grinslade carpenter and company for worke by hym and them don for fyttinge of the Inner drawbridge at Southgate fallen downe and very dangerous for people and horses with their caryages that passed under [*sic*] it . . .'
[Sum unspecified.] 'G. Passemer'.

'The 8th of May 1647. For worke don by Zachary Saunders smyth for Westgate by Mr Mayors order for the Porter there Christopher Harries:
For a Hammer for the gate & 2 eyes for hanginge of it': 2s 6d;
'For 3 hooks and twists and neales for the Porters lodge': 1s 7d;
'For a locke and kay for the Porters lodge and for 2 stapels': 1s 8d;
'For an Iron Crooke for to draw away the filth from the grates': 1s 6d.
. . . [7s 3d.]
'Paid 22th May. George Passemer'.

'The 15th of May 1647.
To Richard Dare the Porter of Eastgate for amendinge of the porteholle of the gate and for a lock and kay for the lodge': 1s 6d.
'George Passemer'.

'The 22th of May 1647
To John Lavers Mason and company for work don att Westgate for the remoovinge of donge, stones, rubbell and other faultes by which meanes the fall of the water was so fild upp and stopt that none could passe that way but brake out the street & howses'. [£1 14s 11d].

'The 7th of June 1647
To Phillip Edwardes porter of Southgate for a bolte of Iron over the wicket att Southgate att the portholl of the ?guine? where throw people might passe att night and else [*sic*] had it not beene don': 2s.
'Paid 17th—George Passemer'.

'The 18th of September 1647
To George Creemer mason and his company for the makinge upp of a clobb wall on the Citties Wall and stoppinge upp of som of the garrettes by meanes whereof (lyinge open) sheepe staylors and other ill affected persons made a thoroughfare of it to the damage of the Citty.
George Creemer cheefe mason 6 dayes att 18*d* a daye': 9*s*;
'Thomas Paule 6 dayes att 16*d* a daye is': 8*s*;
'Richard Trevillyan 6 dayes att 12*d* a daye is': 6*s*;
'For 3 seames of strawe for the morter att 16*d* a seame': 4*s* [torn];
'George Passemer £1 07*s* [torn]'.

'The 23th of September 1647 . . .
More to hym [Arthur Thorne] for setting upp of a new barr at Northgate the old bee [*sic*] broken that the porter could not open nor shut the g[ate?; torn].
To hym and his boy for framinge of it': 2*s* 6*d*;
'To John Reynolls for a peece for the gate': [torn];
[No overall sum recorded on gates—torn]. 'George [Passemer]'.

'The 24th of September 1647. To Zachary Saunders smyth for Ireworke don for the Cities use and for severall workes as under: . . .
For Northgate for a broken barr 25 spukes att 1*d* ech': [torn];
'For 7 long spukes to hold the barr of the gate att 3*d* a pece': [torn];
'For 22 *lbs* of Iron added to the barr of the gate new made att 4*d*': [torn];
'For a Hammer for the gate and an ey to hange it in': [torn];
'Paid 2th October [no sum recorded for gate alone] George Passemer'.

'The 24th of September 164? [torn]. To Richard Dare the Porter of Eastgate for the amend[ing?; torn] of a broken kaye att the Eastgat lock': [torn].
'George Pa[ssemer]'.

[Total expenditure in this year: *c.*£11 9*s*.]

1647–48

Receiver Nicholas Brooking.

[The roll for this year is missing.]

Receiver's Book [DRO, Box 214, Book 19]

[*f.2*] 'Nicholas Broking Receiver Generall for the Chamber of the Citty of Exon . . . is Creditor
Fees & Pencions
Paid to the 4 Porters of the gates of the citty each 4*s* is': 16*s*;
'Paid to the Porter of Westgate for cleansing of the grates': 4*s*;
'Paid to the Porter of the Northgate for cleansing of the grates there': 6*s*;
'Paid to the Porter of the Watergate for keeping of that gate': 6*s* 8*d*.
[Total: £1 12*s* 8*d*.]

[*f.4*] 'Reparations on ye Citties Gates and Walls . . .
10 June 1648 paid Humphrey Locke for 3 Seames of Exsand': 1*s* 6*d*;
'12 [June] paid John Lawrence mason & others': 13*s* 8*d*;
'24 [June] paid John Griffin and others': 6*s* 6*d*;
'July 1 paid George Creemer and others for worke': 9*s* 8*d*;
'Paid George Creemer mason': 19*s* 11*d*;
'29 [July] paid Lewis Greeneslade for planching a place over ye Northgate': £2 7*s* 8*d*;
'August 12 paid Zachary Saunders Smith for Ireworke': 10*s* 4*d*;
'September 30 paid Humphrey Locke': 3*s* 2*d*.
[Total: £5 12*s* 4*d*.]

[*f.10*] [Extraordinary expenses]:
'9 [September] paid Saunders a Smith for a locke & key for Kaygate': 8*s*.

[Total expenditure in this year: £7 13*s* 0*d*.]

1648–49

Receiver Ralph Herman.

[The roll for this year is missing.]

Receiver's Book [DRO, Box 214, Book 20]

[*f.6*] 'Payments
Fees & pencions &c
To the fower Porters of the said Cittie for attendinge the Gates &c *videlicet* to every of them 6*s* 8*d*': £1 6*s*.

[*f.8*] 'Extraordinarie Disbursments . . .
[October 1648] Paid by order of Mr Maior att the tyme of the Murallie Walk, to the prisoners of the High Gaole, Castle Souldiers, prisoners at Southgate, & the poore att severall places': £1 1*s*;
'Paid for Apples for the Boyes att ye same tyme': 4*s* 5*d*.

[*f.9*] [22 November] 'Paid Edmund Hoppinge for mendinge of the locke & key att the Eastgate as Note 30': 1*s*.
[12 January] 'Paid Humfry Lock for sand for wallinge att the Southgate as Note 42': 1*s* 6*d*.

[*f.10*] [31 March] 'Paid John Laurence Mason & others for the amendment of defects in the Citties Walles as Note 61': 10*s* 8*d*;
'Paid Humfrey Lock more for 6 seames of cley for that work as Note 62': 2*s*.

[*f.11*] [15 September] 'Paid John Gibbs Mason & others for mendinge of the Citties Walls att the Palace as Note 102': £1 7*s* 2*d*;
'20 [September] Paid the same men for more work done att the same place as by their note Note 103': 5*s*.
[Total: £3 12*s* 9*d*.]

[Total expenditure in this year: £4 18*s* 9*d*.]

1649–50

Receiver John Dark.

[The roll for this year is missing.]

Receiver's Book [DRO, Box 214, Book 21]

[*f.1*] 'Payments
  Paid John Pasture porter of Northgate for his quarters pencion then . . . due: 2*s* 8*d*;
  'Paid Richard ['Phillipp'—crossed out] Dare Porter of Eastgate for his quarters pencion then alsoe due': 1*s*;
  'Paid Phillipp Edwards Porter of Southgate for his quarters pencion due to him the 25th of March 1650': 1*s*;
  'Paid Christopher Harris Porter of Westgate for his quarters pencion then alsoe due for keeping the gate & clensing the grates': 2*s*;

[*f.2*] 'Paid Christopher Harris Porter of Westgate for his quarters pencion due to him att Midsomer 1650 for keeping the gate & clensing the grates': 2*s*;
  'Paid Richard Dare Porter of Eastgate for the same quarters pencion': 1*s*;
  'Paid the Porter of Northgate for his quarters pencion due att Midsomer 1650 for the gate & grates': 2*s* 8*d*;

[*f.4*] 'More paid him [Adam Bennett] for soe much by him disbursed for mending the locke of the Northgate': 1*s*;

[*f.5*] 'Paid Richard Dare Porter of Eastgate for his pencion due to him the 29th of September 1650': 1*s*;
  'Paid the Porter of Northgate for his quarters pencion then alsoe due': 2*s* 8*d*;
  'Paid the Porter of Westgate for his quarters pencion then alsoe due for keeping that gate & clensing the grate 2*s* & for one yeares pencion then due for keeping Keygate 6*s* 8*d*': 8*s* 8*d*;
  'Paid the Porter of Southgate for halfe of one yeares pencion then alsoe due': 2*s*.

[Total expenditure in this year: £1 7*s* 8*d*.]

1650–51

Receiver Richard Sweete.

[The roll for this year is missing.]

Receiver's Book [DRO, Box 214, Book 22]

[*f.1*] 'Payments . . .
  Paid the Porter of Westgate for clensing the grates there': 4*s*.
  'Paid Arthur Willing for work don on ye Citties Wale in Churchyard': 19*s* 7*d*.

[*f.2*] 'Paid the Porter of Northgate for clensing the grates there for three quarters of one yeare': 5*s*;
  'Paid the Porter of Westgate for keeping the Keygate': 6*s* 8*d*;
  'Paid the 2 Porters of Eastgate & Northgate either of them for 3 quarters of one yeares pencion 6*s*, and to the Porters of Westgate & Southgate either of them for this yeares pencion 8*s* all being': 14*s*.

[*f.11*] 'Paid Walter Strang Hellyer for lyme, sand & plaistering the Walles neere the ledds over Westgate as by a note': 1*s* 6*d*.

[*f.12*] 'Paid John Cann Plumber for worke done on the ledds over the Yarne Markett, over the Great Cunduitt & on the ledds over Westgate as by a note': £3 16*s*.

[*f.13*] 'Paid one [blank] Staple a souldier of the Castle for a rate putt uppon the house over Northgate and Close of ground belonging to that house': 6*s* 8*d*.

[*f.16*] 'Paid Lewes Greenslade Carpenter for timber and Carpentrie worke about repairing the guarde house att Northgate by order of the Chamber as by a note': £2 3*s* 8*d*;
  'Paid Walter Strang hellyer in parte of the charges for healing the guarde house att Northgate': £3;
  'Paid for pitch used about the gutters of the guard house att North Gate': 1*s*;
  'Paid Honnor Crutchett widdow for nailes, iron worke, locke & key used about the guarde house att North Gate and Guildhall pumpe as by a note of the particulers': £1 10*s* 9*d*;
  'Paid . . . [Lewes Greenslade] . . . for one mans labour halfe a daye, & for 3: halfe inch bords used about the guarde house att Northgate': 2*s* 8*d*.
  'Paid Nicholas Band & John Penny each of them 5 dayes about Clensing the vaut under the prison att Southgate and makeing a passage for the water to passe through': 15*s*.

[*f.17*] 'Paid Walter Strange Hellyer in full for healing the guard house att Northgate & for stones & other materialls': £2 10*s*.
  'Paid Peter Halstaffe Lockyer for amending the locke and key of North Gate being broken by the souldiers': 2*s* 6*d*.

[*f.18*] 'Paid John Baker for 10 deale bords used about the guard house att North Gate for the makeing of gutters &c': 10*s*.
  'Paid Walter Strang Hellier for worke done on the poore houses on the Towne Walles neere Northgate as by a note by order of Mr Receiver': 5*s*.

[Total expenditure in this year: £17 14*s* 0*d*.]

1651–52

Receiver Thomas Forde.

[The roll for this year is missing.]

Receiver's Book [DRO, Box 214, Book 23]

[*f.13*] 'Payments . . .
  Paid the fower Porters of the gates of this Cittie': 16*s*.

[*f.14*] 'Paid the Porter of Westgate for clensing the grates there': 4*s*;
  'Paid the Porter of Northgate for clensing the grates there': 6*s* 8*d*;
  'Paid the Porter of Keygate for keeping that gate': 6*s* 8*d*.
  'Paid John Tremlett Roger Peard & two other workemen to fill upp the Trench under the draw bridge without Eastgate, by order from Mr Maior, the Bridge being broken': 4*s* 8*d*.

[*f.15*] 'Paid Honor Crutchett widdow for iron crookes used about the Butchers standings in the Yarne Markett for one iron bolt for Westgate, nailes & amending a staple as by a note': 4*s* 4*d*.
  'Paid 4 Carpenters for takeing downe parte of the draw bridge att Southgate & carrying the timber into a house

for safetie, since used in the Almeshouses without Southgate': 2*s* 6*d*.
'Paid Lewes Greenslade Carpenter for worke done on the sluces and for amending the drawe bridge att Eastgate & a trapp dore over against the Guildhall': 16*s* 6*d*.

[*f.16*] 'Paid Honor Crutchett widdow for iron worke used about Westgate & the Sluces as by a note': 3*s* 10*d*.
'Paid Nicholas Band & John Penny each of them fower dayes about clensing the vaute under the prison att Southgate & making a passage for the water there to passe through': 8*s*.

[*f.17*] 'Paid John Penny & Nicholas Bound laborers, in parte of a more some for clensing the vaute under Southgate': 7*s*.

[*f.18*] 'Paid Nicholas Bickford glasier for amending the glasse windowes in Southgate att the comyng in of Hugh Farthing as by a note': 14*s*.
'Paid John Pennye & Nicholas Bond more in parte of Clensing the vaute under Southgate': 7*s*;
'Paid them more att another time in parte': 27*s*.

[*f.19*] 'Paid Honnor Crutchett widdowe for a crampe of iron waying 12 *lbs* for one of the Sluces & for nailes there used and for nailes & spukes used att Bonehay Bridge & about a dore att Northgate as by a note': 17*s* 6*d*.
'Paid Hugh Farthing for soe much by him disbursed for candles used in the vaute, and for wood used for the melting of ledd and for 4*s* paid by him to Penny & Bound in farther parte for clensing the vaute under the gaole': 7*s*.
'Paid . . . [Lewes Greenslade] for bordes, ledges & making a newe dore to the Porters Lodge att Northgate': 3*s* 10*d*.

[*f.21*] 'Paid him [Richard Clouter, mason] more for himselfe & others for filling upp the drawbridge att Southgate and for takeing upp of great stones there, and att the salley porte in Southenhaye by Mr Deebles order as by a note': £2 3*s* 4*d*.

[*f.23*] 'Paid Emanuell Hodge carpenter for 4 deale bords, one paire of twists waying 19 *lbs* att 4*d per lb*: nailes & labour for a dore for the Porters Lodge att Eastgate, by order in the Chamber': 13*s*.

[*f.24*] 'Paid John Cannn Plummer for ledd used about the casting in of hookes & a Staple into the stone walle for the dore of the Porters Lodge att Northgate': 4*s*.

[Total expenditure in this year: between £8 14*s* 8*d* and £10 16*s* 10*d*.]

1652–53

Receiver James Pearse.

[The roll for this year is missing.]

Receiver's Book [DRO, Box 214, Book 24]

[*f.14*] 'Fees & pencions
Paid the 4 Porters of the gates of this Cittie for their pencions': 16*s*;

[*f.15*] 'Paid the Porter of Westgate for clensing the grates': 4*s*;
'Paid the Porter of Northgate for clensing the grates there': 6*s* 8*d*;
'Paid the Porter of Westgate for keeping the Keygate': 6*s* 8*d*.
[Total: £1 13*s* 4*d*.]

[*f.17*] 'Other payments . . .
Paid by order of Mr Maior & Justices, to the schoole, Gaole & severall poore people in goeing the murall walke': £1 13*s*.

[*f.18*] 'Paid James Ellys by order of the Chamber towards his losse of a gelding breaking his legg att the drawe bridge without Southgate': £2.
'Paid John Wood & John Glanfeild by order of the Chamber for filling upp a deepe trench without Southgate wherein one Gould was latelie drowned': £2.

[*f.21*] 'Paid the Porter of Southgate for amending the locke & key of that gate as by a note': 1*s* 9*d*.
[Total: £5 14*s* 9*d*.]

[Total expenditure in this year: £7 8*s* 1*d*.]

1653–54

Receiver James Marshall, merchant.

Receiver's Roll [N.B. This roll is in English]

[*m.2v.*] 'Pencions & fees paid to the Maior & other Officers . . .
To the fower porters of the Gates of the said Cittie for their pencion': 16*s*;
'To the porter of Westgate for Clensing the grates neere the gate': 4*s*;
'To the porter of Northgate for Clensing of the grates there': 6*s* 8*d*;
'To the porter of Westgate for keeping of the Keygate': 6*s* 8*d*.
[Total: £1 13*s* 4*d*.]

Receiver's Book

[*f.3*] 'Payments
'Paid & given to severall poore people by Mr Maiors order in goeing the Murall Walke': 16*s*.
'Paid John Griffyn mason for worke done att the prison att Southgate as by a note': 11*s* 2*d*.

[*f.4*] 'Paid John Griffyn Mason for worke done att Southgate as by a note': £1 7*s* 6*d*.

[*f.7*] 'Paid John Griffyn Mason for worke done att Southgate prison & about the grates att Westgate and for lyme sand & seame stones as by a note': £1 10*s*.
'Paid John Crutchett Blacksmith for amending the grate within Westgate and for nailes used about the Sluces as by a note': 5*s*.

[*f.8*] 'Paid John Glanfill Richard Sillye & Reynold Badcock Laborers for digging away the earth of the batterie lying on the Barbigan att the Snaile Tower, for the more better passage there, and for prevention of danger of children from falling out over the walles of the Cittie there': 16s 11d.

[*f.9*] 'Paid . . . [John Griffyn, mason] . . . for other worke done att the new stone weare & uppon the Cittie Walle neere Keygate as by a note': £1 14s 6d.
'Paid John Griffyn Mason for stopping upp the passage through the Cittie Walles neere Keygate, & for straw for a wall as by a note': £2 8s 4d.
'Paid John Crutchett blacksmith for spukes nailes & iron worke used about Keygate as by a note': 9s 6d.
[Total: between £4 10s 9d and £8 3d.]

[Total expenditure in this year: between £6 4s 1d and £9 13s 7d.]

1654–55

Receiver Christopher Lethbridge.

Receiver's Roll [N.B. This roll is in English]

[*m.1v.*] Pensions and fees paid to the mayor and other officers:
'To the fower porters of the Gates of the said Cittie for their pencion': 16s;
'To the porter of Westgate for Clensing the grates neere the gate': 4s;
'To the porter of Northgate for Clensing of the Grates there': 6s 8d;
'To the porter of Westgate for keeping of the Keygate': 6s 8d.
[Total: £1 13s 4d.]

Receiver's Book

[*f.3*] 'Payments . . .
Paid Richard Clowter for ta'keing downe of two garretts of the Towne Wall and for copeing the same for Lyme & Sand to finish it 20s': £1.
'Paid at the Maiors walking about the walls at the High Gaole to the prisoners 6s 8d & the poore in that lane 3s 4d is all—10s': 10s;
'To the scholler in the Free Schoole that made an oration . . .': 10s;
'To the usher of the Free Schoole . . .': 5s.

[*f.4*] 'Paid John Griffin for worke done about the sallie port in the Pallice': £1 16s 4d.
'Paid John Tucker for filling up of two trenches without Southgate': £1 19s.

[*f.5*] 'Paid John Griffin for worke done about the Towne Walls': 6s 7d.
'Paid John Audery for two hodds [of] Lyme used at Eastgate': 10s.
'Paid John Griffin for worke done one the Towne Walls neare Northgate': 9s 5d.
[Total: £7 6s 4d.]

Receiver's Vouchers [Box 3]

'December 9th 1654 Received then of Christopher Lethbridge receaver generall of the Citty of Exon for

takeing downe of two Garretts of the Towne Wall behind Alhallands [All Hallows] Church & for copeing of the same & for lyme and sand to finnish the same the summe of Twenty Shillings.
Witness: James Pyn. The signe of Richard Cloutter'.

'March the 17th 1654 [i.e. 1655]. A note of wourcke donne for the citty att the Pallis aboute the Sallieporte by John Griffen masonn & his companie.
John Griffin 1 daye & halfe att 1s 8d *per* daye': 2s 6d;
'Roger Follett 3 dayes att 1s 6d *per* daye': 4s 6d;
'William Owesly 3 dayes att 1s 6d *per* daye': 4s 6d;
'George Croote 3 dayes att 1s 2d *per* daye': 3s 6d;
'Nicholas Wyett 3 dayes att 1s 2d *per* daye': 3s 6d;
'Richard Travillion 1 daye att 1s 6d *per* daye': 1s 6d;
'Rennolle Wattkins 2 dayes att 1s 2d *per* daye': 2s 4d;
'Phillip Baylie 3 dayes att 1s *per* daye': 3s;
'George Seely 1 daye': 1s;
'For 2 Hoggheds of lymbe': 10s;
'John Sprague. £1 16s 4d'.
'Received in full of this note, thirty six shillings fower pence I say received. The marke of John Griffin'.

'Aprill the 9 1655. Receved of Mr Lethebridge . . . Receiver Generall . . . the some of 39 shill[ings] wich is for the fillin[g] of t[w]o poles of water without the Southgat of this Cittie, I say received £1 19s 0d John Tucker'.

'June the 29th 1655. A note of wourcke donne for the cittye aboute the Towne Walles neere the Churchyarde Gate.
Nicholas Wyett 2 dayes att 1s 2d a daye': 2s 4d;
'William Owesly 1 daye': 1s 6d;
'For halfe a seame of strawe': [torn].
. . . [Reverse:] 'John Griffen is note 30 June 1655. 6s 7d'.

'August . . . [torn] . . . Work done for the City on the Towne Wall neere Northgate by John Griffins Company William Woosly 1 day at 18d': 1s 6d;
'George Crait 1 day at 14d': 1s 2d;
'Nicholas Wiat 1 day at 14d': 1s 2d;
'Roger Atkins 1 day at 14d': 1s [torn];
'George Scilly 1 day 12d': 1s [torn];
'One man & 2 horses to carry Earth for the worke: on day': 2s [torn];
'Halfe a seame of straw 7d': [torn];
'3 seames of watter 6d': [torn];
[Sum torn.]
'Then received for this note': [torn].
'Nine shillings 5d I say': [torn].
[On reverse: '9th August 1655'].

'September 22 1655. Paid for mending the loke & the barr at South Gate': 1s 6d.

[Total expenditure in this year: £9 1s 2d.]

1655–56

Receiver Bernard Bartlett.

Receiver's Roll [N.B. This roll is in English]

[*m.1v.*] Pensions and fees paid to the mayor and other officers:

'To the fower Porters of the Gates of the said Cittie for their pencion': 16s;
'To the Porter of Westgate for Clensing the grates neere the Gate': 4s;
'To the Porter of Northgate for Clensing the grates there': 6s 8d;
'To the Porter of Westgate for keeping of the Keygate': 6s 8d.
[Total: £1 13s 4d.]

Receiver's Book

[f.3] 'Payments called extraordinarie disbursements 1655 1656 as follows . . .
Paid mending the locke at the Northgate': 1s 6d.
'Paid John Griffin for work done on the Towne Walls': 9s 11d.
'Paid mending the kay of the Kay Gate': 2s.
'Paid & given the prisoners & others when Mr Maior went the Murall walke': 10s;
'To the scholler in the Free Schoole that made an oration': 10s;
'Paid Mr Farthing towards his Banquett': 15s.
'Paid for work done on the lodg at Westgate': 2s 7d.

[f.4] 'Paid Fox bringing sand to mend the howses on the walls': 4s 8d.
'Paid Walter Strangg & others for worke done on the howses on the wales nere Northgate': £4 11s.
'Paid John Griffin for work done at Eastgate': 18s 11d.

[f.5] 'Paid for aples when Mr Maior went the Murallia walke': 2s 6d.
[Total: £8 8s 1d.]

[Total expenditure in this year: £10 1s 5d.]

1656–57

Receiver Henry Prigg.

Receiver's Roll [N.B. This roll is in English]

[m.2v.] Pensions and fees paid to the mayor and other officers:

[m.1v.] 'To the fower porters of the Gates of the said Cittie for their pencion': 16s;
'To the Porter of Westgate for Clensing the grates neere the Gate': 4s;
'To the Porter of Northgate for Clensing the Grates there': 6s 8d;
'To the Porter of Westgate for keeping of the Keygate': 6s 8d.
[Total: £1 13s 4d.]

Receiver's Book

[f.3] 'Paymentes Called extraordinarie disbursments . . .
Given severall persons at Mr Mayors perambulation . . .': £2 6s.

[f.5] 'Paid Mr Can for worke done at Westgate & for soder': 6s 8d.

[f.6] 'Paid John Ellis for 2 doores one at Westgate and the other without Eastgate': 5s 6d.
'Paid John Fox for worke done at Northgate': 4s 8d;
'Paid him more for worke done at Westgate': 10s 8d.
[Total: £3 13s 6d.]

[Total expenditure in this year: £5 6s 10d.]

1657–58

Receiver Henry Gandy.

Receiver's Roll [N.B. This roll is in English]

[m.1v.] Pensions and fees paid to the mayor and other officers:
'To the fower porters of the Gates of the said Citty for their pencion': 16s;
'To the porter of Westgate for Clensing the Grates neere the Gate': 4s;
'To the porter of Northgate for Clensing the Grates there': 6s 8d;
'To the porter of Westgate for keeping of the Keygate': 6s 8d.
[Total: £1 13s 4d.]

Receiver's Book

[f.3] 'Payments . . .
Paid for mending the wickett of the gate att Westgate': 3s.
'Given to Mr Bradford for his boyes orations': 15s;
'Given more to the poore prisoners in the High Gaole': 5s;
'Given more to the poore in goeing about the murall walke': 9s.

[f.6] 'Paid John Wood for filling upp a trench att the higher end of Southenhaye as by a note': £2.
[Total: £3 12s 0d.]

[Total expenditure in this year: £5 5s 4d.]

1658–59

Receiver Walter Deeble.

Receiver's Roll [N.B. This roll is in English]

[m.2v.] Pensions and fees paid to the mayor and other officers:

[m.1v.] 'To the fower Porters of the Gates of the said Citty for their pencion': 16s;
'To the Porter of Westgate for clensing the grates nere the gate': 4s;
'To the Porter of Northgate for clensing the grates there': 6s 8d;
'To the Porter of Westgate for keeping the Keygate': 6s 8d.
[Total: £1 13s 4d.]

Receiver's Book

[f.3] 'Payments betweene Michaelmas 1658 and Michaelmas 1659 as follows:

Paid for Stones and worke done att Southgate': 15s 11d.
'Paid the Porters for opening the gates by night to the souldiers in their watching': 5s.
'Paid for clensing the vaut att Southgate as by a note': 5s 4d.
'Paid & given the schollers of the Free Schoole att the goeing about the Murall Walke': 18s;
'More paid & given the prisoners the same time': 6s;
'More paid then for Aples for the boyes': 3s 6d.
'Paid Thomas Kelland & 9 others for worke done in filling and leavelling severall pitts in Southenhaye as by a note': £3 7s 1d.

[f.4] 'Paid workemen att Southgate as by a note': 5s 10d;
'Paid them more as by another note': 9s 11d;
'Paid them more as by another note': £1 7s 4d;
'Paid them more as by another note': £1 2s;
'Paid them more as by another note': 7s;
'Paid them more as by another note': 18s 5d;
'Paid for worke on Southgate as by a note': 16s 11d;
'Paid for other worke there as by a note': £1 4s 11d;
'Paid for worke done att Southgate as by a note': £2 1s 4d;
'Paid Lewes Greenslade Carpenter for other worke there done as by note': £2 16s 11d;
'Paid Nicholas Bond Blacksmyth for worke done att Southgate as by a note': £4 7s 10d;
'Paid for worke done att Southgate as by a note': 10s;
'Paid John Griffyn Mason for worke done att Southgate as by a note': 11s 5d.

[f.5] 'Paid for worke done att Westgate as by a note': 5s 6d.
'Paid for worke done att Southgate as by a note': £1 13s 3d;
'Paid for other worke there done as by a note': £1 16s 9d;
'Paid for worke done att Southgate & Backgrate for carrying ruble': £1 6s 10d.
[Total: £28 13s 0d.]

[Total expenditure in this year: £30 6s 4d.]

1659–60

Receiver William Bruen.

Receiver's Roll

[m.2v.] Pensions and fees paid to the mayor and other officers:

[m.1v.] Paid the 4 porters of the gates of the city for their pension: 16s;
Paid the porter of West Gate for cleansing the grates for conducting rainwater there: 4s;
Paid the porter of North Gate for similar labour there: 6s 8d;
Paid the porter of Watergate for his pension: 6s 8d.
[Total: £1 13s 4d.]

Receiver's Book

[f.3] 'Extraordinary Payments . . .
Paid John Griffing for worke at Key Gate by note': 18s 6d.
'Paid and given the schollers of the Free Schoole at the Perambulacion': £1;
'Paid to the prisoners in Castle Lane and Southgate': 13s;
'Paid for Aples for the boyes': 4s 3d;
'Paid for Carriage of Aples and attendance at ye Murallie Walke': 3s 6d.

[f.4] 'Paid for mending the Towne Wall by Sneal Tower to Thomas Hill': 12s.

[f.6] 'Paid Richard Taylor for worke done at Northgate by note': £8 13s 11d.
'Paid John Griffen for mending the Cittie Wall by note': £1 5s 2d.
'Paid Henry Taylor for worke on the Towne Wall by note': 2s.
[Total: £13 12s 4d.]

[Total expenditure in this year: £15 5s 8d.]

EXPENSES IN REPELLING PERKIN WARBECK, 1497

This extraordinary account, which is taken from the Receiver's Roll for 1496–7, lists the sums of money which were laid out by the citizens during Perkin Warbeck's assault on Exeter in September 1497.

[*m.3*] Expenses within the city for repelling Perkyn Usbeck and his rebels:

Firstly paid for 382 *lbs* of 'Gunpowder' bought from diverse men at 6*d* a *lb*: £10 17*s*;

For 2 hogsheads of wine bought and sent to North Gate and East Gate: 40*s*;

For 2 barrels of 'beer' sent to the said gates: 8*s*;

For carriage of 'lez gonnez' to (*ad*) the City Gates: 9*d*;

For 2 men called 'Gonners' for 2 days and nights: 2*s*;

For 6 other 'Gonners' hired for 4 days and nights, each at 12*d per* day and night: 24*s*;

For 500 *lbs* of lead to make 'ledyn peletts' at 5*s per* 100 *lbs*: 25*s*;

For making those 'peletts': 6*s* 8*d*;

Paid for 7 sheaves of arrows bought at 16*d* a sheaf: 9*s* 4*d*;

For 'lez arrow heddez': 3*s* 4*d*;

Paid men to remove 'lez bulworks' to allow men to enter the city: 2*s*;

For 4 'Gonners' hired for 1 day: 4*s*;

Paid men to make 'lez bulwarkez': 8*d*;

Paid Thomas Andrewe for 1½ *cwt* of iron bought and lost at North Gate: 6*s*;

Paid for 400 *lbs* of lead bought and lost at East Gate at 5*s* for 100 *lbs*: 20*s*;

Paid for 1 *cwt* of iron [bought and] used: 4*s*;

Paid John Sengell for several ironwork tasks (*operibus ferreis*) both for 'lez Gonners' and for iron nails and other necessities, as appears in the book of expenditure shown on this account [lost]: 12*s* 11½*d*;

Paid for 'Tampionz' for 'lez Gonners': 4*s* 8*d*;

[*m.3v.*] Paid for 1 man to seek and salvage broken iron lost at North Gate: 4*d*;

For carriage of 1 piece of timber to West Gate to support 1 'Gonne': 4*d*;

For 1 piece of timber bought for 'le Stokkyng' of a 'Gonne': 16*d*;

To men hired to make that piece by night: 14*d*;

Paid a certain King's messenger [?] with letters, as a reward: 3*s* 4*d*;

For candles used both at the City Gates and at the Guildhall for the men charged to watch the city: 3*s* 2*d*;

Paid a certain King's messenger [?] sent with letters of proclamation between the said lord the King and the Scots: 20*d*;

Paid for certain horses bought to serve the King's servant called 'lez postez': 10*s*;

Paid Brian Grene, the city's messenger [?], sent to Cornwall to the Earl of Devon: 8*s* 4*d*;

[Total: £21 ½*d*].

[Source: DRO, Exeter Receiver's Roll, 1496–7.]

DOCUMENT 3

EXTRACTS FROM THE CHAMBER ACT BOOKS, 1511–1545

These extracts from the earliest surviving Chamber act books all relate to the expenditure of money on the city enceinte: expenditure which is not otherwise recorded in the surviving sequence of receivers' accounts. In addition to a series of Chamber orders connected with the rebuilding of East Gate during 1511–13, the extracts include two orders of 1528 directing that £10 should be spent on the city walls yearly; three orders of the 1540s concerning the payment of various fines towards the upkeep of the enceinte and a list of contributions which the members of the Council of Twenty-Four made to the 'Benevolence', or voluntary gift, of 1545.

Chamber Act Book 1, 1509–38

[*f.19*] 8 March 1511
'East Gate
The whiche aggre that Robert Poke of Thorverton shall bilde & make Estgate & the Cite to fynde all maner of stuffe & he to have for his labor £28 & to bilde 6 botores'.

[*f.20*] 18 March 1511
'Also they aggre that [blank] Vawterd shall take downe Estgate & whan it is taken downe he to caste all the sonde & rubbyll, havyng for his labor 26*s* 8*d*'.

[*f.25*] 16 December 1511
'The whiche aggre that Mr Andrewe, for his attendance and laying oute of money for [superscript: 'the bildyng of '] Est Gate, shall have for his rewarde the libertie & fredom of his son Richard'.
'Also they aggre that John Bradmore, late ressevor of this Cite, shall paye unto Mr Andrewe for the money whiche Mr Andrewe laid oute for Est Gate £30'.

[*f.29v.*] 20 March 1512
'The whiche aggre also that the Ressevor shall sell 6 acres of Duryurde wode for the bildyng of Estgate'.

[*f.45*] 30 September 1513
'Item they aggre that Nicholas Abell, Stayner, shalbe mad freman of this Cite, payng nothyng for his fyne excepte he shall paynte the tabernacle & the Kyng in the Est Gate with goolde lyce & oyle, all the hole fronte that is to be paynted at his owne propre costes and charges and suretys for fulfyllyng of the same John Calwodley thelder & John More and the Cite to geve unto the seid Nicholas 40*s*'.

[*f.121*] 21 April 1528
'£10 upon walls yerelye
Whiche holy agre that every Recever frome hensforth for the tyme beyng shalbe stawe apone the Citie Wallys £10 yerely with owt there be a resonabyll lett or cause

shawyd & seyn by Mr Mair & Brotheren for the tyme beyn and that there shall be 4 mene of the number of 24 to have the over seyth of the sayd byldyng by the Nomenacion of Mr Mair for the tyme beyn and here follow the namys of the 4 mene that now be apoynted by Mr Mair viz. William Hurste Mr Henry Hamlyn Robert Hoker & William Peryham'.

[*f.121v.*] 14 July 1528
'They also agree that Mr Receyvor shall have owte of the Comyn Coffer £10 towards the buyldyng of the Cytie Walles, now beyng in werke at the West Gate, the whiche wasse delyveryd hem this present day parcell of the arrages [i.e. arrears] apon the accompt of John Holmer the yonger & the resydue of thit mony wasse put yn the Comyng Coffer'.

Chamber Act Book 2, 1509–60

[*f.58*] 12 September 1542
'Which day Mr White recevor of the Cetie hath made his offer for as mych as he shall be dischargid for his dener att Michaelmas to pay for the recompens of the same £5 sterling to [be] bestawit uppon the walles, the which £5 is payd to John Maynerd recever of the Cetie'.
'Item that John Holmer doyth confesse & grant to pay to the Cities Walles 66*s* 8*d*'.

[*f.68v.*] 30 July 1545
'A benevolens to the walls reparacions.
Which holy agree that ther shalbe a certayne benevolens Getherid amongs the Comons of the Cetie for the mayntenans & makyn of the walles of the Cettie for the defens of the Cetie & the Kynges enmys nowe yn the tyme of the warrs. Which benevolens schalbe getherid by the good wylles of the inhabitans of the Cetie by 2 honyst men assigned by Mr Meer of every parishe with yn this Cetie'.
[A list of contributions from the members of the Chamber is given as follows:]
From Thomas Prestwode, mayor, 10*s*;

From William Hurst 10s;
From Henry Hamlyn 5s;
From John Britnall 5s;
From John Blakealler 5s;
From Thomas Hunt 5s;
From William Bucknam 5s;
From Gilbert Kirke 6s 8d;
From William Peryham 5s;
From John Buller 5s;
From Robert Toker 3s 4d;
From John Holmer 2s 6d;
From John Midwynter 5s;
From John Maynard 3s 4d;
From John Wolcote 2s 6d;
From Nicholas Lymet 3s 4d;
From John Tuckefyld 3s 4d;

From Richard Colwyll 3s 4d;
From Richard Ratclyfe 6s 8d;
From John Thomas 2s 6d;
From John Drake 3s 4d;
From Thomas Spurway 5s;
From William Tottell 3s 4d;
Sum £5 11s 10d.

[f.70] 21 September 1545

'Item is dely is delyvered [sic] for a certayne horsse that was thif stolyn & the partie putt yn gage for the seid horse 10s yn case he can attayne the seid thif for the felonious takyn of the seid horse then to have his 10s agayne which 10s is delivered to Mr Thomas Prestwode & was bestowyd yn his Charges for the newe makyn of the Ceties Walles'.

PURCHASE OF ORDNANCE FOR THE CITY, 1545

During the French invasion scare of 1545, the Exeter Chamber decided to purchase a collection of artillery pieces to strengthen the city defences. The first of these extracts from the contemporary act book records the names of those who were appointed to buy the guns, the details of the weapons they bought and the sums of money which the members of the Council of Twenty-Four and two other prominent citizens offered to lend to the city in order to pay for the new ordnance. The two subsequent extracts list the actual amounts of money which were handed over soon afterwards for this purpose—including two payments of guns 'in kind'— and the repayments which were eventually made to the councillors, their heirs and assignees in 1547.

Chamber Act Book 2, 1509–60

[Extract 1]

[*f.67v.*] 18 June 1545

'An Acte made [for] the provision of the ordynances for the Cetie . . .

Provision for ordinances or great Gunnes

Which wholy agre that, wher as every of the 24 have of ther good willes leyn to be disbursid such summys of mony as it apperith uppon every mannys hedd, that when so ever any nede shall requyer for the sayd besynys or that they & every of them shall pay, uppon request therof made, the one moytie or halfyndell of all such sumez uppon them assessid and the other moytie to be payd after that tyme when so ever any other nede for defens of the said Cetie shall happen'.

'And also all such sumez of mony that any person shall disburse or ly oute as is aboveseid, the said persons shalbe repayd ageyn of the revenys & proffits of the Cetie att the next accompte'.

'Also ther is appoynted to b[u]y ordynances for the Cetie *videlicet* John Wolcote John Thomas & John Drake And they to receve the mony of every man as is above seid'.

'*Nota* payd to John Thomas for the gunnys & ordynances £39 3s 4d;

Wherof payd for 2 slynges & 3 half slynges bought att Dertmouth [Dartmouth] oute of the hulke with 9 Chambers £18;

Item for Charges for preysyng of the gonnys & freyght 8s 10d;

Item payd to Skydmore for 3 peeces of ordynances £12;

Item paid to Mr Wolcote for 2 doble versis & 1 syngle verse £6 13s 4d;

Item for Cariage of the Gonnys to Opham [Topsham] & to Exeter 14s 10d;

Item for the expensis for 5 days 13s 4d;

Summa Totalis £38 10s 4d;

Et remanet 13s'.

[A total of 26 contributors and each individual's assessment are listed as follows:]

Thomas Prestwode, mayor, 10 marks;
Robert Toker £4;
William Hurst 10 marks;
Henry Hamlyn £5;
John Britnall £5;
John Blakealler £4;
William Peryham £5;
Thomas Hunte £5;
Thomas Spurway £5;
William Bucknam £5;
John Buller £4;
John Holmer £3;
John Midwynter £4;
John Maynerd £3;
John Wolcote 40s;
Nicholas Lymet £3;
John Tuckefild £3;
Richard Colwyll £3;
John Thomas 40s;
John Drake £4;
Gilbert Kyrke £5;
Richard Ratclyff £4;
William Tottyll 40s;
Hugh Pope 40s;
William Webbe £3 6s 8d;
William Hals 20s.

[Extract 2]

[*f.68*] [Monies received from the above assessments are listed as follows:]

From Mr Mayor [Thomas Prestwood] 5 marks;
From Mr Blakealler 40s;
From John Drake 40s;
From John Tuckfyld 30s;
From Thomas Spurway 50s;
From Thomas Hunte 50s;
From William Tottyll 20s;
From Mr Peryham 50s;
From Richard Colwyll 30s;
From John Buller 40s;

From William Bucknam 50*s*;
From John Holmer 30*s*;
From Robert Toker 40*s*;
From John Midwynter 40*s*;
From Henry Hamlyn 50*s*;
From John Thomas 20*s*;
From William Hurst 5 marks;
From Nicholas Lymett 30*s*;
From Richard Ratclyff 40*s*;
'Item payd by Mr John Bricknoll yn ordynances bought of Stawell 50*s*';
'Item payd by Mr Gilbert Kirke yn ordynances bought of Stowell 50*s*';
From John Wolcote, merchant, 20*s*;
Sum £45 3*s* 4*d*.

[Extract 3]

[*f.82v.*] 16 March 1547
'. . . £40 9*s* 3*d* is payd to the masters of the 24 for ther mony that they laid oute for the Ordynances of the Cetie as apperith by the acte before made the 18 day of June . . . [1545] yn the tyme that Mr Prestwode was Meyor as herafter foloyth . . .'

[*f.83*] [Payments made to members of the Chamber are listed, as follows:]
To Mr Britnall 50*s*;
To William Hurst 66*s* 8*d*;
To Henry Hamlyn 50*s*;
To John Blakealler 40*s*;
To William Peryham 50*s*;
To Thomas Hunte 50*s*;
To Thomas Spurway 50*s*;
To William Bucknam 50*s*;
To John Buller 40*s*;
To Thomas Prestwode 66*s* 8*d*;
'Item to Mr Prestwode for John Holmer for that Mr Prestwode leyd oute for hem upon the walles 30*s*';
To John Midwynter 40*s*;
To John Wolcote 20*s* 'by the hands of Mr Britnall';
To William Totthill 20*s*;
To Richard Colwyll 30*s*;
To Nicholas Lymett 30*s* 'delyveryd to John Tuckefilld recever';
To John Tuckfild 30*s*;
To John Thomas 20*s*;
To John Drake 40*s*;
'Item to the hands of Mr John Britnall Meer for Mr Kirkes mony 50*s*';
To Richard Ratclyff's wife 40*s*.
'*Summa* of this payment afforeseid £37 16*s* 8*d*;
& remaynyth 52*s* 7*d* wherof is payd to Mr Prestwode for that he layd oute to the walles as apperith upon his accompte 36*s* 8*d*;
Et remaynyth 15*s* 11*d* delyveryd to John Tuckefild and Chargid yn his Accompt'.

DOCUMENT 5

EXPENSES IN THE 'COMMOTION', 1549

More has been written about the Prayer Book Rebellion of 1549—'the Commotion' as it was known to contemporaries—than about almost any other event in the history of the Tudor South West. Yet, as one eminent scholar of sixteenth-century Devon has recently observed, documentary evidence relating to the disturbances of 1549 remains tantalizingly slight, and little new information has emerged since the publication of Frances Rose-Troup's pioneering study of the revolt in 1913. The two newly discovered documents which are reproduced below cast fresh light on this most mysterious and intriguing of Tudor rebellions. Drawn up by Alderman William Hurst and Mayor John Blackaller—two prominent members of the Exeter Chamber—the documents are financial accounts, or bills of charge, which list the monies expended by the two men on the city's behalf during the fateful summer of 1549. Most of the entries relate to defensive measures undertaken during the rebel siege of Exeter between 2 July and 6 August. Hurst and Blackaller presented their accounts to the city authorities for repayment a few weeks later and it may well be that other members of the governing elite submitted similar bills. This is not the place to interrogate the accounts in detail (those entries which make specific reference to the town defences have already been drawn on in the general discussion of the siege which appears in Chapter 5). It should be noted in passing, however, that the bills expand our knowledge of the rebellion in several significant ways: not least by underlining the severity of the punishments which were subsequently handed out to the defeated rebels. Both sets of accounts refer to the erection of gallows, while Blackaller's reference to 'the first payre of galaws made' has an especially sinister ring to it.

[NB—Because the original manuscripts are scrappy, damaged in places and written in unusually villainous hands, a handful of words have proved impossible to decipher. Rough approximations of all such words are provided in the transcriptions below.]

Document 1

[*f.1*] 'Here after folloithe all sowche things as I, Wyllhelmus Hurst, have dellvyeryd owt for the Cytie of Exetror syncs the 9 day of Julyi *in anno* 1549
Item dellyveryd Wyllhelmus Cook for the sytie 4 *lbs* of bremstoune at 2*d*': 8*d*;
'Item mor bowght of Gombyes wyff quarter of oyelle at': 8*d*;
'Item mor dellyveryd Mr Drack 12 dohell platts at 8*d*': 8*s*;
'Mor 100 of borde naylls at': 12*d* [crossed out];
'Item mor to Barnarde Dovell & master Drack 100 hachenaylls': 6*d* [crossed out];
'Mor dellyveryd Robart Hont & to Wylylmus Cook to paye labrows [labourers]': 20*s*;
'Mor dellyveryd Harry Mander steward for to bye bowes for the syties': 40*s*;
'Item mor dellyveryd unto Norbrooke to paye Laberowes': 5*s* 2*d*;
'Mor dellyveryd Mr Cary 8 bords off ellme for to mack paveses at the walls over West Yeat': 6*s* 8*d*;
'Item mor dellyveryd to ye mackyng of the mownt 100 naylls at': 12*d* [crossed out];
'Mor dellyveryd master Drack [hole in paper]': 50*s*;
'Item mor dellyveryd Thomas Ellet to mack corn powder 5 *lbs* of Sarpentyn powder at': 5*s* [sum crossed out] 2*s* 6*d*;
'Item mor dellyveryd unto Sir Roger Blewet & Barnard Dovell for to mack bawerycks 100 [?] yards [?] of fyne creger [?] at': 52*s*;

'Item mor dellyveryd to the mackyng of the mownt & otherwys in Lyer Kas[?] & mands to the vallew of': 16*s*;
'More to the Reserver 50 hayche naylys': 3*d*;
'Received but': 2*d*;
'4 styds of sqware tymbar of 7 fot the pes and 1 bords of 7 fott at': 16*d* [crossed out] 8*d* [crossed out];
'Item mor dellyveryd Thomas Ellot [superscript: Emet (?)] 6 *lbs* of powder at': 6*s* [sum crossed out] 3*s*;
'Item mor dellyveryd unto Master Ennes the gonneres brother 4 *lbs* powder': 4*s* [sum crossed out] 2*s*;
'Mor to Levermore servaunt Westoren & Hychenng at to sondry tymes 12 *lbs* of powder': 12*s* [sum crossed out] 6*s*;
'Mor to Norgat dellyveryd for the Rampyre 5 ellmen bords at 7 fot': 2*s* 6*d*;

[*f.1v.*] 'Item mor dellyveryd unto Hychenng Mores Levarmores servaunt 6 *lbs* of powder': 6*s* [sum crossed out] 3*s*;
'More delyveryd Morets Levermore ys servant Wetteryn & Heychens': £12 12*s* [crossed out];
'Item mor dellyveryd to James Power and Sir John ['Hart' crossed out] Williames for the sytie 16 *lbs* powder at 12*d*': 16*s* [sum crossed out] 8*s*;
'Item more paid Mr Becham': £6 13*s* 4*d*;
'Item more to master Cary': 40*s*;
'Item mor dellyveryd Mr Cortenny 3 Large sprews skynnes att 8*s* the pes Some': 24*s*;
'Mor 4 wen lode tymeber to make the galowys att 10*s*': 40*s*;

'Item to Rychard Prestewod 100 lathes': 6*d*;
£21 18*s* [*sic*: although the figures in fact appear to
amount to £23 4*s* 5*d*].
'Sum of the payment affor seid': £21 18*s*;
'Item more delyveryd to Mr Buckman after this
Accompt the Sum of': 20*s*.

[*f.2*] 'The accompt of Mr Hurst.
A bell for the Cetty of £22 18*s* the furst of September
1549'.
'Mr Hursts byll of chargs in the commotion'.
'The Chargs of Mr William Hurst'.

[*f.2v.*] 'Received of Isork Bellewter 2 bowes and 4 sheves of
arrowes whytch the syte most pay for: nott Chargid'.
'*Summa* of the payments': £20 4*s* 5*d*;
'*Et debet* 15*s* 7*d* payd to Mr Buckman for the payment
of the mason the Saturday the 30 of August'.

[Total sum spent on the defences by Hurst: £22 18*s* (?).]

Document 2

[*f.1*] '[The] accompte of Mr John Blakealler mayor of the
Cetie of Exeter maken before William [. . .] Midwynter
& others the 23 of August Anno . . . Edward VI 3 [i.e.
1549]

In primis Recevyd by me of John Soowell for that mony
that he Recevyd oute of the Comyng Cofer to by Corne
& malt the Sume of': £20;
'*Summa*': £20.

'Item Recevyd of the Seid Soowell for the proffit of the
Sale of the seid Corne': 20*s*;
'*Summa*': 20*s*.

'*Summa Totalis* Receipts': £21.
'Wherof payd in Chargs of the Cetie as herafter foloyth
Payd to Mr Hull [?] one of the burgis of the parliament
for his Charges [. . .] the parlyment for the Cety's affirs
upon his accompte by the [. . .] the 24': £9 14s 2d *
'[Item pay]d to the Towneclerke att Easter terme *Anno*
. . . Edward VI 3 towards his Ch[arges in the] Cety's
besynys': 41*s* *
'[Item payd] to Lancastell for 56 *lbs* of gonnepowder':
28*s*;
'[Item payd] to the seid Lancaster [*sic*] for 8 *lbs* of
powder': 4*s*;
'[Item to] 2 men that brought yn Gibbis man': 6*s*;
'[Item] to my lord Gray is milstrells of reward': 4*s*;
'[Item] payd ? [illegible] the Ciridge [?] of the first
payre of gallaws made': 12*d*;
'Item payd to the Trumpetters that cam with my lord
levetenant': 15*s*;
'Item payd to one that went for masons for the Cetie
Walls': 8*d*;

'Item payd Thomas Tolmey': [blank];
'Item payd to Harry Mawnder for the Cety's besynys':
41*s*;
'Item payd unto William Chirche for the Cetie 50
hacchenayls': 4*d*;
'Item payd to Vyell [?] for the Cetie 50 hacchenaylls &
50 bordnayls': [13*d*—crossed out] 12*d*;
'Item payd to Sawlus [?] to wayt 100 hacchenayls': 4*d*;
'[Item] payd to the workemen 100 hacchenayls for
pavycs': [10*d*—crossed out] 8*d*;
'[Item] payd to Splatt one yron shott weyyng 5 *lbs*
quarter att 3*d* the *lb*': 15*d*;
'[Item pay]d for [30—crossed out] 26 *lbs* of pawder att
5*d* the *lb* amount': 10*s* 10*d*;
'[Item payd] Thomas Ducke for Clensyng of the wheyt
that was recevyd [. . .] ? [illegible]': 8*d*;
'[. . .] hem also for hes attendans to the receyt of the
wheyt': 12*d*;
'*Summa*': £17 7*s* 11*d* [*sic*: in fact, £17 10*s* 11*d*].

[*f.1v.*] 'Item payd to Rycherd Hauks & James Clase for 6
days attendens a pece of them [. . .] ? [illegible] of
Cattall that cam frome the campe taken frome the
rebellorns': 4*s*;
'[. . .] Thomas Ducke Richerd Martyne Walter Martyne
for 4 days also': 5*s* 4*d*;
'[. . .] to Thomas Ducke & Thomas Treble for 2 days
every of them': 16*d*;
'Item payd to Splatt for 7 days after Seynt John is day
after 8*d* the day unto the 2nd day of *Julii*': 4*s* 8*d*;
'Item payd to Splatt for 14 days after the comyng of my
lord privy Seale is Comyng to the Cetie frome the
Saturday Seynt Laurans day unto the Sonday uppon
Seynt Bartholomewe is day after 12*d* the day': 14*s*;
'Item to Water Marten for 7 days after Seynt John is
day att 8*d* the day untill the 2nde day of *Julii*': 4*s* 8*d*;
'Item pad [*sic*] to Water Marten for 6 days before the
Sonday after Bartolomewe is day [. . .] 8*d* the day': 4*s*;
'[. . .] William Knolls for the same for 4 day this last
wyke': 2*s* 8*d*;
'[. . .] James Bore A nother gonner for 6 days': 4*s*;
'[. . .] John Croke A nother gonner for 7 days': 4*s* 8*d*;
'[. . .] to Water Marten for 2 pounde of gon
[superscript: 'Corne'] pouder 2*s*;
'[. . .] payd to Ducke for 10 pillitts wayyng 24 pounde
of yron shoytt for Gonnys': 4*s* 2*d*;
'[. . .] payd to Ducke for a Gon & Chambers of a basse':
12*d*;
'*Summa*': 56*s* 6*d*.

[Total sum laid out on the defences by Blakealler:
£8 12*s* 3*d*.]

[N.B. those items of expenditure marked with an asterisk
' * ' have not been included in this total.]

[Source: DRO, Exeter Receivers' Vouchers, Box 1.]

DOCUMENT 6

LIST OF THE CITY ORDNANCE, 1556

This detailed breakdown of all the weapons which were in the Chamber's possession in the fourth year of Queen Mary's reign was compiled by John Hooker, the city chamberlain: a man who—fortunately for posterity—had a passion for lists and catalogues of all sorts. It includes a collection of arms which were on semi-permanent loan from Francis Russell, second Earl of Bedford, the city's aristocratic patron.

'The ordynance & artyllerye of the Lord Fraunces Erle of Bedford, delyvered to the Custody of the Cittie of Exon by Mr Gyles Gefry, surveyor to the saide Lorde
Inprimis delyvered the 22th day of [August—crossed out] September 1556:
14 hedde bylls;
48 blacke bylls;
57 pykes whereof 2 lacke hedds;
2 chasyng stafes;
63 shovells [showed] with Iron;
6 stopes [?];
150 shefes of Arowes;
17 sycles;
46 iron shote of sacres;
102 ledde shote of fawkenettes;
284 matches;
20 handgonnes whereof one is broken;
2 basses with 3 chambers;
2 bowes & 3 endes;
9 chestes;
2 beames of a tent;
A chest of broken harneys fast nailed;
4 barells of gonne powder weyng 444 [?] with the barells;
Item the last day of August:
2 sacres of Iron cast;
3 porte peces & a halfe slynge;
9 chambers.
The ordnance & artillerie of, or apperteninge to, the Citie of Exon and lieing within Saynt Johns at the East Gate of the Citie & delyvered by me John Hoker to thandes or Custodie of William Knolles cutler & gonner of the Citie the 24 of February 1559
Inprimis one pece of ordinance called a three quarter slinge with too Chambers & a forelocke to the same belonginge;
Item 8 halfe slinges with 8 Chambers & so many Iron forelocks;
Item 9 foulers with Chambers & forelocks;
Item 3 whole peces without Chambers;
Too quarter slynges with Chambers & forlockes;
Item 2 serpentynes with Chambers & forelocks;
9 basses with Chambers & forelocks;
Item 30 tymbers [?] whereof 12 be for greate ordinance;
Item 3 broken peces;
Item 3 forelockes;
7 ladells for cast peces;
Item 2 lytle gonnes whereof one is of brasse;
Item a chest with a key & locke;
Item a Chest full of shotte;
Item 6 Prichelles [?] & a fuller;
A great stage;
Item a barell of gonne powder;
Item 40 picks;
Item 58 pykes & 6 Chambers of therle of Beddfords'.

[Source: DRO, ECA, Book 57, Memorandum Book of John Hooker.]

INSTRUCTIONS FOR THE DEFENCE OF THE CITY, 1643

These orders were issued by the Parliamentarian authorities in Exeter in January 1643. Designed to safeguard the city against future Royalist attacks, they illustrate the exceptionally wide-ranging nature of the defensive measures which were undertaken at Exeter during the Civil War. Of those who are mentioned by name in the document, 'Captain [Peter] Baxter' was the city's retained 'engineer', or military expert, while 'Generall Stamford' was parliament's overall commander in the South West. 'Doctor [Anthony] Salter', 'Mr [James] Rodes' and 'Thomas Orchard' were all Royalist sympathizers whom the city authorities suspected of plotting to admit the Cavalier forces. (N.B.—words placed in parenthesis are taken from a rough draft of the original document.)

'Anno 1642. January. 23th daye.

1. That the Magasin be forthwith viewed & made up as follows:

Powder.	80 Barrils
Match:	40 *C* waight
Musket Bullets of severall sizes	30 *C* weight
Carbine Bullets	04 *C* weight

   Cannon Shott. 1,000 of severall sizes *per* the gunners' direccion.

   Two chambers to every stock fowler & 2 or 3 stock fowlers more to be procured.
2. That more gunners be procured, men to be confided in.
3. That a douzen iron rods with wormes & scowrers be made for the musketts, & some to be at each gate & the Castle.
4. That 4 or 5 companyes of volunteers of the country be procured.
5. That 40 inhabitants of the citty, men to be confided in, may be added to the captains & officers of the volunteers to take their turnes to be over the watches at the severall *corpe de gards*.
6. That some choice men be considdered for the Castle.
7. That the dikes (about the) citty be made deeper, & more falling & people summoned by the drum for expedition: & the walls & (houses) removed.
8. That the Great (Church) be kept continually shut & a guarde ther by night: & a trusty man to keep the keyes.
9. That flankers (be made, *per*) Captain Baxter's direction.
10. That turnepikes (be set at) each gate & att the bridge foot.
11. That dikes & drawbridges (be made) at each gate to prevent blowing up the (gate).
12. That Topsham (&) the (river be effectu)ally secured, & that (Powderham) Castle (be demolished) or secured, & Radford House fortified.
13. That some fortification be made (at) Cowley Bridge so as to command the way from Stoke [Stoke Canon].
14. That the remote parts of the suberbs be baricaded &c.
15. That there be a strict restraint of the prisoners & none suffered to speake with them, but by order of the Deputie Lieutenants, & in presence of the corporall of the watch, & (none to preach there but by permission).
16. (That all) malignants & disaffected (persons be secured or dismiste).
17. (That noe women) or children nor (howsehold goods be passed out of the citty without) order of the Deputie (Lieutenants).
18. (That in case) of fire some aldermen (be named with the sheriffe to cleer) the streets by a proclamacion: (that the Comitty may attend it) who are to prepare bucketts & crooks &c beforehand.
19. That all hay & straw be removed from about the Guildhall.
20. The proclamation be made to require every man to make povision of corne, pease, & other needfull thinges & also of fewell.
21. That hand mills be procured from the country &c, there being one in St Thomas parish.
22. That all disaffected persons be throughly disarmed & their howses dewly searched.
23. That, for securing the mills, the cliffs at Head-ware bee made good.
24. That St Davids hill be secured wher there's most command.
25. That the wall twixt Eastgate & the Castle be viewed, & that some common passage be opened & the High Geole & Orchard's howse be carefully looked unto having out-lets to the said wall & a hollow tower (in the said wale to be repaired) & a vaut from the Geole.
26. That Doctor Salter, Mr Rodes, Thomas Orchard and others who came lately in to be secured or put forth of the cittye.
27. That the Winners [Wynards] (be made goode and the) street before itt.
28. That the guildhall (without Eastgate) be secured for the passage from Paris (Street and the) lane going into Southenhay by Crosses the smith (to be) damned up.
29. That the trees in (Southenhay be) cut downe & brought into the cittye & (some of those) in the Bonney [Bonhay].
30. That the trees (in the) old church yard be carryed to every gate some.

31. That more *corps* (*de guard*) howses be appointed.
32. That strict (discipline may) be (observed) towards all souldiers that neglect (their) duty.
33. [torn] . . . particuler faithfull men to . . .[illegible] . . . that a considerable quantitie of match, bullet . . . balls, & if you can procure some morter peces, they will be very useful.
34. To order that some turnepikes, flankers, or galleries according to former description be made presently without the walls.
35. To take an exact muster of the men, and their armes which are now within this citty: as well trayners [i.e. members of the trained bands] as volunteers, & also those that are fitt to bare armes & have none, as also that each howse holder present to [blank] within his parish what quantity of armes & what sort of armes he hath within his howse, to the intent that on any extraordinary occasion they may be brought forth, & not otherwise: and if any shall refuse to certify the number of their armes, that those that doe soe shall be severely punished & loose their armes.
36. That this being done, Mr Mayor & the Deputyes expresse how many souldiers they think needfull to be called into the citty and when.
37. That one particuler time be assigned to meete to consult during these times & exactlie observed.
38. That an expresse be sent to the Parliament with desires for armes &c as above said.
39. That a letter be written to Generall Stamford to desire his care of this place.
40. That a constant courier . . . [illegible; 'be had'?] . . . for

to have intelligences, & scouts settled so that when one . . . [illegible; 'comes in'?] . . . another may goe out.

[Additional Directives]

[1] [torn] . . . round to . . . heapes of stones, which may be taken from the battlements, or turrets.
[2] The walls to be exactly searched without and within the walls in all houses & sellers that are adjoyning, specially Orchard's house at Eastgate, & Southgate prison.
[3] No watches to be sent to their courts of gard . . . [illegible; 'or'?] . . . to any quarter till examined if they have powder, match & bullets.
[4] Let all the centinells be firelocks & snapances.
[5] Let every souldier have 4 bandoleers of powder, 4 bullets, & 2 yards of match worne about his arme, & one to view them every pay daie, & allowe out of their wages for any thing mispent.
[6] No bells to ring for any dead, or clocks to strike, while the city is beseeged.
[7] A *corps de garde* to be kept in the old churchyard, & to sit in St Maries [St Mary Major] tower and bellfrie with 2 centinells on ye toppe of the tower.
[8] The watch to be set at an exact time at the ringing of Guildhall bell which shall ring, about ½ a quarter of an howre: and punishment for the absent & for late comers.
[9] All corporalls should be directed in what cases to beat an allarum.'

[Source: DRO, DD36995 A and B.]

LIST OF THE CITY ORDNANCE, 1643

This document lists all of the cannon which were mounted around the defensive perimeter at Exeter when the city was captured by the Royalists in September 1643. The Cavalier officer who compiled it clearly made his way around the city walls in a clockwise direction from the Castle, noting the position and the weight (in pounds) of each piece of ordnance as he went. Most of the gun-positions referred to stand in positions which remain readily identifiable to this day, but a handful are more obscure. Of these, 'Reeds Battery' lay between Quay Gate and West Gate, and 'Brodnidge battery' on the city wall at the end of Bradninch Lane (near the present-day Arts Centre). 'Horse Poole'—a sizeable pond in which the citizens of seventeenth-century Exeter were accustomed to water and wash their horses—lay just outside West Gate. The position of the 'Maine Guard' is uncertain, but it may well have been located in the north-west gateway of the Castle.

'A list of all such guns as are now on the Castle Walles and about the Citty of Exeter on batteries

In the south east of the Castle
2 high sacars all of iron, neare in weight—2,200 ⅓
1 sacar cut weigheth neere—2,100 ⅓

In the north west of the Castle
1 Demy culverin of iron neere—3,200
1 high sacar in weight neere—2,200
1 low sacar cut, neere—2,100

In Eastgate below
1 murtherer gros
1 iron drake in the blockhouse & a base with her chambers

On the other side on the toppe of the gate
2 mynyons of iron neere each—1,306

On the walles neere East Gate on the first and second
   batteries
2 low sacars neere in weight each—1,123

On the next battery
1 high sacar neere in weight—1,324

On the same walles neere Southgate
2 iron guns, one sacar, neere—1,520
1 mynyon neere in weight—1,125

In Southgate below
1 broken sacar

On the toppe of the gate
2 mynyons neere each—1,255

On the battery neere Southgate
1 mynion of iron neere in weight—1,283

On the Key Battery
2 mynyons of iron neere—1,211

On Reeds Battery
1 sacar yt was crack't but amended neere—2,231

Under Westgate
1 murtherer gros

At Horse Poole without the gate
2 iron guns, one high sacar, neere—2,522
1 long mynyon crack't, weight—935

On the Bridge
2 broken iron guns, one sacar & a faulcon

On the Snaile Tower battery
3 iron guns, one high sacar, neere—2,323
2 low sacars, weighing each—1,313

On the new battery near Northgate
1 high mynyon—910

On the toppe of Northgate
2 mynyons neere each—1,110

Under the gate
1 grosse murtherer

On Brodnidge battery on the walles neere the Castle
1 mynyon neere—1,124

All these are iron.

Below in the Castle
1 whole culverin of bras[s] whose mussell is broken away
   being on his field carriadge and wheeles

On the Maine Guard
1 drake of bras[s]

The store in the Magazeene in Exeter
Of powder   2,500
Match   10,000
Demyculverin shot 40
Sacar shot   90

Mynyon shot   60
Faulcon shot   40
Faulconet shot   20
Ravenet shot   [Blank]

Peeces of all kinds = 41'.

[Source: BL, Add.MSS, 27402, f.81.]

ANNUAL EXPENDITURE ON THE CITY DEFENCES, 1485–1660

TABLE

Key
— = Accounts missing
* = Imperfect data
+ = Maximum figure

Accounting Year	Expenditure recorded in the receivers' accounts			Additional expenditure			Total expenditure over the decade		
	£	s	d	£	s	d	£	s	d
1484–85	3	11	9						
1485–86	—								
1486–87	1	5	6						
1487–88	3	6	9						
1488–89	2	12	4						
1489–90	7	5	0½				18	1	4½
1490–91		13	10						
1491–92		12	0						
1492–93	1	12	1						
1493–94		12	4						
1494–95		15	0						
1495–96	29	6	9½	21	0	0½			
1496–97	3	3	2						
1497–98	18	1	1½						
1498–99	5	6	0						
1499–1500	21	15	4				102	17	8½
1500–01	32	08	6						
1501–02	2	12	0						
1502–03	—								
1503–04	2	9	11						
1504–05		12	6						
1505–06	5	3	9½						
1506–07		14	8						
1507–08		12	0*						
1508–09		12	0*						
1509–10		12	0*				45	17	4½
1510–11		12	0*						
1511–12		12	0*	59	6	8+			
1512–13		12	0*						
1513–14		12	0*	2	0	0			
1514–15		12	0*						
1515–16		12	0*						
1516–17		12	0*						
1517–18	—								
1518–19		12	0*						
1519–20		12	0*				66	14	8
1520–21		12	0*						

Accounting Year	Expenditure recorded in the receivers' accounts			Additional expenditure			Total expenditure over the decade		
	£	s	d	£	s	d	£	s	d
1521–22		12	0*						
1522–23	—								
1523–24	1	0	0						
1524–25		19	5½						
1525–26		15	10½						
1526–27	1	7	1						
1527–28	29	6	4						
1528–29	24	3	6						
1529–30		18	7				59	14	10
1530–31	32	18	10						
1531–32	—								
1532–33	2	1	4						
1533–34	2	3	4						
1534–35	4	11	2½						
1535–36		15	11						
1536–37		12	0*						
1537–38	1	2	9						
1538–39	20	12	6						
1539–40	241	4	4½				306	2	3
1540–41	—								
1541–42	20	12	0						
1542–43	28	8	0						
1543–44		12	0*						
1544–45	37	2	9+	39	3	4			
1545–46		12	0*						
1546–47	1	2	0						
1547–48		12	0						
1548–49	79	8	7						
1549–50	87	17	6	31	10	3	327	0	5
1550–51	48	18	9½						
1551–52		12	0*						
1552–53	—								
1553–54	87	17	11½						
1554–55		12	0						
1555–56	17	3	9						
1556–57	27	4	0½						
1557–58	—								
1558–59	68	5	11½+						
1559–60	8	4	5½*				258	18	11½
1560–61	12	16	0*						
1561–62	71	13	10½*						
1562–63	31	0	2½						
1563–64		16	0*						
1564–65		16	0*+	N.B. 109 8 9 spent on Watergate and the Quay					
1565–66	1	0	0*+	N.B. 104 15 8 spent on Watergate and the Quay					
1566–67		16	0*						
1567–68		16	0*						
1568–69	13	0	9*						
1569–70	1	9	4*				Between 134 4 2 and 348 8 7		
1570–71	22	4	4*						
1571–72	12	19	0½						
1572–73	2	0	0						
1573–74	12	6	5						
1574–75	1	2	8*						
1575–76	1	12	0						
1576–77	4	13	11						

Accounting Year	Expenditure recorded in the receivers' accounts			Additional expenditure			Total expenditure over the decade		
	£	s	d	£	s	d	£	s	d
1577–78	11	6	6						
1578–79	42	16	0*						
1579–80	42	13	7				153	14	5½
1580–81	3	17	8						
1581–82	33	4	1						
1582–83	91	17	6½						
1583–84	18	8	0						
1584–85	2	2	11						
1585–86	19	15	7						
1586–87	3	7	5						
1587–88	2	0	8+						
1588–89	8	19	9						
1589–90	2	13	7				186	7	2½
1590–91	30	6	7½						
1591–92	3	9	2						
1592–93	5	17	6						
1593–94	3	0	3						
1594–95	2	17	3						
1595–96	18	8	8						
1596–97	5	17	7						
1597–98	3	6	0						
1598–99	3	6	5						
1599–1600	8	14	0				85	3	5½
1600–01	18	12	8½						
1601–02	2	17	9						
1602–03	7	8	4						
1603–04	4	2	9						
1604–05	4	13	5						
1605–06	2	12	8						
1606–07	4	5	9½						
1607–08	1	13	4*						
1608–09	10	10	11*						
1609–10	4	13	0				61	10	8
1610–11	3	7	9						
1611–12	5	13	5						
1612–13	17	17	10						
1613–14	10	1	3½						
1614–15	3	19	2						
1615–16	5	2	1						
1616–17	20	7	7						
1617–18	3	11	6						
1618–19	18	11	9						
1619–20	6	16	5				95	8	9½
1620–21	1	0	0*						
1621–22	1	13	4*						
1622–23	3	10	5*						
1623–24	2	3	10						
1624–25	4	14	0						
1625–26	11	8	1						
1626–27	1	13	4*						
1627–28	6	10	4						
1628–29	6	8	0						
1629–30	3	1	6				42	2	10
1630–31	3	2	6						
1631–32	23	14	3						
1632–33	33	19	0						
1633–34	44	14	8						
1634–35	24	14	10						
1635–36	14	15	4						
1636–37	23	19	3						

Accounting Year	Expenditure recorded in the receivers' accounts			Additional expenditure			Total expenditure over the decade		
	£	s	d	£	s	d	£	s	d
1637–38	16	10	0						
1638–39	2	3	4*						
1639–40	33	8	7*				221	1	9
1640–41	119	5	5*						
1641–42	—								
1642–43	173	16	9	4,374	0	0			
1643–44	369	17	10½						
1644–45	171	3	8						
1645–46	24	18	7*						
1646–47	11	9	0*						
1647–48	7	13	0*						
1648–49	4	18	9*						
1649–50	1	17	8*				5,259	0	8½
1650–51	17	14	0*						
1651–52	8	14	8*						
1652–53	7	8	1*						
1653–54	6	4	1+						
1654–55	9	1	2						
1655–56	10	1	5						
1656–57	5	6	10						
1657–58	5	5	4						
1658–59	30	6	4						
1659–60	15	5	8				115	7	7

Grand Total = £7,539   9   2½

GRAPH

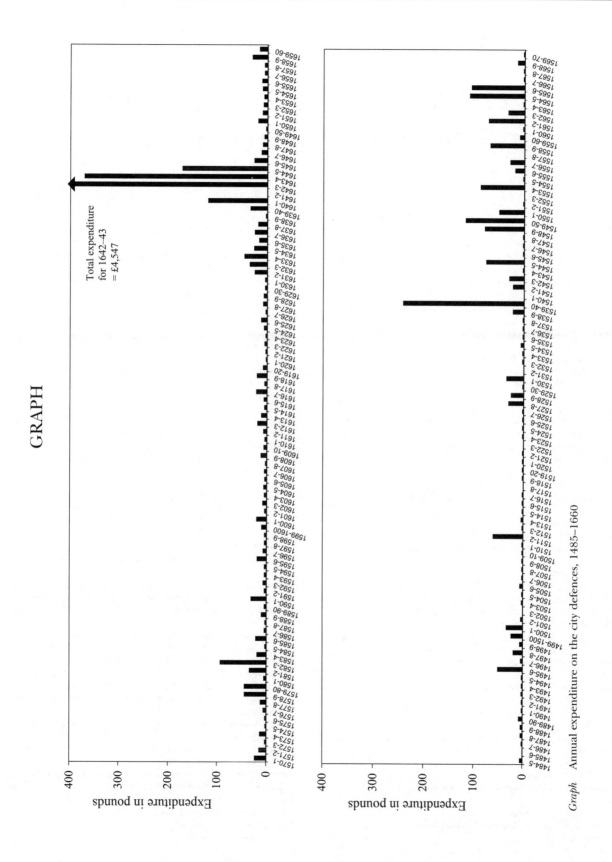

Total expenditure
for 1642–43
= £4,547

Graph Annual expenditure on the city defences, 1485–1660

GLOSSARY OF TERMS USED IN THE DOCUMENTS

barbigan, **barbygan**: the barbican, the broad earthen bank running behind the city wall.

barle berers: barrel-bearers, or porters.

base: a small cannon, or artillery piece.

bawerycks: baldrics, i.e. belts or girdles, used to carry weapons.

beedell: a beadle, a parish official.

berewe: a barrow.

Berly stones: stones from Barley, near Exeter.

borde nayle, **bordnail**: a (flat-headed?) nail for boards.

borrys stonys: burr-stones.

botters: a buttress.

brasis: braces.

bremstoune: brimstone, i.e. sulphur, used in the manufacture of gunpowder.

Bridewell: the House of Correction.

bruere: heather.

burdenayll: *see* **borde nayle**.

burres: blocks of stone.

bushell: a measure of capacity, containing 4 pecks or 8 gallons.

butteras: a buttress.

buttes: targets for archery practice.

byll: a bill, i.e. a long-handled infantry weapon.

C: *see* **hundred**.

cade: a cask, or barrel.

carbine: a firearm used chiefly by cavalrymen.

carnyll: a carnel, i.e. an embrasure or battlement.

cask: a measure of capacity.

cayge: a cage, a place of temporary confinement, a lock-up, constructed of bars of metal or wood.

chamber: a detached charge piece put into the breech of a gun.

Chidly lyme: lime from Chudleigh.

clench, **clynche**: a kind of nail.

clobb: cob, i.e. a mixture of mud and straw used for building walls.

cocke: a spout and tap from which water was obtained.

coffell, **covel**: *see* **cowl**.

coin: a quoin.

comter: *see* **Counter**.

comyn coffer: the common chest of the city.

coole: *see* **cowl**.

corne powder: grained gunpowder.

corpe de gard: a body of soldiers posted on guard duty.

cosk: *see* **cask** (?).

Counter: the city prison, kept at South Gate from the mid-sixteenth century onwards.

cowl: a small tub or vat in which liquids could be stored.

coyn: a quoin, or corner-stone.

crampe: cramp, a metal clamp used to hold stonework together.

crampettes: little cramps.

cresse, **creste**: a ceramic crest or ridge roof tile.

croke: a hook.

culverin: an artillery piece of 5½ inch bore.

cwt: *see* **hundred**.

cyntern: the wooden frame on which an arch is built.

d: penny, or pence.

dale: a trough or conduit for carrying off water.

delebords: deal boards, i.e. planks.

demy culverin: a demi-culverin, an artillery piece of 4½ inch bore.

Derewod: Duryard Wood, from which the city obtained most of its timber supplies.

dike: the defensive ditch around the city wall.

drake: a small artillery piece.

draste: refuse, or dirt (?).

draught-house: a privy.

dyall, **dyoll**: a dial, the face of a clock.

ellmen: of, or pertaining to, elms or elm-wood.

enterclose: a screen, partition or space partitioned off.

ewesborde: *see* **ovisbord**.

fanes: vanes, ornamental metal plates, commonly attached to the top of important buildings.

faulcon: a falcon, an artillery piece of 2½ inch bore.

fawkenette: a falconet, an artillery piece of 2½ inch bore.

fillingstone: rubble or chippings, used to infill walls.

firelocks: firearms using locks to produce a spark, thus igniting a gunpowder charge.

flake, **vlake**: a wicker hurdle used as a platform in scaffolding.

flanker: an earthwork position in which guns were placed to cover the city gates.

fotmal, **fotmel**: a fotmel, a measurement of weight for lead, usually equivalent to 70 *lbs*.

fottes: faults.

fouler, **fowler**: *see* **stock-fowler**.

fyldebrigge: a drawbridge (?).

fyllett: a strip of lead, or other metal.

gage: a pawn, or pledge.

galleries: covered walkways with musket-proof sides.

garet, gariette, garrett: a merlon or parapet on the battlement surmounting the city wall.

gemys: 'gemews', a kind of hinge virtually identical to the modern butt-hinge.

goolde lyce: gold lace.

goone: a gun, or cannon.

grate: a framework of metal bars, fixed in a door, window or other outlet. Often used to describe the metal grilles at the city's gates, which permitted the outfall of liquids from the gutters and drains but prevented unauthorized ingress.

hachenail, hachenayle: a kind of nail.

halfyndell: the half part, half.

hapse: a hasp.

harneys: harness, i.e. armour.

haychenayle: *see* **hachenail**.

healing, heling: slating, or tiling.

Heavitree stones: stones from the quarries at Heavitree.

hellier, helyer: a roofer, slater or tiler.

helyngpynne: small wooden pegs for securing roofing slates.

helyng stone, heylinge stone: roofing slate; cf. **tylestone**.

hogesyde, hoggishede: a hogshead, a large cask, holding approximately 52½ gallons of liquid.

hoke, houkye: a hook.

hood: a hod.

hot lyme: quicklime.

hundred, C, cwt: measures of variable size. For nails, stones and tiles the so-called long hundred, i.e. 120 *lbs*, was usual.

inprimis: firstly.

ive, ivee: ivy.

jakes: a privy.

kreste: *see* **cresse**.

lath nayle: nails used for fixing laths.

lazer people: lepers.

lede: lead.

legge: a wooden bar set across a door or gate for reinforcement.

lenye: linney, a kind of open-fronted out-building.

lyern, lyers: a connecting (piece of) timber, probably one set at right-angles to a beam.

lynseed oyle: oil derived from the seed of flax, used as a medium for paint.

lyntern: a lintel, a horizontal piece of timber or stone placed over a door, window or other apperture.

mach, match: a wick, cord, or rope of hemp used in the firing of guns or cannon.

maunds: wicker baskets.

mewralye, mural, muralye: the Mural Walk, an annual perambulation of the city walls undertaken by the mayor and other dignitaries for the purpose of inspection.

Milberry stones: stones from the quarry at Milberry, in Exminster parish.

mount: a substantial defensive work built of earth.

murtherer: a murdering piece, a small cannon used to clear a passageway or gateway.

mynyon: a minion, an artillery piece of 3½ inch bore.

nonschenk: nuncheon, an allowance of food or money for a worker's midday meal.

offendiculum: [stumbling-block], perhaps a barrier placed over the road at the entrance to the city.

orely nayles: a type of nail.

orlake nayles: a type of nail.

ovisbord: an eavesboard, a curved timber, often taken from old barrels, set at the lowest edge of a roof to direct rain-water away from a wall.

pales, palles: stakes driven into the ground to form a fence.

pament: pavement, paving.

paniyers: panniers, i.e. baskets.

pantes, pantys: a pentice, a small projecting roof.

parut: as appears.

paveses, pavyes: pavis, i.e. a screen or shelter used as a defence against archery.

Peamore stone: stones from Peamore quarry, in Shillingford parish.

pecke: a peck, a measure of dry goods equivalent to 2 gallons of liquid.

pillers: pillars.

pillory: stocks or other device in which an offender was exposed to public ridicule.

pipestavys: (curved) staves from a pipe, or barrel.

planchur: planking, laying of planks.

planke, plonke: plank.

plat: plate, a flat piece of timber or metal.

playster: plaster.

plump: a pump.

poncent, poncover: posnet, i.e. a small metal pot or vessel for boiling.

port-piece: *see* **murtherer**.

pose, posse: a (timber) post.

potte: a basket.

poundfold: pinfold, i.e. a pound or fold for sheep or cattle.

prevy, privye: a latrine.

pykes: pikes, long-handled infantry weapons.

pynnys: pins.

quarter: a quarter of a **hundred**, equivalent to a **seam** [q.v.].

quintal: a hundredweight, i.e. 120 *lbs*.

rampyre: a rampart.

ratch: sense unclear.

ravinet: rabinet, an artillery piece of 1½ inch bore.

redyng, riddinge, rudinge, ryddyng: clearing out, disposal (of unwanted matter) or scouring.

rep: rip, i.e. to cut, pull, tear, split or cleave.

rester: sense unclear.

robell, robill, robull, robyll: rubble, builders' debris.

robyes, rubuys: rubbish, rubble.

roftris: roof-trees.

rowcastyng: rough-casting (of walls).

rud, rude: reed.

rynnyngbarre: a sliding bar to secure a door or gate.

s: shilling, or shillings.

sacre: saker, an artillery piece of 3½–4 inch bore.

saers: sawyers.

sawder, sawdier: solder.

scablinge, skabelyng: scappling, that is to say the hewing of material into approximately square or rectangular blocks; the rough-dressing of stones.

scaffell: a scaffold.

scaple stones: stones which have been hewn into blocks.

scowrer: scourer, i.e. a contrivance for clearing out the bore of a gun.

seam, seme: a pack-horse load, the amount that would be carried in packsaddles on a horse; generally equivalent to a **quarter** [q.v.].

serpentyne: serpentine, a cannon, or artillery piece.

sholshed, sokeshede [?]: sense unclear.

shyllyng: sense unclear, but possibly slates (known locally as 'heling stones').

Silferton stones: stones from the quarry near Silverton.

skene pinnes: sense unclear (?).

slegg: sledge, i.e. a hammer.

slynge: a sling, a type of cannon.

snap[h]ances: muskets of the flintlock type.

sparrys: (timber) roofing spars.

spek, spekenayle, spyke, spykenayll: an iron spike.

spill: a rod or stalk.

spook: *see* **spucke**.

sprange: an iron spring (?).

spucke, spuke: (1) a bar or rod of wood; (2) a spike, or large nail.

staple: an iron staple on which the pintle of a gate was hung.

stock-fowler: a small artillery piece.

stode: a stud, a supporting timber, especially an upright.

stoopes: posts, or pillars.

stropp: a (leather) strap.

stuffe: stuff, i.e. cloth or material(s).

syntern: *see* **cyntern**.

tampion: a block of wood placed into the muzzle of a gun in order to keep out rain-water.

task: work at task, a specified piece of work, the extent of and payment for which were set out in advance in a contract.

thacchere: a thatcher.

tolehousse: a toll-house.

town sege: town-seat, i.e. the common latrines of the city.

turnepike: a spiked barrier, usually fixed across a road or passageway.

twyste: an (iron) twist to fasten a door, a gate or a window.

tylestone: roofing slate.

vanne: *see* **fanes**.

vaut, vawte: a vault, cellar or archway.

vente: vent, an entrance to, or air vent from the city's 'underground passages'.

verse, versis: *see* **base**.

videlicet: that is to say.

vlakis: *see* **flake**.

vlotmel: *see* **fotmal**.

wagge: a wedge.

waits: a small group of musicians retained by the city.

walplate: a horizontal beam at the top of a wall to support the timber frame of a roof.

wekett, wickett, wiket, wyket: a wicket, a small gate, especially as set within a larger one.

wen lode: a wain-load, or wagon-load.

Wonfordeston: stones from Wonford near Exeter. An alternative name for Heavitree stone.

workmanshepp: craftsman's wages, labour costs.

wormes: screws used for removing the charge or wad from a muzzle-loading gun.

wyenbrigge: a wainbridge, i.e. a bridge for wagons.

wylly: a willy, i.e. a basket.

wyndyete: flexible rod, or withies, used in making or repairing walls.

yate: gate.

Yeldhall: the Guildhall.

yer: iron.

yvys: *see* **ive**.

ABBREVIATIONS

AJ	*Archaeological Journal.*
BL	British Library.
Bod.	Bodleian Library, Oxford.
CBA	Council for British Archaeology.
CJ	*Commons Journals.*
CSPD	*Calendar of State Papers, Domestic.*
DAS	Devon Archaeological Society.
DCA	Dean and Chapter Archives, Exeter.
DCNQ	*Devon and Cornwall Notes and Queries.*
DCRS	*Devon and Cornwall Record Society.*
DRO	Devon Record Office, Exeter.
EA	Exeter Archaeology.
ECA	Exeter City Archives, kept at the Devon Record Office.
ECAB	Exeter Chamber Act Book, kept at the Devon Record Office.
EMAFU	Exeter Museums Archaeological Field Unit.
EPD	J.Z. Juddery and P.R. Staniforth (eds), *Exeter Property Deeds, 1150–1450* (5 vols, EMAFU, Reports Nos. 91.45–48 and 92.29, 1991–92).
ERB	Exeter Receivers' Books, kept at the Devon Record Office.
ERR	Exeter Receivers' Rolls, kept at the Devon Record Office.

ERSB	Exeter Receivers' Summary Books, kept at the Devon Record Office.
ERV	Exeter Receivers' Vouchers, kept at the Devon Record Office.
EQSMB	Exeter Quarter Sessions Minute Book, kept at the Devon Record Office.
HERG	*History of Exeter Research Group.*
HMC	Historical Manuscripts Commission.
Hooker	W.J. Harte, J.W. Schopp and H. Tapley Soper (eds), *The Description of the City of Exeter, by John Vowell, alias Hooker,* (3 vols, *Devon and Cornwall Record Society*, 1919 and 1947).
MA	*Medieval Archaeology.*
OED	*Oxford English Dictionary.*
PMA	*Post-Medieval Archaeology*
PRO	Public Record Office, London.
RCHM	Royal Commission on Historical Monuments.
SL	S. Moore (ed.), *Letters and Papers of John Shillingford, Mayor of Exeter, 1447–50,* (*Camden Society*, New Series, 2, 1871).
SP	State Papers.
TDA	*Transactions of the Devonshire Association.*
TRHS	*Transactions of the Royal Historical Society.*
WCSL	West Country Studies Library, Exeter.

NOTES

Part I   Introduction

1   See R. Pickard, *The Population and Epidemics of Exeter in Pre-Census Times* (Exeter, 1947), p. 18; W.G. Hoskins (ed.), *Exeter in the Seventeenth Century: Tax and Rate Assessments, 1602–99*, (DCRS, New Series, 2, 1957), p. xvi; W.T. MacCaffrey, *Exeter, 1540–1640: The Growth of an English County Town* (second edition London, 1975), pp. 11–13; W.B. Stephens, *Seventeenth Century Exeter: A Study of Industrial and Commercial Development, 1625–88* (Exeter, 1958), p. 40; E.M. Carus-Wilson, *The Expansion of Exeter at the Close of the Middle Ages* (Exeter, 1963), p. 31; and C.G. Henderson, 'The City of Exeter from AD 50 to the early nineteenth century', in R. Kain and W. Ravenhill (eds), *Historical Atlas of South West England* (Exeter, 1999), pp. 492–94.

2   On the Chamber, see MacCaffrey, *Exeter*, especially pp. 16–17, 26–53; and M. Stoyle, *From Deliverance to Destruction: Rebellion and Civil War in an English City* (Exeter, 1996), pp. 14–15.

3   On Exeter's medieval trade, see Carus-Wilson, *Expansion of Exeter*; W.R. Childs, 'Devon's Overseas Trade in the late Middle Ages', in M. Duffy *et al.* (eds), *The New Maritime History of Devon* (2 vols, Exeter, 1992), I, pp. 79–89, especially pp. 79, 88; and M. Kowaleski, *Local Markets and Regional Trade in Medieval Exeter* (Cambridge, 1995).

4   C.G. Henderson, 'The Roman Walls of Exeter', *Devon Archaeology*, 2 (1984), pp. 13–25; P.T. Bidwell, *Roman Exeter: Fortress and Town* (Exeter, 1980), especially pp. 59–66; Henderson, 'City of Exeter', pp. 484, 486, 493.

5   H.L. Turner, *Town Defences in England and Wales: An Architectural and Documentary Study, 900–1500* (London, 1970), p. 13.

6   See, for example, Turner, *Town Defences*; J.R. Kenyon, *Medieval Fortifications* (Leicester, 1990); D.M. Palliser, 'Town Defences in Medieval England and Wales', in A. Ayton and J.L. Price (eds), *The Medieval Military Revolution: State, Society and Military Change* (London, 1995), pp. 105–20.

7   See J.D. Tracy (ed.), *City Walls: The Urban Enceinte in Global Perspective* (Cambridge, 2000).

8   G. Oliver, 'The Castle of Exeter', *AJ*, 26 (1850), pp. 128–39; H.G. Godsall, *The Castle of Exeter* (Exeter, 1956, 28 pp.); and E.T. Vachell, 'Exeter Castle: Its Background, Origin and History', *TDA*, 98 (1966), pp. 327–48. See also J.B. Phear, 'Recent Discoveries at the Castle, Exeter', *TDA*, 23 (1891), pp. 318–22; J.B. Phear, 'Additional Discoveries at the Castle, Exeter', *TDA*, 24 (1891), pp. 147–50; and J.B. Phear, 'Recent Repairs to the Castle at Exeter', *TDA*, 27 (1895), pp. 137–43.

9   C.B. Lyster, 'Exeter City Wall as it was Originally Built', *DCNQ*, 7 (1913), pp. 161–71; G.T. Carter, 'Exeter City Wall', *DCNQ*, 8 (1915), pp. 209–10. In addition, a very brief account of the wall is given in A.H. Harvey, *The Castles and Walled Towns of England* (London, 1925), pp. 214–16.

10 A. Jenkins, *The History and Description of the City of Exeter* (Exeter, 1806), pp. 15–17, 83, 92–93, 126, 213, 217, 220, 281, 376–78, 405–6; C.J.G. Sprake, *The Gates and Other Antiquities of the City of Exeter* (Exeter, 1832); K. Cherry, 'Lollard's Tower', *Exeter Flying Post*, 29 July 1911; E. Lega-Weekes, *Some Studies in the Topography of the Cathedral Close, Exeter* (Exeter, 1915), pp. 94–109, 135–42; F. Rose-Troup, *Lost Chapels of Exeter*, HERG, Monograph 1 (Exeter, 1923), pp. 25–31, 51–52.

11 I. Burrow, 'The Town Defences of Exeter', *Transactions of the Devonshire Association*, 109 (1977), pp. 13–40.

12 See, for example, S.R. Blaylock, *Exeter Castle Gatehouse: Architectural Survey, 1985*, EMAFU, Report No. 87.04 (1987); S.R. Blaylock, *Exeter City Defences: Excavation and Survey on the City Walls from the North Gate to the Castle, 1978–88*, EMAFU, Report No. 88.13 (1988); J.Z. Juddery *et al.*, *Exeter City Defences: Expenditure on the Walls and Gates Recorded in the Receivers' Accounts, 1339–1700*, (5 vols) EMAFU, Reports Nos. 88.14–88.16, 89.09–89.10 (1988–89); S.R. Blaylock and R.A. Higham, 'Exeter Castle', *AJ*, supplement to vol. 147 (1990), pp. 35–39; S.R. Blaylock, *Exeter City Defences: A Fabric Survey of the City Wall, Part I: The Exterior*, EMAFU, Report No. 93.66 (1993); S.J. Simpson, *Exeter City Defences: West Gate to South Gate, Survey and Excavation in the West Quarter*, EMAFU, Report No. 93.73 (1993); J.B. Bedford and M.E.P. Hall, *Exeter City Defences: Observations at Princesshay Memorial Fountain, 1992*, EMAFU, Report No. 94.41 (1994); J.B. Bedford and M.E.P. Hall, *Exeter City Defences: Fabric Recording of the City Wall between Southgate and Watergate, 1992*, EMAFU, Report No. 94.41 (1994); S.R. Blaylock and R.W. Parker, *Exeter City Defences: Fabric Recording of the External Elevation of the City Wall in Northernhay Gardens adjacent to Athelstan's Tower, 1993–94*, EMAFU, Report No. 94.92 (1994).

13 S.R. Blaylock, *Exeter City Wall Survey* (Exeter Archaeology, 1995). See also S. Blaylock, 'Exeter City Wall' (DAS Field Guide, No. 12, Exeter, 1998).

14   Hoskins, *Exeter in the Seventeenth Century*, p. xix.

15   On the receivers' accounts in general, see M.M. Rowe and J.M. Draisey (eds), *The Receivers' Accounts of the City of Exeter, 1304–53*, (DCRS, New Series, 32, 1989), p. vii.

1 The Nature of the City Defences

1   W.T. MacCaffrey, *Exeter, 1540–1640: The Growth of an English County Town* (second edition London, 1975), p. 13.

2   I. Burrow, 'The Town Defences of Exeter', *TDA*, 109 (1977), pp. 17–18; S.R. Blaylock, *Exeter City Wall Survey* (Exeter Archaeology, 1995), pp. 1–3, 31; and C.G. Henderson, *The Roman Walls of Exeter*, Devon Archaeology, 2 (1984), p. 22.

3   A. Jenkins, *The History and Description of the City of Exeter* (Exeter, 1806), p. 17.

4   Burrow, 'Town Defences', p. 13; Blaylock, *City Wall Survey*, p.1; and C.G. Henderson, personal communication. For the purposes of comparison, it may be noted that the walls of Bristol were 8 feet thick, those of Newcastle 7 feet thick, those of Bath 6 feet thick and those of Southampton just 2½ feet thick, see J.R. Kenyon, *Medieval Fortifications* (Leicester, 1990), p. 187.

5   ERR, 1527–28, m.3*v*.; Blaylock, *City Wall Survey*, pp. 51–53; E. Lega-Weekes, *Some Studies in the Topography of the Cathedral Close*, Exeter (Exeter, 1915), p. 100; and ERB, 1634–5, f.5. The term was in common use during the sixteenth century, see, for example, H.M. Colvin *et al.* (eds), *The History of the King's Works; Volume III, 1485–1660* (London, 1975), Part one, p. 264.

6   ECA, Book 100 ('Presentments of Nuisances', 1554–88), ff.36, 46. Cf. A.D. Saunders, 'The Defences of Southampton in the Late Middle Ages', in L.A. Burgess (ed.), *The Southampton Terrier of 1454*, Southampton Record Series, 15 (1976), p. 24.

7   S.R. Blaylock, *Exeter City Wall: Fabric Recording of Civil War Period Crenellations at Trinity Lane*, EMAFU, Report No. 93.71 (1993).

8   HMC, *Exeter*, p. 286; DRO, Book 100, f.317.

9   ECA, Book 100, ff.36, 180, 268, 285; and ERB, 1573–74, f.3*v*. One or two private individuals also erected steps leading up to the city wall-walk. One such flight of stairs, the so-called 'Archdeacon's steps', still survive, to the rear of Holy Trinity church. These were probably built in the early seventeenth century, see p. 46.

10   ECA, Book 100, ff.98, 192.

11   See, for example, ERR, 1526–27, m.4*v*.; ERB, 1586–87, f.5; and ERB, 1589–90, f.2.

12   Similar banks of earth are known to have been incorporated within the fortifications of many other English cities, see, for example, A.E. Wilson, 'The Archaeology of Chichester City Walls' (Chichester Papers, 5, Chichester, 1957), pp. 4–9, 15; E. Gooder, C. Woodfield and R.E. Chaplin, 'The Walls of Coventry', *Transactions of the Birmingham Archaeological Society*, 81 (1966), pp. 93–94; and C. Green, 'Excavations on the Town Wall, Great Yarmouth, Norfolk, 1955', (Norfolk Archaeology, 35, 1973), pp. 109–17.

13   HMC, *Exeter*, p. 199.

14   ECA, Book 100, f.31.

15   Hooker, II, p. 163; and ECAB, B 1/8 (1634–47), f.286.

16   Lega-Weekes, *Topography of the Cathedral Close*, p. 102.

17   HMC, *Exeter*, p. 199.

18   Hooker, II, pp. 161–65; *SL*, pp. 87–88, 102–3, 110–12; and Lega-Weekes, *Topography of the Cathedral Close*, pp. 139–42. A similar arrangement had been made between the Archbishop and the civic authorities of medieval York; see C. Coulson, 'Battlements and the Bourgeoisie: Municipal Status and the apparatus of Urban Defence in Later Medieval England', in S. Church and R. Harvey (eds), Medieval Knighthood, V: Papers from the Sixth Strawberry Hill Conference, 1994 (Woodbridge, 1995) p. 165.

19   ERB, 1636–37, f.21; and ERR, 1430–31, m.2.

20   M.J. Stoyle, *A History of Exeter South Gate to 1642*, EMAFU, Report No. 94.59 (1994), pp. 1–4.

21   Jenkins, *History*, pp. 377–78.

22   HMC, *Exeter*, pp. 286–87; and ERR, 1446–47, m.3.

23   Ibid; ERR, 1355–57, m.3; ERR, 1361–62, m.2; ERR, 1443–44, m.2; and F. Rose-Troup, *Lost Chapels of Exeter* (*HERG*, Monograph 1, Exeter, 1923) pp. 25–31, 51–52.

24   ECAB, B 1/1 (1508–38), f.18. See also Chapter 5, below.

25   Jenkins, *History*, p. 220.

26   HMC, *Exeter*, p. 286; and ERR, 1430–31, m.2.

27   ERR, 1483–84, m.4; and ECAB, B 1/2 (1509–60), f.112.

28   ECAB, B 1/2, f.320. See also Chapter 4, below.

29   Jenkins, *History*, p. 213.

30   For the Cornish Chough, see W.J. Harte, *Gleanings from the Commonplace Book of John Hooker* (Exeter, n.d.), p. 29; and ECA, Book 100, f.229.

31   HMC, *Exeter*, p. 287; DRO, D1/16⁄26 (indenture between the City and Hugh Bidwell); and DRO, Box 214, Book 19 (Account of Nicholas Brooking, 1647–48), f.1.

32   ERR, 1379–80, m.3; ERR, 1451–52, m.2; and ERR, 1483–84, m.4.

33   Jenkins, *History*, p. 406.

34   ERR, 1371–72, m.2; ERR, 1430–31, m.2; ERR, 1503–4, m.4*v*. Similar structures lay beneath several of the gates of Tudor York, see RCHM, *An Inventory of the Historical Monuments in the City of York: Volume II: The Defences* (London, 1972), p. 42. In both cities the drains were known as 'grates' during the early modern period.

35   See, for example, ERR, 1527–28, m.4*v*.; ERR, 1528–29, m.2*v*.; and ERR, 1529–30, m.4*v*.

36   ECA, Book 100, f.229.

37   ERR, 1404–5, m.2; ERR, 1409–10, mm.1–2*v*.; and ERR, 1411–12, m.2.

38   Burrow, 'Town Defences', pp. 33–34; and Blaylock, *City Wall Survey*, p. 2. By the mid-Tudor period the towers were already regarded as ancient. During his visit to Exeter in *c*.1540, John Leland noted that 'as the [city] waulles have be[en] newly made, so have the old towers decayed', see L. Toulmin Smith (ed.), *The Itinerary of John Leland . . . Parts 1 to 3* (London, 1907), p. 227.

39   Blaylock, *City Wall Survey*, p. 38; and DRO, DD. 36995 B.

40   DRO, Miscellaneous Roll 6, m.22*v*.

41   Blaylock, *City Wall Survey*, pp. 101–03; and Burrow, 'Town Defences', pp. 31–32.

42 Hooker, III, p. 750; ERR, 1599–1600, m.2; and ERR, 1653–54, m.2.

43 Jenkins, *History*, p. 16.

44 DRO, Letter Book 60D, No. 247.

45 Ibid. See also No. 246.

46 G. Scott-Thomson, 'Exeter and the Russell Earls of Bedford', *DCNQ*, 17 (1932–33), pp. 17–23. The footbridge at Exeter is parallelled by the 'swivel bridge' which the Dominican friars of Newcastle were permitted to erect over the city ditch in 1312, in order to allow them to come and go through their postern gate through the town wall, see Coulson, 'Battlements and the Bourgeoisie', p. 158.

47 *SL*, p. 84.

48 Hooker, II, pp. 165–66; *EPD*, II, p. 119.

49 Hooker, II, pp. 165–66.

50 *SL*, pp. 85, 100.

51 Hooker, II, p. 212.

52 ERR, 1541–42, m.3v.

53 *SL*, pp. 87–88.

54 K. Cherry, 'Lollard's Tower', *Exeter Flying Post*, 29 July 1911.

55 Blaylock, *City Wall Survey*, pp. 89–92; and Burrow, 'Town Defences', pp. 26–29.

56 *SL*, pp. 15–16, 88. For another use of a tower as a clerical prison, see A.D. Saunders, 'The Cow Tower, Norwich: An East Anglican Bastille?', *MA*, Vol. 29 (1985), p. 109.

57 ERR, 1376–77, m.3; ERR, 1384–85, m.1v.; ERR, 1385–86, m.1; and ERR, 1414–15, m.2.

58 Blaylock, *City Wall Survey*, pp. 88–90.

59 See Chapter 5.

60 W.G. Hoskins, *Two Thousand Years in Exeter* (Exeter, 1960), p. 152. It is interesting to note that, during the early sixteenth century, a structure known as 'the Snail Tower' was incorporated within the English fortifications of Calais, see Colvin, *King's Works III*, Part One, pp. 342 and 352.

61 *EPD*, I, p. 68; ERR, 1480–81, m.4; ERR, 1492–93, m.2.

62 Blaylock, *City Wall Survey*, pp. 70–71.

63 C.G. Henderson, 'The City of Exeter from AD50 to the early nineteenth century', in R. Kain and W. Ravenhill (eds), *Historical Atlas of South West England* (Exeter, 1999), p. 493; J. Allan, C. Henderson and R. Higham, 'Saxon Exeter', in J. Haslam (ed.), *Anglo-Saxon Towns in Southern England* (Chichester, 1984), p. 397; and C.G. Henderson, personal communication.

64 *EPD*, I, pp. 31, 37; DRO, DD. 36995 B; and T.N. Brushfield, 'The Financial Diary of a Citizen of Exeter, 1631–43', *TDA*, 33 (1901), p. 267.

65 Blaylock, *City Wall Survey*, pp. 2–3.

66 ECA, Law Papers, Box 40 (Northernhay and Southernhay Suit), depositions of Easter 1633, f.39.

67 Ibid., depositions of 24 September 1633, f.40; and depositions of Easter 1633, f.78.

68 J.Allan, C.G. Henderson and R. Higham, 'Saxon Exeter', in J. Haslam (ed.), *Anglo-Saxon Towns in Southern England* (Chichester, 1984), p. 397.

69 M.R. Ravenhill and M.M. Rowe, *Early Devon Maps* (Exeter, 2000), p. 21.

70 G. Oliver, 'The Castle of Exeter', *AJ*, 26 (1850), p. 10.

71 On the Castle, see Blaylock, *City Wall Survey*, pp. 39–54.

72 ECA, Book 51 (Commonplace Book of John Hooker) f.322; and W. Shakespeare, *Richard III*, Act 4, Scene 2.

73 R.B. Dobson, 'Urban Decline in Late Medieval England', *TRHS*, 5th Series, 27 (1977), p. 5.

74 M.M. Rowe and A.M. Jackson (eds), *Exeter Freemen, 1266–1967* (DCRS, Extra Series I, Exeter, 1973), p. 27; and DRO, Miscellaneous Roll 6, m.34. For the use of 'springolds' in urban fortifications elsewhere, see B.H. O'Neill, 'Southampton Town Walls', in W.F. Grimes (ed.) *Aspects of Archaeology in Britain and Beyond* (London, 1951), p. 246; and Coulson, 'Battlements and the Bourgeoisie', p. 195, note 299.

75 ERR, 1483–84, m.5; and ERR, 1484–85, m.4.

76 DRO, Box 214, Book 5 (Account of Robert Midwynter, 1556–57), f.10; ECAB, B 1/3 (1560–81), f.88; and ECAB, B 1/2, f.295. Tudor York, too, possessed its 'Gunhouse', see RCHM, *York: II*, p. 49.

77 See, for example, ERB, 1596–97, f.1; ERB, 1604–5, f.1v.; and ERB, 1614–15, f.1.

78 See ECAB, B 1/2, ff.230, 259, 321.

79 Hooker, II, pp. 819–20.

80 ECA, Book 51, f.344; and PRO, SP 16, 407, Item 27 ('A list of the captaynes . . . of . . . the . . . Cittie of Exeter').

81 On the Exeter Trained Bands, see MacCaffrey, *Exeter*, pp. 235–36; and HMC, *Exeter*, pp. 10–11, 83, 85.

82 Hooker, II, p. 820.

83 Ibid.

84 See, for example, ECAB, B 1/5 (1587–1601), f.221 and ECAB, B 1/8, f.278.

85 ERR, 1560–61, m.2v.

86 ECAB, B 1/3 (1560–81), f.169.

87 ECAB, B 1/5, f.460.

88 DRO, Box 214, Book 21 (Account of John Dark, 1649–50), f.5.

89 ECAB, B 1/5, f.207; ERB, 1634–35, f.9; ERB, 1635–36, f.18; and ERB, 1636–37, f.23.

90 See, for example, ECAB, B 1/8, ff.215, 282, 350; ERB, 1603–4, f.3v.; ERB, 1605–6, f.5; and ERB, 1635–36, ff.16–17.

91 ECAB, B 1/2, f.112.

92 Hooker, II, pp. 742, 747; and ERB, 1600–1, f.2.

93 ERB, 1602–3, f.1v.

94 EQSMB, 61 (1618–21), f.105.

95 ECAB, B 1/13 (1684–1731), f.110; and ECAB B 1/8, f.197.

96 *EPD*, II, pp. 150, 164; and ECA, Book 100, f.30.

97 ERB, 1590–91, ff.3–5.

98 ERB, 1619–20, f.1; and *OED*.

99 ERR, 1480–81, m.4.

100 M.J. Stoyle, 'A Medieval Watergate?', in J.Z. Juddery, P.R. Staniforth and M.J. Stoyle, *Exeter City Defences: Expenditure on the Walls and Gates, 1450–1570*, EMAFU, Report No. 89.10 (1989), pp. 51–57; ECA, Book 100, ff.31, 36, 60, 146; DRO Law Papers, Box 40 (*Exeter versus Frye*), and DRO, Box 214, Book 11 (Account of Edward Brydgeman), f.3.

101 ERR, 1527–28, m.3v.

102 ECAB, B 1/1, f.121.

103 ECAB, B 1/8, f.214.

104 ERB, 1571–72, f.10.

105 ECA, Book 100, ff.31, 36, 42.

106 ERB, 1628–29, f.12.

107 J.Z. Juddery and M.J. Stoyle, *The Aqueducts of Medieval Exeter*, EA, Report No. 95.44 (1995), pp. vii–xix.

108 ECA, Law Papers, Box 40, depositions of Easter 1633, ff.79–80; and ERB, 1636–37, f.21.

109 ECA, Book 101 ('Presentments of Nuisances', 1620–57), f.57.
110 ERR, 1391–92, m.1*v*.; ERR, 1395–96, m.2; and ERB, 1614–15, f.5*v*.
111 For the 'framing poasts' of the grate, see ERB, 1645–46, f.1*v*.
112 *SL*, p. 89.
113 Hooker, II, pp. 167–72.
114 ECAB, B 1/8, f.200; and Lega-Weekes, *Topography of the Cathedral Close*, pp. 138–39.
115 ECA, Book 100, f.36; ERB, 1595–96, ff.4*v*.–5*v*.; ERB, 1634–35, f.6; ERB, 1637–38, f.26; ERB, 1658–59, ff.3–4.
116 ERB, 1595–96, ff.4*v*.–5*v*.; ERB, 1637–38, f.25; and ERB, 1633–34, f.12.
117 DRO, Box 214 (Account of Richard Sweete, 1651–52), ff.16–19; and ECAB, B 1/10 (1652–63), f.6.
118 Jenkins, *History*, p. 377.
119 ECA, Book 100, ff.46, 98.
120 HMC, *Exeter*, pp. 199–200. The encroachment of latrines on the wall-top caused similar problems in many other English cities, see Coulson, 'Battlements and the Bourgeoisie', p. 139, note 74.
121 Hooker, II, p. 751; and ERR, 1653–54, m.1.

2 Purpose and Function

1 ECAB, B 1/2 (1509–60), f.137.
2 HMC, *Exeter*, p. 21.
3 DRO, Letter Book 60D, No. 247; ECAB, B 1/7 (1611–34), f.645; ECAB, B 1/8 (1634–47), f.409. See also W.T. MacCaffrey, *Exeter, 1540–1640: The Growth of an English County Town* (second edition London, 1975), p. 235.
4 For a brief general discussion of this subject, see N. Orme, *The Cap and the Sword: Exeter and the Rebellions of 1497* (Exeter, 1997), p. 4.
5 ECAB, B 1/8, f.208; and ERV, Box 2, bill of 18 September 1647.
6 Hooker, III, pp. 819–20.
7 I use the term 'hammered' advisedly. As the city accounts reveal, hammers were hung outside each gate in order to ensure that even the most sleepy-headed porter could be summoned instantly, see ERB, 1601–2, f.2; ERB, 1627–28, f.7; and ERV, Box 2 (1633–47), bills of 8 May 1647 and 24 September 1647.
8 M.M. Rowe and J.M. Draisey (eds), *The Receivers' Accounts of the City of Exeter, 1304–53* (DCRS, New Series, 32, 1989), p. 93; and MacCaffrey, *Exeter*, p. 79. See also ERR, 1532–33, m.2*v*. for the erection of a 'tolehowsse at South Gate' on the occasion of the annual St Mary Magdalen Fair.
9 ECAB, B 1/8, ff.209, 211–13, 215, 332; and J.Z. Juddery and M. Stoyle, *Exeter City Defences: Expenditure on the Walls and Gates recorded in the Receivers' Accounts, 1650–1700*, EMAFU, Report No. 88.16 (1988), pp. vi–vii.
10 ERB, 1615–16, f.1; and ERB, 1617–18, f.1.
11 In 1497 and 1642, for example. See ECA, Book 51 (John Hooker's Commonplace Book), f.327*v*.; and ECAB, B 1/8, f.276.
12 EQSMB, 61 (1618–21), f.240.
13 See R.A. Higham, 'Castles, Fortified Houses and Fortified Towns in the Middle Ages', in R. Kain and W.

Ravenhill (eds), *Historical Atlas of South-West England* (Exeter, 1999), p. 142.
14 J. Bond, *A Doore of Hope, also Holy and Loyal Activity: Two Treatises delivered . . . in Exeter* (1641), p. 49.
15 L. Toulmin-Smith (ed.), *The Itinerary of John Leland . . . Parts 1 to 3* (London, 1907), p. 227; and T. Risdon, *The Chorographical Description, or Survey of the County of Devon* (Barnstaple, 1970 edition), p. 103. See also I. Burrow, 'The Town Defences of Exeter', *TDA*, 109 (1977), pp. 13–40, p. 37.
16 ERR, 1553–4, m.2*v*.; A. Jenkins, *The History and Description of the City of Exeter* (Exeter, 1806), p. 377; ERB, 1558–59, f.21; and ECAB, B 1/1 (1509–38), f.45.
17 ERR, 1451–52, m.1*v*. Cf. RCHM, *An Inventory of the Historical Monuments in the City of York: Volume II, The Defences* (London, 1972), pp. 20, 22.
18 ERB, 1558–59, f.24; ERB, 1619–20, f.3; and ERB, 1643–44, f.4.
19 ERB, 1643–4, ff.4–5, f.20; ERB, 1642–43, f.7; and S.R. Blaylock, *Exeter City Wall Survey* (Exeter Archaeology, 1995), p. 35. Several date-stones still survive within the fabric of the city wall, though sadly their inscriptions are no longer legible. See Blaylock, *City Wall Survey*, pp. 61–62, 86, 89, and plates 93–96. Similar date-stones may be found at York, see RCHM, *York II*, p. 54
20 ERR, 1501–2, m.5; ERR, 1553–54, m.2*v*.; ERB, 1562–63, f.25; A. Jenkins, *The History and Description of the City of Exeter* (Exeter, 1806), pp. 220, 377. Royal and civic coats of arms were similarly displayed above the gateways of many other English cities, including Chester, London, Norwich, Rye, Southampton and Winchester, see RCHM, *York: II*, p. 54.
21 ECA, Book 51, f.227.
22 ERR, 1532–33, m.2*v*.
23 ERR, 1483–84, m.5; and ERB, 1617–18, f.1. This was common practice in all English cities of the period, see, for example, C. Pythian Adams, *The Desolation of a City: Coventry and the Urban Crisis of the Middle Ages* (Cambridge, 1979), p. 177; and P. Ackroyd, *London: The Biography* (London, 2001), p. 291.
24 ERB, 1562–63, f.25; ECA, Book 100 (Presentments of Nuisances, 1554–88), f.335; ERB, 1611–12, f.18*v*.; ERB, 1610–11, f.12*v*.; and DRO, CC 867 Moger (unpaginated), entry for 24 July 1619.
25 *OED*; and ERR, 1478–79, m.1*v*. At York, too, stocks and whipping posts were placed beside the city gates, see RCHM, *York: II*, p. 55.
26 EQSMB, 61, f.237.
27 EQSMB, 62 (1621–30), f.4*v*.
28 M.J. Stoyle, *A History of Exeter Southgate to 1642*, EMAFU, Report No. 94.59 (1994), pp. 3–4. A prison also seems to have been briefly established at North Gate in the aftermath of the 1497 risings, see ERR, 1497–98, m.4. For the long-standing association of gates with prisons, see R.B. Pugh, 'The King's Prisons before 1250', *TRHS*, 5th Series, 5 (1955), p. 21; and RCHM, *York: II*, p. 4
29 M. Stoyle, *From Deliverance to Destruction: Rebellion and Civil War in an English City* (Exeter, 1996), p. 192.
30 ECAB, B 1/2, f.324.
31 ERB, 1558–9, f.14; HMC, *Exeter*, p. 317; and ERB, 1588–89, f.1*v*.
32 ERB, 1602–3, f.1*v*.
33 ECA, Book 51, f.322.
34 W. Cotton and H. Woollcombe, *Gleanings from the*

Municipal and Cathedral Records . . . of Exeter (Exeter, 1877), p. 35.

35 E. Walker, *Historical Discourses Upon Several Occasions* (1705), p. 47. On this subject more generally, see J. Gidley, *Notes of Exeter, Comprising a History of Royal Visits* (Exeter, 1863), *passim*. For similar welcoming ceremonies laid on at other English cities, see RCHM, *York: II*, p. 39.

36 DRO, Box 214, Book 11 (Account of Edward Brydgeman, 1562–63), f.5.

37 Stoyle, *History of Exeter South Gate*, p. 5; and DRO, Box 214, Book 19 (Account of Nicholas Brooking, 1647–48), f.1. See also HMC, *Exeter*, pp. 286–87.

38 H. Lloyd Parry, *The Founding of Exeter School* (Exeter, 1913), p. 64.

39 *SL*, p. 88. Cf. B. Losch, 'The City Walls of Glurns', in G. Perbellini (ed.), *Les Enceintes Urbaines Áu Moyen Age* (Europa Nostra Bulletin, 53, The Hague, 2000), p. 37.

40 ECAB, B 1/8, f.212.

41 ECAB, B 1/10, (1652–63), f.99.

42 ERB, 1660–61, ff.2, 14.

43 See Lloyd Parry, *Founding of Exeter School*, map facing p. 78.

44 ECAB, B 1/5 (1587–1601), f.140.

45 K. Cherry, 'Lollard's Tower', *Exeter Flying Post*, 29 July 1911.

46 See, for example, J. Maclean, *The Life and Times of Sir Peter Carew* (London, 1857), p. 153; and ECAB, B 1/3 (1560–81), f.288.

47 EQSMB, 64 (1642–60), f.112.

48 ECA, Law Papers, Box 40 (Northernhay and Southernhay Suit), depositions of Easter 1633, f.25.

49 Ibid., f.74; J. Youings, 'Bowmen, Billmen and Hackbutters: The Elizabethan Militia in the South-West', in R. Higham (ed.), *Security and Defence in South-West England before 1800* (Exeter, 1987), p. 61; HMC, *Exeter*, p. 63; EQSMB, 62, ff.82–85.

50 ECA, Law Papers, Box 40, depositions of Easter 1633, ff.74, 89; and depositions of September 1633, f.124.

51 ERR, 1530–31, m.5v.; ERR, 1537–38, m.4v.; ERR, 1544–45, m.4v.; ECAB, B 1/2, f.107; ERR, 1555–56, m.2v.; ERB, 1558–59, f.16; ERB, 1571–72, f.7; ERB, 1575–76, f.4; ERB, 1576–77, f.4v.; ERB, 1582–83, f.1v.; ERB, 1586–87, f.7v.

52 ERB, 1612–13, f.38; ERB, 1613–14, ff.19–25; and S. Izacke, *Remarkable Antiquities of the City of Exeter* (London, 1723), p. 145.

53 PRO, STAC 8, 161/10, f.22; and ECA, Law Papers, Box 40, depositions of Easter 1633, ff.85, 146.

54 Similar gardens were established on the town ramparts of late medieval Coventry, see E. Goodber, C. Woodfield and R.E. Chaplin, 'The Walls of Coventry', *Transactions of the Birmingham Archaeological Society*, 81 (1966), pp. 88–138.

55 ECA, Book 100, f.98.

56 ECAB, B 1/5, f.190.

57 E. Lega-Weekes, 'Some Studies in the Topography of the Cathedral Close, Exeter', *DCNQ*, 8, part 2 (1915), p. 108.

58 EQSMB, 64, f.62v.

59 Ibid., f.326v.

60 Maclean, *Life of Peter Carew*, p.5. For the dialect term 'meechinge' (still current in Exeter when I was a schoolboy during the 1980s), see HMC, *Exeter*, p. 145.

61 ERB, 1653–54, f.8.

62 EQSMB, 64, f.111.

63 A. Jenkins, *The History and Description of the City of Exeter* (Exeter, 1806), pp. 405–6.

64 ERB, 1604–5, f.2.

65 EQSMB, 61, ff.103, 105; and ECA, Book 101 (Presentments to the Court, 1620–57), f.17v.

66 ECAB, B 1/8, f.142. For the symbolism of the wine-bush, see A.E. Richardson, *The Old Inns of England* (London, 1934), pp. 50–51; and H.A. Monckton, *A History of the English Public House* (London, 1969), p. 15.

67 ECAB, B 1/8, f.142.

68 Jenkins, *History*, p. 220.

69 ECAB, B 1/2, f.194.

70 EQSMB, 64, ff.16v.–17.

71 For these disturbances, see F. Rose-Troup, *The Western Rebellion of 1549* (London, 1913), pp. 200–01; Stoyle, *Deliverance*, pp. 65–67; and S.K. Roberts, *Recovery and Restoration in an English County: Devon Local Administration, 1646–70* (Exeter, 1985), pp. 138–39.

72 Similar accidents occurred at the gates of other English cities, cf. B. Cunliffe, 'The Winchester City Wall', *Proceedings of the Hampshire Field Club*, 22, part 1 (1961), p. 53.

73 ECAB, B 1/10, f.21v.; and DRO, Box 214, Book 24 (Account of James Pearse, 1652–3), f.18.

74 Ibid.

75 ECA, Law Papers, Box 40, depositions of Easter 1633, f.78.

76 Ibid., *passim*.

77 Stoyle, *History of Exeter South Gate*, pp. 3–7.

78 For the gaol garden, see HMC, *Exeter*, pp. 198–99; DRO, CC Moger 867, entry for 17 February 1616; and PRO, STAC 8, 17/19.

79 For the madfolks' house, see ERB, 1590–91, ff.3–4. For Helliar's Almshouses, see ECAB, B 1/4, ff.442 and 579; ECAB, B 1/5, ff.140 and 467; and ECA, Book 101, f.10v. By 1656 the building had gone, brought down by a collapse of the city wall, see ECAB, B 1/9, f.72v.

80 F. Nesbitt (ed.), 'Exeter Holy Trinity Burials, 1563–1729' (typescript, 1930–31, copy held in WCSL), p. 48.

81 Rather surprisingly, the records of the court leet do not appear to have been utilized by any previous historian of early modern Exeter.

82 ECA, Book 100, ff.29–30.

83 Ibid., f.46; and HMC, *Exeter*, pp. 199–200.

84 ECA, Book 101, f.12. For the scavengers and their duties, see ECA, Book 51, ff.177–78.

85 Ibid., f.78v.

86 ECA, Book 100, f.13.

87 DRO, CC Moger 867, entries of 28 June and 14 July 1617.

88 PRO, STAC 8, 17/19.

89 Ibid.; and DRO, CC Moger 867, entries of 17 February 1616, 29 October 1616 and 13 March 1618. Tales of the 'violence and rapacity' of early modern prison-keepers are legion, see, for example, G. Salgado, *The Elizabethan Underworld* (Stroud, 1992), pp. 174–76, 180; and Ackroyd, *London: The Biography*, pp. 247–49.

90 ECA, Book 100, ff.31, 296v.

91 Ibid., f.337; and ECA, Book 101, f.13.

92 ECA, Book 100, ff.32, 274; and ECA, Book 101, ff.49, 96*v*.

93 ECA, Book 100, f.31; and ECA, Book 101, f.1*v*.

94 ECA, Book 101, f.14*v*.

95 Rowe and Draisey, *Receivers' Accounts*, pp. 3, 4, 47, 76; *EPD*, p. 134; and ECA, Law Papers, Box 40, depositions of September 1633, ff.84, 130.

96 ERB, 1625–26, f.2; ECA, Book 100, f.103.

97 ECA, Law Papers, Box 40, depositions of Easter 1633, f.36.

98 H.G. Godsall, *The Castle of Exeter* (Exeter, 1956), p. 24; ECAB, B 1/8, f.243; ECAB, B 1/3, f.253; and J.F. Chanter, *The Bishop's Palace, Exeter, and its Story* (London, 1932), p. 87.

99 ECAB, B 1/8, f.286.

100 ECA, Book 100, f.60.

101 Ibid., f.98; and ERB, 1556–57, f.13.

102 ECA, Book 100, ff.73, 267.

103 ECAB, B 1/3, f.429.

104 ECA, Book 100, f.338; and ECAB, B 1/10, f.9*v*.

105 W.B. Stephens, *Seventeenth Century Exeter: A Study of Industrial and Commercial Development, 1625–88* (Exeter, 1958), p. 6. See also W.G. Hoskins, *Industry, Trade and People in Exeter, circa 1688–1800* (Manchester, 1935), pp. 22, 37.

106 Hooker, III, p.757.

107 ECAB, B 1/8, f.224. The Chamber order does not elaborate on the precise nature of the damage caused.

108 ECAB, B 1/9, f.139.

109 For the overseers of the city's works, see ERB, 1612–13, f.18; ERB, 1613–14, f.9; and DRO, DD 39,137. For the 'princely sums' which those who oversaw the construction of the city defences could occasionally command, at least during the late medieval period, see M. Kowaleski, *Local Markets and Regional Trade in Medieval Exeter* (Cambridge, 1995), p. 105.

3 Maintenance and Repair

1 For an excellent general introduction to this subject, see D.M. Palliser, 'Town Defences in Medieval England and Wales', in A. Ayton and J.L. Price (eds), *The Medieval Military Revolution* (London, 1995), pp. 110–13. For some interesting French comparisons, see A. Rigaudière, 'Le Financement des Fortifications Urbaines en France du milieu du XIVe siècle à la fin du XVe siècle', *Revue Historique*, 273 (1985), pp. 19–95; and M. Wolfe, 'Walled Towns during the French Wars of Religion', in J.D. Tracy (ed.), *City Walls: The Urban Enceinte in Global Perspective* (Cambridge, 2000), pp. 317–48, especially pp. 322, 328–36. Cf. RCHM, *An Inventory of the Historical Monuments in the City of York: Volume II, The Defences* (London, 1972), pp. 20, 22.

2 See, for example, M. Dawes (ed.), *Register of Edward, the Black Prince* (3 vols, London, 1930–33), II, p. 36; and I. Burrow, 'The Town Defences of Exeter', *TDA*, 109 (1977), pp. 13–40, p. 35.

3 *OED*; and Hooker, II, p. 163. (The date to which Hooker ascribes this document—1330—is incorrect, see E. Lega-Weekes, *Some Studies in the Topography of the Cathedral Close, Exeter* (Exeter, 1915), p. 140.)

4 During the late sixteenth and early seventeenth centuries, the walk was almost always undertaken between 6 and 13 October, see ERB, 1572–1660, *passim*.

5 Hooker, II, p. 212. Similar inspections were held at Coventry from 1534–35 onwards. See E. Gooder, C. Woodfield and R.E. Chaplin, 'The Walls of Coventry', *Transactions of the Birmingham Archaeological Society*, 81 (1966), p. 95.

6 ECA, Book 51 (John Hooker's Commonplace Book), f.164*v*.

7 Probably so called because he was charged with keeping an eye out for the illegal gutters which did so much damage to the fabric of the wall, see Chapter 1.

8 J. Cossins, *Reminiscences of Exeter Fifty Years Since* (Exeter, 1877), p. 7.

9 See ERR, 1495–96, m.3; and ERR and ERB, 1572–1660, *passim*. The lack of any references to the mural walk in the receivers' accounts for 1497–1571 is a puzzle, for the procession clearly continued to be staged throughout this period.

10 S.R. Blaylock, *Exeter City Wall Survey* (Exeter Archaeology, 1995), figures 3–4 (map of John Roque, 1744, and map of Charles Tozer, 1792). For an evocative photograph of Goldsmith Street in its final days, taken as a woman with a beehive hairdo passed along the sunlit pavement, see P. Thomas, *The Changing Face of Exeter* (Stroud, 1995), p. 57.

11 Hooker, III, p. 754.

12 For a payment to 'the Beedells for clensinge the walles', see ERB, 1581–82, f.4*v*. See also ERB, 1611–12, f.1.

13 HMC, *Exeter*, pp. 198–99.

14 See, for example, ERB, 1657–58, f.3; ERB, 1654–55, f.5; and ERB, 1659–60, f.3.

15 See, for example, ERB, 1593–94, f.1; ERB, 1595–96, f.1; and ERB, 1599–1600, f.2.

16 For the protracted struggle between the Chamber and the Cathedral Chapter over the school, see W.T. MacCaffrey, *Exeter, 1540–1640: The Growth of an English County Town* (second edition London, 1975), pp. 118–25.

17 Ibid., p. 119; and H. Lloyd Parry, *The Founding of Exeter School* (Exeter, 1913), pp. 74, 78–79.

18 ERB, 1634–35, f.6; ERB, 1635–36, f.14.

19 See, for example, ERB, 1637–38, f.30.

20 ERB, 1618–19, f.1*v*.; ERB, 1572–73, m.2*v*.; ERB, 1580–81, f.5.

21 ERB, 1588–89, f.1. The receivers' accounts for 1629–35 record a whole string of payments made to 'Mistress Sibley', consort of the prison-keeper Robert Sibley, for her 'bankett[s]'.

22 M.J. Stoyle, *A History of Exeter South Gate to 1642*, EMAFU, Report No. 94.59 (1994), p. 5.

23 For the 'fine prospect' which could be obtained from the gate, see A. Jenkins, *The History and Description of the City of Exeter* (Exeter, 1806), p. 378. The Chamber's decision to institute a yearly banquet on top of the South Gate may well have been inspired by the example of the aristocratic Thynne family, who, some years before, had caused miniature 'banketting houses' to be erected on the roof of their splendid mansion house at Longleat, in Wiltshire, see M. Girouard, *Robert Smythson and the Elizabethan Country House* (London, 1983), pp. 48–49. I owe this reference to Stuart Blaylock.

24 ERB, 1632–33, f.7; and ERB, 1637–38, f.30.

25 ERB, 1634–35, f.6; and ERB, 1635–36, f.14.

26 See, for example, ERB, 1573–74, f.1; ERB, 1576–77, f.9.

27 ERB, 1612–13, f.1; ERB, 1659–60, f.3.
28 As late as 1911, one respectable scholar was made distinctly uneasy by the 'obscure lanes and unsavoury alleys' down which he had been forced to tread in his perambulation of the city walls at Exeter, see A.H. Harvey, *The Castles and Walled Towns of England* (London, 1911, 1925 edition), p. 214.
29 ERB, 1587–88, f.4*v*.; ERB, 1601–2, f.1.
30 Cossins, *Reminiscences*, p. 7.
31 R. Newton, *Eighteenth Century Exeter* (Exeter, 1984), p. 149.
32 Cossins, *Reminiscences*, p. 7.
33 The episcopal rabbits were presumably kept in a warren in the grounds behind the Bishop's Palace.
34 ECA, Book 100 ('Presentments of Nuisances, 1554–88'), ff.103–5.
35 Ibid., ff.112–13.
36 ECAB, B 1/10 (1652–63), f.31*v*.
37 ECAB, B 1/8 (1634–47), ff.258, 279, 281, 285.
38 ECA, Book 100, f.13.
39 HMC, *Exeter*, p. 200.
40 ECA, Book 100, ff.98, 113.
41 Ibid., f.141.
42 ECAB, B 1/3 (1560–81), f.214; ERR, 1571–72, m.2*v*.; and ERB, 1571–72, f.10.
43 ECA, Book 100, f.31; and ERB, 1579–80, ff.1–3.
44 ERR, 1528–29, m.2*v*.
45 ECAB, B 1/8, f.137.
46 ECAB, B 1/1 (1509–38), f.19; and ERR, 1500–1, m.3*v*.
47 ECAB, B 1/1, f.8; ECAB, B 1/2 (1509–60), f.320; ECAB, B 1/3, f.10.
48 ECAB, B 1/2, f.320.
49 York had its 'muremasters', for example, Chester its 'murengers' and Montpellier its 'obriers', see D.M. Palliser, *Tudor York* (Oxford, 1979), pp. 70, 82; RCHM, *York: II*, p. 36 and K.L. Reyerson, 'Medieval Walled Space: Urban Development versus Defense', in Tracy (ed.), *City Walls*, pp. 98–114.
50 ERR, 1499–1500, m.2*v*.; and ECAB, B 1/1, f.25.
51 See ERB, 1612–13, ff.18–19; ERB, 1613–14, f.9; ERB, 1618–19, f.2; and ERB, 1625–26, f.2.
52 ERR, 1527–28, m.3*v*.; and ERR, 1528–29, m.2*v*.
53 ECAB, B 1/3, f.454.
54 ERV, Box 1, 'Accompte of Mr John Blakealler'; and ERB, 1643–44, ff.5, 20.
55 ERB, 1556–57, f.13 and ERB, 1562–63, f.18. See also ECA, Book 100, f.98.
56 ERB, 1573–74, f.4*v*.; ERB, 1576–77, f.9*v*.; and ECAB, B 1/5 (1587–1601), f.140.
57 Palliser, *Tudor York*, pp. 75, 172; and RCHM, *York: II*, p. 36. See also M.M. Elbl, 'Portuguese Urban Fortifications in Morocco: Borrowing, Adaptation and Innovation along a Military Frontier', in Tracy (ed.), *City Walls*, p. 377; and H. Swanson, *Medieval Artisans: An Urban Class in Late Medieval England* (Oxford, 1989), p. 91.
58 ECAB, B 1/5, f.197. Deymond had been hired by the receiver to repair the prison at South Gate as early as 1580, see ERB, 1579–80, f.3. He was also the foremost ordinary mason on the Guildhall works in 1592–94, see S.R. Blaylock, 'Exeter Guildhall', *Proceedings of the Devon Archaeological Society*, 48 (1990), p. 141. John Deymond, perhaps his son, later rose to local prominence as a monumental mason and statuary, see A. Wells-Cole, *Art and Decoration in Elizabethan and*

Jacobean England: The Influence of Continental Prints, 1558–1625 (London, 1997), pp. 63, 90, 149. It is interesting to note that, in 1599, 'Richard Deymond and John Deymond' were working together on East Gate bridge, see ERB, 1599–1600, f.4. I am most grateful to John Allan and Stuart Blaylock for discussing the Deymonds with me.
59 Deymond's last known appearance on the city walls was in November 1611; five months later he was dead. See ERB, 1611–12, f.18*v*.; and F. Nesbitt (ed.), 'Exeter Holy Trinity: Burials, 1563–1729' (typescript, 1930–31, copy held in WCSL), p. 11.
60 M.M. Rowe and A.M. Jackson (eds), *Exeter Freemen, 1266–1967* (DCRS, Extra Series, 1, 1973), p. 109; and ERB, 1583–84, f.4*v*.
61 DRO, DD.391 (Exeter Siege Accounts), ff.35*v*, 39, 41*v*.
62 Ibid., f.39; and ERB, 1643–44, f.5.
63 BL, E.319 (21), *A Continuation of Certain Special and Remarkable Passages*, 23–30 January 1646.
64 ERB, 1650–51, f.16; and ERB, 1651–52, ff.15–16.
65 M. Stoyle, *From Deliverance to Destruction: Rebellion and Civil War in an English City* (Exeter, 1996), pp. 209–10.
66 The best introduction to contemporary building techniques remains L.F. Salzman, *Building in England down to 1540* (Oxford, 1967). See also Swanson, *Medieval Artisans*, pp. 82–106.
67 ECA, Law Papers, Box 40, depositions of Easter 1633, ff.38–39.
68 ERB, 1579–80, f.1*v*.
69 See, for example, ERR, 1538–39, m.3*v*.; and ERB, 1619–20, f.6.
70 On flakes, see Salzman, *Building in England*, p. 320.
71 ERR, 1539–40, m.3*v*.
72 ERR, 1538–39, m.3*v*.
73 ERB, 1633–34, f.6; and ERB, 1643–44, f.5. See also Salzman, *Building in England*, p. 322.
74 For the use of these terms, see ERV, Box 2 (1633–47), bills of 17 January and 18 September 1647. See also Swanson, *Medieval Artisans*, p. 90.
75 See, for example, ERB, 1580–81, f.7; and ERB, 1619–20, f.6.
76 ERV, Box 2, bill of 17 January 1647; and ERV, Box 3 (1653–57), bill of 17 March 1655.
77 ERR, 1539–40, m.3*v*.
78 Those of William Arnold, Zachary Brothers, William Heard, John Lawrence, John Rumpson, George Saunders and Arthur Williams, see DRO, DD.391, ff.35–43.
79 See ERB and ERR, 1485–1660, *passim*; and ERV, Box 3, bill of 17 March 1655.
80 ERR, 1488–89, m.2; ERB, 1505–6, f.3; ERB, 1636–37, f.24; ERB, 1642–43, f.7.
81 On this subject, see MacCaffrey, *Exeter*, pp. 67–68.
82 ERB, 1642–43, f.4; and EQSMB, 63 (1630–42), f.335.
83 ERR, 1538–39, m.3*v*.; ERR, 1539–40, m.3*v*.; ERB, 1558–59, f.22; and B. Cherry and N. Pevsner (eds), *The Buildings of England: Devon* (London, 1989), p. 263.
84 ERB, 1643–44, f.9. The limestone was probably brought to the kilns at Topsham from quarries in South Devon, see A.H. Shorter, W.L.D. Ravenhill and K.J. Gregory (eds), *South-West England* (London, 1969), p. 136.
85 Burrow, 'Town Defences', pp. 15, 17–18; and Blaylock, *City Wall Survey*, pp. 2–31.

86 On those occasions when the type of stone used to repair the city walls is specifically stated in the early modern accounts, the material alluded to is almost invariably breccia.

87 ERB, 1583–84, f.5v.; ERB, 1585–86, f.8. Much of the trap used in medieval and early modern Exeter came from quarries in Northernhay, see ECA, Law Papers, Box 40, depositions of Easter 1633, ff.83, 98, 113, 148; and Blaylock, *City Wall Survey*, p. 31.

88 ERR, 1376–77, m.2. On Raddon Quarry, see I. Stoyle, *Thorverton, Devon* (Thorverton, 1993), pp. 14–16.

89 ECAB, B 1/1, f.19.

90 ERR, 1538–39, m.3v.; and ERR, 1539–40, m.3v.

91 ECAB, B 1/8, f.280.

92 Ibid., f.331.

93 ECAB, 1/10, f.354; ERR, 1534–35, m.3v.; ERB, 1582–83, f.2v.

94 ECAB, B 1/1, ff.20, 45. See also Rowe and Jackson, *Exeter Freemen*, p. 66.

95 On the towers, see Hooker, II, pp. 167, 212, 214; on the gates, see ECAB, B 1/2, f.177; and ECAB, B 1/3, f.62.

96 ERR, 1496–97, m.2v.; ERR, 1497–98, m.4v. For Grymstone, see also F. Rose-Troup, *Lost Chapels of Exeter* (*HERG*, Monograph 1, Exeter, 1923), p. 30.

97 ERR, 1539–40, m.1v.

98 ECA, Book 51, f.345.

99 ECAB, B 1/2, f.116; and ERSB, 1 (1539–78), ff. 50–51.

100 ECA, Book 51, ff.336v, 348v; and ECAB, B 1/2, f.224.

101 ECAB, B 1/8, f.409.

102 On murage in general, see C. Allmand, 'Taxation in Medieval England: The Example of Murage', in M. Bourin (ed.), *Villes, Bonnes Villes, Cités et Capitales* (Caen, 1993), pp. 223–30. On murage in Exeter, see Burrow, 'Town Defences', pp. 15, 33–34; M.M. Rowe and J.M. Draisey (eds), *The Receivers' Accounts of the City of Exeter, 1304–1353* (DCRS, New Series, 32, 1989), pp. ix, xviii, 93–94; and M. Kowaleski, 'Tax Payers in Late Fourteenth-century Exeter: The 1377 Murage Roll', *DCNQ*, 34 (1978–81), pp. 217–22.

103 Stoyle, *Deliverance*, pp. 91–92.

104 ECAB, B 1/2, f.294; ERSB, 1, f.179; and DRO, DD.391, f.45.

105 See Chapters 4 and 5, below.

106 HMC, *Exeter*, p. 22.

107 DRO, DD.391, f.45.

108 See PRO, SP 28, 153 (Account book of Charles Vaughan), 'Receipts of money assessed by order of Colonell Ruthin'; and Stoyle, *Deliverance*, pp. 71–74.

109 C.H. Firth and R.S. Rait (eds), *Ordinances and Acts of the Commonwealth and Protectorate* (3 vols, 1911), I, p. 64.

110 PRO, SP 28, 153, 'Receipts of moneyes assessed by vertue of an ordinance of the Parliament'.

111 PRO, SP 23, 184, f.813.

112 SL, p. 76.

113 ECA, Law Papers, Box 40, *Breviat per civit' Exon* (undated), f.4.

4 The City Defences under the Tudors

1 On the abortive rising of 1483, see S.B. Chrimes, *Henry VII* (London, 1972), pp. 20–28; P.M. Kendall, *Richard III* (London, 1972), pp. 260–82; M. Van Cleave Alexander, *The First of the Tudors: A Study of Henry VII and his Reign* (London, 1981), pp. 18–21;

and W. Cotton and H. Woollcombe, *Gleanings from the Municipal and Cathedral Records of Exeter* (Exeter, 1877), pp. 20–23.

2 ERR, 1483–84, m.5.

3 A. Jenkins, *The History and Description of the City of Exeter* (Exeter, 1806), p. 127.

4 ERR, 1487–88, m.4v.; ERR, 1488–89, m.2; and ERR, 1489–90, m.3.

5 ERR, 1492–93, m.2. On the fears of French invasion which circulated in England at this time, see B.H. O'Neill, *Castles and Cannon: A Study of Early Artillery Fortification in Engand* (Oxford 1960), p. 41.

6 ERR, 1495–96, m.3. In addition, over £14 was laid out on 'repairs to the foundation of East Gate' and for 'a vaulte made there'. This 'vaulte' was a stone-lined inspection tunnel, built to facilitate access to the city's underground water pipes at the point where they passed into Exeter beneath East Gate. See J.Z. Juddery and M.J. Stoyle, *The Aqueducts of Medieval Exeter*, EA, Report No. 95.44 (September 1995), pp. xv–xvi.

7 I. Arthurson, *The Perkin Warbeck Conspiracy, 1491–99* (Stroud, 1994), pp. 110–17.

8 For the attack of May 1497, see I. Arthurson, 'The Rising of 1497: A Revolt of the Peasantry', in J. Rosenthal and C. Richmond (eds), *People, Politics and Community in the Late Middle Ages* (Gloucester, 1987), pp. 1–18.

9 ECA, Book 51 (John Hooker's Commonplace Book), f.327v.

10 For Warbeck's assault on Exeter, see Cotton and Woollcombe, *Gleanings*, pp. 29–42; and Arthurson, *Perkin Warbeck*, pp. 183–86.

11 ECA, Book 51, f.328.

12 Ibid.

13 N. Longmate, *Defending the Island: From Caesar to the Armada* (London, 1989), p. 359.

14 ECA, Book 51, f.328.

15 Ibid.

16 Ibid.

17 ERR, 1496–97, mm.3–3v.

18 Cotton and Woollcombe, *Gleanings*, p. 44.

19 ECA, Book 51, f.328v.

20 ERR, 1497–98, mm.4–4v.

21 ERR, 1498–99, m.1v.

22 ERR, 1500–1, m.3v.

23 ECA, Book 51, f.333.

24 ECAB, B 1/1 (1509–38), f.18.

25 Ibid., f.19.

26 Ibid., f.20.

27 C. Pythian-Adams, *Desolation of a City: Coventry and the Urban Crisis of the Late Middle Ages* (Cambridge, 1979), p. 62.

28 ECA, Book 51, f.333v. See also O'Neill, *Castles and Cannon*, p. 43.

29 ECAB, B 1/1, f.25.

30 Ibid., f.29v.

31 Ibid., f.45; and Jenkins, *History*, p. 220. Similar statues were subsequently to be erected above the gateways of many other English cities: that of Belinus at Bristol, for example, that of Elizabeth I at London and that of James I at Newcastle, see RCHM, *An Inventory of the Historical Monuments in the City of York: Volume II, The Defences* (London, 1972), p. 55.

32 ECAB, B 1/1, f.47.

33 For the use of the term 'blockhouse' to describe this structure, see BL, Add. MSS, 27402, f.81. Artillery blockhouses are known to have been built at sites throughout the South West between 1490 and 1520, see M. Duffy, 'Coastal Defence and Garrisons, 1480–1914', in R. Kain and W. Ravenhill (eds), *Historical Atlas of South West England* (Exeter, 1999), p. 158.

34 See M. Stoyle, *Exeter in the Civil War* (Devon Archaeology, 6, 1995), pp. 16–17. The blockhouse was later extended to form what appears to have been a primitive *caponier* (i.e. a covered passageway across the city ditch). For a comparable structure erected at Craignethan Castle, Lanarkshire, in the 1530s, see A. Saunders, *Fortress Britain: Artillery Fortifications in the British Isles and Ireland* (Liphook, 1989), pp. 31–32.

35 ERR, 1526–27, m.5*v*.

36 ERR, 1527–28, m.3*v*.

37 ECA, Book 51, f.340. See also ECAB, B 1/1, f.121.

38 ECAB, B 1/1, f.121*v*.

39 ERR, 1527–28, m.3*v*.

40 ERR, 1528–29, mm.2*v*.–3*v*.

41 ERR, 1530–31, m.4*v*. It seems probable that the work carried out on this occasion took place along that section of the wall which today stands beneath the railings of St Bartholomew's Cemetery, see S.R. Blaylock, *Exeter City Wall Survey* (Exeter Archaeology, 1995), p. 68.

42 ERR, 1532–33, m.2*v*.; and ERR, 1534–35, m.4*v*. For Denys, see W.T. MacCaffrey, *Exeter, 1540–1640: The Growth of an English County Town* (second edition London, 1975), p. 213.

43 For the Hunne affair, see A. Ogle, *The Tragedy of the Lollards Tower: The Case of Richard Hunne, with its aftermath in the Reformation Parliament* (Oxford, 1949).

44 Hooker, II, p. 214.

45 A.G. Little and R.C. Easterling, *The Franciscans and Dominicans of Exeter* (*HERG*, Monograph, 3, Exeter, 1927), pp. 27, 49; and J. Youings, 'The City of Exeter and the Property of the Dissolved Monasteries', *TDA*, 84 (1952), pp. 122–46.

46 Youings, 'Property of the Dissolved Monasteries', pp. 129–30.

47 The fact that the receiver's roll for 1536–37 is missing makes it conceivable that major repairs were undertaken for which no evidence survives. The lack of any references to work on the defences at this time in the surviving Chamber act books, however, militates strongly against this notion. For the Northern rebellion of 1536–37, see M.H. Dodds and R. Dodds, *The Pilgrimage of Grace and the Exeter Conspiracy* (Cambridge, 1915), *passim*.

48 There were mutters of local support for the Pilgrimage of Grace, see ECA, Book 51, f. 343*v*.

49 For the invasion scare of 1538–39, see O'Neill, *Castles and Cannon*, pp. 48–62; J.J. Scarisbrick, *Henry VIII* (1970) p. 362; Longmate, *Defending the Island*, pp. 376–88; Saunders, *Fortress Britain*, pp. 36–48; and A.D. Saunders, 'The Defences of Southhampton in the Later Middle Ages', in L.A. Burgess (ed.), *The Southampton Terrier of 1454*, Southhampton Record Series, 15 (1976), pp. 29–31.

50 ERR, 1538–39, mm.3*v*.–4*v*.

51 ECA, Book 51, f.345.

52 Ibid., f.344. For Russell, see also D. Willen, *John Russell, First Earl of Bedford: One of the King's Men* (London, Royal Historical Society Studies in History, No. 23, 1981), pp. 62–67; and MacCaffrey, *Exeter*, pp. 205–10.

53 ECA, Book 51, f.345.

54 ERR, 1538–39, mm.1*v*.–3*v*.

55 ECA, Book 51, f.345.

56 ERR, 1539–40, mm.2*v*.–3*v*. Some of the work carried out in Southernhay at this time almost certainly took place on the two towers occupied by the Bishop (see Chapter 3). The fact that Prestwood made a small payment to 'Mr [William] Horssay' suggests that the city's workmen may also have been active on the ruinous tower which adjoined the latter's house.

57 ECA, Book 51, f.346*v*.

58 ERR, 1541–42, m.3*v*. It seems probable that Duffield's work involved the construction of a new stretch of curtain wall to replace the collapsed archdeacon's tower, see Chapter 1.

59 For Duffield, see W.J. Harte (ed.), *An Account of the Sieges of Exeter . . . by John Vowell, alias Hooker* (Exeter, 1911), pp. 77–79; and Cotton and Woollcombe, *Gleanings*, p. 193.

60 For the invasion crisis of 1545, see Scarisbrick, *Henry VIII*, p. 454; Longmate, *Defending the Island*, pp. 389–98; and Saunders, *Fortress Britain*, p. 50.

61 ECAB, B 1/2 (1509–60), f.67*v*. See also ERR, 1544–45, m.4*v*.

62 *CSPD*, 1545, part I, p. 542.

63 ECAB, B 1/2, f.68*v*.

64 ERR, 1544–45, m.3*v*.

65 *CSPD*, 1545, part II, p. 68.

66 ECAB, B 1/2, f.70.

67 Ibid., f.74*v*.

68 Harte, *An Account of the Sieges of Exeter*, p. 68. On religious feeling in Exeter, see F. Rose-Troup, *The Western Rebellion of 1549* (London, 1913), pp. 167–83.

69 ECAB, B 1/2, ff.103–103*v*.

70 Harte, *An Account of the Sieges of Exeter*, p. 68.

71 For the siege of 1549, see Cotton and Woollcombe, *Gleanings*, pp. 47–71; Rose-Troup, *Western Rebellion*, pp. 184–210, 278–90; J. Cornwall, *Revolt of the Peasantry, 1549* (London, 1977), pp. 73–136 and 160–92; J. Youings, 'The South-Western Rebellion of 1549', *Southern History*, I (1979), pp. 99–122, especially pp. 112–13; Willen, *John Russell*, pp. 69–77; and E. Duffy, *The Voices of Morebath: Reformation and Rebellion in an English Village* (Yale, 2001), pp. 129–34.

72 Harte, *An Account of the Sieges of Exeter*, p. 69.

73 Ibid., p. 71.

74 ERR, 1548–49, m.2*v*.; and ECAB, B 1/3 (1560–80), f.67.

75 Harte, *An Account of the Sieges of Exeter*, p. 93.

76 Ibid., p. 71.

77 Ibid., p. 69.

78 Ibid., pp. 69, 87.

79 ERV, Box 1, 'Mr Hursts Byll of Chargs in the Commotion'.

80 Harte, *An Account of the Sieges of Exeter*, p. 69.

81 One of the rebel mines was dug under West Gate. The 'sap' which excavators discovered near East Gate in the 1930s may well have been another. See Exeter Excavation Committee, *c*.1932, *Report on the Underground Passages in Exeter*, pp. 195–97.

82 ECAB, B 1/2, f.103*v*; and ECA, Mayor's Court Book, 1545–57, ff.179–81*v*.

83 Harte, *An Account of the Sieges of Exeter*, pp. 67, 70, 74, 77–78; and ERV, Box 1, 'Mr Hursts Byll of Chargs' and 'The Accompte of Mr John Blakealler'.

84 For the 'camp' at St David's Down, see Duffy, *Voices of Morebath*, pp. 134–39. For the lifting of the siege, see Harte, *An Account of the Sieges of Exeter*, p. 93.

85 ERV, Box 1, 'Mr Hursts Byll of Chargs' and 'The Accompte of Mr John Blakealler'.

86 Ibid.; and ERR, 1548–49, m.3*v*. On 16 August 1549 Lord Russell observed that he had been 'credebly informed that the defence of the cytie hathe ben vary chargeable', see HMC, *Exeter*, p. 22. A royal charter of 1550 stated that the citizens had had to undergo 'intolerable costs, expenses and burdens' during the siege, see Rose-Troup, *Western Rebellion*, p. 379.

87 Rose-Troup, *Western Rebellion*, pp. 289–90; and MacCaffrey, *Exeter*, p. 206.

88 ECA, Book 51, f.348*v*.

89 ERR, 1549–50, m.2*v*.; ERR, 1550–51, m.2*v*.; ERR, 1551–52, m.2*v*.; ERSB, 1 (1539–78), pp. 80, 94.

90 ECAB, B 1/2, f.114.

91 Ibid., f.115.

92 ERSB, 1, p. 94.

93 On the Carews' abortive rising, see D.M. Loades, *Two Tudor Conspiracies* (Cambridge, 1965), pp. 35–46; A. Fletcher and D. MacCulloch, *Tudor Rebellions* (London, 1997), pp. 81–83; and J. Wagner, *The Devon Gentleman: A Life of Sir Peter Carew* (Hull, 1998), pp. 154–90.

94 J. Maclean, *The Life and Times of Sir Peter Carew* (London, 1857), pp. 146, 151, 179.

95 ERR, 1553–54, m.2*v*.

96 ERB, 1556–57, ff.11–11*v*.

97 ECAB, B 1/2, f.160.

98 Ibid., f.162.

99 Ibid., f.170*v*.

100 ERB, 1558–59, *passim*.

101 ERR, 1561–62, m.4*v*.

102 ERB, 1562–63, *passim*.

103 HMC, *Exeter*, p. 28; and MacCaffrey, *Exeter*, pp. 126–32.

104 ECAB, B 1/3, f.160.

105 Ibid.

106 ERR, 1564–65, m.2*v*.

107 J. Black, *The Reign of Elizabeth, 1558–1603* (London, 1965), pp. 145–46.

108 ECAB, B 1/3, f.253.

109 ERR, 1570–71, m.2*v*.

110 ERB, 1571–72, ff.10–11*v*.

111 ECAB, B 1/3, f.288.

112 Ibid., f.288. The Chamber had been engaged in a long-running legal dispute with John Frye, Robert Frye and others over the ownership of the barbican in this area ever since 1555, see ERR, 1555–56, m.2*v*.; ERB, 1556–57, f.6*v*.; ERR 1558–59, m.2*v*. and DRO, Law Papers, Box 40, '*Exeter v. Frye*'. It seems probable that the town governors exploited the scare of 1572 in order to stamp their authority on the disputed piece of land. For the use of very similar tactics during the 1620s, see Chapter 5.

113 ECAB, B 1/3, f.289; and ERB, 1572–73, m.2.

114 ECAB, B 1/3, f.413.

115 Ibid., f.435.

116 ERB, 1579–80, f.1.

117 ECAB, B 1/3, f.448.

118 Ibid., f.454.

119 ERB, 1581–82, f.1.

120 ERR, 1582–83, m.4*v*.

121 ERB, 1583–84, ff.4*v*.–6.

122 ERB, 1587–88, f.2*v*.; MacCaffrey, *Exeter*, pp. 237–39. See also, more generally, J. Roberts, *Devon and the Armada* (East Wittering, 1988), pp. 47–55.

123 Ibid.; and Rowe and Jackson, *Exeter Freemen*, p. 100.

124 ERR, 1590–91, m.3*v*. See also ERB, 1589–90, f.2*v*.; ERB, 1590–91, ff.3–5; and ERSB, 2 (1586–1622), 99.

125 See ECA, Law Papers, Box 40, 'Northernhay and Southernhay Suit', depositions of Easter 1633, ff.14, 77–78.

126 Youings, 'Property of the Dissolved Monasteries', p. 140.

127 ERB, 1602–3, ff.1*v*.–3; and ERB, 1603–4, f.3.

5 The City Defences under the Early Stuarts

1 ERB, 1602–3, f.1*v*. For local anxieties on Elizabeth's death, see M. Stoyle, 'The Counterfeit King: Popular Reaction to the Accession of King James I, 1603', in T. Gray (ed.), *Devon Documents* (Tiverton, 1996), pp. 177–83.

2 ERB, 1612–13, ff.18–19.

3 HMC, *Exeter*, p. 105. The reference to the walls as 'walkes' hints at a shift in contemporary perceptions of the rampart's primary function. See also ECA, Law Papers, Box 40, 'Northernhay and Southernhay Suit', depositions of Easter 1633, f.26.

4 DRO, Letter Book D, No. 247, item 7.

5 ERB, 1613–14, f.9.

6 ECA, Book 100 ('Presentments of Nuisances, 1554–88'), f.191.

7 ERB, 1616–17, f.14*v*.; and G. Scott-Thomson, 'Exeter and the Russell Earls of Bedford', *DCNQ*, 17 (1932–33), pp. 22–23.

8 ERB, 1616–17, f.11.

9 ERB, 1618–19, f.2.

10 On the great plague of 1625–26, see R. Pickard, *Population and Epidemics of Exeter in pre-Census Times* (Exeter, 1947), pp. 36–38; P. Slack, *The Impact of Plague in Tudor and Stuart England* (Oxford, 1985), pp. 115–17; and ERB, 1625–26, f.1.

11 *Acts of the Privy Council of England, 1626* (Lichtenstein, 1974 edition), pp. 66–67; and ECAB, 1/7 (1611–34), f.322.

12 Ibid.

13 ERB, 1625–26, f.2.

14 ECAB, B 1/7, f.322.

15 It was common for bishops living in urban communities elsewhere to secure the right to a similar door through the city wall, see, for example, K.L. Reyerson, 'Medieval Walled Space: Urban Development versus Defence', in J.D. Tracy (ed.), *City Walls: The Urban Enceinte in Global Perspective* (Cambridge, 2000), p. 107. Cf. RCHM, *An Inventory of the Historical Monuments in the City of York: Volume II, The Defences* (London, 1972), pp. 20, 22.

16 HMC, *Exeter*, p. 17. See also E. Lega-Weekes, 'Some Studies in the Topography of the Cathedral Close, Exeter', *DCNQ*, 8, part 2 (1915), pp. 101–6; and I. Burrow, 'The Town Defences of Exeter', *TDA*, 109 (1977), p. 26.

17 ERB, 1625–26, f.2.
18 ECAB, B 1/7, f.322.
19 For Puritanism in Exeter before the Civil War, see M. Stoyle, *From Deliverance to Destruction: Rebellion and Civil War in an English City* (Exeter, 1996), pp. 1–45.
20 HMC, *Exeter*, p. 131.
21 PRO, SP 16/377, f.91.
22 For Carpenter, see HMC, *Exeter*, p. 85 and ERB, 1617–18, f.1. For Jurdain, see Stoyle, *Deliverance*, Chapter 2.
23 HMC, *Exeter*, p. 177.
24 The two 'drawbridges' which Carpenter alleged that the plotters planned to rebuild were those which had formerly crossed over the Castle's defensive ditch at the Devil's Cradle, and at the head of Castle Lane. The component pieces of the former bridge had clearly survived until as late as 1577–78, when the receiver laid out 6 pence 'for setting up againe of the bridg for the arche[r]s to pass over in Northinghey', see ERB, 1577–78, f.1.
25 HMC, *Exeter*, p. 177.
26 ERR, 1631–32, m.1*v*.
27 T. Gray, 'Turkish Pirates and Early Stuart Devon', *TDA*, 121 (1988), pp. 159–71.
28 E.A. Andriette, *Devon and Exeter in the Civil War* (Newton Abbot, 1971), pp. 31–33. See also *CSPD*, 1629–31, pp. 44, 80, 232; and W.B. Stephens, *Seventeenth Century Exeter: A Study of Industrial and Commercial Development, 1625–88* (Exeter, 1958), pp. 14–21.
29 W. Ravenhill, 'Maps for the Landlord', in P. Barber and C. Board (eds), *Tales from the Map Room* (London, 1993), pp. 96–97; BL, Add MSS, 6027, ff.80*v*.–81; and ECA, Law Papers, Box 40, 'Northernhay and Southernhay Suit', depositions of Easter 1633, f.29.
30 Ibid., *passim*; R. Fisher, 'Sir Peter Balle of Mamhead (1598–1680): A Study in Allegiance', *TDA*, 129 (1997), p. 83; and ECAB, 1/8 (1634–47), f.184.
31 ECA, Law Papers, Box 40, 'Northernhay and Southernhay Suit', *Breviat per Civit' Exon*, ff.3–4; and depositions of Easter 1633, f.33.
32 ECAB, B 1/7, f.421*v*.
33 ERB, 1632–33, f.6.
34 ERB, 1633–34, f.6; and ECA, Book 101 ('Presentments to the Court, 1620–57'), f.42.
35 *CSPD*, 1634–35, pp. 210, 225.
36 ECAB, B 1/8, f.25; and ERB, 1634–35, f.5.
37 ECAB, B 1/8, f.25.
38 K. Cherry, 'Lollard's Tower', *Exeter Flying Post*, 29 July 1911.
39 ERB, 1634–35, f.5; and ECAB, B 1/8, f.36. For a complaint of 1630 about the condition of the barbican in this area, see ECA, Book 101, f.52*v*.
40 ERB, 1635–36, ff.10–11.
41 ECAB, B 1/8, f.57.
42 ERB, 1636–37, ff.21, 24, 26 and ECAB, B 1/8, f.102.
43 ERB, 1637–38, ff.23–25. See also ECAB, B 1/8, f.137.
44 ECAB, B 1/8, ff.147, 159–60. It is possible that these orders were connected with the presence of Sir Jacob Astley in the West Country during the summer of 1638. His mission was to inspect the condition of the local militia, see M. Fissell, *The Bishops' Wars: Charles I's Campaigns against Scotland, 1638–40* (Cambridge, 1994), p.197.
45 ECAB, B 1/8, ff.164, 170, 172, 182, 189.
46 ERR, 1639–40, m.1*v*.
47 ECAB, B 1/8, f.205. Sadly, the original presentment by the law jury has not survived.
48 ERR, 1640–41, m.2*v*.
49 ECAB, B 1/8, f.219.
50 ERR, B 1640–41, m.2*v*.
51 ECAB, B 1/8, f.212.
52 J. Youings, 'The City of Exeter and the Property of the Dissolved Monasteries', *TDA*, 84 (1952), p. 140. The use of a mural tower as a civic magazine is paralleled at Southampton, see A.D. Saunders, 'The Defences of Southampton in the Later Middle Ages', in L.A. Burgess (ed.), *The Southampton Terrier of 1454*, Southampton Record Series, 15 (1976), pp. 24, 27.
53 ECAB, B 1/8, f.243.
54 Ibid., ff.253–54.
55 See A. Fletcher, *The Outbreak of the English Civil War* (London, 1981), p. 225.
56 ECAB, B 1/8, f.258.
57 Ibid., ff.266, 269. Payments made to craftsmen for work carried out on the city wall in 'Minsons garden' in Southernhay in December 1642 may well mark the date at which the Bedford Postern was finally walled up, see ERB, 1642–43, f.5; and ERB, 1616–17, f.14*v*.
58 For the events of April–August 1642, see Stoyle, *Deliverance*, pp. 58–61.
59 See M. Stoyle, *Loyalty and Locality: Popular Allegiance in Devon during the English Civil War* (Exeter, 1994), pp. 93–110.
60 See, for example, W. Cotton and H. Woollcombe (eds), *Gleanings from the Municipal and Cathedral Records . . . of Exeter* (Exeter, 1877), pp. 73–111; M. Coate, 'Exeter in the Civil War and Interregnum', *DCNQ*, 18 (1935), pp. 338–52; Stephens, *Seventeenth Century Exeter*, pp. 60–64; R.J.E. Bush, 'The Civil War and Interregnum in Exeter, 1642–46', *DCNQ*, 29 (1962), pp. 80–87, 102–9, 132–38, 171–76; Andriette, *Devon and Exeter in the Civil War*, *passim*; M. Stoyle, *Documentary Evidence for the Civil War Defences of Exeter*, EMAFU, Report, No. 92.10 (1992); Stoyle, *Loyalty and Locality*, pp. 93–111; M. Stoyle, *Exeter in the Civil War* (Devon Archaeology, 6, 1995); and Stoyle, *Deliverance*, *passim*.
61 See W.G. Ross, *Military Engineering during the Great Civil War, 1642–49* (London, 1984 edition), p. 62; P. Harrington, *Archaeology of the English Civil War* (Princes Risborough, 1992), p. 27; and R. Hutton and W. Reeves, 'Sieges and Fortifications', in J. Kenyon and J. Ohlmeyer (eds), *The Civil Wars: A Military History of England, Scotland and Ireland* (Oxford, 1998), pp. 201–4.
62 This was the phrase used by the contemporary mayor of Chester, see S. Ward, *Excavations at Chester: The Civil War Siegeworks, 1642–46* (Grosvernor Museum Archaeological Excavation and Survey Reports, 4, Chester, 1987), p. 6.
63 ECAB, B 1/8, f.280.
64 For the demolition and filling of the towers, see Lega-Weekes, *Topography of the Cathedral Close*, pp. 100–1; and Burrow, 'Town Defences', pp. 19, 32, 36. This practice was frequently resorted to, both in England and elsewhere, when adapting a medieval enceinte to meet the needs of 'modern' warfare, see J.R. Kenyon, 'Early Artillery Fortifications in England and Wales: A Preliminary Survey and Re-appraisal', *AJ*, 138 (1981), pp. 223–25; M. Atkin and W. Laughlin, *Gloucester and*

the *Civil War: A City Under Siege* (Gloucester, 1992), p. 52; and M.M. Elbl, 'Portuguese Urban Fortifications in Morocco', in Tracy, *City Walls*, pp. 372, 376.

65 ECAB, B 1/8, ff.281, 285; ERB, 1642–43, ff.4–9; and J. Loftis and P.H. Hardacre (eds), *Colonel Joseph Bampfield's Apology* (London, 1993), p. 41.

66 ECAB, B 1/8, f.289.

67 Stoyle, *Documentary Evidence*, pp. 18–19.

68 ECAB, B 1/8, f.281; and Stoyle, *Deliverance*, pp. 64, 205–07.

69 ERB, 1642–43, f.7.

70 DRO, Letter Book 60F, DD.391, 43*v*.

71 Ibid., ff.43*v*.–45; ECAB, B 1/8, ff.287, 294; and Stoyle, *Deliverance*, pp. 72–74.

72 ERB, 1643–44, f.4.

73 ECAB, B 1/8, f.311.

74 ERB, 1643–44, f.9.

75 There had been no doorway or 'sally port' through the Lollard's Tower prior to the Civil War, but by 1647, at the latest, one had appeared, see J.F. Chanter, *The Bishop's Palace, Exeter, and its Story* (London, 1932), pp. 88, 91. A reference made in the receiver's accounts to the 'leavelling of the barbican' behind the city walls in Southernhay during May 1644 provides a possible date for the construction of this structure, for a section of the earthen bank, or 'counter-mure', would have had to be removed before the doorway could be built, see ERB, 1643–44, f.4. Cf. Kenyon, 'Early Artillery Fortifications' p. 225.

76 Ibid., ff.4–20.

77 For some comparative figures from Bath, see J. Wroughton, *A Community at War: The Civil War in Bath and North Somerset, 1642–50* (Bath, 1992), p. 149.

78 ECAB, B 1/8, f.326.

79 ERB, 1644–45, ff.3–5.

80 Stoyle, *Exeter in the Civil War*, pp. 29–33; and M. Stoyle, 'Whole Streets Converted to Ashes: Property Destruction in Exeter during the English Civil War', *Southern History*, 16 (1994), pp. 67–84.

81 Stoyle, *Exeter in the Civil War*, pp. 29–33.

82 J. Sprigg, *Anglia Rediviva: England's Recovery* (London, 1647), table between pages 334 and 335; and Stoyle, *Deliverance*, pp. 112–14. During autumn 1645, one parliamentary journalist wrote that 'as for Excester, its conceived to be as strong a place as in England of the King's', see BL, Burney Collection, *The Moderate Intelligencer*, 23–30 October 1645.

83 ERB, 1646–47, f.2a; ERV, Box 2, Bill of 17 January 1647.

84 ECAB, B 1/8, f.416.

85 ERV, Box 2, Bill of 18 September 1647.

86 Bush, 'Exeter during the Civil War', pp. 107–9.

87 Bod., Tanner MSS, Volume 57, No. 69, 'A true relation of what hath passed betwixt the citty of Exon, and Sir Hardress Waller', f.129; and *CJ*, 5 (1646–48), p. 571.

88 M. Stoyle, 'The Gear Rout: The Cornish Rising of 1648 and the Second Civil War', *Albion*, 32, No. 1 (Spring 2000), pp. 37–58; and ECAB, 9 (1647–55), f.15.

89 See ECAB, B 1/10 (1651–63), ff.59*v*., 121*v*., 128*v*.; ERB, 1651–52, ff.14 and 21; ERB, 1652–53, f.18; ERB, 1653–54, f.8; ERB, 1654–55, f.2; ERB, 1657–58, f.6; and ERB, 1658–59, f.3. In this respect, Exeter's experience parallels that of Gloucester, where the earthwork bastions which had been thrown up around

the town during the Civil War were demolished in 1653, see Atkin and Laughlin, *Gloucester and the Civil War*, pp. 130–34.

90 ECAB, B 1/10, f.72*v*.

91 Ibid., f.31*v*.

92 Ibid., f.50.

93 ERB, 1653–54, f.9.

94 ECA, Book 101, f.117*v*.

95 ECAB, B 1/10, f.139; ECAB B 1/11 (1663–84), f.262.

96 ECAB, B 1/10, f.65*v*.

97 Ibid., f.60. See also ERB, 1654–55, f.4; and ERV, 1654–55, bill of John Griffin, 17 March 1655.

98 Ibid., f.69*v*.

99 ECAB, B 1/8, f.224.

100 ERB, 1654–55, ff.3–4; and ERB, 1657–58, f.3.

101 ERB, 1655–56, f.4.

102 ERB, 1658–59, ff.3–5.

103 ERB, 1659–60, ff.3–6.

104 Cotton and Woolcombe, *Gleanings*, p. 183; and S.K. Roberts, *Recovery and Restoration in an English County: Devon Local Administration, 1646–70* (Exeter, 1985), pp. 138–39.

105 *CSPD*, 1659–60, p. 309.

106 ECAB, B 1/9, f.133.

107 Ibid.

108 ECAB, B 1/10, ff.166*v*., 177; ERB, 1662–63, f.2; and ERB, 1663–64, ff.4–5.

Conclusion

1 The same message was reiterated by the city authorities in many different ways during the 1660s: not least through their decision that the receivers' rolls and other civic records, which had been kept in English during the 1650s, should again be written up in Latin. See ERR, 1658–59 and ERR, 1659–60.

2 A. Hughes, 'Coventry and the English Revolution', in R.C. Richardson (ed.), *Town and Countryside in the English Revolution* (Manchester, 1992), p. 96; A.R. Warmington, *Civil War, Interregnum and Restoration in Gloucestershire, 1640–72* (Woodbridge, 1997), p. 182; R. Hutton and W. Reeves, 'Sieges and Fortifications', in J. Kenyon and J. Ohlmeyer (eds), *The Civil Wars: A Military History of England, Scotland and Ireland, 1638–1660* (Oxford, 1998), p. 233; and J. Savage, *The History of Taunton in the County of Somerset* (Taunton, 1822), pp. 429–30.

3 W.G. Hoskins, *Two Thousand Years in Exeter* (Exeter, 1963), pp. 79–80.

4 *SL*, pp. 75–76. The decline of the city circuit after 1700 is traced in S.R. Blaylock, *Exeter City Wall Survey* (Exeter Archaeology, 1995), pp. 16–25.

5 See A. Saunders, *Fortress Britain: Artillery Fortification in the British Isles and Ireland* (Liphook, 1989), p. 19; N. Longmate, *Defending the Island: Caesar to the Armada* (London, 1989), pp. 263, 266, 276–84, 295–302, 308; and S. Porter, *Destruction in the English Civil Wars* (Stroud, 1994), p. 70.

6 W.T. MacCaffrey, *Exeter, 1540–1640: The Growth of an English County Town* (second edition London, 1975), p. 54.

7 See, for example, I. Roy, 'The City of Oxford, 1640–60', in Richardson (ed.), *Town and Countryside*, p. 146; and P. Harrington, *Archaeology of the English Civil War* (Princes Risborough, 1992), p. 29.

8 Even the cost of the ship canal constructed between *c.*1563 and *c.*1640—usually seen as the most ambitious civic project undertaken in early modern Exeter—was only £6,950, see MacCaffrey, *Exeter*, p. 68.

9 On this subject more generally, see M.J. Stoyle, 'Whole Streets Converted to Ashes: Property Destruction in Exeter during the English Civil War', *Southern History*, 16 (1994), pp. 67–84.

10 See, for example, *SL*, pp. 75–76.

11 On the similar persistence of 'medieval public-works traditions' in France, see M. Wolfe, 'Walled Towns during the French Wars of Religion, 1560–1630', in J.D. Tracy (ed.), *City Walls: The Urban Enceinte in Global Perspective* (Cambridge, 2000), pp. 335–36.

12 See, for example, ERB, 1664–65, f.4.

Part II   Introduction

1 On the receivers and their duties, see Hooker, III, pp. 809–10; W.T. MacCaffrey, *Exeter, 1540–1640: The Growth of an English County Town* (second edition London, 1975), pp. 36, 48–49, 63; and M. Rowe and J. Draisey, *The Receivers' Accounts of the City of Exeter, 1304–1353* (*DCRS*, New Series, 32, 1989) pp. ix–xi.

2 Hooker, III, p. 925.

3 MacCaffrey, *Exeter*, pp. 37–38.

4 Hooker, III, p. 924.

5 Ibid., p. 925.

6 MacCaffrey, *Exeter*, p. 36.

7 Ibid; and ECA, Law Papers, Box 40, 'Northernhay and Southernhay Suit', depositions of 24 September 1633, f.92.

8 Ibid.

9 ERR, 1599–1600; ERR, 1600–1; ERR, 1653–54; ERR, 1654–55; ERR, 1655–56; ERR, 1656 57; ERR, 1657–58; ERR, 1658–59; and Rowe and Draisey, *Receivers' Accounts*, p. vii. The 'English' rolls of the late Elizabethan period—which have previously gone unnoticed by scholars—were presumably produced in response to a Chamber order of 25 June 1601 'that all the accompts of the Cittie shalbe from henssefurthe made and sett fourthe in Englische', see HMC, *Exeter*, p. 320.

10 ERR, 1499–1500.

11 ERB, 1505–6.

12 See, for example, ERR, 1513–14, m.5*v*.; ERR, 1544–45, m.4*v*.; and ERR, 1534–35, m.4*v*.

13 DRO, Box 214, Books 2 and 3.

14 ERV, Boxes 1–3.

15 ERR, 1372–73, m.2; ERR, 1393–94, m.2; and ERR, 1480–81, m.4.

16 ECA, Box 214, Book 20 (Account of Ralph Herman, 1648–49), *passim*.

17 ECA, Law Papers, Box 40, 'Northernhay and Southernhay Suit', depositions of 24 September 1633, f.92.

18 The Chamber employed Dr George Oliver to draw up a calendar of some of the more important civic documents during the 1820s, see HMC, *Exeter*, p. ix. Oliver himself later published an abstract of one of the fourteenth-century receivers' rolls, see G. Oliver, *History of the City of Exeter* (Exeter, 1861), pp. 319–23. For one of the first published accounts of the Exeter records, see T. Wright, 'The Municipal Archives of Exeter', *Journal of the Archaeological Association*, 18 (1862), pp. 306–17.

19 HMC, *Exeter*, p. ix. The three-volume calendar of the receivers' accounts which Moore subsequently prepared remains in use in the Devon Record Office to this day.

20 HMC, *Exeter*, p. ix; and H. Lloyd Parry, *The History of the Exeter Guildhall and the Life Within* (Exeter, 1936), pp. 140–41, 168–69.

21 HMC, *Exeter*, p. ix; and Lloyd Parry, *Exeter Guildhall*, p. 141.

INDEX I
PLACES AND SUBJECTS

References in **bold** refer to major entries.
References in *italics* refer to plate numbers.

223

INDEX II
PERSONS

Hals, William, 188
Halstaff, —, 159
Halstaffe, Peter, locksmith, 171–73, 180
Hamlyn, —, 128, 151
Hamlyn, Henry, receiver, 121
Hamlyn, [Mr] Henry, 186–89
Hamlyn, Nicholas, 126, 128
Hamlyn, Nicholas, receiver, 115
Harres, Thomas, public notary, 2
Harries, see Harris
Harris, Christopher, porter of West Gate, 178, 180
Harris, Philip, 176
Hawkes, Richard, 191
Hawkes, Richard, mason, 133, 134
Haydon, John, 126
Hayne, John, receiver, 166
Heard, William, 173
Heathfield, —, 126–28
Heathman, —, 151
Hedgeland, Caleb, 1
Helier, see Hellier
Hellecomb, Walter, 125
Helliar, see Hellier
Hellier, —, 151, 172
Hellier, Jerome, founder of Hellier's Almshouses, 47
Hellier, John, 126
Hellier, Richard, hellier, 137
Hellier, Thomas, 121
Hellier, William, 172
Hellyen, John, 128
Hellyer, see Hellier
Helmore, John junior, receiver, 129
Helyer, see Hellier
Helyet, Robert, server, 126
Helyet, William, 125
Henderson, Chris, 4
Henry VI, 39, 68
Henry VII, 3, 17, 40, 69–73
Henry VIII, 72, 73, 75–78
Herman, Mr —, 166
Herman, Ralph, receiver, 111, 179
Hethefyld, Hethfild, Hethfyld, see Heathfield
Hethman, see Heathman
Hew, Laurence, 157
Hew, William, mason, 132, 133, 134
Heychens, see Hitchens
Heythfild, Heythfyld, see Heathfield
Hill, Thomas, 184
Hilliard, Jeremy, 155
Hitchens, —, 190
Hocker, see Hooker
Hockwell, Mr —, 173
Hodder, Robert, 143
Hodge, Emanuel, carpenter, 181
Hodge, Thomas, receiver, 123
Hogenberg, Remegius, 4, 18, 24
Hoigge, see Hodge
Hoker, see Hooker
Holmore, John, 186–89
Holmore, John junior, 186
Holwell, —, 162
Honicombe, John, mason, 167, 168, 170
Hont, Robert, 190
Honyland, —, 139
Honyland, John, carpenter, 116, 117
Honyton, —, 127
Hooker, Mr —, 135, 136
Hooker, John, chamberlain, 3, 5, 7, 11, 16, 22, 29, 30, 40, 49, 52, 55, 72, 75, 76, 78–80, 109, 149, 192
Hooker, John, receiver, 114
Hooker, Robert, 186
Hooker, Robert, receiver, 121
Hooper, John, 125
Hooper, Richard, fuller, 50
Hooper, Thomas, 125
Hooper, William, 125, 129
Hoppkyns, Elizabeth, 123
Hopping, —, 164
Hopping, Mr —, 169
Hopping, Edmund, 168, 179

Horither, John, 126
Horwell, —, 152
Horsey, Mr William, archdeacon, 75, 126
How, —, 122
Howcker, see Hooker
Howell, John, receiver, 148
Howenton, Gilbert, 125
Huish, William, 143
Hull, Mr —, 139, 191
Hull, Henry, receiver, 150
Hull, John, receiver, 117
Hull, Matthew, 138
Humfrye, porter of East Gate, 31
Hundaller, John, porter of Water Gate, 150–52
Hunne, Richard, 75
Hunt, —, 140
Hunt, —, chandler, 146
Hunt, Henry, 142
Hunt, John, carpenter, 133
Hunt, Peter, carpenter, 133
Hunt, Thomas, 187–89
Hunt, Thomas, receiver, 120, 124
Hurst, John, receiver, 130
Hurst, Mr —, 137, 145, 191
Hurst, [Mr] William, alderman, 66, 186–91
Hutchings, Richard, 126, 127

Jacob the Dutchman, gunner, 80, 81
James I, 62, 86, 88–90
James, John, porter of Water Gate, 139
Jarman, see Germyn
Jeffrey, Dorothy, 44
Jeffrey, Francis, 143
Jeffrey, Mr Giles, surveyor to the Earl of Bedford, 192
Jeffrey, John, 125
Jeffrey, Thomas, 140, 144
Jeffrey, William, labourer, 125, 129
Jenkins, Alexander, 12, 15, 17–19, 22, 36, 44
Jerman, see Germyn
Johnson, Michael, 140
Johnson, Robert, carpenter, 137
Jones, John, hellier, 121
Joselyng, Thomas, 125
Jube, Henry, 140
Jurdain, Ignatius, alderman, 89, 156
Jurdain, John, receiver, 162

Kelland, Thomas, 184
Kelly, —, widow, 60, 174, 176
Kennick, —, 163
Kennick, Christopher, 61, 178
Kente, —, archdeacon, 47
Keroll, John, mason, 138
Keroll, Stephen, mason, 138
Kettell, —, 129
Kettell, —, mason, 134
Kettell, John, 132
Kettell, Richard, mason, 129, 132, 134
Kettell, Stephen, 132
Keyser, Richard, 137
King, —, 135, 163
King, John, 157
King, Thomas, 177
Kirke, see Kyrke
Knight, —, 140
Knight, — junior, carpenter, 138
Knight, John, carpenter, 137, 138
Knight, Simon, receiver, 138
Knolles, William, cutler and gunner, 131, 137, 140, 145, 149, 191, 192
Koke, see Cook
Kychyn, Richard, 127
Kyrke, Mr —, 189
Kyrke, [Mr] Gilbert, 187–89
Kyrke, Gilbert, receiver, 122
Kyrkham, James, 41

Labbden, William, mason, 123
Lake, John, 114
Lake, Robert, mason, 146
Lambal, see Lambert
Lambert, Mr —, 157

Lancastell, see Lancaster
Lancaster, —, 191
Lane, Mr —, 157
Lang, William, 137
Lante, John, receiver, 155
Laud, William, Archbishop of Canterbury, 89, 91
Lavers, John, mason, 178
Lawman, Thomas, 132
Lawrence, —, 127, 128, 157, 163
Lawrence, John, mason, 59, 61, 171–79
Lawrence, William, mason, 59, 60, 145, 146, 151, 158, 159, 165–70
Leach, —, 172
Leach, Mr —, 44, 155
Leland, John, 38
Lethbridge, Mr Christopher, receiver, 182
Levermore, —, 190
Lévermore, John, gentleman, receiver, 146
Levermore, Maurice, receiver, 130, 190
Lewis, —, 152
Lewis, Geoffrey, receiver, 120
Limmett, see Lymett
Locke, Humphrey, 166–73, 176, 177, 179
Locke, Thomas, 128
Lockyer, John, 138
Lowton, John, 118
Loyntters, Thomas, 140
Lye, Robert, 125, 127
Lymett, Edward, receiver, 138
Lymett, Nicholas, 187–89
Lymett, Nicholas, receiver, 78, 130
Lynne, John, receiver, 162
Lynnett, see Lymett
Lympyn, John, receiver, 119
Lytell, William, 123

Madock, —, 153
Mager, William, thatcher, 138
Maior, see Mayor
Major, Avis, 38
Mallock, Mr Roger, mayor and receiver, 165, 169
Marks, William, 41, 148–49, 159–61
Marshall, James merchant, receiver, 181
Marshall, John, receiver, 156
Martin, —, smith, 128, 135
Martin, Edmund, mason, 134
Martin, John, 121
Martin, John, receiver, 176
Martin, Nicholas, gentleman, receiver, 163
Martin, Nicholas, receiver, 139
Martin, Peter, of Teignmouth, mason, master craftsman, 59, 174, 176
Martin, Richard, 191
Martin, Richard, receiver, 123
Martin, Thomas, receiver, 141, 157
Martin, Walter, 191
Martin, William gentleman, receiver, 145
Mary, Queen of England, 81, 82
Marys, see Morris
Mason, John, 122
Mason, William, 123
Mathew, labourer, 134
Maunder, —, 163
Maunder, —, senior ('the old'), 163
Maunder, —, constable, 168
Maunder, Anthony, 142
Maunder, Harry, steward, 190, 191
Maynard, John, 66, 129, 130, 187, 188
Maynard, John, receiver, 129, 186
Mayne, Alexander, receiver, 152
Mayne, William, 125
Mayor, John, mason, 117
Mendust, James, 38
Menifie, Richard, 159
Middleton, John, 128
Midwinter, —, 191
Midwinter, John, 131, 187–89
Midwinter, John, receiver, 128
Midwinter, Robert, receiver, 131
Minson, —, 160, 172
Mitchell, John, 115
Miwall, John, mason, 139
Modeffilde, see Modyfild